# SLINGS AND ARROWS

## THEATER IN MY LIFE

# SLINGS AND ARROWS

## THEATER IN MY LIFE

Robert Lewis

Slings and Arrows: Theater in My Life
by Robert Lewis


***Library of Congress Cataloging-in-Publication Data***

Library of Congress Card Number: **96-85219**

*British Library Cataloging-in-Publication Data*

A catalog record of this book is available from the British Library.

**APPLAUSE BOOKS**

211 West 71st Street
New York, NY 10023
Phone (212) 496-7511
Fax: (212) 721-2856

A&C BLACK

Howard Road, Eaton Socon
Huntington, Cambs PE19 3EZ
Phone 0171-242 0946
Fax 0171-831 8478

Distributed in the U.K. and European Union by A&C Black

To the memory of Harold Clurman

Books by Robert Lewis

*Method—or Madness?*
*Advice to the Players*

# Acknowledgments

Material from "Literary Gangsters" by Gore Vidal reprinted from *Commentary*, March 1970, by permission; all rights reserved.

Material from a letter to Robert Lewis from Cheryl Crawford regarding his production of *The Sea Gull* reprinted by permission of Cheryl Crawford.

Material from *Albums of Early Life* by Stanley Kauffmann, copyright © 1970, 1971, 1972, 1973, 1975, 1977, 1978, 1979, 1980 by Stanley Kauffmann, reprinted by permission of Ticknor & Fields, a Houghton Mifflin Company.

Material from a letter to Robert Lewis from Elia Kazan reprinted by permission of Elia Kazan.

Material from *Kazan on Kazan* by Michel Ciment reprinted by permission of Martin Secker & Warburg Limited.

Material from the following reviews in *The New York Times*, copyright © 1942, 1954 by The New York Times Company, reprinted by permission. "Mr. Saroyan Tosses on a Show," by Brooks Atkinson, August 23, 1942; a review of *Teahouse of the August Moon* by Drew Middleton, May 2, 1954; a review of *Teahouse of the August Moon* by W. A. Darlington, June 13, 1954.

Material from *The Street Where I Live* by Alan Jay Lerner, W. W. Norton & Company, Inc., Copyright © 1978 by Alan Jay Lerner, reprinted by permission of the publisher.

Material from *Building a Character* by Constantin Stanislavski used by permission of the publishers, Theatre Arts Books, 153 Waverly Place, New York, N.Y. 10014. Copyright 1949 by Elizabeth Reynolds Hapgood. Copyright renewed 1977 by David Ten Eyck Hapgood. Copyright under the International Copyright Union. All rights reserved under Pan-American Copyright Union.

Every effort has been made to trace copyright holders of material used in this book. The publishers apologize if any material has been included without permission.

# Contents

# SLINGS AND ARROWS

CHAPTER 1

# Brooklyn 1909-1929

EVEN THOUGH HE was our efficient family doctor and lived next door to us in the Brownsville section of Brooklyn, where I was born in 1909, I knew very little about the private life of Dr. Samuel Greenberg. But in recent years I read *The Last Angry Man,* the book his son Gerald Green wrote about him. According to Gerald, who was one of my boyhood friends on the block, if the walls of our two-family houses were thinner, I could often have heard the good doctor screaming, "The bastards won't let you live," when some tough guys would ring his bell at three o'clock in the morning, having dumped a beat-up body on his doorstep; or when any other insulting torments were inflicted on him that mocked the dignity of his profession. How many times on my own bumpy ride through the theatrical jungle would I echo Dr. Greenberg's cry against philistines in my profession: conniving producers, egomaniacal stars, selfish designers, obnoxious critics. "The bastards won't let you live."

Even on his deathbed, when he knew his coronary attack would prove fatal, Dr. Greenberg's feistiness didn't desert him. "What's all that crap for?" he asked the doctor who was bringing in an oxygen tank.

When my father was stricken with his coronary in 1941, the famous diagnostician Dr. Emmanuel Libman consented to drive from Manhattan to Brooklyn to examine Pop's heart. Libman, refusing to cut his enormous fee, had chosen rather to offer his services to us gratis. I remember looking out of our front window at the kids on the block crawling all over his huge black limousine while the doctor was examining my father. When he was through he called me into the next room and told me my father had only a week or so to live. He then asked me what I did for a living. "I am an actor," I said.

Beaming with pride, Dr. Libman told me he had been the personal physician attending Sarah Bernhardt on her last American tour.

"She was the greatest actress who ever lived," he maintained.

"What about Duse?" I asked.

"I don't know," said Libman. "She never called me in."

My father, who worked in a jewelry firm, was a genuine innocent. His first act upon arising every day was to place a saucer of breadcrumbs for the birds on the sill outside the kitchen window. He referred to those birds as his "chippies." He also called young girls "chippies."

Wondering at Pop's habit of sleeping with a hammer under his pillow, I asked him one day why he did.

"Well," he answered, "if a burglar comes in the middle of the night I'll hit him on the head with my hammer." It seemed to me at the time unlikely that, one, a burglar would bother to visit our house, where that hammer was probably the most valuable piece of loot, and, two, that my father would hit anyone with anything. But Pop could sleep soundly, knowing he was protecting his family. Now, sitting beside him as he lay dying, I heard his last words, "Excuse me." Although I loved the gentleness of my father, I knew that in my chosen profession I would have to be more like Dr. Greenberg to survive.

"The gentleness of my father"

If he had placed his ear to the wall in his house at almost any time of day or night, Dr. Greenberg might have heard from our front room, as we called the parlor, the famous golden voice of Enrico Caruso emanating from our wind-up Victrola. He might also have been surprised if he could have seen me, one arm outstretched and the other on my heart (I had seen the famous picture of Caruso as Canio in *Pagliacci* in *The Victrola Book of the Opera*), mouthing the words along with the great tenor's singing, imagining myself on the stage of the Metropolitan Opera House.

I was encouraged in my love for opera by Uncle Louis, my Aunt Beck's foreign-born husband. He was not liked very much by the rest of the family because he acted and sounded too "European." My mother and father were both born on the Lower East Side of Manhattan. Louis used to go to the opera by himself and when he came to our house in Brooklyn he invariably brought me a Red-Seal Victor record of some great singer he'd heard at the Met. So it was that, while other families on the block who had Victrolas might have owned a McCormack, a Galli-Curci, or Fritz Kreisler's version of "The Old Refrain," I was weaned on the likes of Emmy Destinn, the Bohemian soprano.

While most of the kids were in the street playing stickball, I was closeted in our front room doing my pantomime record act to "Vesti la giubba" from *Pagliacci.* Sometimes the turntable didn't stop automatically at the end of the aria, and I had to reach over and lift off the machine's heavy tone arm. I hated that because it destroyed the illusion for a moment before I started my bowing. I had read in the newspapers that one night Caruso took twenty-six curtain calls, and I wasn't about to be cheated. Back and back again the wild applause would call me. I'd try to beg off. No use. Panting, but happy, I'd return to the center of the stage waving to my bravoing fans in the top gallery.

Top gallery and way over to the side ("limited viewing" they called it) was where I sat and craned my neck the only time, as a child, I was ever in an opera house in person. My mother, who had herself been a contralto in the Frank Damrosch chorus when she was a single girl, recognized my love of singing and saved up the price of two Saturday matinée seats. It turned out to be *The Barber of Seville* with Giuseppe de Luca as Figaro.

My mother: "A contralto in the Frank Damrosch chorus"

Going from our house in Brooklyn to the Thirty-ninth Street Metropolitan Opera House in Manhattan was, for us, in those days, a dangerous safari. There was no subway in Brooklyn then, and we had to take a streetcar to the bridge. ("Which car? Bergen Street? Fulton Street?") Then if we got over the bridge to lower Manhattan we could take the subway ("Which subway? Seventh Avenue? Lex?")

After several wrong choices, my mother and I finally arrived, quite late of course, at the opera house. Now there was the climb to the top, which was not unlike conquering Mount Everest. Wild with anxiety, I finally found my seat. Finding de Luca was harder. Occasionally, I'd see this speck of a baritone barber cavorting over to the small corner of the stage visible from our part of the gallery. You can be sure that when I attended de Luca's farewell West Coast recital in the forties, when I was working in the movies, I sat way down front in the orchestra.

In the lower half of our two-family house lived another angry man, my uncle Wolf, who was totally blind. Wolf had a sharp mind and was perpetually incensed by his incapacitation. He only laughed when his daughter Augusta's boyfriend, Mr. Vogel, came to call. Augusta, not too pretty or too young, but interested in "culture," accepted Mr. Vogel's attentions because, although he too was blind, he was a musician. He also had a bitter wit, referring to Wolf's other blind friends as "blinkers." Mr. Vogel played the piano to accompany the silent movies around the corner at the Paradise movie house where we kids could get in two for a nickel. I can still hear the street-cry: "I got three cents, anyone got two?" Once in, we would stay most of the day, seeing a William S. Hart western or some other feature and a Pearl White serial over and over in the smelly house, which we nicknamed the "Paradump."

Mr. Vogel had to be prompted by those sitting down front as to what was going on up there on the screen, so that he could play appropriate music on his piano. Some rotten kids would, on occasion, fool him, and we'd get extra laughs by hearing "chase" music accompanying Theda Bara's dilating nostrils in a hot love scene.

Augusta and Mr. Vogel were, after Uncle Louis, the two great musical influences of my childhood. Every Sunday evening they went to Charles D. Isaacson's free concerts in the De Witt Clinton High School Auditorium in Manhattan and took me along. One memorable night, Isaacson filled the stage with bits of old operatic scenery as a background for one of his prize offerings, Johanna Gadski. The great Wagnerian soprano of the Metropolitan Opera Company had gone home to Germany in 1917 after the United States entered the war, and now she was back for some concerts. Thus I added another name to my list of what I was one day to call my "dead singers." The appellation came from a salesman at the Schirmer-Wilshire record shop, where I bought many operatic records when I was making my first real money as an actor in Hollywood in the forties. There were two young people who sold records in the store, a boy in charge of the jazz department and a girl who presided over the classical. As I opened the door one day, I heard the boy turn to the girl and say, "Here he comes. Have we got any dead singers today?"

Sympathetic with my operatic aspirations, my mother finally agreed to take me to a Brooklyn vocal teacher to have my voice tested. This was my very first audition, and it set the pattern of agony for all subsequent ones, mine and those of others I eventually had to judge. "Sing 'The Star Spangled Banner,'" commanded the teacher. With no accompaniment offered to sustain me, my voice wobbled around, sometimes even coming near the pitch. Caruso I wasn't.

"If he likes music so much," said the teacher, "why don't you let him take up an instrument?" The guy was probably trying to be helpful. How could he know he was plunging a knife into my heart? I still shudder thinking of this first important rejection. From that moment on all the activities of my life—acting, directing, teaching, whatever—I'm sure have been attempts to sublimate my original aim to be an opera singer. On my desk as I write this, is a beautifully framed photo of an elegant mustachioed Caruso taken in London in 1906.

The violin was the usual instrument stuck into the hands of kids whose parents hoped to spawn another Mischa Elman. My mother was not too keen on the years of a scratching fiddle she would be forced to endure. "What's that other lower-sounding instrument in there?" she asked one day when I was playing a recording of a trio for piano, violin, and cello. And so it turned out that I marched into the Brooklyn Music School Settlement next door to the Academy of Music and sat down to the three-quarter size cello they handed me.

In addition to classes in harmony, theory, and sight-singing, which went along with my cello and secondary piano lessons, the school offered a Little Theatre group under the direction of a gnomelike woman called Jane Kerley. Little Theatre groups proliferated all over the country in those days, and at the end of each season there was a nationwide contest. Each group did a scene or an act of a play in a marathon performance and prizes were given to the best entries. I joined Jane Kerley's hopefuls. It seemed closer to Caruso than cello playing.

Miss Kerley was a stickler for the voice and diction aspects of acting. As an example to her actors she recited, with great expression, the words of the "One Fine Day" aria from *Madama Butterfly*. Although she didn't follow the tune set down by Puccini, she had a pretty good one of her own going as she sang out her vowels and clipped her consonants. As far as consonants were concerned, she was fond of saying things like "In that 'tryst tonight,' dear, I want to hear the 't' at the end of tryst and the 't' at the beginning of tonight. They both pay taxes and have a right to vote."

As our Little Theatre contest entry, Miss Kerley chose a dubious Greek number called *Marsyas the Faun.* Marsyas was this Pan-like god of nature who presumed to challenge Apollo to a flute-lyre contest. Our hero not only lost but was flayed alive. At one rehearsal, the actor playing the title role had laryngitis, and Miss Kerley asked me to stand in for him. When you're a young and enthusiastic actor, you know everyone's lines. Actually I didn't exactly look like a Greek god. In fact, I looked more like my cello. But this was just a rehearsal.

That evening something remarkable happened. Stretched out on the floor as Marsyas, crying out in my blank-verse agony, I experienced a sensation of the most ineffable happiness filling me. I never felt like that embracing my cello. Deep down I knew then the road I had to take. True, I kept up my music studies, and a good thing too; they would help me in my future theater work in many ways, not only when directing operas or musicals, but as a guide to dynamics and a feeling for form in straight plays.

"I never felt like that embracing my cello."

My search for great performers to study and worship, which had gone from Caruso to Pablo Casals, now switched to Jane Cowl and Bertha Kalich, when they held forth at the Majestic Theatre in downtown Brooklyn not too far from the Music School Settlement. My mother always gave me twenty-five cents for lunch, and on matinée days I could get a seat in the second balcony for that. I also saved up my quarters for a trip to Manhattan to see Raquel Meller, the great Spanish diseuse, who was touring America.

These three great ladies confirmed my belief that the theater was to be my life. I hung dangerously over the second balcony rail as Jane Cowl, all in white as Juliet, held her potion high and cried out in her melodious voice, "Romeo, I come! This do I drink to thee." As she sank gracefully onto her

Jane Cowl as Juliet: "How I loved that bowing."

bed, the scene-curtains closed. Along with everyone else in that theater I clapped my hands wildly. It may not have been the end of the act, but it was the end of a great "aria," and through the curtains came Jane Cowl, bowing again and again (as I had done as Caruso), finally begging off so she could finish the play. How I loved that bowing.

Then there was the glamorous Bertha Kalich in the title role of *Magda*. She was the incarnation of the grand manner. She just didn't come onto the stage. She made an entrance. And what an entrance. As the play opens Magda, a famous opera singer, is to return to her home from which her tyrannical father had thrown her out earlier in her life. First we see the maids tidying up the living room in preparation for the great lady's arrival. Carriage wheels are heard. They rush to the window. False alarm; it's not Magda. Back they go to tidying up and chattering about the expected one. Again sounds of a carriage. Again the rush to the window. Oh, God! This time it really is Bertha—I mean Magda. They run offstage to meet her. The room remains empty and it is quiet enough for me to hear my heart thumping. Suddenly, her voice is heard as the front door slams. We may not be seeing her yet, but we are hearing those low throaty tones from the vestibule. Next we follow her fruity laughter coming down the hall toward the upstage center drapes of the living room. Suddenly, those drapes are flicked open, and with both arms flung out to the sides, there stands the dark beauty that is Bertha Kalich. I nearly fell out of the balcony.

Bertha Kalich as Magda: "I nearly fell out of the balcony."

You would think this opening and the ovation it received would be difficult for Mme. Kalich to top. Not at all. There was the grape-eating scene. As everything she did was larger and, if I may say so, more glorious than life, so was her grape eating memorable. Draped on the arm of a chair, she reached over to a bowl of fruit on the table and grabbed a large bunch of grapes. Supporting herself with one hand, she arched her head way back, and with the other hand, lifted the grapes up and onto her lips. Snapping off a grape with her pearly teeth, she dispatched the seeds in a graceful arc clear across the stage before swallowing the fruit—a maneuver unsurpassed even when Greta Garbo, in *Queen Christina,* passionately kissed a bunch of purple grapes while John Gilbert looked on hungrily.

It was Kalich's daring theatrical spirit that excited me. It exuded the same heady atmosphere of glamour I sought to evoke with my Caruso number in our parlor and light years away from the real life in our kitchen. Little did I know that my early years as an actor would be in the Group Theatre of the thirties, where I would find myself right back in that Odetsian kitchen hearing little Ralphie Berger, in *Awake and Sing,* moaning, "All my life I want a pair of black and white shoes and can't get them."

The next beautiful stage artist I encountered late in the twenties seems now to have differed from the others by having used all her genuine theatricality to uncover the truth of her material rather than to exploit her extraordinary personality. This was the Spanish diseuse, Raquel Meller. She, of all my ladies, became the lodestar of my own artistic path, although I was only dimly aware of it at the time. Not being able to afford the staggering opening night prices, even for my gallery seat, I went on the second night. The rave newspaper reviews had acknowledged that the extravagant publicity campaign preceding her arrival in this country was more than justified. As a result, when she made her initial appearance on the stage, the audience greeted her with a deafening welcome. The lighthearted mood she came on with for her opening number, a little song about a girl dressed up in her grandmother's clothes, soon gave way, under the prolonged ovation, to such strong feeling, that it was quite wrong for her needs. Up went her hand to halt the music. Breathing deeply, she circled the stage a few times, trying to shake off her emotion, so she could get started properly, which she presently did. This not only had a stunning effect on the audience, but taught me an early lesson in the use of emotion for serving the character, rather than for the aggrandizement of the performer.

In one of her songs she accomplished a feat of acting, the nature of which I was only to understand years later. "Flor del Mal" was two verses and two choruses long but, as in all her numbers, it contained enough acting material for a complete characterization embodied in a compact drama. Meller played a prostitute sitting at an outdoor cafe casing imaginary passersby for a prospective customer. During her singing of the first verse and chorus you could read in her eyes the particular people she was looking at—an unattractive man, a pair of lovers, a woman with a child, and so on. Then came the unforgettable moment in the orchestral interlude before the second half. Meller languidly took a cigarette from her purse, placed it in her mouth, and reached for a match. It required several genuinely painful tries for her to strike the match, and the ensuing exhaustion, which followed that effort as she put the flame to the cigarette and summoned up strength to blow out the match, revealed something fundamental to her characterization: bone-aching fatigue, plus boredom. During the last chorus, she apparently saw a prospect give her the eye and she slowly gathered her things together, pulled herself up from her chair with difficulty and, lifting up her head, ambled off to work.

Raquel Meller:
"Of all my ladies, the lodestar..."

The illuminating manner in which she lighted her cigarette to express fatigue, a basic ingredient of her profession, would be what Michael Chekhov, the great Russian actor and nephew of Anton Chekhov, later would call "psychological gesture." He defined this as an archetypal gesture, as distinguished from the natural and usual gestures we use in life or on the stage. It is, in condensed form, a revelation of the *essence* of your part—a guide to your entire characterization. I would one day witness Chekhov himself illustrate this concept in performances and lectures. In the meantime, here was Raquel Meller offering an early contribution to my theatrical storehouse. Incidentally, Charlie Chaplin had wanted to make a film with himself as Napoleon and Meller as Josephine but it was not to be. However, Chaplin did use "La Violetera," Meller's lighthearted closing number, in his *City Lights* musical score.

My year with Jane Kerley ended with the participation of our Little Theatre Group in a gala pageant staged in the opera house of the Brooklyn Academy of Music (BAM) next door to the Music School. The director was Princess Matchabelli. She was the statuesque Maria Carmi, who had been in Max Reinhardt's *The Miracle*. This was, technically, my debut on any stage. I experienced the same feeling of joy that I had rehearsing the Greek faun as I sat in the dressing-room chair, looking at a mirror as my face was being transformed by the make up man. When Harvey Lichtenstein, in the sixties, was planning the renovations of the Academy of Music to house his BAM theater groups, he invited me on a tour of the old building. As I went from dressing room to dressing room backstage at the opera house, I was sure I'd suffer a shattering emotional memory. Nothing. BUT—when I crossed the great stage where Caruso had hemorrhaged during the first act of *L'elisir d'amore* in December 1920, leading up to his fatal illness, I did undergo a genuine emotional experience.

Although I spent another year, after the Brooklyn Music School Settlement, at the Institute of Musical Art in Manhattan, soon to be renamed the Juilliard School of Music, I was already weaning myself away from the cello. A summer job in the Catskills as a social director gave me the chance to act in plays and skits. I also got five dollars for a week as "Scoop," a reporter, in Michael Arlen's *The Green Hat* on the Wee and Leventhal Stock Company Circuit. But it was not until I joined Sue Hastings' Marionette Company, which toured a lot, that I had to make the break not only from my music lessons but from my family.

My mother was frantic. As a musician, even if I didn't become a soloist, I could always give cello lessons, make a living. But an actor—what was that? I certainly didn't look like one. "Fat-face fiddler," my charming French teacher had called me when I played in the high school orchestra. Off my mother dragged me to have a talk with Uncle Sidney, who was the principal of a high school and therefore the family authority on everything.

"You don't look like . . . Walter Hampden," said Uncle Sidney.

He then proceeded to be rather rough on me, talking of "disgracing the family" and the like. In a few years, he would come backstage to congratulate me after a Group Theatre play I acted in. I was unforgiving and wouldn't see him.

Anyway, I found a tiny room (no windows and the toilet down the hall) on the same floor of the commercial building where Sue Hastings' Marionette Company was located. I've kept a copy of a letter I wrote my hurt mother from Horne's Department Store in Pittsburgh where our marionette company was playing an Easter engagement. Trying to explain my need to be free to pursue my new life, I ended the letter with this dramatic reference to one of my new stage idols: "Ruth Draper, in one of her sketches, tells of a soldier, killed in the war, whose spirit visits his mother. The woman, seeing the form of her son, weeps bitterly. The son replies to her sobs, 'Give over weeping, mother, lest my wounds bleed anew.'"

I also started the practice of enclosing in my letters some money from my weekly salary. I only mention this because my older brother Frank had aspirations to be a business tycoon and although he was out of work most of the time and lived at home, he always derided my ambition to be an actor. Once I started with the marionette show I went from one theater job to another, always making some kind of living, but so strong was the legend of actors being a shiftless lot and businessmen the backbone of the community that Frank, rarely working and sharing, in my mother's house, the money I sent home, continued forever to patronize me. "When you gonna play the Palace?" he'd say every time he saw me. Even when I had a steady ten-year job with the Group Theatre during the depression while he was a member of the vast unemployed, Frank would still smile at me in a condescending way as if *I* were the one goofing off. (He had the same attitude toward my younger sister, Golda, who also left home at an early age to become a painter.) Years later when *Variety,* the bible of show business, listed me among the stage directors with the highest incomes, Frank would come to my town house on the East Side of New York, look around and snicker, "Where'd you steal all this?" Legend is stronger than reality.

So I came to the end of my teens playing all kinds of parts in the marionette plays. This was certainly good practice for the versatility I would need later as a character actor. For the children's shows I was a puppeteer using every voice from the villainous giant in *Jack and the Beanstalk* to Eeyore, the donkey, in *Winnie the Pooh.*

Touring helped me keep up my affair with opera greats, too. In Chicago I saw Mary Garden as *Louise.* Unforgettable. Not only was she a superb actress but, to this day, I remember strokes of stagecraft that point up her talent as a director—or "directa," as she called herself when she took over the administration of the Chicago Opera Company. In the second act

Montmartre scene, the entire huge stage of the opera house was alive with dancers and singers. Down front right leaning against the proscenium was red-haired Garden, as Louise, in a simple black dress. Careful not to move an inch, she watched the busy, colorful, choreographed spectacle unfolding. Whom do you think all the opera glasses were focussed on? Our Mary, of course.

Another director's trick I remember was the moment when it came time for the high B in "Depuis le Jour." The talk about Garden was that her acting was always great, but her singing not so reliable. Listening to her exquisite 1912 Columbia recording of "Depuis le Jour" will cast some doubt on that gossip. In any case, we opera buffs were on our guard as she got close to the B. Up to that point in the scene she again kept absolutely still as she poured out her song to Julien, her lover, seated in a chair downstage of Louise, but facing her. A second before the B, our heroine suddenly ran forward to Julien, throwing her arms around him in a wild embrace. By the time the audience recovered from the startling movement the B was long gone.

A prime example of an actress saving a scene occurred in the last act where Louise quarrels with her father and he throws her out of the house. The baritone, in the time-honored way of some opera singers, lumbered around the stage after Louise. But Garden, literally knocking over chairs in her flight from him, gave the impression of genuine danger and, in a sense, to create believability for herself, was playing *his* part for him as well as her own.

With Sue Hastings, in whose marionette company "I got to play Romeo."

Most satisfying for me were the adult marionette performances Sue Hastings booked for evening shows all over the country. In addition to songs and dances, we did one-act plays and scenes from classics. My favorite was the balcony scene from *Romeo and Juliet,* as I got to act Romeo, well hidden of course, on a platform behind the black drapes of the marionette stage. When I returned to New York City to "make the rounds" and landed in a production of *Romeo and Juliet* with live actors at the Civic Repertory Theatre I had to settle for two bit-parts: Gregory, a servant to Capulet, and a wordless watchman in the final tomb scene. I didn't get to play the romantic lead this time.

CHAPTER 2

# The Civic Repertory Theatre 1929

GROUP THEATRE ACTOR Luther Adler used to tell of his visit to a plastic surgeon. Sick of being cast in character rather than romantic roles when still young, Luther went to this physician to have his nose fixed. "Doctor," he said, pointing to various areas on his nose—the bridge, the underneath part, both nostrils—"I want you to cut this off, and this, and this." "But Mr. Adler," the surgeon interrupted, "if I cut all that off, your face will lose its character." "Doctor," commanded Luther, "*wherever* you see character, cut it off!"

Short and rotund as I was, I reluctantly accepted the "character" category. Therefore, in my search for an acting job I kept my eyes open for a chance to join a company where, even if I didn't get a big leading part, I might get a lot of little character ones. I hied myself up to Sixty-fourth and Broadway where Walter Hampden held forth with one of the two permanent companies then housed in New York performing plays with large casts. There I was told that I was not tall enough for the towering Mr. Hampden's company. Down I went to the Civic Repertory Theatre on Fourteenth Street presided over by the shorter Eva Le Gallienne.

At the stage door I was again turned away, this time with the admonition that I was too late for that season; the company was set and was at that very moment in rehearsal. Desperate, I walked around to the front of the theater and, even though I had heard it was unprofessional for actors to come in through the front of the house, I carefully opened the door and found myself in the deserted lobby. Afraid to enter the orchestra in case I would be caught and thrown out, I sneaked up the stairs to the balcony and eased myself into a seat in the back row.

There they were on that stage rehearsing *Romeo and Juliet.* Miss Le Gallienne was directing some actors and others, not in that scene, were scattered around in the orchestra seats, watching. In the front of the balcony I noticed a woman behind a huge camera set on a tripod, with one of those black cloths you throw over your head when snapping the shutter. She was taking rehearsal pictures. Slowly I edged my way down to her side. I later found out her name was Helen Lohman, an assistant to Miss Le Gallienne and the staff photographer. As she pulled one of the large wooden frames out of the front of her camera after taking a shot, I reached up and carefully took it out of her hand and set it down on a seat. Miss Lohman peaked out from under the black hood and said, "Thank you." "You're welcome," I replied. No doubt she thought I was one of the new apprentices from downstairs who was not needed in the scene on stage. I kept making a neat pile of her photographic plates for her, and when she was through taking pictures from that distance, she started to lift her camera to move downstairs. I grabbed it quickly and, slinging it over my shoulder, followed her down to the middle of the orchestra, where we set up business for closer shots. I was now obviously her assistant, so no one questioned me. When Miss Lohman had taken all the photos she wanted, she grabbed her camera and disappeared. I sat still as a mouse.

Presently Miss Le Gallienne, who was rehearsing one of the street scenes, turned to the auditorium and said, "I need a couple of more people here. Is there anyone out there who can be in this scene?" I could, and up went my hand with a few others in the house. "Come on up here then—quickly," called the director. I soon found myself in the Veronese crowd and I didn't care if I was a Capulet or a Montague.

At lunch time Thelma Chandler, the stage manager, assuming I must be a late addition of Le Gallienne's, gave me a card to fill out with my name and address. I was in five plays there that season.

Looking over my script of *Romeo and Juliet,* which I still have (I've saved every scrap of paper relating to my theater activities), I'm reminded that Donald Cameron was Romeo to Miss Le Gallienne's Juliet and J. Edward Bromberg, later a colleague of mine in the Group Theatre, a rather too portly Mercutio. Burgess Meredith was Peter, servant to the Nurse, and in a tiny walk-on as a page, May Sarton, now the well-known novelist. The most interesting casting, however, was Jacob Ben-Ami, star of the Yiddish stage, as Prince Escalus. In permanent companies, as I was to discover again in the Group, actors are often forced to "stretch" themselves, sometimes to the breaking point. Ben-Ami was a very great actor, far and away the best in the Civic Rep Company, but he had an accent that didn't quite fit the Prince of Verona. It was a weird mixture of a highly elegant manner of speaking with certain distinctly Yiddish pronunciations. Escalus's opening salvo, delivered from the top of a huge flight of steps to the brawlers down below on the stage floor was, "Rebellious subjects, enemies to peace." In Ben-Ami's version, the Bard's line came out, "Ribalious sobjects, animies to piss." At this point, Burgess (called Buzz) Meredith, who had quickly become my friend in the company, always stared at me, bugging his eyes, in a wicked attempt to break me up.

The Prince's closing lines of the play didn't help us keep straight faces either. It was the Tomb Scene and in the solemn final tableau Buzz would face as far upstage as possible, covering his face with his hand as he kneeled in reverence, the better to hold his shaking head. As the curtain slowly fell on Tchaikovsky's *Romeo and Juliet* music being played in the pit, Ben-Ami's beautifully lyrical voice intoned the final words of a "sturry of murr woe than this of Juliatt and her Rummeo."

Of course if he ever forgot his lines, as he did once in a preview performance, Ben-Ami was up the creek. It isn't easy to improvise your way out in Shakespeare, especially if English isn't your first language. After Tybalt is slain, the Prince exiles Romeo and explains why: "My blood for your rude brawls doth lie a-bleeding" etc. Ben-Ami went "higher than a kite," as actors say. He knew he had to explain the banishment but he couldn't think of the damn words. We all tried to prompt him under our breaths, but every actor who knows the panic that overtakes you in a moment like that, will attest to the fact that your senses, including hearing, tend to go dead. Finally, in desperation, Ben-Ami pulled himself together and with royal bearing, and with the quick-witted trumpeters heralding him forth, sailed off majestically crying "I have my rizzons for all dot."

The bits I acted in the various plays at the Civic were not as important to my development as the fact that I had a theatrical home. Since I could never be satisfied with playing small parts forever, my creative juices spilled over into the next logical possibility: directing. Egon Brecher, one of Miss Le Gallienne's character actors, directed a studio production of Gorki's *The Lower Depths* with a cast of the new young actors, and I was in it as Bubnov, the shoemaker. Brecher made his own English translation from a German version of the original Russian and I helped him with it. Soon I was his assistant. It then was only a step for me to assemble my own project to direct. I chose a one-act play, *The Twelve Pound Look* by J. M. Barrie, because I had seen the regal Ethel Barrymore in it at the Palace. Although I don't remember if I copied her production to the letter, I thought it wouldn't hurt to have a guide for my very first directing job. I rehearsed it in the cellar of the theater with two other young company members, Arnold Moss and his soon-to-be-wife, Stella, in the Barrymore part. The audience for our single showing consisted of whatever actors in the company cared to attend.

Miss Le Gallienne's direction of the plays performed by the Civic Repertory Company was always intelligent and faithful to the text. She had proclaimed that the main objective of her enterprise was "to make a library of good plays at popular prices." And this she surely did. Imaginative directorial flights weren't featured. What is now called the "conceptual" approach didn't really hit the New York theater until Orson Welles's talent exploded a decade or so later. In his productions, Orson defined a new posture for the modern American director. He made it clear that all the elements of the production—scenery, costumes, lights, music, style of acting—stemmed from a single artistic source. These choices, combined, would express a single interpretation, or concept, derived from the material of the playwright. That was the rightful business of the director.

One of Orson's most famous concepts, of course, was his Blackshirt version of *Julius Caesar*. In *Danton's Death* (Büchner) he covered the entire back wall of the theater with hundreds and hundreds of human skulls as a telling background of the French Revolution. Richard Wright's *Native Son* was set in a tiny room overpowered on three sides by a huge brick wall that pressed down on the playing area and never let us forget the environment that bred the tragedy of the black man.

Eventually abuses of this conceptual approach crept in, with some directors employing "clever" concepts not deriving from the nature of the material they were supposed to be interpreting, but rather forcing them on to the text, often destroying it.

But, conceptual or not, Miss Le Gallienne was able, as producer and director, to deliver some fine actors in a number of highly professional

"In Tolstoi's *The Living Corpse* he was unmatched." Jacob Ben-Ami (on the floor) in Fedya's death scene. The old man in the "bald wig" framed in the door is Bobby Lewis as a 20-year-old Civic Rep apprentice.

performances in the course of each season. Among these actors were Alla Nazimova and Jacob Ben-Ami in *The Cherry Orchard* and *The Sea Gull.* Miss Le Gallienne herself has never been surpassed as Masha in *The Sea Gull* and Varya in *The Cherry Orchard.* No one could remain unmoved by her acting as Sister Joanna of the Cross in Sierra's *The Cradle Song* and no actress since has come close, in my opinion, to the wild excitement of her *Peter Pan.*

The most influential experience I had at the Civic Rep was my association with Jacob Ben-Ami. His accent may have tickled us in *Romeo and Juliet* but in the plays of Chekhov and Tolstoi's *The Living Corpse* he was unmatched. Ben-Ami—I sensed this even though I was a beginner myself—was not only the finest artist on that theater's stage; he was, in some mysterious way, *different.* And I was determined to find out why. I recognized in him something akin to what I perceived in Raquel Meller. They worked in two different mediums, of course, but both seemed to be able to be theatrical without losing their sense of inner truth. The "outside," so to say, seemed to be justified by the "inside" and vice versa. I had a vague feeling that this was unique, and it steered me to glean what secrets I could from Ben-Ami.

I was lucky enough to be in the same scene with him in *The Living Corpse.* He played the lead, Fedya, and I was the waiter serving him champagne in the private room of a restaurant. I still have a trauma about pulling the cork out of a champagne bottle as a result of the series of onstage disasters I perpetrated as poor Fedya was trying to write his farewell note before he would kill himself. The cork took forever to come out; or it came out at once without popping; or it would pop so forcefully as to endanger Ben-Ami. My two other variations were, one, to spill the gushing wine over the suicide note or, two, when the cork wouldn't emerge at all, to stand in front of the whole table and fake the pouring. But as soon as I was mercifully offstage I'd stand in the wings to watch the great scene that followed. In Tolstoi's script it seems straightforward enough:

(*Fedya* locks the door, takes up the revolver, cocks it, puts it to his temple, shudders, and carefully lowers it again. Groans.) *Fedya*: "No, I can't. I can't. I can't!" (Someone knocks at the door) "Who's there?"

Now I had seen the Reinhardt company, which was visiting New York then, in its production of *The Living Corpse.* Their leading actor, Alexander Moissi, had made this scene so famous that it was noted in the actor's biography at the back of the program. We were actually exhorted to watch for this high moment. I recall our grade-school teacher telling us that if we wanted to see how another famous "moment" was accomplished, to keep our eyes riveted on the apple in a production of *William Tell* in German that our class was taken to see at the Irving Place Theatre. The entire stage crowd of villagers had settled down, as the father, on one side of the stage, pulled his bow back preparatory to shooting the arrow through the apple on the head of his son way on the other side. Every character stood stock still and after the boy said, bravely, "Vater, ich fürchte mich nicht" ("Father, I'm not afraid") there was a deathly silence. Suddenly, upstage in the crowd and furthest away from the apple, there was some sort of disturbance. For a moment, all audience eyes were automatically deflected to the place where the sound and movement came from. In the next second, someone close to the boy with the apple on his head yelled, "He did it! The father did it." When we looked back, there was the arrow straight through the heart of the apple.

Well, Moissi's rendering of the attempted suicide in *The Living Corpse* was certainly spectacular, too. He slowly raised the gun to his temple and then lifted his justly famous tenor voice in a cry as memorable as Olivier's in *Oedipus.* "Ich kann nicht," he wailed at top volume. "Ich k—a—a—nn nicht!" Then as he heard the knock at the door, he whispered something like "Who is it?" over and over. The dynamic shock from fortissimo to sudden pianissimo added to the pyrotechnics of the moment. But, in the end, it was just that—the thrilling pyrotechnics of a very colorful actor.

In Ben-Ami's case, equally theatrical, by the way—and that's the point—an altogether different result was achieved. As the gun slowly reached his temple, something happened inside him that invariably made the audience gasp quite audibly. They actually felt he really was going to kill himself. In Moissi's case the wonderful physical thrill the public got from his acting lasted as long as the moment lasted. Ben-Ami's choices, theatrical though they were, were devoted to the illumination of the character he was playing rather than to the exploitation of his acting effects. As a result, while Moissi got a thunderclap of applause for his heroic efforts, the audience at Ben-Ami's Fedya not only experienced the genuine inner terror with him, but were impressed, when the scene was over, with the realization that this weak man was a failure, even at killing himself. I have since used this example of two different techniques whenever I talk in class to actors about total acting—"inside" plus "outside." I then advise them to read George Bernard Shaw on the different approaches of Duse and Bernhardt in Sudermann's *Magda.*

One day, seeing Ben-Ami through the open door of his dressing room studying his lines, I asked him if he'd like me to cue him. He accepted with thanks, and that got me inside the dressing room. Soon I was tidying up his makeup table daily and helping him with his costume changes. Now I could pick his brains. Like all sensitive artists, he didn't much like to discuss his inner workings, but, after much prodding, I got him to reveal the secret of his suicide moment.

"Not having blown my brains out very often," he said, "I had to find some substitute that, with my imagination, could help me believe in such an act." One of the component parts, he felt, must be the fear of the actual physical pain of the bullet entering the brain as Fedya lifted the gun to his temple. "You'll laugh," he said, "when I tell you what I finally came up with." A most agonizing anticipation of pain for him to endure, Ben-Ami explained, was that terrible moment just before stepping into an ice-cold shower. All his muscles would tense, his eyelids would flutter, he'd hold his breath, and then plunge into the painful knifelike spray. If he could truthfully recreate the sensation of that pre-plunge terror, that experience, plus the actuality of the slow raising of the gun to his temple, would insure belief in the audience that he was actually going to kill himself. And, I must say, it worked every time. The collective gasp never failed to come. I was finding out that acting could be a creative activity, far more complex and exciting than merely delivering your dialogue with intelligence and expression and moving to the positions that the director had blocked.

Did I learn anything from being in the other plays? Well, I learned how to be a whirling dervish in *The Would-Be Gentleman* and an Indian in *Peter Pan*. In the latter play, I also learned not to fool around with the star when you're a bit player. One matinée, some kid in the audience had a most peculiar laugh, which broke the audience up every time he let loose. It was like a staccato bleat from a goat. Now we Indians, whenever the Great White Father Peter Pan approached, had to raise our right hands in a sort of fascist salute, and with impassive faces, cry "Ooh, ooh, wa—ah!" Miss Le Gallienne, as Peter, always used to stand in the wings before her entrance, trying to break up us Indians onstage by making all sorts of faces. This particular afternoon, as if by prearranged signal (actually it wasn't), all the Indians felt it would be fun to greet Peter's entrance with an "Ooh, ooh, wa—ah," in which the "wa—ah" was a replica of the goat bleat. The audience howled, but this time it was Miss Le Gallienne's face that was impassive. When she came off, she threatened to fire us all for unseemly conduct on stage. Everyone, especially the Indians, thought the punishment was too heavy for the crime, and old Egon Brecher finally interceded for us. Miss Le Gallienne relented, and we didn't fool around anymore that whole year.

At the end of the season, Miss Le Gallienne called all the young apprentices together for a critique and to announce who would be kept on and who would be let go. I was let go and was told why. "Bobby, I feel you definitely have a place in the theater; but it is not as an actor." I wasn't sure what she meant by a "place in the theater." I only knew this was my second big rejection—I couldn't be an opera singer, and now, I shouldn't be an actor. Staggered by the blow, I sat still in my chair, unable to look at Miss Le Gallienne or the other actors and kept saying to myself, "I'll show you. I'll show you." And in the Group Theatre I did, indeed, do some damn colorful, small-part character acting. But my main activities, in the years to come, were to be directing and teaching. So maybe Miss Le Gallienne wasn't too far wrong.

CHAPTER 3

# Group Theatre–the First Summer 1931

I DIDN'T HAVE to sneak into the Group Theatre. This time, I was chosen legitimately. Still believing in the idea of a "home" with a company of players as the best way for me to advance, I joined a group called "The Actors' Workshop." They were presenting a revival of Maxwell Anderson and Harold Hickerson's play *Gods of the Lightning* at the Provincetown Playhouse, on MacDougal Street in Greenwich Village. Yes, there was an off-Broadway then, too, and the Provincetown had a distinguished record, having housed the early Eugene O'Neill plays.

*Gods of the Lightning* was a sympathetic account of the arrest, trial, and execution of the anarchists, Sacco and Vanzetti. I played Capraro, the counterpart of Vanzetti, and I hoped that Miss Le Gallienne didn't miss my personal reviews in the newspapers: "Mention must be made of Robert Lewis for his admirable portrayal of Capraro, one of the doomed men"; "Outstanding was the work of Robert Lewis as Capraro, the gentle anarchist"; "Lewis possesses a tenderness, a sincerity that wins him sympathy and respect on every hand."

Naturally, I was ecstatic with these notices; that is, I was until Lee Strasberg arrived backstage one night with *his* critique. Harold Clurman and Strasberg had come to see their friend, Sanford Meisner, who was playing the defense attorney in the play. After the performance, Sandy introduced them to me. Whatever Harold said is wiped out of my mind by the memory of Lee's icy question, delivered through taut lips and clenched teeth and accompanied by a steely-eyed expression: "What—were—you—trying—to—do?" I didn't have a clue then what he meant, but I know I experienced that same bowel-crumbling sensation of guilt so many other actors would ultimately feel under the same punishing examination. Sam Wanamaker says he carried his load of Strasbergian guilt all the way from America to London where, even though he established himself there as a successful actor and director, he couldn't wipe it out. One year, he had occasion to go to Germany where he met Bertolt Brecht who, in no time at all, and with a few fierce, caustic, scatological words, exorcised Wanamaker's guilt forever. Mildred Dunnock also told of how she had once knocked herself out preparing a scene to present to Lee at the Actors Studio. Like many other distinguished players, Millie attended classes there because she felt she had to stretch herself. She didn't mean on the rack, of course; so that when Lee, after the usual deadly silence that follows the presentation of a scene at the Studio, asked his ominous question, "What were you trying to do?" Millie, infuriated, replied, "I was trying to do a damn fine performance" and stalked out.

**Lee Strasberg:**
**"What were you trying to do?"**

As I stared at Strasberg backstage at the Provincetown, feeling immobilized with fear at the intensity of his probing, he let fly his next salvo. "Do you think that was real emotion you felt up there? You were just indicating." I didn't know then what that meant, either, but I could tell it was a dirty word. Still, there was something so impressive about this Svengali that I accepted his, and Clurman's, invitation to attend some meetings they were having to organize a new theater project. I realized later, of course, that Clurman, and even Strasberg, must have sensed some qualities in my acting they were interested in, or they would never have invited me.

The meetings were held in Steinway Hall, on Fifty-seventh Street, every Friday night at 11:30, that season (1930-1931). Employed or unemployed actors in whom they were interested were invited to attend by Clurman,

Strasberg, and Cheryl Crawford, the third member of the triumvirate that was to constitute the leadership of the Group. The Group was always the way the future theater enterprise was referred to in the meetings, so it was natural that it eventually was officially named the Group Theatre.

Cheryl, Lee, and Harold all worked for the Theatre Guild at the time. Cheryl was the casting director, Lee a stage manager, and Harold the foreign play reader. They had all been influenced by the presence in New York of Richard Boleslavsky, an early defector from Stanislavski's Moscow Art Theatre, who had established the American Laboratory Theatre. Earlier, Harold also got to rub elbows with the great Frenchman, Jacques Copeau, here to direct his dramatization of *The Brothers Karamazov* for the Theatre Guild. To make the Group leaders' theatrical seeds universal, there were the theories published by England's Gordon Craig on what would later be referred to as "Total Theatre."

Strasberg, Clurman, and Crawford would have liked to establish a studio to explore their ideas within the Guild setup, but, luckily for them, they were turned down, and this led to their ultimate resignations from the Guild and the establishment of the Group. At the Steinway Hall meetings, Cheryl occasionally spoke on the administrative aspects of theater, Lee on artistic matters, and Harold on everything. Most passionate and evangelical of the three, Harold exhorted us all to relate the theater to life. He defined the word *theater* as something that need not only be the presentation of a production for the entertainment of the public. He spoke of an ensemble of dedicated artists—actors, playwrights, directors, designers—collaborating, through a common technique, to create unified presentations of plays that would reflect, for their audience, the life of their times. He, without question, was the inspirational backbone of these Steinway Hall meetings as well as of the ten years of the Group that followed. If truth be told, the echoes of his exhortations can still be heard reverberating wherever there is evidence of theater, as opposed to show business.

Boris Aronson, the Group's favorite stage designer, was present one evening during one of the theater's summer rehearsal periods when Harold was haranguing the company for his usual four or five hours. Some of the actors had fallen asleep on the floor. Others downed black coffee. Gadget (Elia) Kazan and I were performing our favorite pantomime: pasting our ears back on our heads. Panting heavily, veins distended on his forehead, Harold finally ground to a halt. Said the awestruck Boris, "I understand him now. If he hadn't become the director of the Group, he would have been an evangelist like Father Divine."

The excitement of Harold's fervent talks made the thought of going home to sleep after the Steinway Hall meetings impossible. Many of us would repair to the Child's Restaurant then on Columbus Circle and sit throughout the night talking some more about how we had to save the American theater and, incidentally, change the world. A beautiful young

Harold Clurman:
"He would have been Father Divine."

girl who attended one meeting wasn't impressed. She was, at the time, only an understudy. When asked at the end of Harold's talk what she thought, she said, "This may be all right for you people, if you want it, but you see, I'm going to be a star." We were all properly shocked. Eunice Stoddard, later a Group member, who brought this independent girl to the meeting told us her name was Katharine Hepburn. In 1943, playing one of my many Japanese parts, this time in MGM's *Dragon Seed,* starring Hepburn, I told her how remarkable it was for her to have known herself so well at the start of her career. And how honest. She never could have submerged her extraordinary personality in the ensemble theater company being planned. She kidded me, "Bobby, you and Gadget were the only ones mean and tough enough to come out of those ten years with the Group completely untouched." "Yes," I replied, "except for two or three complete nervous breakdowns, it didn't touch me at all."

At the end of that season of the Steinway Hall meetings, the three directors chose twenty-eight actors they felt had the material needed to build their kind of acting company. I was chosen as one of those who would trek, for the summer, to Brookfield Center, Connecticut, for rehearsals, lectures, and training. Each actor was asked to contribute ninety dollars for room and board for the entire period. Democracy being what it is, the poor (like me) were expected to pay the same amount as the rich (like Franchot Tone). Ninety dollars was a walloping sum to anyone in my circle, in those days. But this was obviously going to be the most important step in my career, and I was desperate. There was one rich man I knew only casually, but I thought I'd take a chance. "You're an investor," I said, when he agreed to see me. "You invest in stocks and bonds. Here's a chance to invest ninety dollars in someone's life. When I start to earn some money, I promise to pay you back." I got the money, but by the time I saved up ninety dollars from the pittance the Group paid me, I read in the newspaper that the man had died. I never did get the chance to pay him back for my life.

The average age of the company that first Group summer in the country was twenty-seven. At twenty-two, I was the youngest, although I wasn't going to let the others know that. I left the honor of being the baby of the group, with its attendant ragging, to Herbert Ratner, who, being more naive than I was, was better cast for the part. He used to sit out on the lake, alone in a rowboat, playing classical records on his portable Victrola and reciting speeches from Shakespeare. Herbert was one of those actors who, though in love with acting and capable of real emotion, was never able to acquire enough technique to be very useful as a working professional. Permanent companies all over have the devil's own time dealing with these faithful and well-meaning disciples.

The first production the directors put into rehearsal was Paul Green's play about the South, *The House of Connelly,* released to the new group by the Theatre Guild, which owned it. I was given the first of many infinitesimal bits I was to play in the early productions. To take the curse off, they were referred to as "cameos" and, to stress their importance to the ensemble idea, we were reminded of the Stanislavkian dictum, "There are no small parts, only small actors." I quickly revised that to read, "There are no small parts, only small salaries."

Restless and unsatisfied at just being in the crowd scenes, I was quick to notice that Strasberg, the director of *Connelly,* made daily individual,

The Group Theatre Acting Company: "To change the world."

private, rehearsal calls with the lead actors which the rest of the company didn't attend. I went to Cheryl Crawford and asked her if the Group stage manager was definitely set. "Yes," she said, "It's Alixe Walker." "Who's her assistant?" I asked. "She has none as yet," replied Cheryl. "She has now," said I, and went off to sweep out the rehearsal hall and set up the chairs. Now I was able to be in on those private rehearsals where the nitty-gritty stuff took place. The education I received as a future director was invaluable. To this day, I'm convinced it's the best way for a prospective director to learn his craft: apprenticing himself to a good director. It's the same as being an assistant choreographer or an assistant conductor. Any student can learn in a conducting class how to beat time, but only by being in on the actual rehearsal work can you observe the process of getting your interpretation realized by the musicians.

I certainly got more from the job than I contributed to it, since I turned out to be the very worst assistant stage manager in history. A couple of examples: distractedly ambling around backstage one night during a performance of our second play, *1931—*, I spotted a fascinating-looking box with metal knobs all in rows. I tapped one lightly and a fearful gun shot rang out right in the middle of one of Franchot Tone's quiet scenes. He didn't like it.

Another failing of mine, which often delayed the rising of the curtain, was forgetting the all-important call of "fifteen minutes," which warned the actors of the impending start of the show. The reason was simple. I was in Stella Adler's dressing room picking her brains about some acting point, as I had done at the Civic with Ben-Ami. Not only was Stella most knowledgeable about the craft of acting, she was the most glamorous one in the company and reminded me of the great ladies I had previously worshipped.

I was too young to have seen her father, Jacob P. Adler, a giant of the Yiddish theater, but I did witness an extraordinary display of great acting performed by her mother, Sarah Adler, on the occasion of her fiftieth anniversary on the stage. In life, Mrs. Adler remained very colorful into her great age. In her eighties she kept up with the latest social dances by taking rhumba lessons. On the stage, however, she had the simplicity that must have characterized the playing of Eleanora Duse. And like Duse, her acting was as revealing as a mirror. Sarah Adler chose, for her contribution to the anniversary gala, a scene from an adaptation of Tolstoi's *Resurrection.* It was a moment at the end of this scene that told us we were in the presence of a queen of acting. Her emotion rising gradually in a frenzied crescendo, she finally sank to the floor, cursing wildly. The audience started to applaud. Without the slightest break in her concentration, the actress's left hand, as though it belonged to someone else, shot up and turned the applause off like a twist on a faucet. She was not finished yet. Brought up short in her cursing by noticing an icon on the wall, she begged forgiveness for her

**Group Theatre Acting Company: the first summer, 1931. One of Harold Clurman's "fervent" talks. Bobby sitting on the bench, taking notes.**

blasphemy as she crossed herself. *Now* they could clap. And so they did, like thunder.

Starting in that summer of 1931 at Brookfield Center, Clurman and Strasberg delivered a series of lectures to the company which, when made concrete in the rehearsals and classes, constituted a training program that forged the group of actors into a powerful, realistic ensemble that was to influence the acting style of a whole generation. Clurman first defined for us the component parts of the Stanislavski System, which the great Russian director maintained were the elements present when a good actor was playing truthfully and artistically. Harold and Lee had absorbed the workings of the system at Boleskavsky's American Laboratory Theatre. Although Clurman was careful to point out that the system was not an end, but a means, this approach, which Stanislavski himself never stopped investigating, was eventually frozen by careless practitioners into a dogma called the Method. It is, to this day, fetishized by its defenders and derided by its detractors.

Harold was not only interested in the truth of our acting, he wanted to give shape to our life attitudes—especially our relation as individuals to the Group. Taking as his text Gordon Craig's principle, "After we've reformed the art of the Theatre, we must remake the life of the Theatre," Harold encouraged us to develop what he called "dynamic humility." It was sort of "ask not what the Group can do for you, ask what you can do for the Group." The peculiarities of each of us were not the issue; the work of the group was. The differences between us, he maintained, were accidental; the similarities were important. Rightly or wrongly, Harold felt the amount of talent we had was not as crucial as what that talent was, and could become. In case some actors were wondering about the size of the talent of some of the others, we were told not to judge, but to concentrate on what we could get from each other, and what we could give, too, through the love of what we were trying to do. Harold pointed out that, too often, acting was used in a neurotic way for its therapeutic value, as self-escape, rather than for self-expression. In a strong theater one would work out of a sense of fullness. Copeau had said he wanted to play so many parts that he would die exhausted. Perhaps the most important technical point Harold stressed, at the time, was that our emotion onstage ought not to be self-indulgent, but should be used artistically, for the play. He used the well-worn analogy of the respective emotional qualities of Bach and Tchaikovsky—the former making the world's suffering his, the latter making his suffering the world's. This proposition of Clurman's, put forth that first summer of the Group Theatre, was forgotten by latter-day Method-ists.

While Clurman's talks were inspirational, Lee Strasberg's were Talmudic. He was fond of circumlocutions like "A whole apple is better than half a pear—especially if you want an orange." Often he'd begin a talk by announcing, "In the first place, there are two things." Lee was much more than an intellectual Sam Goldwyn, however. One of his most persistent efforts, the first summer of the Group, was his insistence on truthful, not simulated, emotion on stage. That was what he called "indicating." To help us arouse feelings which could be used as fuel in our acting, Strasberg taught us how to do "affective memory" exercises. Boiled down to the simplest explanation, this process was designed to kindle emotion by recalling, in detail, an event in your past that had made a profound-enough impression to regenerate some feeling, which could then be used in a scene. One danger inherent in this work was the inability, or unwillingness, of some actors to play the *scene* with the feeling that was captured. Instead, they played the emotion. They blindly held on to the feeling for its own sake, and the points in the scene's situation often got washed away in the tears. It feels just great to experience that groundswell of emotion rising in you and the temptation to self-indulgence is almost irresistible.

Another hidden danger in the careless use of emotional memory is the matter of choice. Often the actor comes up with feelings that may be true to *his* reaction to a particular situation, rather than the emotion the character should have. *That's* the truthful feeling we should be looking for. This would lead us to *theatrical* truth, not the personal behavior and feeling indulged in by so many practitioners of what they think is the Stanislavski System.

In 1947 when Kazan and I held our classes in the first year of the Actors Studio, we tried to remedy this fault. We reminded the actors, first, about their choice of emotional material. And, second, if, and when, they did an emotional memory exercise, they should release themselves from the exercise when entering the scene and play the situation, allowing whatever feeling they may have aroused to work fluidly, as real emotion does, rising and falling naturally in context with each moment played. This would prevent that "psychological grip" so identifiable with malpractitioners of Stanislavski's System.

After a full day of rehearsals, classes, and lectures at Brookfield Center, it was always a pleasure to look forward to the evening hours of relaxation. Some actors listened to classical music on their phonographs (Morris Carnovsky and Clifford Odets); some played chess (Franchot Tone and Roman Bohnen) and Stella Adler told theater stories. My favorites were the ones about her years in the Yiddish Theatre. The most colorful anecdotes concerned a certain Honigman, an actor who, in life as well as on the stage, managed to get everything upside down and backwards.

The night the kidnapping of the Lindbergh baby was on the lips of everyone in the world, Honigman rushed into the Café Royal, the renowned actors' restaurant on Second Avenue, and called out, "Did they find the Goldenberg baby yet?" He then sat down, sadly, put salt in his coffee, tasted it, and complained, "Who put pepper in my tea?"

In one highly emotional scene in a play, Honigman stood sobbing and staring at the gesture of his shaking hand spread out in front of his face and pleaded for mercy: "I'm the father of—five-grown-up—fingers!"

A colossal Honigman blooper occurred in some play about the pogroms against the Jews in Czarist Russia. A young Jewish student (accent on the second syllable) son of a Rabbi, was spirited out of the ghetto and over the border to freedom so he could tell the outside world about the persecution of his people. Honigman had the crucial second-act curtain line. As he rushed, panting, into the room the assembled Jews cried out to him, "Well? What happened? Did he get over the border safely? Did he get past the Cossack guards?"

"No," was Honigman's agonized reply. "They shot and killed him."

"Killed him?" the others screamed. "Why? Why?"

Honigman's line was to be the big tearjerker: "Why? Because he's a Jew!" Slow curtain.

But what did Honigman say this particular night? He said, "Why? Because he's a goy!" And the curtain fell—fast.

Well, you can imagine the rumble of excitement that spread through the audience at this startling turn in the plot. Backstage, the actors stared, dumbfounded, at Honigman. Then they hit him a lot. They only had ten or fifteen minutes of intermission to think up a whole new finish to the play. The best they could come up with by the time the curtain rose on the third act was that the student, when a newborn baby, was left by his no-good goyish parents on the doorstep of the Rabbi who brought him up as a good Jew.

When a favorite Yiddish actor, Leon Gold, was given his fiftieth anniversary benefit, it was Honigman, of course, who was chosen to present the old actor with a gold watch after the performance, as a tribute from his colleagues. Honigman's accompanying speech was a classic: "My dear golden friends, on this golden occasion of the golden anniversary of our golden friend, Leon Gold, we now present him with this silver watch."

Clifford Odets, who was to be the most notable playwright the Group spawned from its company, was, that first summer in Connecticut, its most intense actor. A frustrated musician, Clifford would sit for long periods releasing his tension by pounding out a stream of E-minor chords on the piano. As if that were not annoying enough, one night he took to throwing billiard balls at the bedroom door of one of our actresses, Margaret Barker, who was heartlessly refusing him entrance. From the top of the stairs came the booming voice of Stella Adler: "Clifford, if you don't turn out to be a genius, I'll never speak to you again."

Being Clurman's girl friend, and later his wife, Stella's evaluation of him may have been slightly less reverent than the other actors. I once asked her why she thought Harold had a habit of staring at himself in the mirror so much, studying first one side of his face, then the other. "He's trying," said Stella, "to imagine how he's going to look on that horse when he's a statue in Central Park."

Some years later, visiting Harold in Hollywood, I had the dubious pleasure of sharing a bedroom with him and so being a captive audience at a concert of nocturnal sounds emanating from his mouth. Although Harold expressed himself with passionate fanaticism during the day, his night sounds were even more volcanic. As he slept, cries of rage alternated with delicate purrings. Then there were such sounds of clicking teeth as a castanet player would envy. Stella, fed up one night, says she awakened him and demanded, "Harold, don't sleep like a great man. Just sleep."

If Stella Adler was our grande dame, Franchot Tone was our only leading man. Like Stella, Franchot had reservations about group encounters. Scion, as they say, of a wealthy family, he wasn't too sympathetic to the plethora of intellectual talk and classical music that permeated the night air. On the Fourth of July, proclaiming "I am an American," he let loose an answering barrage of firecrackers. It was one of the ironies of the time that, during the McCarthy period, his patriotism was questioned. During the Spanish Civil War Franchot and his wife, Joan Crawford, had donated an ambulance to Loyalist Spain. Joan simply invited a dozen or so of her movie star sisters to lunch one day and put a check for one thousand dollars at each place setting to be signed by the guests. Although Joan was excited by the non-Hollywood theater names she learned from Franchot, such as Stanislavski, Chaliapin, and the like, she was less interested in her political education. In the Spanish Civil War, for instance, it was impossible for her to remember which side she was on. "Rebels" sounded so exciting. Yet Franchot insisted they were Franco's soldiers; therefore, on the fascist side. The "Loyalists," he said, were our boys. At a party I gave in my apartment one Christmas in the late thirties, when Franchot brought Joan to New York to meet his former Group Theatre colleagues, she sat listening with the rest of us to the radio reports of the war, knitting away like Mme. Defarge. "The rebels are advancing," announced the news commentator. Hopefully, Joan looked up at Franchot. "Is that us, dear?"

The person I felt closest to that first summer was the great Negro actress, Rose McClendon. (The term "black" was still some years away.) I had become friends with Rosa, as I called her, during my year at the Civic Rep. A few of us used to go to Harlem several times a week after the evening performance and stay through the night. One of our favorite hangouts was the Theatrical Club, where Fats Waller held forth at the piano. At Tillie's Kitchen we'd have some fried chicken at the next table from the gourmandizing Heywood Broun who, upon scanning the huge and seductive menu had proclaimed, "I see nothing to object to here." After a stop at Jimmy Daniels's place to hear him sing, we'd end up at the Five O'clock Club. A

**Summer with the Group: Franchot Tone, "I am an American."**

subway ride downtown, a bit of breakfast and we were ready for our first session at the Civic: a ballet class under Blake Scott. This was followed by a fencing lesson with George Santelli, the Olympic champion, who staged Miss Le Gallienne's sword fights for her. The afternoon was for rehearsals of one of the plays (or a performance on matinée days). Then came the evening show and off to Harlem again. We slept on Sundays.

In between stops at the various uptown clubs, I had often visited with Rose McClendon whom I met through Carl van Vechten. Along with Nancy Cunard and some others, he was in the vanguard of those who worked for the promotion of Negro artists. Rosa's house was a social center for many of the most interesting personalities in Negro art. In her salon, one could meet Paul Robeson, Langston Hughes, Countée Cullen, and many others, including the marvelous blues singer, who was one of Rosa's closest friends, Alberta Hunter.

Rose McClendon had been suggested by Cheryl Crawford to play Big Sue, a cackling field hand on the plantation, in Paul Green's *The House of Connelly,* the Group's first production. Cheryl knew her from the *Porgy* days at the Guild when Cheryl was casting director, and Rosa had given her memorable performance as Serena. As a field hand in the Paul Green play she was about as miscast as she could be, since she was a tall, slender, elegant woman with the carriage of a queen. Richmond Barthé, the sculptor, made a full-length statue of her as Nefertiti. However, there were few parts offered in those days for actresses like Rose McClendon that weren't servants or slaves. The beautiful Edna Thomas, for example, who made such a staggering success as Lady Macbeth in the Orson Welles Federal Theatre production, was in almost nothing else until she played a bit of a blind Mexican woman crossing the stage in *A Streetcar Named Desire* calling out, "Flores para los muertos."

In 1926, Rose had played the proud Madam of a house of prostitution in Arthur Hopkins's production of *Deep River.* Hopkins, noticing Ethel Barrymore standing in the back of the theater one night during the Philadelphia tryout, asked her to be sure to stay until the last act "and watch Rose McClendon come down those stairs. She can teach some of our most hoity-toity actresses distinction." It was Miss Barrymore who sought out Arthur Hopkins at the end of the play to tell him, "She can teach them *all* distinction." This then was the artist who attended all the rehearsals of her scenes in *The House of Connelly* but never the lectures given by Clurman and Strasberg since there were no blacks in the Group. But I happen to know that she listened from behind her window, like a good "house nigger," to the goings on of the quality folk on the lawn below. While Strasberg thrilled us with stories of the great Eleanora Duse's contributions to the art of acting, Rosa heard it all sitting in her room in the back of the artistic bus—she who was described by Alexander Woolcott in the *New York World* as "the lost loveliness that was Duse."

Rose McClendon: "The lost loveliness that was Duse."

CHAPTER 4

# The Group Theatre—First Season 1931

THE GROUP THEATRE started its ten years of production with *The House of Connelly* on September 23, 1931, at the Martin Beck Theatre. The other two plays that first season were Claire and Paul Sifton's *1931*—and Maxwell Anderson's *Night Over Taos. Connelly* was an immediate critical success. More important, astute observers recognized the special ensemble nature of the performance that was to characterize the Group's best work and would justify the directors' approach in building a permanent company. Brooks Atkinson, in *The New York Times,* said, "Between Mr. Green's prose poem and the Group Theatre's performance, it is not too much to hope that something fine and true has been started in the American Theatre." Not only were all the performances knitted together into a harmonious whole, but some of the individual actors had true elegance, a word not used often in describing the Group players. Clifford Odets's plays—of which we did a number—being about lower-bourgeois families, resulted in the assumption that the actors were specialists only in "kitchen" drama. In *The House of Connelly,* Franchot Tone, as the tormented son, was a picture of repressed inner power with no viability, using his own natural quality of refinement to advantage. Morris Carnovsky was a pathetic old gentleman of a dying South, to the letter. And Stella Adler, as the elder sister, deeply aware of the crumbling values around her, was full of proud dignity.

Superb as Lee Strasberg's handling of the actors was in *The House of Connelly,* the tiniest seeds were being sown for what was to grow into a widespread fault in the application of the Stanislavski System in American acting. That failing consisted of creating a sense of truth that, while being genuinely derived from the inner life experience of the actor himself, often represented *his* emotional reaction to a situation rather than the character's. Further, there developed an unnecessary concentration on emotional

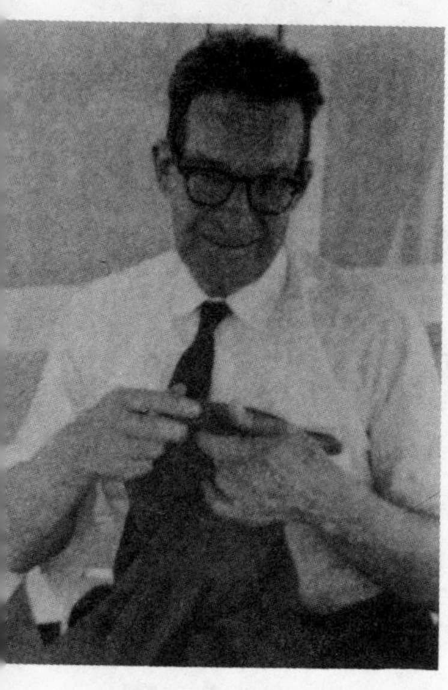

**Paul Green, author of *The House of Connelly*: "Something fine and true has been started."**

preparation in moments where the simple playing of the points of the scene would generate a sufficiently truthful result.

As assistant stage manager of *The House of Connelly,* one of my jobs was to take charge of an offstage crowd of mocking Christmas revelers that gradually approached the main house of the Connelly plantation and eventually invaded the dining room, where the family was having supper. We, the actors in the crowd scene, assembled in the Martin Beck Theatre basement a long time before our cue and started our "preparation." This "taking a minute," as it was called, before each entrance, in order to get emotionally prepared, was one of the elements of the so-called Method that became a fetish. After each individual character in the crowd was thoroughly prepared, I gave a signal for an improvisation to begin. None of the early part of this fascinating scene, of course, was ever heard or seen by the audience and was only to give a sense of believability to the actors. Gradually, as our "situation" developed, we climbed the stairs to the stage floor, where we "adjusted" to the Connelly house and the fancy people eating inside. On a cue, we burst into the room, and our onstage improvisation blended in with the family scene. Now, in Lee's defense, there isn't a shadow of doubt that our "cellar acting" paid off in the reality it achieved when all the members of the crowd finally arrived on stage. But when I saw Leo Bulgakov's production of *The Lower Depths,* at about the same time I couldn't help wondering why the audience was so thrilled when his offstage crowd, starting pianissimo in the distance and swelling gradually to fortissimo, burst onto the stage. It's quite possible those actors may not have been as "truthful" as we were, but there is no doubt in my mind now, that the *dynamic design* of the building crowd noise contributed mightily to the excitement of the entrance that brought forth a solid round of applause. All right, maybe applause is not the point. But, why, in heaven's name, is it not possible to orchestrate a performance and *not* lose your sense of truth? What is an artist, if not a *designer* of truth?

*1931-* was the title of the second play of the Group's first season. It opened on December 10, 1931, and closed nine days later, in time to prevent its title from going out-of-date. The late Claire and Paul Sifton were journalists, and this play about unemployment was their first. They didn't write many more, and one of our Group members, Friendly Ford, may just have had something to do with that. It was never too clear how Friendly got into the Group acting company in the first place, since he seemed to exist on a planet totally devoid of the smell of theater. He looked more like a hayseed than an actor. Being a vegetarian, he didn't partake of nice pastrami sandwiches on seeded rye like the rest of us. He seemed to be satisfied with just the seeds. Harold Clurman, who had a fuzzy tongue, invariably called Friendly "Truly."

The initial period of sitting around the table before putting the play on its feet was unusually long in the early Group days. First, there was the analysis of the play and its relation to the world. Then, there was the work on the inner life of the characters, the principle being, if that were understood thoroughly, the external manifestations, in terms of movement, would flow naturally and, therefore, be more justified than the usual

Max Gorelik: "I was there once, but I didn't take any notes."

arbitrary "blocking." This last part of the work, the staging, not coming until quite late, caused a bit of worry for the actors, as well as the playwrights this time, since Mordecai (called Max) Gorelik had designed a handsome, but complicated, unit set for *1931-* to accommodate some twenty scenes located all over New York City—in the park, under the "el," in a squalid bedroom, and so on. In front of all this, giving a chilling sense of the mercilessness of the times, were three wide, menacing-looking, corrugated iron doors which rose and fell like giant guillotines. A slightly ill-timed entrance or exit through one of these doors meant certain decapitation. It was natural, therefore, for the actors, to want to get "on their feet" in time to acquaint themselves with Gorelik's floor plan.

Max's sense of humor was as steely as his set for *1931-*. When he later designed Odets's *Rocket to the Moon,* the director, Harold Clurman, gave Gorelik instructions for the scenery: "Max, although the set is just a dentist's office, I don't want just a dentist's office. These characters are all hemmed in by life. I want the scenery to seem to stifle the people—to press in on them. I want it to give the effect of a womb. Do you understand, Max, a womb?" Said Max, "Well, I was there once but I didn't take any notes."

So it was then that, late in the rehearsal period of *1931-*, the cast was still sitting around on the stage listening to Strasberg discuss some philosophical point in the play. The Siftons, who had been waiting for days on end to see their play on its feet, dozed in the darkened auditorium. Finally, Lee finished his discourse to the actors, and the Siftons shook themselves awake.

"Did you all understand what I said?" Lee inquired.

"I didn't," said Friendly Ford.

"Good," said Lee. "I'll explain it another way." And off he was again. The poor Siftons collapsed in their seats once more. After another hour or so of Strasberg patiently taking his point on a trip around the world, he asked, "Now is it clear?"

"Nope," said Friendly.

This really warmed Lee up, and he sailed into still another explication. Paul Sifton blew a gasket. Leaping up in the aisle, he shouted, "If that guy doesn't understand, why don't you tell him to march?"

The effect on us all, of this otherwise sensible challenge, was staggering. Up to that point in the Group life, no one had seriously questioned any of Lee's actions. He was our theatrical god. The word *guru* wasn't popularized till later. Now all the actors were frozen in anticipation. How would Lee deal with this heretical author? Paul Sifton could in no way have been prepared for what he heard. Lee, turning very slowly in his chair until he faced the offender, barely moved his lips as he icily informed the angry writer, "Mr. Sifton, we are not here to rehearse your play." The poor playwright of course had been laboring under the delusion that that was exactly what we were there to do. The actors, however, understood at once what Lee meant. He meant we were there to build the Great American Theatre, we were there to bring culture to the masses—lots of "big" things. Both of the Sifton faces froze in terror as they absorbed the staggering pronouncement. Then they fled from the theater.

I'm sure they never could have known how Friendly finally ended his Group Theatre days. At the conclusion of the first season, since he seemed less and less to fit into the Group's pattern of life, Friendly was called into the office for a chat with Clurman.

"Truly," Harold began, "I've been observing you for some time now, and I'm beginning to wonder if you are really happy in the Group, or even right for it. Maybe acting isn't the ideal career for you. I thought we'd have this little talk to get at the inner problem. For example, what is it that moves you most in life?" Friendly didn't have to probe long for the answer to that one. "The smell of manure," he replied. "Well," said Harold, encouragingly, "Why don't you become a farmer?" Strangely enough, no one had ever suggested that to Friendly before. "I think I will," he said happily, and was gone. Listening to as much show business crap as I have over the years, I have often thought, enviously, of Friendly Ford out there, somewhere, plowing through some honest manure.

Having played walk-ons, and served as assistant stage manager in the first two productions, I was sure the Group directors would reward me with at least a bit part in the third play, *Night Over Taos,* which had lots of little Mexican-type characters in it. When the actors gathered around for the first read-through, our sides were handed out. Sides are six-by-eight-inch pieces of paper with the dialogue and cues typed on them and bound with a blue, manila cover. When I received mine, I smiled foolishly at my colleagues as I weighed it in my hand. A butterfly would have been heavier. The dialogue is usually typed in black, and the stage directions in red. Cold fear growing in my heart, I slowly opened the cover. There was only a single, thin sheet of paper, and all the typed material was red. My unbelieving eyes were greeted by, "Act 1. Scene 1. You are an old Indian. When the curtain rises you are finishing cleaning up the ashes from the fireplace and you leave the stage." End of part.

Sensing all the other actors were staring at me, I sat perfectly still, head down, and made a silent vow that, before I was through, this would be a play about an old Indian. My first move was to go to the great Robert Edmond Jones, who had designed the décor, and beg him to work with me on my costume and makeup. He complied at once, thrilled that an actor with such a tiny part would care that much. We got up my slave character in a marvelously colorful outfit, topped by a huge Indian blanket folded and wrapped around my middle. A spectacular wig of long, black shiny hair was dressed with a headband and many bows of colorful rags. A good-sized blob of putty was fashioned into a hooked Aztec nose. I then mixed my makeup, the skin base being a dark, but luminous, red color. For

Bobby Lewis in *Night Over Taos*: "A play about an old Indian."

physical behavior, I perfected a wobbly running gait, achieved by turning my toes in, which I read, in my extensive research, that the Indians employed to grab the earth as they ran.

My simple characterization completed, I now had to plot a way to get into every damn scene. This was not as impossible as it may sound since Strasberg, the director, always improvised the play's situations in rehearsal and I, as the household slave, found easy justifications to be present on every single occasion. Lee was delighted with my inventiveness, his only objection being that I was too comic. Every day on his page of rehearsal notes I'd see the same entry: "Bobby—not funny Indian." Laughter of any kind was obviously out of place in Maxwell Anderson's turgid poeticism. There was one big plotting scene where Stella Adler, J. Edward Bromberg, and Franchot Tone huddled over a map spread out on a table. I stood, immobile, in the corner, arms folded, body turned slightly away, but obviously listening hard to their important dialogue. The bewildered audience mused, "Keep your eye on that Indian. He knows something."

I was shameless, too, at the very opening of the show when Franchot had to make his first entrance into the adobe house. As the faithful servant, I preceded him with my running gait and, in a grand flourish, took the colorful blanket which draped the door frame and flung it high in the air like a welcoming banner. By the time Franchot came on—well, forget it. He was so furious with my shenanigans that, at the end of the first preview, he left his place in the center of the full company call, walked all the way to the end of the line where I, the least of the characters, was standing, and pulled me back to the center with him and, locking my arm under his, forced me to bow alongside the principal actors.

They never gave me a walk-on again.

CHAPTER 5

# The Group Theatre Decade 1931-41

WHATEVER MAY BE said concerning the merits of the twenty-five play scripts the Group Theatre produced from 1931 to 1941, there can be no doubt about the enormous influence the theater itself had. The high quality of the actors' performances, and the basic idea behind the Group's existence, plus the experimental work done during the summer rehearsal periods, set a standard for permanent theaters anywhere.

First, the performances. The ensemble nature of the Group acting was compared favorably by the respected critics of the day with that of the Moscow Art Theatre.

Second, the idea. Clurman's premise was that acting, and all the other elements of theater, can never really be properly understood except as parts of the whole for which they exist—the theater itself—and that the theater should exist because of a need shared by its members—actors, directors, designers—who have a dream of a social life they want to live in common. Most "shows," Harold taught, since they exist by and for themselves, lead to an occupational loneliness caused by their separation from the whole of the theater. Also, the training of actors, when disassociated from theaters can lead to artiness and pretension. From this, he said, theatrical sterility results.

Third, the training. The classes and lectures of Strasberg and Clurman in the thirties spawned an army of directors, teachers, and actors who have, along with their progeny, influenced the technique of acting at home and abroad. Whether accepted or squabbled over, the results of the work inaugurated in those Group rehearsals and classes, have infiltrated countless American stages, films, and acting schools. The impact of the Group's success with their London appearance in *Golden Boy,* in 1938, led to the establishment of English ensembles similar to the Group Theatre. The Unity Theatre played *Waiting For Lefty,* and individual artists, such as

Joan Littlewood, were influenced by the Group company's ability to create realistic truth on the stage. Michael Billington, in *The New York Times* of March 23, 1980, claims that, "Groups like La Mama, the Open Theatre, and the Living Theatre electrified Londoners in the late sixties with a gut-tearing (and frequently gut-exposing) kind of ensemble attack they (the English) hadn't seen before." Each generation has to discover America, I suppose. The same words were used to describe the Group in 1938. "Gutsy," they called us, not only in reviews, but in editorials. James Agate, in the *London Times*, said of *Golden Boy*, "The acting attains a level which is something we know nothing at all about."

**Sandy Meisner, Kermit Bloomgarden, Gadget, and Bobby on the way to open *Golden Boy* in London: "'Gutsy,' they called us."**

If the Group Theatre, then, was so valuable why did it break up? Why couldn't it survive longer than ten years? Many theories have been propounded, one of the favorites holding that internal dissension and defections to Hollywood were the causes. Well, tell me of a permanent theater anywhere in the world free of intramural quarrels. God knows, the Group had its fair share, but it always rode out the storms and pressed on. As for the movies, the only big loss in the early years was Franchot Tone, and his type, at least, was replaced by Alexander Kirkland who played in *Men in*

*White* and *The Case of Clyde Griffiths.* Actually, Franchot himself returned toward the end of the Group's life to appear in Irwin Shaw's *The Gentle People* and like a good, repentant sinner, was its major financial "angel." By the time Julie Garfield left the Group for the films, it was 1938, three years before the theater's final collapse. But his defection was not the cause.

The next explanation of the relatively short life of the Group comes from Harold Clurman himself. Relative, I may say, only to the Moscow Art Theatre and La Comédie Française, since there have been precious few examples of the Group set up to compare it with in America. Harold, writing his own theater's obituary in *The New York Times,* said "that while we tried to maintain a true theater policy artistically, we proceeded economically on a show-business basis." That was true. Each play was set up and financed individually. We always seemed to be waiting for the mail from North Carolina to deliver a third act from playwright Paul Green, or for Mr. Lee Shubert to decide he liked a play of ours well enough to put part of his real estate empire behind us.

My own theory is that the very spine of the Group contributed to its undoing: "To present new plays that reflected the life of its time." First of all, how many really first rate new plays in a season are written and would be submitted to a theater company committed to a set group of actors? And why did it have to be a new script that would reflect the life around us? Why couldn't a classic or a revival be done with a directorial eye modern enough to be able to illuminate the script in terms that would render it analogous to existing problems? Giuseppe Verdi, no mean producer of theatrical works himself, said, "Let us return to the past—and it will be progress." And I don't mean you are bound to go in for the updating of every classic play or to transplanting it from Illyria to the South Bronx. With a body of classics and revivals to draw on, plus whatever good new scripts they'd have been able to acquire, bolstered by some sort of subscription (unions, for example) that could have been sought with a backlog of established plays in hand, and in a permanent home, the Group idea might have gone on and on.

I'm sure the directors have given many reasons why this didn't happen. But what about this theory: the artistic directors of the Group were most comfortable with contemporary theatrical material. Clurman often referred to *Awake and Sing* and *The House of Connelly* as poetic plays in trying to defend the Group against accusations that it was a realistic theater, "lifelike as a newsreel," as it was said at the time. Helen Westley, the Theatre Guild actress, once remarked that sitting at a Group performance was as real and exciting as watching an accident take place. But there is a vast difference between the poetic sensibilities of Odets or Paul Green and the acting and directing problems of verse, costume, period, and all the other aspects of speech and movement one encounters in classics.

In the season of 1935-36, Harold wrote a paper celebrating the fifth birthday of the Group in which he explained that our method of work was based on Stanislavski, but tailored to our American needs. He also defined what social comment meant to the Group: "A comment on the aims, defeats, accomplishments of ourselves and our fellow man." Then, in a parenthesis he said, "And, of course, we will produce Shakespeare because, like all great artists from Phidias through Dickens, he is chock full of social content." We never did.

At about the same time, I received a letter from Lee Strasberg in answer to one of mine harping, as I always was, on the problem of style in our repertory. He says, "The point you make about the value of gesture, etc., in a purely realistic form, is very important. Most people at present completely misunderstand the problem and come to two extremes: either they believe the road of the future to lie along the path of stylization, or they accept realistic truth as the acme of perfection (and to hell with the audience!). One leads to an exaggerated gesture and movement where the style is perceived separate from the material (content) it deals with, and at best becomes a highly skillful individual manner which is bound to twist material into one's own shape or form; the other is even worse because it usually deteriorates into an acceptance of one's own emotion and truth (usually no more than personal comfort) as the standard."

Reading these wise words now, in 1980, from two important theater men, makes one wonder at the wide chasm that exists between yearning and accomplishment. For if the Group had been able to tackle classics with the expertness they brought to realism, they might not only have survived, but, with the influence they would have generated, there may have been fewer examples of the mangling of language, the smart-aleck mockery of classical writers, and all the other self-indulgences of directors, canonized by some critics eager to accept any novelty as "avant-garde."

Therefore, the problem remains. Many of the fine realistic American actors, descendants of the Group, or the Group ideas, still don't tackle parts much different from themselves. With the need to conquer problems of language and movement due to the decentralization of the theater, and the actors having to face up to the world repertory in regional theaters, we have turned to the English for guidance. The tables are turned. The Group invasion of England in the thirties has ended in the counterrevolution of the sixties and seventies. When the good American actors discover they can infuse parts in *whatever* style with that command of truth they inherited from the Group techniques, provided they look for that truth in the material as well as in themselves, they can recapture their preeminence. And when the talented new directors find out that form need not be *pasted* on to the content, but should derive *from* it, the American theater will be on its way again. All talk of a true National Theatre is empty rhetoric without facing up to this basic problem of style.

Whatever charges of limitations in matters of style one could level at the Group's productions each winter, there could be no doubt that a genuine urge to expand the boundaries of realism was manifested in Strasberg's summer classes. The experimental nature of some of the work in these sessions was, for me, the most exciting activity of the whole Group project. It was also the most valuable part of the work for my future career as a director and teacher. I lapped up acting études based on music or painting, often staying up the whole night preparing props and staging for a "number" I was to present the next day in class. Eventually, I held my own classes during the theater seasons in New York City and carried on this work, always searching for further ways to extend the sense of truth so precious to the Group's acting style into material that depended not only on psychology, but on movement, speech, period, and so on.

One of these classes was in the basement of the Broadhurst Theatre where we were holding forth for a full season (1933-34) with the Group's first financial success, *Men in White*, by Sidney Kingsley. Burgess Meredith, my pal from the Civic Rep, was one of the actors in that class (he tried to get into the Group, but never quite made it—their fault, not his). Present also was a kid called Julius Garfinkle. He subsequently changed his name to Julie Garfield for the stage and to John Garfield in the movies. Clifford Odets, who had volunteered to hold some acting sessions at the Theater Union, found Julie there. He had recently graduated from Angelo Patri's school for what were called "delinquents." Cliff brought him to my class. He had the manner of a street kid, but it didn't take long to uncover a warmth, sincerity, and genuine sweetness underneath.

Laurette Taylor, when I interviewed her later on, asked me about Julie. His eyes, she said, were particularly extraordinary to her. "It's as if he's looking inside himself." Many classes later when I had his daughter, also called Julie Garfield, in my workshop, it always startled me to look down the aisle to where she was sitting and be greeted by those same eyes and that same look.

To lay on him, at once, the problem of speech and movement that would be foreign to his own, I suggested he work on a Picasso painting of a young boy. The exercise required him to accomplish a number of steps. First, to recreate the exact pose of the painting, down to the minutest detail of posture and facial expression. Next, to fill out the inner life of the pose and expression with whatever he felt the boy was thinking. Then to walk, sit, run, and move about in the manner the pose and the costume suggested, all the while creating a specific silent improvisation derived from the sense of the picture. A further step was to pick a poem to be used as a text that would be consistent with the characterization evolving and use that poem as though it were the dialogue of a situation in a play this character might inhabit. Finally, appropriate music was to be chosen which would enhance the life of the étude.

The end result that he came up with, was so imaginative and so beautifully executed that I went upstairs to the Group office, nabbed Clurman and Strasberg, and made Julie repeat the number for them. The next summer they took him away with us and he became a Group member with a small part in Melvin Levy's *Gold Eagle Guy,* which the theater was rehearsing for the following season.

It turned out that it was also possible to relieve, in a modest way, the Group's continuous financial distress by charging a nominal tuition (one hundred dollars for ten weeks) when Kazan and I conducted still another Group Theatre Studio in the beginning of the 1937-1938 season.

Gadget and I also enjoyed the dance instruction we got in the summertime, and if I may speak for the two of us, we were pretty good at it. So much so, in fact, that Gluck-Sandor and Felicia Sorel, our teachers one summer, invited us to work with them the following winter in their ballet company's production of *Salome.* José Limon was John the Baptist, and a teenage member of the company was Jerry Robbins.

My favorite of all our dance teachers was the late Helen Tamiris at Dover Furnace, New York, in the summer of 1932. She herself was a superb, dynamic performer. A pioneer in the Modern Dance movement in America, she had commanding arms and hands and a leap that carried her into next week. She developed the actors' creaking bodies relentlessly, until some of us could actually move with genuine authority.

Away from her role as brutal trainer of sluggish bodies, she was a lusty and humorous companion. When Lincoln Kirstein became head of the dance project of the WPA, she said he called all the dancers and choreographers on the government payroll together to announce his first production. It would be a cavalcade of the great dancers of history, to be impersonated by those present.

"For example," he explained, "Gluck-Sandor, you could dance the part of Nijinsky. Felicia Sorel, you might be Taglioni, and Tamiris, you could play Isadora Duncan."

"Yeah," said Tamiris, "but then who'll play me?"

Tamiris: "Who'll play me?"

My interest in movement led to the extraordinary occasion of my appearance as Agnes de Mille's partner in one of her numbers at a Sunday night concert at the Guild (now Virginia) Theatre. Agnes had just returned from a three-year period in England and needed a dancer for a duet that was to be part of her homecoming program. She telephoned John Martin, then dance critic of *The New York Times,* and inquired if he knew someone who could portray a Spanish ambassador at the court of Elizabeth I. The Queen and the Ambassador not only had to dance a Galliard and Canaries at a ball, but needed to act out a drama of political intrigue and antagonism while executing those Elizabethan court dances. The lute and recorder music of the period were to be in the capable hands of Suzanne Bloch, daughter of the composer, Ernest Bloch.

Now John Martin had seen me, with Kazan as my drummer, at many benefit performances doing my impersonations of Shan-Kar, Mary Wigman, Martha Graham, etc., and knew I could move, at least in a funny way. Lincoln Kirstein, never a champion of Modern Dance, had written in his review of Tamiris in the *Nation,* "Bob Lewis' imitation of Wigman, which followed one of her (Tamiris') numbers, was funnier and a more savage criticism than one would take the trouble to write about her." *Variety,* under "New Acts" had commented that my dance burlesques were "smart, devastating, and hilarious and would be surefire in a sophisticated or intimate revue." Considering the fact that I impersonated only the greatest dancers in the world at the time, I thought *Variety* got carried away when it went on to say, "His satires are better—and funnier—than the original dancers." Although none of this qualified me to dance in a serious recital as Agnes de Mille's partner, John Martin, in all innocence, recommended me to Agnes.

In answer to her telegram, I phoned her and emphasized the fact that I was an actor who could move rather than a dancer who could act.

Summer with the Group: Bob Lewis satirizing Mary Wigman: "Funnier than the original."

"Why don't we start to rehearse," suggested Agnes. "If you don't think you can do the steps, say so, and if I don't think you can, I'll say so."

It was an offer I couldn't refuse. After a few sessions, Agnes seemed to think I might make it. As for me, one view of myself in the rehearsal hall mirror gliding around in that courtly manner and I lost my head completely. Nijinsky was not as narcissistic in *Afternoon of a Faun.* My Group Theatre colleagues kidded the hell out of me, wrapping my precious feet in blankets to protect them, and advising me against smoking to save my wind for my pirouettes.

Meantime, Agnes's mother, daughter of the author of *Progress and Poverty,* Henry George, was saving money by sewing me a beautiful doublet-and-hose costume. I prepared a makeup based on the Velasquez portraits of Philip IV of Spain, Bourbon lower lip and all. Since my Ambassador was from a wealthy court, I covered every one of my fingers with glittering rings.

In her book, *Dance to the Piper,* recounting her agonies as a young dancer trying to get a foothold on the stage, Agnes explains her choice of me as follows: "The brilliant and highly trained young men who abound today were not around in '35. I had to settle for two partners; one a musclebound, overgrown athlete who could move to a small degree, and the other a nimble member of the Group Theatre who could act. The latter was Robert Lewis, who has since become a director of distinction. He was chosen, at this point, for his pantomime abilities, but he footed a Galliard with friskiness and aplomb." Well, dear Agnes, that's very generous of you, but considering the disaster I was, I wonder whether it is kindness or blessed forgetfulness on your part.

When the Guild Theatre curtain rose there was Agnes, magnificently costumed as the first Elizabeth, facing front, with me poised at her side. My left hand was on my hip, my right arm and hand extended in front of me. That pose of the two of us, standing there majestically in the royal ballroom, proved to be the high point of the number. As I took my first step downstage, the audience burst into hoots of laughter. Agnes slowly turned her queenly head to see what the hell I was doing. So far I hadn't done anything, but I, too, was panic-struck at the laughing since this was the evening's most dramatic number. I had completely forgotten (and Agnes had never known) that the audience was the very same small group which, in those days, were the devotees who attended every modern dance event and knew me only as a burlesquer of dancers. The blinding glitter caused by the front spotlights hitting all my huge, fake diamond rings didn't help, either. Now we started downstage together, Agnes steaming, and me working much too hard to succeed in suppressing the audience's giggling. Reversing our direction, we proceeded upstage. You must believe me when I tell you that the movement Agnes choreographed required me to leave my arm and outstretched hand behind me as I turned and danced away from the audience, the rings thereby getting the benefit of the front spots again. The laughter swelled. Agnes' eyeballs rolled upward. Then came the big, dramatic moment. Elizabeth let a rose fall to the floor, and as I dropped gracefully to one knee to retrieve the flower for her, she had to grind her heel into my hand. This royal cruelty was greeted, not with the gasp Agnes was used to in her appearances in England, but with a tidal wave of laughter. When the curtain fell, mercifully, Agnes, near tears, had no time to dwell on what went wrong, having to change quickly for her next number. At the end of the evening, Martha Graham came backstage. At parties she had always laughed at my impersonation of her in one of her great dances, "Extasis." She was a bit more restrained on this occasion. "Bobby," she said, "you kept your mood all through." John Martin, probably feeling guilty in his lukewarm review of the whole evening, tactfully omitted any reference to my debut (and farewell) as a serious dancer.

Thereafter, when my services were enlisted for various charity benefits, I stuck to numbers that did not rely primarily on dance movement. One of these came to be known as the "Red Hamlet." This piece resulted from an exercise I performed in one of Strasberg's summer classes. By taking a speech from a Shakespeare play and adding movements as well as meanings from another context, one could come up with a new synthesis. These early experiments in the Group Theatre summers were, in reality, sketchy forerunners of the later experimentation employed by Charles Marowitz, the American director practicing in England, with his conceptual approach to Shakespeare in *The Marowitz Hamlet, A Macbeth, An Othello, Variations on the Merchant of Venice,* etc. I was present at an audition Marowitz held for a proposed American production of his version of *The Taming of the Shrew*. He asked the auditioners to do a speech of Petruchio's in the character of Hamlet, Macbeth, a nineteenth-century Shakespearean actor, and so on. The idea was to test the actor's ability to transform himself regardless of the explicit sense of the chosen text. Although we were experimenting with similar techniques, mostly in exercises and "numbers" in the thirties, openly zealous avant-garde directors nowadays, sometimes find difficulty in differentiating between imaginative interpreting of classics and crude tampering with them.

For my "Red Hamlet" speech, I took the "To be or not to be" soliloquy and, in the character of a political orator haranguing a crowd, illustrated each of the phrases with poses and meanings based on cartoons by Gropper and other social-minded cartoonists of the day. Starting with the attitude of a worker in chains (what else?), on the first phrase I broke my bonds, flung my arms in the air, and proclaimed a victorious "To be!" On "or not to be," I sank into a sitting position, thumbs under my armpits and assumed the manner of a fat, capitalist bastard (those two words were always spoken as one). "That is the question" propelled me up and into my character of a mediator, making the contrasting points of capital versus labor—and so on to the end. At the finale, "And lose the name of action," the word *action,* accompanied by a raised fist, was a thunderous cry to revolt. You can't imagine how popular this number was during the depression. Heywood Broun, who acted as master of ceremonies at one of the benefits where I did this Hamlet number, remarked to the audience when I finished, "I didn't know Shakespeare was a communist."

Another staple I had originated in class was a setting of Walt Whitman's "I Sing the Body Electric." In the character of an old Milquetoast of a man, I began asleep in bed, huddled under a blanket. The alarm woke me and, shivering from cold, I went to the bathroom to take my morning shower. I turned on the hot water faucet and nothing came out. Quaking with fear, I touched the cold water faucet, and holding my breath, turned on the freezing water. As it hit me I screamed, "I sing the body electric!" Then, as I praised the glories of each organ recounted in the poem, I soaped it (you can be sure I mixed my organs up a bit), finally drying my shriveled body quickly and jumping back under the covers.

Another political foray (practically everything we did was politically oriented in the theater activities of the thirties) was my takeoff on Herbert

**As Herbert Hoover: "Everything we did was politically oriented."**

Hoover. I put little balls in my cheeks to stretch out my face, wore the highest stiff collar I could find, and read from a seemingly prepared political speech. Only it was Robert Browning's "Pippa Passes." Hoover had promised prosperity in the form of a chicken in every pot, and as I got to "God's in his—," I came to the bottom of the page. Turning to the top of the next page, I obviously couldn't find the next word. Leafing madly through my papers, dropping some to the floor, I conducted an insane search for the whereabouts of God. The last sight of Herbert Hoover was on the floor frantically pawing the pages and not finding "heaven" anywhere.

Sometimes I even performed these and other numbers at two different benefits in one evening, after I left my theater dressing room. One benefit I organized for our own acting company took place just before the Group was to go away for the third summer to sing for its supper at Green Mansions, a hotel in the Catskills. We were also to prepare *Men in White* for the following season. The benefit to help raise funds for the summer work was held at the Majestic Theatre. I stage managed it, too, and there was an extraordinary array of artists, from Martha Graham to the Hall Johnson Choir, who volunteered their services. I went to Heywood Broun's apartment to persuade him to do his usual gracious Master of Ceremonies duties for us. I found the huge, benign, rumpled man eating jam out of a pot. I hadn't seen that since I'd been a puppeteer and manipulated Winnie the Pooh in the same delicate maneuver.

Anyone who has run a big benefit knows that the toughest job is arranging the order of the program. The various artists arrive at different times. Each wants to get on as soon as possible and go home. My problem was to keep the waiting performers happy in the dressing rooms. The venerable Cissie Loftus and her partner, Hilda Spong, had their own idea about how to keep happy, and by the time their turn arrived, they were blissfully feeling no pain. Instead of choosing to do a few of her brilliant impersonations, as I had hoped she would, Miss Loftus insisted on a lengthy park bench scene between two indecipherable cockney characters. To accompany their mumbled dialogue, Miss Loftus had called for atmospheric, dark blue night lighting. Late as it was in the program, having settled unsteadily onto their bench, Loftus and Spong seemed reluctant to leave it in this life. From the wings, I could hear the audience's reaction going from boredom, to restlessness, to outright hostility. Hoping to brighten the piece up in whatever feeble way I could, I called to the electrician, "Bring the footlights up a quarter." Broun, standing nearby, added, "And bring Miss Loftus up a half."

My own attempts to explore acting styles other than the purely realistic finally extended beyond classroom exercises. I organized a production of Chekhov's *The Marriage Proposal* in the Group summer of 1936 at Nichols, Connecticut. The one-acter is a farce showing the attempts of a hypochondriac trying to win the hand of a landowner's daughter and being frustrated by the continuous quarrels of the two of them. The characterization I planned for my timid suitor was based on a mouse. I held the fingers of my hands together like little paws; I made a moustache of a couple of mouselike whiskers and sniffed at my hoped-for bride as though she were a piece of cheese. For this part, I cast Paula Miller, a Group member who'd also been in the Le Gallienne company with me. This was the Paula who rose from small-part actress to the wife of Lee Strasberg, and the crutch of Marilyn Monroe, and whose great talent was to develop herself into a maternal monument for other artists with assorted weaknesses to lean against. Jack Cole, the choreographer who created the dances for three musicals I directed, told me this story: Marilyn Monroe played a member of a little theater group in her film with Yves Montand called *Let's Make Love.* George Cukor was the director, but Paula was the power behind the camera as far as Marilyn was concerned. For several thousand dollars a week, Paula not only administered Marilyn's life, but stood behind the camera and humiliated the director by being, at Marilyn's insistence, the final arbiter as to whether a shot was to be printed or not. A nod would be agreement, but a shake of the head meant "one more time."

This particular day, Marilyn's simple task was to arrive at a rehearsal already under way and, so as not to disturb what was going on, slip into her seat as unobtrusively as she could. When the shot was set up, Cukor called, "Action," and Marilyn wiggled in, hands fluttering, and took her seat. "Cut," cried Cukor. "Marilyn," he said, "that was lovely, but you see, she is late and doesn't want to disturb the other actors; so just come in as simply as you can and sneak into your seat." On this, Marilyn went into a corner with Paula, her acting coach, and after a conference, George called, "Action," again. Again, the wiggling and the fluttering. Again, the cry of "Cut," and the director's plea for simplicity. Then Marilyn's inevitable conference with Paula. Jack Cole, employed on the picture to help Monroe with her "My Heart Belongs to Daddy" number, was standing at the rear of the set watching these maneuvers with growing interest. "I decided," Jack told me, "that I had to find out what Paula was telling her that was creating this impasse. I slunk down the side of the wall to where I could listen, unobserved, to the coaching conference. Paula was saying, 'More like a bird, Marilyn, more like a bird.'"

To complete the cheese image in *The Marriage Proposal,* I dressed Paula, who already had yellow hair, in a floor-length yellow dress. She looked like a mouth watering Brünnhilde. Knowing that, left to my own devices, I'd either go too far in executing my metaphor, or fail to justify all the comic business I had in mind, I sought the restraining hand of Stella Adler and asked her to be my director. Stella was wary of my approach, having once compared me in the following manner with Norman Lloyd, an Orson Welles actor, who was even more stylized than I was. "At least Bobby's an animal," said Stella. "Norman's a vegetable."

Paula Strasberg and Bobby Lewis in *The Marriage Proposal* by Chekhov: "I sniffed away at Paula."

Stella demanded, "What's your approach?" "Simple," I replied, "I see him as a mouse and the girl he's proposing to as a piece of cheese." "You're sure?" Stella's eyes widened, but great coach that she was, she didn't try to change my mind but helped me to be the best damned mouse in the world. Nose twitching, wisps of rodent hair quivering on my upper lip, I sniffed away at Paula and nibbled on her ear a lot. Even the purest Stanislavkyites in the Group company laughed.

My first attempt to experiment in a directorial way with the approaches in style I was reaching for as an actor was a summer of 1934 laboratory production of a play about the condition of the Kentucky coal miners, at that time called *In New Kentucky*. Samuel Ornitz had only finished one act, but it was written in a nonrealistic manner, with opportunities for choral work and many special effects that I wanted to create vocally. For instance, there was, at one point, the effect of a train approaching and passing the scene of the action. I got my offstage crowd to repeat the phrase "somebody said so" over and over, starting low and building to a climax, then fading away. By dividing my voices into sections that overlapped each other and then adding in some clacking sounds, I was able to create an imaginative reproduction of a train passing. All the other sounds in the text were likewise created by the cast and became part of the choral aspects of the script. Not many Group members were thrilled about the idea of spending part of each day rehearsing this sort of thing, so I worked mainly with apprentices. The play script was never finished, and the production never got on, but I was grateful to Strasberg and Clurman for encouraging me to try my directorial wings on this kind of unusual material. Lee felt I had potential in the direction of Vachtangov, one of the "big three" of Russian directors. Stanislavski was the master of realism, Meyerhold was a-psychological, and Vachtangov was known for his heightened ("fantastic") realism. When Lee returned from a trip to Russia and saw the work I had done on *In New Kentucky,* he generously said it was as good as the Vachtangov productions he saw there.

But looking back now on my rehearsal techniques at that early time, I realize how intimidated I was by Strasbergian "truth." Ever since I had conducted the offstage crowd in *The House Of Connelly,* I felt that every breath, of every actor, at every moment had to be truthfully felt. Therefore, for the effect of the train, I couldn't just instruct the chorus in the required sounds and dynamics. I had to give them an improvisation about a bit of gossip being passed around in order that the words "somebody said so" would be justified, and each wheel clack could be a disapproving tongue cluck. The cast felt individually truthful, I'm sure, with their improvisation, but the *theatrical* truth required for that moment was the effect of a train passing. However I would have felt like a sinner if they just made the proper offstage sounds, no matter how brilliantly orchestrated. That feeling of guilt again!

Then came August 7, 1934. It was the summer period at Mt. Menagha Inn, in the Catskills. There occurred that day an event which was volcanic for the Group and crucially important to American actors everywhere. That was the day Stella Adler delivered her comprehensive report to the Group Theatre acting company on her visit and work with Stanislavski himself, for about six weeks in the Bois de Boulogne, in Paris, where the master was recuperating from an illness. Stella told him that the Group was using his System and that she, and others, were unhappy with the results. Stanislavski suggested that perhaps we weren't applying it properly and agreed to work with her, using a scene from a Group play which had been directed by Strasberg, and in which Stella had played a role. From her explanations, Stanislavski felt we had placed a wrong emphasis on emotion by relying too heavily on "affective memory" exercises. Stanislavski gave Stella a chart of his System, which included all the elements that go into the art of acting, internal *and* external. These and many more pointers from the master himself had an enormously salutary effect on the actors, when Stella made her presentation. Lee Strasberg, however, blew his top. The very next day he called a meeting in which he declared to the startled actors that he taught the Strasberg Method, not the Stanislavski System. He also stated that we used the practice of Affective Memory in our own way, for our own results. The most amazing part of his rebuttal was his contention that in the Group we went beyond Stanislavski's verisimilitude, that our productions had more intensity than the Moscow Art Theatre's at any time, and that Pushkin and Shakespeare productions were failures in the Moscow Art Theatre because they had no sense of period. Talk about projecting. We never did any classics at all, and even Lee's post-Group productions of *The Three Sisters* and *Peer Gynt* were hardly hailed as stylistic triumphs. Anyway, it was an ugly reception for Stella's errand of mercy, an errand which just may have saved whatever respect for the Stanislavski System is still abroad in the land. Lee ultimately re-adopted Stanislavski after the latter's death, as he also bestowed belated recognition on Brecht when he died. There is a kind of theatrical necrophilia in the theater that makes it easier for us to worship the safely dead.

The net effect of Stella's report to the Group, however, was to drive a chink into what was, up to then, Lee's impenetrable armor and also to let some fresh air into the fetid atmosphere in America surrounding the theories of Stanislavski.

The decade of the thirties was not only a time of depression, it was a time of talk—radical talk. Group Theatre actors sat up half the night in Stewart's cafeteria and instead of moaning, "What a world," cried, "Change the world." Although we usually had very little money in our pockets, if there was enough for a ten- or fifteen-cent bowl of bean soup, we were in luck because there was the free condiment counter. Here were laid out such delicacies as pickles, beets, cole slaw, chow-chow, apple sauce, olives—green and black. These, heaped on a plate, plus the bread that came with the soup, constituted a tasty and colorful depression meal.

Some of the talk, of course, was a serious attempt to find solutions to the problems of the times. Much of it was the silly spouting of instant converts to the revolution. One of these members of the lunatic fringe was a beautiful, blond girl introduced to me by a Group actor, with whom I was sharing a dressing room. I was struck not only by her beauty and her Bergdorf Goodman attire but by the fact that when Rose McClendon, the elegant black actress, formerly from *The House of Connelly,* arrived at the dressing room to pick me up one night after the show, this blond beauty sniffed and stalked out of the room. Well, I thought, that's the end of her, since I knew my dressing-room mate was one of the left-wingers in the company. We were all surprised, therefore, to read one morning in the society pages of the *New York Herald-Tribune* that this daughter of a prominent society family had married our Group comrade. But wait. That surprise was nothing compared to what greeted our eyes shortly thereafter.

During a rehearsal break, in walked our débutante, wearing distinctly proletarian clothes, with no makeup on, and sporting the obligatory straight, stringy hair. She was practically unrecognizable. The following summer session she spent in the kitchen organizing the help, while it was the poor actors eating frankfurters and beans in the dining room who were the real underprivileged.

Tony Kraber, Joe Bromberg, and Gadget Kazan: "Like a Red Sea on the march."

Typical examples of left-wing "infantilism" would invariably turn up at the May Day parades, in which some Group members occasionally participated. One year they made themselves into a float with a huge red cloth pierced with holes for the actors' heads to peep through, like a Red Sea on the march, whether Russian or biblical was not clear, since some of the actors were faithful Catholics, and it must have been schizoid for them to reconcile their religious beliefs with Soviet atheism. The richest actress in the Group, daughter of a wealthy Southern railroad tycoon, brought her maid along to the workers' May Day parade, whether to convert her, or in the event the "honorary proletarian" needed some sustenance on the long march down Eighth Avenue, wasn't clear.

On these occasions, I always enjoyed the majestic presence of Stella Adler, who had proudly proclaimed that she could live in any communist country as long as she were the queen. One May Day, after waiting at least

Summer with the Group: Stella Adler, "La Pasionaria."

ten minutes on the side street for the cue when our float would join the marchers on the avenue, Stella glanced at her wristwatch and announced imperiously, "That's enough; I have an appointment at Jay Thorpe's," and off she went in a taxi. I dubbed her "La Pasionaria," after the Spanish Civil War heroine.

People have often wondered how I escaped involvement with the House Un-American Activities Committee in the fifties, when so many theater artists close to me were tapped. I can only put it down to luck and/or bureaucratic bungling. It couldn't be simply because I never joined the Communist party. Some completely nonpolitical people were persecuted, often by the most accidental association. Will Hare, a good actor who was in my class the first year of the Actors Studio and later in the road company of my production of *Witness for the Prosecution* was a tragic case in point. He had been signed for a leading part in a Lux radio show when he was suddenly canceled out. After pressing for an explanation, Will was told the sponsor threatened to withdraw since, they said, Will was a communist, his membership in the Actors Studio being presented as evidence. He maintained that not only was he not a communist, but he was completely apolitical. Upon investigation, it was proven that Will Hare was right, and somehow his name had gotten mixed up with Will Geer, an actor who was blacklisted. When Will Hare was still not reinstated in his job, he inquired again. This time he was told the sponsors didn't want anyone whose name was associated with the Will Hare-Will Geer controversy. The sponsor remarked, "Will Hare, Will Geer. What's the difference? They're all communists."

For my part, I was "guilty" of giving a benefit in Harlem to raise money for the release of the Scottsboro Boys. I had also spearheaded the *Sailor, Beware!* case in Actors Equity. This was the play whose producer had asked the actors to take pay cuts because it was losing money. They did. When these same actors found the show's intake had built and was now making a profit, they felt they should have a share since, without their sacrifice, that couldn't have happened. Actors Equity failed to help them, and a reform movement was started in that union for cuts boards, rehearsal pay, etc. At one particularly stormy meeting, one of those speaking in behalf of the liberalization movement was Albert van Dekker. Trying to parry the standard accusations of "un-American" leveled at us by the old guard in Equity, van Dekker (he soon dropped the "van") searched his brain for a country as remote as possible as he cried "I'm an American. I'm not—a—a—a—Czechoslovakian." Blanche Yurka arose and pridefully boomed out "I AM!" Bedlam of laughter, cheers, and applause. Sensing the meeting was verging on the burlesque, I arose and reminded the assembly that only the week before there was a "100 percent American" meeting in the city where some of our fellow citizens had gotten their "goddamn heads broken." Well, it was as if a bomb had exploded in the hallowed halls of Thespis. You would think none of those jokers had ever heard the word *goddamn* before. Such a hissing, such a tongue clucking you never heard. I was reprimanded by the chair (the very staid Frank Gillmore) and prevented from making any further "incendiary" remarks, or any other remarks, for that matter. I knew in that moment I didn't have the stomach to be a mass figure in an actors' revolution.

I was further put off from allowing myself to be signed up in the party by a functionary who used to hang around the Group. Every time I'd ask him about certain abuses of individual liberties I heard existed in the Soviet Union, he explained that the first obligation the revolution had was to make sure everyone had bread, *then* they'd get around to such matters as human rights. I didn't believe it then, and I don't believe it now.

Finally, there was the day a darling but neurotic girl, an acting student of mine, was chosen, idiotically, to recruit me personally. She was a striking beauty whose chalk-white face, flaming red hair, and sexy body convinced her antediluvian father that she must be what he called a "bad girl." When she'd come home too late at night, he'd be certain she was out with "fellers" and give her a good whack. He'd have killed her if he knew she was actually at meetings of her "cell." As a protest against her tyrannical father, she never ate the expensive meals served in their lavish apartment but lived exclusively on tuna fish sandwiches and cardboard cartons of black coffee. This, then, was the revolutionist they sent to my apartment one day to sell me on the glories of the Communist party. I accepted her bribe of half a tuna fish sandwich, but in no time at all we got around to exchanging theater gossip and giggling a lot, and the revolution was completely forgotten. I wish I could report that this innocent, charming girl outgrew her childish rebellion and had a happy life when the "radical" thirties ended. She didn't. What she did do was drive her car into the side of the exclusive apartment house where her father lived and kill herself.

CHAPTER 6

# The Group Theatre Productions 1931-41

THE WORLD OF entertainment which measured success by money, personal beauty, or notoriety made it difficult for some to remain good Group members. For me, there was no better choice than to have a place where I could grow as an artist. Add to that the fact that belonging to a permanent organization insured some kind of continuous wage, no matter how small. Although the Group salaries were generally less than those Broadway offered, a survey in *Fortune* magazine came up with the amazing discovery that, over the long haul, Group members came out better financially than most average Broadway actors.

Charismatic people such as Franchot Tone, independently wealthy and handsome as well as talented, had an understandably hard time remaining part of an ensemble company. The "need to sin," as Clifford Odets called it when he subsequently went to Hollywood, overcame Franchot early on and he became the Group's first important defector. He left in the second season during the run of John Howard Lawson's *Success Story*. Sandy Meisner and I were very fond of Franchot, and we accompanied him to Grand Central Station to say goodbye from the platform. He stood on the steps of the famous Twentieth Century Limited club car, teary-eyed, and as the train started to pull out of the station, he called to us, "Keep your line."

Walking across Forty-second Street, I turned to Sandy and observed, "Did you hear what he said? Here we are, going back to our struggling new Group while he's off to Hollywood to make a movie with Lilyan Tashman and he tells *us* to keep *our* line."

Said Sandy, "He meant keep it for him."

Franchot Tone was missed in *Success Story*, but there was still that amazing last scene of Stella Adler's. Franchot had played the boss of a business firm, and Stella was his secretary. She was in love with a man, played by her brother Luther, who started as an office boy and ruthlessly pushed his way to the top of the firm. Constantly using the secretary and accepting her love, Luther, on the way up, betrayed not only his ideals but her, too, by having an affair with a rich lady. In the final scene of the play, Luther and Stella are in the office in the middle of the night, and although she has tried to wipe him out of her heart, he pleads once more for her to save him from himself. In the ensuing struggle, with Stella trying to free herself from his grasp, she grabs the gun he has brought along and fires it into his side. Holding his body in her arms, all the while paraphrasing the biblical *Songs of Solomon* ("Make me a wilderness," etc.), Stella set up a kind of keening that was shattering to her and to the audience. She had taken as her emotional reference the legend that, during World War I, young British soldiers, under the unbearable pressure of relentless shelling, had been heard to speak Chaucerian English. It was found that when agonized by overpowering, relentless stress you can suffer a regression not only to your own earlier age, but to a period long before your time. Anyone who witnessed that acting feat of Stella's might well wonder when he would see the like again. It occurred at the close of the play, and many well-known actors would come in and stand at the back of the Maxine Elliott Theater to catch those hair-raising final moments. I was the assistant stage manager and used to peek out to check the celebrities who came nightly to study Stella. Among them, I remember specifically Ruth Chatterton and Noel Coward.

I got my first small part (as opposed to a walk-on or a bit) in Sidney Kingsley's *Men in White,* which turned out to be the Group's first "hit." It also won the Pulitzer Prize. The first doctors and nurses play, *Men in White,* was the forerunner of a deluge of television hospital series. I played a comic intern, Shorty, and for a scene in the hospital library where the young doctors gathered, presumably to study, Lee Strasberg, who directed the play, instructed me as follows: "Bobby, in this scene I want you to do ten funny things." Did you ever try to be funny on command? I started by taking a comb, putting tissue paper around it, and playing it like a kazoo. Disaster. Harold Clurman finally saved my life with one helpful remark. "It's easy, Bobby," he said. "Stop worrying. He's just the kind of kid who sees a pretty nurse coming toward him in the corridor and calls out 'Hi, sweetie. Gettin' plenty? Oops, I'm sorry. I forgot you're a Catholic!'" That did it. I was O.K. from then on. I had the needed comic spirit. Even my idol of comedy, Fanny Brice, who came backstage during the run, was kind enough to say to me, "You couldn't have been an inch funnier." If you think it's immodest of me to mention it, you just don't know what that kind of remark from someone like Fanny Brice means to a young actor.

The opening of the season of 1934-1935 found the Group on the road with *Men in White*. It was in the actors' dressing rooms located, naturally, in the basement of the Shubert Theatre, in Boston, that *Waiting for Lefty* was born. The company had been committed to play a benefit for some "progressive" organization, as they liked to be called, while we were in town. Clifford Odets decided to write a one-act play about a taxi drivers' strike with emphasis on the corruption of the union leadership. Since there would be no possibility of a physical production at the benefit, Cliff arranged the stage in the style of a minstrel show with a number of "acts." There was a semicircle of chairs which held the entire cast of taxi drivers, including people from other professions who had taken to driving cabs due to depression unemployment. As each scene came around, the players rose, went to the center of the semicircle, and returned to their chairs when their section was over. The assumption was that the members of the audience were all taxi drivers, too, and the theater was their union meeting hall. Since each scene had only two or three characters in it, they were rehearsed separately in dressing rooms, supervised by Odets and Sandy Meisner.

When the day of the performance arrived, we were informed that the benefit was called off. It seems the fire department had condemned the hall we were to play in as a "hazard," a condition that always seemed to arise when radical causes were being espoused. So *Lefty* sat on the shelf for awhile.

Early in 1935, the Group was asked to give another benefit, this one on a Sunday night at the Civic Repertory Theatre in New York City, proceeds to go to the *New Theatre* magazine. *Lefty* was brushed up and performed on the night of January 5. The dialogue, aside from its social content, reflected a kind of street poetry that brought roars of approving recognition from the audience, starting with the very first scene. No one left the premises after the wild ovation at the finish. Hordes of people stormed backstage to get a glimpse, not only of the actors, but of this fellow called Odets. He had been discovered by the playgoers as an exciting, new voice in the social drama of the thirties. It was a night to remember.

Further Sunday night performances were scheduled, with the critics getting their first introduction to the new playwright on February 10. Subsequently, Cliff wrote another one-acter, *Till the Day I Die,* and coupled with *Lefty,* these two short plays opened for a run at the Longacre Theatre. *Lefty* confirmed for me that, used judiciously, and in certain specific instances, the application of an Emotional Memory exercise can have a startling effect. I played the part of the labor spy, who was exposed at the union meeting by his brother (Gadget Kazan). When the union boss (Morris Carnovsky) wanted to know how Kazan was so sure I was guilty of being a fink, Gadget would look at me and say "He's my own lousy brother!" On this, my face invariably turned a deep red. Since the blush worked every night there was speculation that it was some kind of trick: holding my breath, for instance. Actually, I had found a very strong emotional reference of a time when I was caught in a most compromising situation, and the simple substitution of Gadget for the person who had

**Kazan and Lewis in *Waiting for Lefty*: "He's my own lousy brother!"**

surprised me "in the act" always resulted in the strong feeling of shame and fright that caused my blazing cheeks to be visible all the way to the back of the theater.

The scariest performance of *Lefty* for me to get through was a benefit night when the audience was made up of real taxi drivers. I expected my lines to be greeted with boos, but when I had to make my hurried exit up the center aisle, through the audience, and out the front door of the theater, some guy stuck out his leg and tripped me. I went scrambling up the aisle while all the taxi drivers stood and cheered wildly the comeuppance of the fink. Incidentally, in his *Memoirs,* Tennessee Williams says that "*Camino Real* (1953) was the first time on Broadway of which I know when actors ran down the aisles and went out into the audience." *Camino*'s director, Gadge Kazan, at least, knew we did it in *Lefty* about twenty years earlier. And of course there are examples earlier than that.

Nineteen thirty-five was also the year Sol Hurok brought Michael Chekhov and his company to the Majestic Theatre, and all eyes were opened to what could, for once, accurately be described as "total" acting. By that I mean each part Chekhov assumed was minutely executed from the point of view of physical characterization—the walk, the gestures, the voice, the makeup—all were meticulously designed to illuminate the character he was playing. Even more remarkable was, that, at the same time, his emotions were full, all equally chosen, and experienced according to the minds and hearts of the personages he acted. Here was the supreme example of the complete "inside" coupled with the complete "outside," each deriving from the other. Never again could one willingly accept the proposition that emotion was all-important, and that if one felt truthfully, characterization would take care of itself. Or, conversely, that the delineation of the physical behavior of a part, coupled with intelligible line-readings, was satisfactory without the inner life, thought, and feelings being experienced by that particular character.

Chekhov played a repertory consisting of a couple of full-length plays, *The Inspector General* and *The Deluge,* and a ravishing evening of sketches based on short stories of his uncle, Anton. His Khlestakov in the Gogol play was a prime example of total acting. To create the characterization of an arrogant fop Chekhov, himself a short man, stretched himself taut as he pranced three steps forward and two back. In his hands he held gloves in such a way as to elongate his fingers. All his sounds and movements were musicalized. Yet so forceful was Chekhov's inner momentum in his phantasmagoric drunk scene at the curtain of one act, that we Group actors staggered up the aisles of the theater, having caught his intoxication.

*The Deluge,* by Henning Berger, was a sort of morality play, and in it Chekhov demonstrated, in one unforgettable moment, what he called "psychological gesture." The play was set in a bar peopled by a bunch of disreputable characters. Chekhov played an American businessman named Fraser. In the second act, when all the patrons waited, terrified, for the approaching waters of a broken dam that would surely wash them all away, Chekhov was sitting at a table with a business colleague he had bilked some time before. In an attempt to purge himself of guilt before dying, Chekhov confessed to the man that the terrible circumstances of life had led him to cheat and that actually he felt only affection for the man personally. As he acted this speech, Chekhov kept digging his hands into the area of the man's heart as though trying to become one with him, creating a powerfully revealing "psychological gesture" of the nature of love.

The evening of Anton Chekhov sketches was a kaleidoscope of fascinating roles, tragic and comic, each one perfect in terms of physical characterization plus internal truth.

Had it the resources, the Group might have grabbed Chekhov at once and made some life for him here in America, as he was an emigré from the Soviet Union. He was afraid to return there, particularly because he was an anthroposophist and felt his spiritual feelings would endanger him in the new Russia. To the rescue came an American actress, Beatrice Straight, whose mother, married to Lord Elmhirst, had a gorgeous estate called Dartington Hall in Devonshire, England. There Beatrice set Chekhov up in a school that he operated until the Second World War.

The Group season of 1935 also brought forth the second crisis of Strasberg's leadership, the first being the effect of the Stella Adler report on her visit with Stanislavski. We were having a dress rehearsal of *Gold Eagle Guy* by Melvin Levy. Neither of the Adlers were overly enthusiastic about the merits of this saga of the San Francisco earthquake. Stella had announced, "No one wants to see a play about bills of lading," and Luther proclaimed to his fellow actors, "Boys, I think we're working on a stiff." My first foray into oriental parts added to the confusion with one newspaper review referring to me as a "Jap in a top hat" and another as "a marvelous Chinaman." Margaret Barker, called "Beany," played a San Francisco society hostess. A big scene was a tea party where one of her lady guests had to faint suddenly. Although Strasberg's direction did not call for it, at one particular dress rehearsal Beany, with her natural sensitivity, to say nothing of the logic of how a good hostess would ordinarily react, rose ever so slightly in her chair at the other end of the table, as the lady sank to the floor. Realizing her mistake, she sat back down immediately and went on with the scene. Lee, sitting in the auditorium, stopped the rehearsal.

"What were you doing?" he demanded, with tight lips.

"I'm sorry, Lee," said Beany. "It was a mistake. May we go on?"

"What were you doing?" Lee persisted.

"Nothing," pleaded Beany. "I made a mistake. That's all. May we go on?"

But Lee would not be put off. The actors sensed what was up. Beany, daughter of Llewellys F. Barker, President Emeritus of Johns Hopkins, had been brought up a Baltimore society belle. Lee, born in Budzanov in Galicia, was reared on the Lower East Side of Manhattan. Strasberg kept badgering Beany for a reply, at which point he could then explode, admit his well-known lack of formal manners, but insist he was not about to be given a lesson in natural courtesy. Although now drenched in tears, Beany would not give him this opportunity. Ruth Nelson, playing one of the guests in the scene, couldn't take it any longer. A profoundly religious woman, Ruth announced in a calm, steady voice that let it be known with certainty she wasn't kidding, "Now I'm going to kill him." With outstretched hands aimed toward Lee's throat, she started across the footlights, oblivious of the great void of the orchestra pit between herself and her target. Had the other actors not grabbed her and held her hard, she would have taken a bone-smashing plunge. Lee, genuinely frightened, fled from the theater. He did not return to the production, and Harold Clurman took over the remaining rehearsals. It was the first time he held, even temporarily, the directorial reins of a Group production. Although Lee subsequently directed two more Group plays and didn't actually resign until April of 1937, after that *Gold Eagle Guy* incident, and the Stella Adler contretemps, his hold over the actors was never the same.

The very next play the Group produced was assigned to Harold Clurman after one more confrontation of the actors with Strasberg. Following the debacle of *Gold Eagle Guy,* the company was assembled in the basement of the Belasco Theatre to listen hopefully to the directors' plans for our survival, since it was the middle of the season and we had no play to produce. We soon guessed there were no plans since Cheryl Crawford was giving her usual pep talk about how we were waiting for a script from this or that author, that she was trying to get us on a radio show to make some money, etc., etc. Suddenly unable to stand it any longer, Clifford Odets burst out with, "Why don't you read the actors my play?" Silence. Then the slow, frigid reply from Lee Strasberg. "How many times do I have to tell you, Cliff, we don't like your play."

No silence this time. "We have nothing to rehearse tomorrow morning. We don't care what you like. We want to hear the play," came loud and clear from Stella Adler, once more in her role as savior of actors. When Clifford's play, which was *Awake And Sing,* was read to them, the actors drooled, recognizing the many superb parts. As it turned out, Harold Clurman had wanted the Group to do the play, but Lee didn't feel it was good enough, and Cheryl, the third director, always sided with Lee. That made it two against one, and in order to present a united front, Harold hadn't pushed the play. Now, with the enthusiasm of the actors so high, it was not only agreed to go into rehearsal with the play, but that Harold should direct it as his first full production for the Group. It opened on February 19, 1935, and along with *Waiting for Lefty,* established Clifford as a leading playwright of the thirties. Strasberg could boast, with Fiorello La Guardia, that he didn't often make a mistake, but when he did it was a beaut.

Stella, as Bessie Berger, set a standard for Jewish mother parts that has not been approached since; omitting the usual self-pity and leavening the dominating nature of the woman with lofty humor. A strikingly beautiful woman, Stella hated to have to play an old character part. She was particularly exasperated when people would come backstage and address her as Luther's mother, when there was actually only a year's age difference between them. As the play's run continued, I began to notice distinct signs of old Bessie Berger getting a subtle, but unmistakable, face lift. One age line per performance would disappear from the makeup. When she started forgetting to apply pieces of her body padding, I cautioned Stella one night that if she didn't stop, she'd soon end up young as a fetus.

The next defection to Hollywood, on the part of Joe Bromberg, gave me a chance to play his part, Uncle Morty, in the Chicago engagement of *Awake and Sing*, in the spring of 1936. I got away with it, but I was miscast in the part. I was too young and didn't have the inner "weight" required. I have a treasured, if exaggerated, letter of praise from Carl Sandburg dated June 30, 1936: "It was an unforgettable afternoon with you and your associates. If I ever get going on a drama I shall seek you out. Your own characterization of that evening, the speech and the pantomime, will stay among my memories of great roles."

Sandburg was a real stage-door Johnny. He loved to hang out with the actors, admiring the sort of gypsy life he thought we led. Years later, when he was not too well, he received Marilyn Monroe in a New York hotel room. With her thirst for the good, cultural things of life, she had sought him out. When it was time for her to go, he apologized for not rising. Reading of her untimely death in Hollywood a short time later, he remarked, "I wish I had stood up."

My most vivid memory of that Chicago engagement of *Awake and Sing* was a horrifying incident that occurred on the opening night. Throughout the action of the play, Moe Axelrod, the character portrayed by Luther Adler, would remark, "What the hell kind of house is this, it ain't got an orange?" During the intermission some university students went to a store and bought a lot of oranges, and some grapefruit, too, which were even deadlier ammunition. At the end of the play, when the curtain rose on the first company call, a barrage of well-aimed pieces of fruit sailed across the footlights, pelting the actors. Phoebe Brand, who played the daughter, Hennie Berger, was felled by a particularly anti-Semitic grapefruit. Guess who was the first person to rise to the occasion? Right, Stella. Striding down to the footlights, she boomed into the auditorium, "It's up to you ladies and gentlemen out there to protect these actors." And so they did. Some of the fleeing culprits were seized and arrested. The next morning's newspaper headlined an editorial, "Chicago's Shame."

**Bob Lewis as Uncle Morty in the Chicago company of *Awake and Sing*: "What the hell kind of house is this?"**

Lulla Adler Rosenfeld, Jacob P. Adler's granddaughter and biographer, maintains that some years after this event, Saul Bellow told her he was the leader of the student group responsible for the incident. It seems they were believers in Trotskyism and resented what they felt was Odets's Stalinist bias, especially in his delineation of the grandfather in the play who was constantly quoting Marxian ideology. I telephoned Saul Bellow in 1980 to ask him if the story of his implication in the episode in 1936 was true. He replied that although he himself was not in the audience that opening night, the perpetrators were friends of his and were "just having a little fun."

Incidentally, Arthur Miller told Harold Clurman that he was definitely spurred on to become a playwright by witnessing this production of *Awake and Sing* in Chicago when he was a student at the University of Michigan.

The next Odets play the Group produced was *Paradise Lost* (December, 1935). It was prepared at the same time as a little number called *Weep for the Virgins.* The only thing we need to record about that one is the fact that it was written by a woman named Nelisse Child—because her mother was called Nelly.

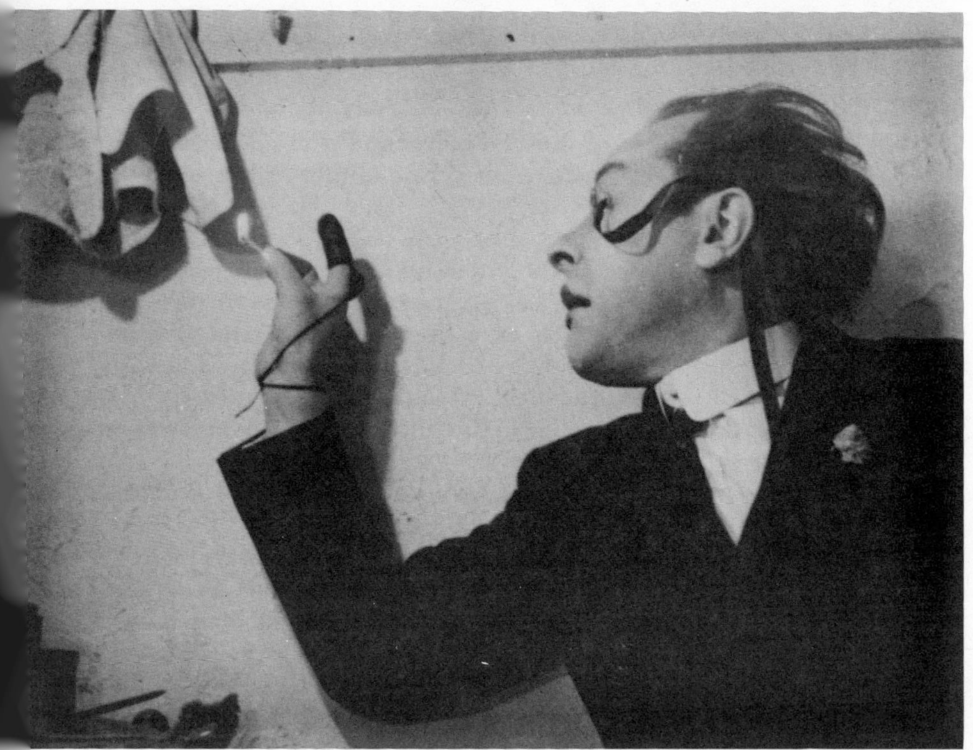

**Bob Lewis in *Paradise Lost* as Mr. May: "A weird little character."**

**Bob Lewis as Mr. May in the firebug scene from Odets's *Paradise Lost,* with Morris Carnovsky and Luther Adler: "A sickly-sweet smile."**

In *Paradise Lost* I played Mr. May, a weird little character who tried to interest Morris Carnovsky and Luther Adler in a scheme whereby their failing factory could "happen" to catch fire so that they could collect the insurance. I dyed my hair red, combed it up at the sides in flamelike wisps, and wore a black leather guard on my index finger, hinting at some unfortunate accident in one of my forays into arson. I used some indeterminate accent, pronouncing my "v"s as "w"s. With a sickly-sweet smile and furtive movements, the few minutes I was on stage in the second act were undeniably theatrical.

Jed Harris was captivated by this delineation of Mr. May, mainly, I suppose, because it had a stylistically different look from the usual Group acting. Harris had no patience with the Group, either with its repertory or the style of its productions. That did not prevent him, however, from trying to woo Odets to let Jed produce his plays instead of Harold Clurman. It also didn't stop him from trying to capture some members of the acting company. He offered Kazan parts if he'd leave the Group and went into full gear in trying to tear me away from the bosom of the Group. His first ploy was to purchase a pair of down-front seats for various performances of *Paradise Lost.* He clocked the time my scene went on, treating it in the manner of a vaudeville turn, and would hurry down the aisle with a different guest each time a few minutes before I was to enter. He'd slouch down in his seat and clap his hat over his eyes pretending to be offended by the other Group actors' performances. As I descended the long staircase into the living room set, he'd nudge his partner and sit up straight, beaming. The second I made my exit, he'd sail up the aisle and out of the theater.

Then one day Jed summoned me to his office and informed me he had asked Daniel Fuchs to dramatize Fuchs's novel *Homage to Blenholt.* One of the leading characters, a Mr. Munves, reminded Jed of my Mr. May. Playing Munves for Jed Harris, he said, would not only spring me from the Group Theatre but elevate me to the status as an actor he felt I deserved. He gave me some jelly beans and sent me on my way. Periodically, I'd get a call from Jed, and he'd sit me down at his desk opposite him. Pushing the bowl of jelly beans at me, he'd lean back in his chair perusing pages of the play script he had received from Fuchs. Every once in a while, as he read to himself, he'd giggle or laugh, presumably at some delicious speech I was to deliver some day in the proposed Jed Harris production. I'd sit there, in exquisite torture, drooling, and not only over the jelly beans. Then he'd put the script away in his drawer and tell me he'd let me know when he got some more scenes. Finally, one day he called me to his office and stood there with the completed manuscript in his hand. Looking at me with that sardonic smile which Laurence Olivier used as a model for his characterization of Richard III, Jed threw the play on the desk. "Here," he said, "this stinks. Give it to Harold Clurman."

Until I read his autobiography, I didn't know the main reason that Jed resented the Group Theatre so fiercely. In 1928, shortly before the Group got started, he himself had planned to give up his "expertly devised entertainments" on Broadway and establish a real theater of his own. Holbrook Blinn, a superb actor, had agreed to be his partner and William Randolph Hearst had promised to put up money and donate land for a fully equipped theater with rehearsal rooms, scene painter's loft, carpenter's shop, etc. In rapid fire order, Blinn was killed in a fall from a horse, the stock market crash cost Harris most of his fortune, and even Hearst, said Jed, put his art collection on sale at Macy's department store. Harris' dream crumbled. Understandably, it rankled Jed, who had planned a repertory of famous European plays, and who had gone abroad to recruit English stars for his company (yes, they were doing it then, too), that the Group was surviving the depression years with new American playwrights and mostly little-known American actors.

*The Case of Clyde Griffiths,* an adaptation in "epic" style by Erwin Piscator of Theodore Dreiser's *An American Tragedy* gave me another chance to pursue my search for a style of acting that would extend beyond realism. Sensing the opposition to my experimentation of some of the more orthodox Stanislavskiites in the Group—one of the actresses in the cast of *Paradise Lost,* observing the preparations for my characterization of Mr. May had observed, "Is he going to start that stuff again?"—Lee Strasberg, the director of *Clyde Griffiths,* generously gave me carte blanche, this time, by asking me to devise and stage my own scene. In Piscator's version of the Dreiser work, the emphasis of the tragedy was not only on Clyde Griffiths's abandonment of his factory-girl sweetheart for a rich one but on his desertion of the class to which he belonged. In my sequence, Clyde came into a shop to buy evening clothes for an upper-class Christmas party with his new girl friend. I got myself up as an elegant mannequin placed in a department store window. In one corner of the stage, I stood a girl trio of Salvation Army singers (Clyde's parents had been street preachers) harmonizing "Silent Night, Holy Night" throughout the pantomime that began as Clyde entered the store. I "came to life" and with the slow movements of a robot, I decked Clyde out in evening clothes, ending up by throwing a white silk scarf around his neck in the manner of a Papal investiture. When Griffiths walked out he was transformed into a representative mannequin of his new class as I lapsed back into my figure of a store window dummy.

Theodore Dreiser, then in his great age, sat in on rehearsals and remarked that this epic style sequence was the essence of his novel, too, which he maintained dwelt in the whole social order and not on an isolated criminal act. Dreiser's approval was most important, of course, although I was gratified when the special style of my staging was recognized in a newspaper review: "The one scene in which Clyde buys his dress suit for his first social false step is a masterpiece of acting and staging, worth all the rest of the show put together, and well worth your time if you are at all interested in how far the theater can extend itself beyond the old-fashioned footlights."

A final word about Dreiser. Since Lee never solicited a suggestion from the grand old man during the weeks of rehearsal, Dreiser just sat in his chair, often dozing. Lee's biggest problem with Alexander Kirkland, who played Clyde Griffiths, had been to get Kirkland to be muscularly free because his physical tensions were inhibiting the flow of his feeling. Lee had finally succeeded in getting Kirkland relaxed. That is, until Dreiser, finally prompted by Strasberg for a word to the cast, rose unsteadily to his feet, fixed Kirkland with his venerable eyes, and proclaimed, "My boy, to succeed in this part there is only one thing you must remember all through—*be tense*!" And with this, Dreiser sank back into his seat. What he meant, of course, was "intense" not "tense." But the look in Strasberg's eyes made me sure it would be a frosty Friday before he asked another playwright for any suggestions.

The next voice that attempted to wean the Group Theatre away from realism was Kurt Weill's. Refugees from Hitler, Kurt and his wife, Lotte Lenya, spent the summer of 1936 in Nichols, Connecticut, with the Group company preparing *Johnny Johnson,* a musical with libretto by Paul Green. A sort of Americanized *Good Soldier Schweik,* laid during the First World War, it was put into rehearsal at the end of the summer. Meantime, Kurt favored the actors with classes on how to sing and act his songs, as well as talks on how Brecht and he arrived at their musical style.

Finding that as a composer he couldn't work with "voice acrobats," Weill gravitated to the theater to write "opera with actors." Emulating the revolt of *The Beggars' Opera* against the Italian opera style at the beginning of the eighteenth century, Kurt and Brecht were led to the form of *The Threepenny Opera.* They insisted that it comprise "songs" (verse and refrain with variations) that were not just "lyrical," but that gave the philosophy of the play. In addition, they opted for a seven-piece orchestra. Not until the opera house developed theatrically as a result of Brecht and Weill's work, Kurt maintained, would he go back to the opera form. He must have thought this miracle had actually occurred because he did get closer to the opera form in *Mahagonny* and other works. Feeling that the American theater had been dominated for a couple of decades by a lifelike realism that could better be expressed in the movies, he hoped our playwrights would attempt some kind of poetic theater—and that music could help them break from prose to poetry. In class, he taught us actors how to eschew the "seminal" singing encouraged by opera teachers. He said this approach took away the personal character of the voice and made for standard sound. The actor should retain his own voice. Phrasing should be guided not only by the melodic line, but by the sense of the words. It was a form of "talking" on the notes.

In his adopted land, Kurt wanted to become a successful American composer—like Richard Rodgers, for example—as fast as possible. And with *The Lady in the Dark* and some others, he did. Janet Flanner, as Paris correspondent for *The New Yorker,* was understandably knowledgeable about Weill's European output; but at a party in my house, when she told Kurt that *The Threepenny Opera* was her favorite, he was not at all pleased. He vowed that what he was doing at that moment—writing American musical comedies—was his most important contribution. He may have been trying to obliterate memories of what had happened to him and other non-Aryan musicians in Germany. But, after his death, the revivals of his earlier scores made it possible to compare the high quality of *Threepenny Opera* or *Mahagonny* with, let's say, *Knickerbocker Holiday, One Touch of Venus,* or *Love Life.*

The actual production of *Johnny Johnson* revealed that all the lectures, classes, and knowledge of the problems of form and content are no substitute for eyes and ears, if you are to direct a musical. Under Lee Strasberg's

Bobby Lewis in *Johnny Johnson* as Clemenceau, "The 'Tiger' of France."

direction, there were fine individual performances, notably Russell Collins in the title role. Morris Carnovsky, as a mad army psychiatrist, rose successfully to the challenge of heightening his acting to conform with the dynamics of a musical. For my part, I played a wide-eyed Mayor in the beginning, and the French Premier in the scene where the heads of the Allied governments meet to decide how many young men each country would throw into the war. Taking my cue from Clemenceau, the "Tiger" of France, I covered my eyebrows and lips with enough crepe hair to suggest that animal and gestured with great over-the-head clawing movements. Again, my attempts at stylization caught the eye of a reviewer: "Bob Lewis' contortions as the French Premier and the Mayor add the quality of dance to the poetry and music of the drama. His rhythmical voice and movements serve as an example, in a perfect though small unit, of the aim of the play form as a whole." But I would not be able to realize my aim at a poetic style in a full production until directing Saroyan's *My Heart's in the Highlands,* a couple of years later.

*Johnny Johnson,* as a production, was my first experience with a play whose best performance was the rehearsal just before the scenery, costumes, and lights are added. "Whatever happened to that touching and funny play I saw in that rehearsal hall?" everyone wants to know at the dress rehearsal in the theater. Well, what happened can be one of two things. Either the rehearsals are not conducted from the beginning with the décor and the size of the theater in mind; or the pieces of scenery and the costumes now overwhelming the show bear little relation to those darling sketches that were originally presented by the designers. In any case, poor Johnny Johnson had to fight not only the First World War but the battle of the scenery. Huge cannons would loom up from the back of the stage, dwarfing the acting at the same time as the orchestra in the pit fought the actors' singing voices onstage.

One particularly embarrassing moment occurred at the end of a song sung by a French Red Cross nurse (Paula Strasberg) in front of the curtain while a huge scenery change was lumbering around in back. The song finished with the words, "Mon ami, my friend." Since Paula, no Edith Piaf, was trapped in the dead center of the forestage, and not two hands were put together in the form of applause at the end, she sidestepped off stage left, in deathly silence, smiling foolishly. One day I made the mistake of offering Lee a simple suggestion to help Paula. Being an old hand at doing "numbers," I wondered why he couldn't tell her to "travel" on her last four bars so she could be at the side of the stage on her last note, leap offstage, and escape her embarrassment. Lee pounced on me hard, maintaining this was "theater, not vaudeville." I never ventured a suggestion again. I had learned the credo of theatrical egoists: do something wrong, then make a theory to defend it.

After the demise of *Johnny Johnson,* the Group activities slowly ground to a halt. Scripts were scarce, and the one we started to rehearse (*Silent Partner* by Odets) never got off the ground. It was decided to discontinue production for a while so the Group could regroup. The actors were officially released to seek employment wherever they could. I got to play another Japanese in a play called *His Excellency,* by Leslie Reade. Harold Clurman, Stella Adler, and Elia Kazan went off to join Clifford Odets in Hollywood, and in April of 1937, Lee Strasberg and Cheryl Crawford resigned as directors of the Group.

The first thing Hollywood studios did in those days was change your name, especially if it had a suspicious ethnic ring to it. Kazan was offered Cézanne but refused it on the grounds that some other guy beat him to it. Stella, who was staying at the Beverly Wilshire Hotel, was asked to change her name to Miss Beverly Wilshire. I said it was a good thing she wasn't living at the Coconut Grove.

I went West, too, but it was to pursue my interest in directing. I had an offer to stage *Gods of the Lightning,* the play that served to get me into the Group Theatre. It was presented by the Federal Theatre Project and played the Mayan Theatre, in Los Angeles. While in Hollywood, I enjoyed my first taste of life among the movie stars. Clifford was married to Luise Rainer and asked me to have dinner with her one night, in their Beverly Hills home, when he was to be away on a quick trip to New York. After dinner, Luise and I took a walk. Pausing to rest on a rock, we both gazed in silence across a magnificent canyon at the lights going on in the houses on the other side. Finally, Luise, with that shy, eyes-cast-down, lips-pursed look that was her cinematic trademark, ventured the following: "Bobby, sometimes I sit here by myself, and look down into that big canyon, and over to those tall mountains on the other side, and then up at the sky and the stars and I say, 'Luise, all that is greater than you.'"

If Joan Crawford wasn't as modest as Luise Rainer she was, at least, as ambitious. Franchot's former Group colleagues were often invited to Sunday dinner at the Tone's. Asked to come in the afternoon for a swim, we'd be yanked out of the pool and into the music room at four o'clock sharp to constitute a small audience for Joan's singing lesson. To prepare her for a possible side trip into opera, a Viennese maestro had been hired to coach Joan. From what I knew of the singing voice, I could tell this joker was forcing Joan's natural mezzo voice up into the soprano range where she could have better operatic starring roles to chose from. The maestro's wife was also present to contribute cooing sounds of approbation at the conclusion of each scale or arpeggio. She'd then turn to the rest of the assemblage, and with her eyes daring us to contradict her, would insist, "What an improvement this week, no?"

Our spiritual requirements satisfied, we were then allowed the cocktail hour—and finally the dinner. At five to six, exactly, Joan would leave the bar and enter the dining room to contribute a personal touch to the food by lighting the chafing dish that contained the kidney beans. Quickly placing three marrow bones on the floor in the corner of the room for her trio of beloved dachshunds, she opened the dining room door for us to enter just as the clock struck six.

In the center of the huge dining table was a miniature replica of the large table, complete with setups of tiny knives, forks, spoons, glasses, etc. Behind each tiny plate were tiny place cards with our names on them which guided us to our proper chairs around the big table. The dachshunds had no place cards and retaliated by rattling their hard, demarrowed bones on the floor all through the meal, making human conversation impossible. After dinner we all repaired to the private screening room for coffee, a short subject, and a feature film. Joan sat in the back row, constantly knitting and studying her sister performers on the screen. Sometimes she'd offer friendly advice. "Uh, oh, Barbara," she'd call to Stanwyck's screen image, "pull that stomach in."

The final chore for the guests came when Joan was neatly tucked into her bed. We were invited to the bedroom to say goodnight before we left. It was only about nine-thirty or ten when she'd retire, because she had to get up very early. Needing her sleep so there'd be no lines under the eyes in the morning, we were admonished not to refer to anything disturbing such as wars, plagues, or uncomplimentary gossip about Joan. We'd all comment, quite accurately, on how beautiful she looked and tiptoe out into the night.

Once when I was a guest at Joan's, her two adopted kids were brought into the bedroom to bid Joan goodnight. "Come kiss your beautiful mother goodnight," she called to them, her arms flung out. I thought, some day one of those kids is going to kill her. Actually, one of them did, with her pen, but not till Joan had gone.

After the elevating social life in the Hollywood of the thirties—Lillian Hellman's father once visited her when she was on the West Coast writing a screen play, and said, "Lillian, what's a nice girl like you doing in a place where they eat salad as a first course and hot grapefruit for dessert?"—it was a relief to get back to the trials of surviving in the theater of the depression. Odets had finished a play about a violinist turned prizefighter, and Harold Clurman returned to New York to reassemble the Group and stage *Golden Boy*. He was also now the sole director of the theater, and I dubbed him "Der Führer."

*Golden Boy* turned out to be the biggest popular success the Group ever had, opening at the Belasco Theatre on November 4, 1937. Joining the Group company, in the leading feminine role, was Frances Farmer, a great beauty and the Marilyn Monroe of her day. By that I mean that although successful in her career, and married to Leif Ericson, a tall, handsome, nice guy, she wanted more out of life. And that more was "culture." Ericson was her Joe Di Maggio, as Clifford Odets was her Arthur Miller. She was eager for an intellectual artist to regale her with stories of how Duse wore no makeup and Isadora Duncan revelled in free love. Sprinkled with a nickel's worth of Marxian philosophy, and accompanied by phonograph recordings of Beethoven's last quartets, the head-turning of a worshipful girl, and her unbalancing, was not too difficult.

I played Roxy Gottlieb, a prizefight promoter, in *Golden Boy*. In type I was not your ideal habitué of Stillman's gym, although I visited there to research the part. The most I came up with was a racing form dangling from my side pocket. In addition, my Rs always sounded suspiciously like Ws. Stuck with me as the closest available choice for the part (the penalty of having a permanent company), the Group put me to work with a speech teacher. Every day I intoned, "pray, pree, pry, pro, pru; tray, tree, try, tro, tru," and so on, in the hope that I would eventually kill the unwanted laugh that greeted my very first line. As the lights came up on the fight manager's office, tough Roxy Gottlieb was heard complaining of the new violinist-turned-boxer, "He's a wegular bwain-twust."

Being in a hit when you feel as miscast as I did can be capital punishment. To compensate, I actively pursued my teaching career. In addition to joining the first of what would eventually be many university drama school faculties (in 1938 it was Sarah Lawrence College in Bronxville, NY), I reactivated the Group Theatre Studio, made up of fifty young actors and actresses chosen from over four hundred who auditioned. Outstanding in the classes (Kazan's and mine) were Martin Ritt, now the film director, Will Lee (of *Sesame Street* fame), and Larry Parks, remembered both for his film impersonation of Al Jolson and his dismemberment by the House Un-American Activities Committee. Most important to me was the contribution the Group Studio members made when I needed them the following year for my casting of *My Heart's in the Highlands*.

I've already documented the impact the Group's ensemble playing had on the London theater world in the summer of 1938, when we produced *Golden Boy* at the St. James Theatre. But I must record the last weekend in June I spent in Devonshire at Dartington Hall, studying the teaching methods of my acting idol, Michael Chekhov. When the Group members saw Chekhov act in New York two years earlier, we heard stories from a member of Chekhov's company of how Stanislavski, who, although considering him the foremost stage exponent of the acting method Stanislavski taught, warned against Chekhov as a teacher. I was determined to see for myself what was meant by this. I attended two full days of classes and activities at Dartington Hall and then went back to London. On July 4, I delivered my report to the Group members playing in *Golden Boy*. I tried first to describe the general atmosphere of the surroundings at the Dartington Hall estate. Chekhov himself was a devout man, and all his pupils seemed to absorb something of the master's spirituality. As I walked over the beautiful grounds, I saw a girl sitting alone on the grass looking at the classroom building with worshipful tears in her eyes. Coming from the

The Group Theatre Studio: Robert Lewis, center, on floor, hair receding: Martin Ritt, at right, white shirt: (below) Larry Parks, pre-Al Jolson; and Evelyn Geller.

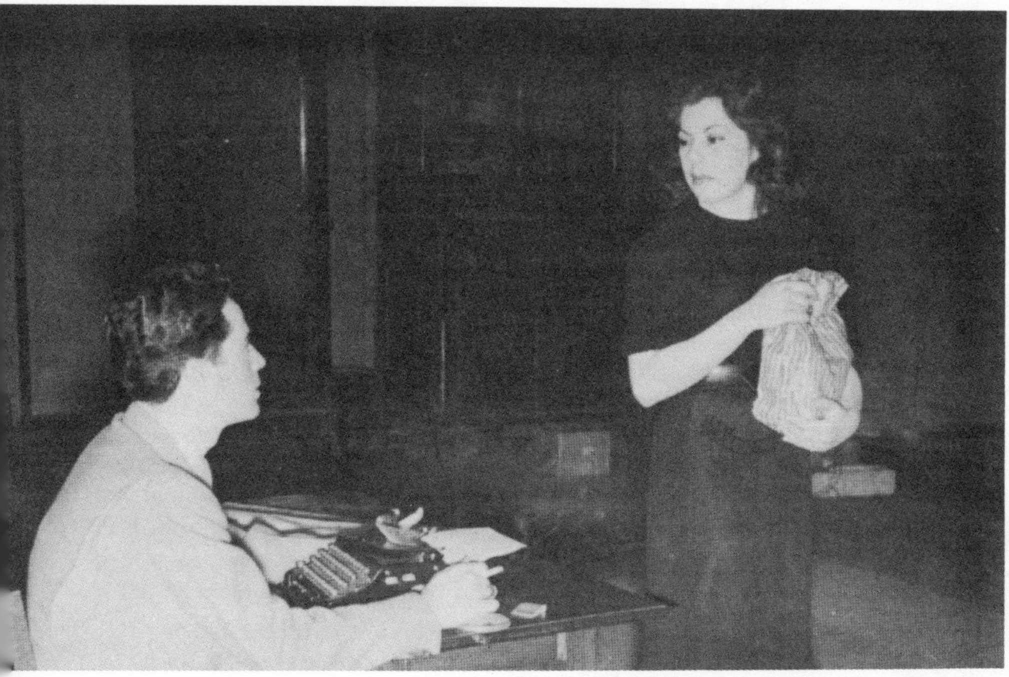

more materialistic and embattled atmosphere of the Group, this seemed remarkable to me. A eurythmy class consisted of group movements, circles spiraling in and out, accompanied by *oo* and *ah* sounds, and based in feelings of love, hate, and the like. A voice class used poems, with accompanying gestures, passing lines from one actor to another with no breaks in rhythm. There was an improvisational exercise in slow "hot" rhythms and quick "cool" ones. Then a theme was added to the movements: departure. I kept sensing that it was essentially movement work useful for dancers who must communicate themes to the audience through movement. With actors, I felt, you might move slowly if you're hot, but your rhythms would come not only from outer designs but from some inner experience, too, which I found lacking in the students. I made a note as I sat there in class, "There is nothing to move them to act. There is everything to move them to move."

There was another improvisation in group composition. The quality demanded was fire danger. The movement (on different platform levels) arrived at was the visual crystallization of the theme, all right. But since there was no emotional sense of fire—or danger—it seemed to me it could have been done simply by assigning space relations in the beginning. The crystallization, I felt, could not be found truthfully without the essence. If the movement could have been added to, or derived from, the psychological groundwork, they would then have approached the acting style of their master, Michael Chekhov, who, as an artist, was always overflowing with true emotion. It seemed to me the pupils were just getting what Chekhov created of his physical characterizations, and that he seemed to take for granted they'd supply the insides. But they didn't really relate to one another or react to any impulse but outward ones. Chekhov, in his remarks to the class, however, did offer them the supreme advice that guided him as an actor: "The highest point of our art is reached when we are burning inside and command complete outer ease at the same time." I stole this quote at once and have used it often.

The class then did an improvisation based on the plot of *The Deluge* in which we had seen Chekhov give such an extraordinary performance. He broke the scene up into headings: suspicion, beginning of storm, dam breaks, chaos, love, and reconciliation. The "qualities" that were to progress from the opening to the end were staccato-heavy-closed to legato-light-open. He indicated two "climaxes": one just before the storm comes, and one at the end of the scene. The dam bursting (for which he would give a signal) was an "accent."

The improvisation started. What the company seemed to be acting were the "qualities" without the psychological underpinnings of the deluge. I realized that this principle of design was great for a director's guide, but without the actors being trained for the inner experiencing of the nature of the situation for each character, it made for effective groupings but poor individual acting. I also made a mental note to be sure to explore, as I developed my own teaching skills in the future, the ways in which the psychological groundwork of the actors craft would be basic to whatever physical expression would be required in terms of characterization, movement, voice, staging, and so on. Then, and only then, might I approach that fusion of the inside and the outside that was the hallmark of Michael Chekhov's acting. This search has continued throughout my entire working life. I ended my report to the Group actors in London that day with this remark: "A great actor might also be a great teacher, but it ain't necessarily so."

My impressions in Dartington Hall of Chekhov's teaching, as opposed to his acting, further confirmed what I had suspected during a lecture on acting he gave at the New School in New York City in 1935. At that time I watched Chekhov illustrate another of his "psychological gestures." He performed a small bit of his characterization of *Eric XIV* (Strindberg). To create the image of a weakling, Chekhov gave us the moment where King Eric shouts an order. His own commanding voice so frightened him that the sound died in his throat, and the imperious movement of his upraised hand was broken at the wrist. What Chekhov was illustrating was the sound and the gesture. What he neglected to mention was the tremendous wave of inner feeling rising up in him, and then being deflated, that propelled those outward manifestations. I wondered what the same moment would be like if another actor, lacking the emotional motor that was such a great part of Chekhov's genius as an actor, just did "what he did."

My third go-around with *Golden Boy* was the important one for me. On our return from England, Harold Clurman asked me to direct the Chicago company of the Odets play which would open on Christmas night, 1938, and star Jean Muir and Phillips Holmes in the Frances Farmer and Luther Adler roles. Although the pattern of direction had been laid down in Clurman's production, I had a chance to be responsible for preparing a new cast for the play. It was another step toward getting my own Group production to direct.

I would act only one more role (Oriental, of course) for the company and that was a Chinese airman in Robert Ardrey's *Thunder Rock*, directed by Elia Kazan. My part consisted of a single word only: "Okay." The trick was that, since I repeated it dozens of times during the play, I had to make "okay" mean something else each time. It was fun to do and, for me, made an amusing farewell to the stage as a performer since I only acted in a few films after that and concentrated the rest of my career on directing and teaching.

The last couple of years in the life of the Group Theatre included *The Gentle People*, which featured the return of Franchot Tone to the company, and *Retreat to Pleasure*, both plays by Irwin Shaw. Odets's last

**With Phillips Holmes and Jean Muir: Chicago company of *Golden Boy*: "The important one for me."**

hurrah for the Group was *Night Music.* Since I wasn't in the cast, I attended the opening performance with my favorite theater companion, designer Boris Aronson. I anticipated some fine, cynical humor, as usual, from Boris, especially since the scenery for the play was by Max Gorelik, his only worthy rival among Group designers. Boris, by the way, was the inspiration for the character of the vastly amusing, old junk dealer in Arthur Miller's *The Price.* After the first act of *Night Music* ended, Aronson's face was wreathed in smiles as we went up the aisle.

"How do you like it so far?" I asked him.

"Marvelous, simply marvelous," he chortled. "It's completely confusing."

After the second act, Boris looked glum.

"What's the matter, Boris," I inquired. "Don't you like it anymore?"

"A—a—ah," growled Boris, "it's beginning to clear up."

What never cleared up was the same tragic flaw in the Odets character that afflicts so many American theater artists. That "need to sin" that Clifford used as an excuse to go to Hollywood eventually became a way of life for him. I, too, know how difficult it is to grab a bit of réclame and, let's face it, some money also, in show business while attempting to retain a measure of integrity in artistic aspirations. It's a disease that weakens you, and unless you have more healthy, artistic blood cells than Cliff obviously did, it eventually kills you. He himself became a Golden Boy who went "off his line" to achieve "success and fame." This hunger for success plagued Clifford even as he was writing his play on the subject. In a letter to me (5/22/37) from Hollywood describing the new play he was working on (*Golden Boy*) he referred to the abandonment of his earlier effort, *The Silent Partner*: "Saw Harold (Clurman) the other night, and we were both dissatisfied with *The Silent Partner* as the first of our new Group productions because it hasn't in it the elements of popular success and you know what I mean." To give Cliff his due, the apologetic words must surely refer to the desire to get the Group back on its feet financially. But it recalled a remark I heard Cliff make when I was in his house in Hollywood, at a party for Charlie Chaplin. Cliff was inveighing, not only against the Broadway theater, but the whole United States, in an attempt to justify his working in movies. There was nothing to write a play about, he fumed, in a country that was spiritually bankrupt. He was challenged on the spot by Paul Rosenfeld, the astute husband of Stella's niece, Lulla Adler. Paul echoed the Roman Pliny the Younger, who, in the first century, remarked, "You say there is nothing to write about, then write to me that there is nothing to write about." To Clifford, Paul put it this way: "If you really believe what you just said, Cliff, why don't you write a play about that spiritual bankruptcy?"

"What," Cliff replied disdainfully, "and have it run three weeks?"

Nevertheless, he tried to express the pain of that just-one-more-picture-and-then-I'll-quit disease with a post-Group play called *The Big Knife* in 1948 and another, *The Country Girl,* a backstage drama, in 1951. The following year found Odets sitting in Barbetta's, an Italian restaurant in the Broadway theater district, with Lillian Hellman, whom he had invited to dinner to ask her what she intended to say to the House Un-American Activities Committee, which had summoned both of them. She allowed as to how she might just answer for herself but would absolutely refuse to talk about others—which is what she did. Cliff agreed to do the same and was buoyed up instantly. (In his first flush of success as a playwright, Cliff had courted Beatrice Lillie for a time, and she summed up their relations this way: "Clifford was a little too serious, there—for a moment.") When faced with the committee, Odets not only named those colleagues he knew had been party members, but he even guessed at some others, though he had no sure knowledge of them. One of those fingered by Clifford was Joe Bromberg, his Group Theatre friend. When Joe died Cliff, in his speech at the memorial service, had accused the House Un-American Activities Committee of complicity in bringing on Bromberg's death.

The last time I saw Odets was when I called on him at the Chateau Marmont Hotel on Sunset Boulevard where many movie people stayed. I waited in the lobby for him to come down. Suddenly he appeared, in wild disarray, hair flying, eyes bulging, looking for all the world like one of Gustave Doré's biblical figures. He headed straight for the desk clerk. Screaming uncontrollably, he demanded that the room maid be gotten off his back. She was always pestering him for permission to make up his room, he complained.

"But she has to go home at five o'clock," the desk clerk informed him, "and you won't let her in your room before then. What can she do?"

"She has no right to tell me what my working hours are to be," bellowed the playwright of the proletariat. "She has delusions of grandeur."

The desk clerk didn't know what to make of that. I did. Although the end was not to come for a couple of years, in that moment I knew he was already dead.

As the Group which spawned Clifford limped to its own finale, I made one more attempt to get over my point about the stultifying absence of styles other than realism in its program. Even the one attempt at a noncontemporary play the company essayed and abandoned in its last summer period—Chekhov's *The Three Sisters*—was afflicted by a fatal absence of a sense of period. Early in 1939, I sent a paper to the Group leadership which, although peppered with some of my highest-flown verbiage, did contain this paragraph: "I say that Group productions lack music, color, rhythm, movement—all those *other* things in the theater besides psychology, and all the things which in theatrical form clarify and make important one's psychology—not that color and movement, etc. are not present one by one on our stage—they are, but they are not fused into a single style which in each production is peculiar to the expression of the talent of the particular author."

If Harold Clurman was offended by this attack, his reply was characteristically generous. A couple of months later he made possible my first directing job on my own of a Group Theatre production, William Saroyan's *My Heart's in the Highlands,* which would challenge me to create on the stage the kind of poetic style I had been talking about.

In the spring of 1941, with the last few productions having turned out to be financial failures, Harold wrote, in an article for *The New York Times,* that without some institutional setup the Group could no longer function.

Elia Kazan and I accompanied Clurman to the Group office in the Sardi building to be with him when he turned the key in the lock for the last time. And so ended a decade of provocative, stimulating, frustrating, influential work. The Group Theatre proved that a company of artists, surviving for a mere ten years, with a commitment to a certain kind of theater, evolving a craft to express its talent, although that craft was not all-embracing stylistically, could be a potent force in theater, here and abroad, in its lifetime and, indeed, for future generations. In other words, the basic idea was right.

CHAPTER 7

# My Heart's in the Highlands 1939

*MY HEART'S IN the Highlands,* my true firstborn, remains my favorite to this day, mainly for the reason that I could build the production from scratch with no serious, outside interference in the creative work from start to finish. One of the hazards of a collaborative artistic enterprise like theater production is the possible dilution of the original concept through the many contributions of the team. The play director's job, therefore, is the unifying of all the departments—writing, acting, settings, costumes, lights, music, movement—into a single expression, each conspiring to say the same thing at the same time and, by so doing, enhance the concept. If the contributing artists' creations don't derive from this central concept, brilliant though they may be in themselves, they may undermine the unity of the production on which its artistic integrity depends. Add to this situation the well-meant help offered by the producer (or producers), agents, lawyers, backers, and all their assorted spouses and concubines, and you begin to see the perils of the journey. I've had suggestions for rewrites from wardrobe mistresses and doormen—some of them quite interesting, too. There was none of this "help" that I soon learned was standard in the case of my first professional directing assignment, because no one but the cast was around at rehearsal time. William Saroyan was in Fresno, California, Harold Clurman was in Havana, and I barred the actors' committee of the Group from the rehearsal hall because of their expressed hostile attitude to the material.

The play script had evolved this way. In 1937 Clurman sent a letter to Bill Saroyan asking if he would be interested in writing for the theater since he had evidenced a flair for lively dialogue in his short stories. Saroyan replied in the affirmative but insisted (and I didn't know this at the time) that if he did write a play, he would have to direct it himself. Bill had on hand a short story called *The Man With the Heart in the Highlands,* which he'd written one afternoon in 1935 and published himself (with three other undergraduates) at UCLA the next year. The writing consisted mainly of dialogue, and so, with Saroyan excising every "he said" and "she said," the play script was ready to submit to Molly Day Thacher (Kazan's wife) who was the Group's play reader. Knowing of my interest in lyric theater, Molly showed me the short play. I saw in it a perfect libretto on which to build a poetic production by adding music, sound, color, and movement to the enchanting dialogue. Since the one-act play was quite short and cried out for expansion, Molly asked Saroyan if he could extend the play. He did, and Clurman offered me the job of director and the promise of five special performances.

I read the completed script to the Group company. Having been nourished on Odets, the actors' reaction to the Saroyan script might have been predicted. Our stage manager, Michael Gordon, later a director himself, called it "a piece of cheese." Even my usually encouraging friend in the Group, Elia Kazan, said the play sounded like "a flute's complaint." Only one Group member agreed to appear in it: Art Smith. I cast him for the part of Jasper MacGregor, the ancient Shakespearean actor escaped from an old people's home. I was relieved when Franchot Tone turned down a special plea from Clurman to play the leading part of the poet. I had visioned the character at the opening of the play, when he is trying to find a rhyme for a poem he is composing, to be on his hands and knees, on top of the kitchen table, scribbling on a scrap of paper, suffering in that idiotic way well-known to artists—the comic agony of creation. Fine though Franchot was as an actor, he had too much innate dignity of manner for such carryings on. I chose, instead, Phillip Loeb, a close friend of the Group. He lapped up the part, having just the right mixture of childish fun and moving frustration. He was completely Saroyanesque.

Most of the rest of the cast I recruited from my Group Theatre studio classes. They included Nick Conte, who was known in his subsequent film career as Richard Conte, and Harry Bratsburg, now Harry Morgan of TV's "M*A*S*H" series. Hester Sondergaard played the grandmother, speaking only Armenian all through. The late William Hansen, who was also to be featured as the Dominie in my 1947 production of *Brigadoon,* delivered a heartbreaking performance as the grocer who couldn't help giving the poet and his son bread and cheese on credit forever. The son, Johnny, was little Sidney Lumet, now big Sidney Lumet, the film director.

For Johnny's girl friend, the grocer's small daughter, who had a tender, frustrated love scene with the boy, I needed a child who was sensitive, but plain and vulnerable. Dawn Powell, the author of the Group's *Big Night,* sent in her friend's daughter, a stunning child who was a pupil at the admirable King-Coit School, where gifted children were trained in all the performing arts. Their yearly Christmas productions, directed in high style, were mandatory viewing for many celebrated actors and dancers of the day. I felt Dawn's entry was too beautiful (even her name was beautiful—Tanaquil LeClercq), too assured, too "successful" looking, even as a little girl, for the part. I needed a "loser" child. To avoid any feeling of rejection, I told Dawn to be sure to tell Tanaquil the reason that she didn't get the part and that it certainly was not on any grounds of talent, with which she was obviously loaded. A few years ago, at the Stravinsky Festival of the New York City Ballet Company, Miss LeClercq sat in her wheelchair in the aisle right next to my seat. She had become the world-famous ballerina of the cool beauty, tragically struck down by polio at the height of her career. It was the first time I'd seen her again (except in her superb dancing performances), and we recalled that day long ago when she auditioned for the part of Esther in *My Heart's in the Highlands.* She said she still had the typed scene of the audition she felt she had failed and told me how much hurt she had suffered when she was turned down. The dancer had not been informed why and was hardly relieved to hear the explanation I gave her thirty-three years late. Ever after, auditions have been even more traumatic to me as a director, than they are to the performers.

To create the scenery and costumes for *Highlands,* I chose a new designer, Herbert Andrews, who had done some sets for the Group Theatre summer shows. A friend of Aaron Copland, Paul Bowles, composed the first of his many superb scores of incidental music for plays, a special talent

Dawn Powell, author of *Big Night.* Group Theatre production, 1932-33.

*My Heart's in the Highlands*: **Philip Loeb, Sidney Lumet, Jackie Ayers. ". . . the poet agonized."**

in which he excelled. This is the same Paul Bowles who is the fine writer of novels with a North African background.

I prepared an opening moment for the production that would not only set the style of the evening but immediately nail to the ground the play's theme, which I had chosen. That theme was the agony of the artist's attempt to create in a hostile world. In the play, the poet, whose writings have been rejected by the *Atlantic Monthly,* cries out, "I must have readers," and the Old Shakespearean actor complains, "They took away my bugle." Toward the end of the overture, which contained echoes of a war, the lights came up on a set revealing the area of the poet's house and the street in front. A huge, stylized tree framed the bare outlines of the set. Up on a platform (the inside of the house) the poet agonized over the problem of finding a rhyme, while his little son, Johnny, dressed identically as the father, sat on the steps to the street, holding the balusters of the railing, looking out, as though through the bars of a prison cell, and drooled as a boy with a double-decker ice cream cone, consisting of two different colorful flavors, went by. The most acrimonious actor-director arguments I had were with the child thespian, Jackie Ayers, over which flavors would call forth his best acting efforts. Failing to cadge even one lick of ice cream from the passing boy, Johnny went on to try some handstands. I synchronized each attempt and fall of the son with the try out and failure of a possible rhyme by the father—all this to the continuing music, of course.

Finally, eureka! With a gleeful shout, the poet found the right word just as the son in the street below accomplished the handstand, following it with celebratory cartwheels. So I established, at the outset, that the psychological points would be made not only through the dialogue, but through the theatricalization of chosen movement, music, and/or sound, costume, props, and so on.

Since a subsidiary theme of the play held that the people are nourished by art, when the old man subsequently played the song "My Heart's in the Highlands" to the assembled villagers, I took as my image: a plant flowering as it is watered. As the old man played his horn (a long, thin Shakespearean-type trumpet) on the porch above, the people below gathered together to listen. I built them up like a tree, from a few in kneeling position, to a child held high on somebody's shoulders. Each person had concealed a colorfully painted article of food, and slowly, as the old man vibrated his trumpet like a tremulous watering can, they held aloft their offerings, which seemed to be growing out of the branches of a large tree. Finally, the whole group swayed slightly as in a wind, and at the end, the child on top proudly held high a gaily colored chicken.

*My Heart's in the Highlands*: Art Smith plays his Shakespearean trumpet.

Toward the end of the four-week rehearsal period, word of these strange goings-on reached the Group actors' committee, and they asked permission to watch me work as Harold Clurman was vacationing in Cuba. I refused for two reasons: one, I knew that my experiments in stylization would not meet with their approval, and, two, being afraid I would not finish my staging in time, I worked so fast that I was ready for my run-throughs after one and a half weeks. For the remaining two and a half weeks, I had to goof off until the announced opening. Since a daily run-through of the short play and the notes given to the actors only consumed a couple of hours, I was hard put to invent ways to waste the rest of the rehearsal time. I didn't want to go through the play more than once a day in order to avoid being overrehearsed. Once, since it was Easter time and there were children in the cast, I organized an egg hunt in the Guild Theatre. It was time, I felt, that the Theatre Guild folk had a good egg hunt in their theater. Phil Loeb inscribed each egg with funny pictures and sayings, and the kids squealed merrily as they unearthed them. Hardly a "rehearsal" I cared to be caught by the dour committee. Infuriated at my high-handed "no admittance" edict, they cabled Clurman for permission to cancel the production, which they said was squandering the Group's (their) money. Harold's reply saved the production while enunciating the play's theme: "The Group is not a bank. Proceed with Saroyan play."

Speaking of money, I had occasion to compare the budgets of this, my first Broadway production, in 1939, with one of my recent efforts: *Harold and Maude,* in 1980. All right, all right, we'll talk about the difference in quality later; let's stick to the budgeting. Both plays employed about twenty actors, both had sets consisting of a central area of a house with little platforms coming on at the sides for smaller scenes, both had incidental music scored for a few instruments. *My Heart's in the Highlands* cost less than nine thousand dollars, and *Harold and Maude* cost three-quarters of a million dollars. That tell you something?

The night before the *Highlands* opening, Bill Saroyan arrived from Fresno, California, and came to the dress rehearsal. It was my first meeting with him, and it was a charming revelation. He seemed to be theatrically ingenuous, walking around the stage after the dress rehearsal like a bemused child, touching the props, the scenery, even the sandbags used as counterweights for the sets. This was his first produced play. "I just realized it," he cried. "My initials, W.S., are the same as Shakespeare's!" One thing was clear: he had not anticipated all the theatrical elements of staging: scenery, lighting, props, music, and sounds. I don't know how he had dreamed of the production in his mind, but if it was anything like a group of actors standing on a stage saying all of his words loudly and clearly, he must have been truly stunned.

After the rehearsal we went for coffee. Bill kept commenting on how much work it must have been for me to get all those production values together, while he had contributed nothing. I assured him he had contributed the most important element, the play itself. No, he insisted, he had done nothing to help get it on, and he wanted to offer something. "Such as what?" I asked, carefully. Well, he could write some new dialogue for us. As gently as I could, I informed him that the play was to open the next night, and I had only called the cast for a little get-together before the première. If he gave the actors too many new lines at the last moment, it might throw them. He assured me there were only a few little places he noticed during the evening that he could improve with some simple changes. "Fine," I said, "I'll see you in the morning at your hotel."

When I arrived at the Great Northern on Fifty-seventh Street the next day, Saroyan handed me a script of the play. Riffling through it, my blood slowly froze. On almost every page there was some little modification. Nothing essential seemed to be altered but everywhere there were tiny rearrangements of wording, the kind of changes that are ball-breakers for actors to learn after four weeks of saying the lines one way. A few "Johnny, you can do it"s after you've been saying "You can do it, Johnny," is a tougher assignment than learning a whole new scene. It was not easy for me to conceal my worry from the playwright. But I didn't want him to think I was arbitrary or uncooperative, and I knew how much he wanted to contribute something to the opening performance of his play. I said I'd take the script home, and although I couldn't promise to get every change in by the evening, I'd do the best I could without upsetting the first night. Actually, there was one addition that Saroyan made that was not only funny but easy for Phil Loeb to insert. When the poet introduces the old man to the neighbors, he had previously said, "Good neighbors, and friends, I want you to meet Jasper MacGregor, the greatest Shakespearean actor of our day." Bill had revised it to read, "Good neighbors, and friends, I want you to meet Jasper MacGregor, the greatest Shakespearean actor of our day—I believe."

That evening, April 13, 1939, I stood at the back of the orchestra and watched the opening performance. Having designed the sound, music, scene-change, and lighting cues with precise dynamics, I held my breath each time a cue came, for fear the timing would be off even a second. Everything clicked along perfectly until the very last moment of the play. I had staged a Hamlet-like exit for the old Shakespearean actor when he died. His body was lifted aloft on the shoulders of two neighbors, and he was carried up the ramp to the "Highlands." His head hung down in back with the long, thin horn dangling from his neck. The cortege was to step out on the right foot and march slowly in tempo to the dirge of a trumpet and an English horn. A bass drum kept the beat. One of the pallbearers stepped out on his left foot and, consequently, was out of step all the way up the hill. This offense to form struck me with the force of a blow, and I fell back against the wall of the theater, hitting my head a damn good

*My Heart's in the Highlands*: "One of the pallbearers stepped out on his left foot . . ."

whack. I then staggered down the stairs, through the lobby, and out onto Fifty-second Street, and collapsed against the front of the theater. I felt the whole evening was ruined, and I did not go back inside to hear the applause at the end. When the audience started coming out, I rushed through the stage door to the dressing rooms. The actors tried to console me by saying it was the only mistake that was made. It was as assuring as telling me a dancer had completed all his turns successfully and had only lost his balance on the last one and fallen to the ground.

After all the actors had been congratulated, Harold Clurman and Stella Adler decided to take Bill Saroyan and me for a bite of food to celebrate. The Guild Theatre was on Fifty-second Street, so we walked across town to the famous 21 Club. I guess none of us was of a high-enough celebrity status for that establishment, because we were stopped at the door with "No tables." We finally ended up at an Armenian restaurant, not a great thrill for Fresno's Armenian son.

In the next few days, I got my first dose of "mixed" reviews. I don't mean each review was mixed, in the context that the word is now understood, namely, that the critic says the play, the direction, the acting and the scenery were all lousy, but the orange juice sold in the lobby had an encouragingly lower uric acid content than usual. I mean "mixed" in the sense that half the critics wrote "raves," while the other half clobbered us mercilessly. Here are some samples of the latter. Wolcott Gibbs in the *New*

*Yorker*: "This collision between the most completely undisciplined talent in American letters and the actors of the Group Theatre bored me nearly to distraction and I would advise you to stay away from it." Gibbs ended his diatribe with "I think we'd better forget all about it as soon as possible."

Sidney Whipple, in the *World-Telegram,* calling it "surrealist" drama, concluded that "this painful experiment was conducted for one purpose—to test the I.Q. of the public and the critics." He advised the Group Theatre "to pay no further attention to Mr. Saroyan's babbling."

The quote dean unquote of New York critics, Burns Mantle, was really violent, taking the attitude some reviewers do that you put the play on just to aggravate them. Referring to the scene of the neighbors gathering for the old man's trumpet solo he declared, "They bring vegetables, too, but do not throw them. And that, I suspect, is a symbol of forbearance."

Fortunately the opposing side could boast the real heavyweights. Among them were Brooks Atkinson, George Jean Nathan, and John Mason Brown. Having called *My Heart's in the Highlands* "wholly enchanting," Mr. Atkinson continued, in his Sunday follow-up review, "The Group Theatre is giving a performance that the Moscow Art Theatre would be glad to accept as worthy of the Stanislavski standard." John Mason Brown touched on my unrealistic approach with, "What the Group Theatre has staged with a formalism that turns its back skillfully on everyday reality, interested and moved me more than most of the produc-

For Robert Lewis, the director of my first play "My Heart's in the Highlands" (*Peace, It's Wonderful**), with great admiration and gratitude, with sincere regards, and with the faith that, as for myself, this play is also, for him, only the beginning of many more plays to know, and to have directed, so splendidly,

Sincerely
William Saroyan

NY April 23, 1939.

* The directing.

"The review that gave me the most satisfaction."

tions I have seen this winter. And I surmise from those around me who had tears in their eyes that they were no less touched than I by what is poignant, charming, and yet indefinable in *My Heart's in the Highlands.*" I was particularly grateful to have succeeded in making the point that emotion can be aroused in an audience without the actors doing all the crying.

The *Herald-Tribune*'s Richard Watts said that "the best tribute I can think of to pay the Group at the moment is to say that after seeing it at work in the Saroyan play one can understand why those who have once played with it never seem happy until they return to its fold." Had he checked his cast list, Mr. Watts would have noticed that only Art Smith of the Group Company was in it.

The review that gave me the most satisfaction came from the playwright himself. Saroyan presented me with a collection of his short stories called *Peace, It's Wonderful.* On the title page he wrote, "For Robert Lewis, the director of my first play, *My Heart's in the Highlands,* with great admiration and gratitude, with sincere regards, and with the faith that, as for myself, this play is also for him the beginning of many more plays to know, and to have directed, so splendidly. Sincerely, William Saroyan, N.Y., April 23, 1939." Next to the title, *Peace, It's Wonderful,* he placed a little cross indicating a reference at the bottom of the page that said, "The directing."

Of the congratulatory letters I received, the most impressive one came from Laurence Olivier, not only because he offered his "heartfelt congratulations and admiration for a really beautiful achievement," but because it was written on stationery with the following address in embossed printing:

LAURENCE OLIVIER
ETHEL BARRYMORE THEATRE
NEW YORK CITY

This sense of the theater (where he was playing in Sam Behrman's *No Time for Comedy*) being a home permanent enough for embossed stationery told me something about the young Englishman's admirable self-confidence. Robert Ross, a colleague from the Civic Rep, and his wife, Margalo Gillmore, from the cast of the Behrman play, was with Olivier the Thursday matinee he saw *Highlands.* Ross reported in a letter to me that Olivier characterized his feelings about the production by saying, "It's the best in America—it is what theatre should be and rarely ever is. It's better than you'll find in London."

One highly prized letter from the nontheatrical world came from the great photographer Alfred Stieglitz. Headed "An American Place—May 11, 1939," it started "My dear Bob Lewis: You gave me something truly beautifully living—It possesses me.—That evening." It was signed, "Your old Stieglitz."

But of all the rewards I enjoyed for my directorial debut, two delighted and amazed me more than all the others. The first was the fact that Renée, the hatcheck girl at Sardi's restaurant, no longer gave me a chit to reclaim my hat. She now knew who I was, and she knew my hat. Receiving this accolade from Renée assured me I was finally "in." The second event put the ultimate imprimatur on me: *The New York Times* sent their obituary photographer around to snap my picture for their morgue. I now know why many ancient people, when they die, look so young on the obituary page.

The five special performances of *Highlands* were extended to five weeks, thanks to the follow-up articles by Brooks Atkinson, George Jean Nathan, and John Mason Brown. Brown tried to shame the Theatre Guild into offering the production to its many subscribers by saying, "Once upon a time the moguls of The Guild would have been the first to receive and the first to produce such a script as Mr. Saroyan's." Initially, the Guild board resisted the extension of the run. They felt it was a mistake to cast Phil Loeb in the lead. They wondered if his face wasn't too "swarthy" for the part. I pointed out that the play took place in Fresno, where it was said there were more Armenians than in Armenia, and since the poet's mother in the production spoke only Armenian, and the poet spoke Armenian to her, it was reasonably safe to assume he must be Armenian—like Saroyan, for instance, himself a rather swarthy type. "Swarthy" was the show-business word used for Jewish, Italian, or any other ethnic group you didn't want to offend when you turned actors down for parts.

Next, the Guild complained that the play only lasted an hour and a half and their subscribers would object. (If it isn't size 7¼, it isn't a hat.) They suggested I add a curtain raiser. I balked at that, feeling the play could, and should, stand on its own. Finally, the Guild gave in and presented the production for its fifth play of the season, but not until they cut the regular subscription price of $3.50 to $2.20. Subscribers were informed they could take their refund in cash or deduct it from the following season's payment. When the five subscription weeks ended, there was so little box-office activity that the play closed at once. But when the Drama Critics met to award their silver plaque for the best American play of the season, there was a deadlock, with votes divided among *The Little Foxes, Abe Lincoln in Illinois, Rocket to the Moon,* and *My Heart's in the Highlands.* As a result, no American play award was given that season. If all the people who had boasted, in the years since 1939, "Ah, yes, I remember *My Heart's in the Highlands,*" had actually seen it, it would still be running.

More important than the satisfaction of having proven to the theater world that I could direct, was the inner security I gained for my creative impulses. I could pursue freely, in directing and teaching, my consuming interest in the problems of style. I now know that to realize, in my first time at bat, one hundred percent of the production values I had originally dreamed up was a miracle. Richard Rodgers, questioned by me once as to whether he had ever heard anyone sing a song of his exactly as he originally heard it in his head, replied immediately, "No." Then, after a pause, he corrected himself. "Yes, one time," he said. "When Bill Tabbert sang 'Younger Than Springtime' in *South Pacific.*" Well, *My Heart's in the Highlands* turned out to be my "Younger Than Springtime." Although I'd direct many other more commercially successful productions, this first baby would be my only pure one, uncontaminated by the crazy, collaborative nature of the Broadway theatrical process. My days as an innocent were over.

CHAPTER 8

# The Time of Your Life 1939

AFTER *MY HEART'S in the Highlands,* Saroyan went to work on what was to become his most commercially successful play, *The Time of Your Life.* He offered it first to the Group Theatre, but Harold Clurman, who admired certain fanciful parts of it, felt too much of Saroyan's writing was undisciplined, self-indulgent, and bathetic. Harold thereby anticipated the rest of the critical fraternity when the playwright got up to bat again a year later. Whenever any charges of formlessness were leveled against Saroyan in the very beginning, influential critics, George Jean Nathan in particular, encouraged him to pay no attention. His flights of imagination were so entertaining that Saroyan, who became buddies with some of the critics, organizing an occasional dice game with some, was warned by them against academicians who would straightjacket him. Then, as though by mutual agreement, these same critics all pounced on the writer for his *Love's Old Sweet Song,* which followed *The Time of Your Life,* and was no more "formless" than his other plays. It has some of his most hilarious "bits," like the ticking off of all the names of *Time* magazine's editors. But by then (only the next year—1940) we find John Mason Brown, one of Saroyan's early boosters, saying the play "grows tiresome and thin. Its silliness is redeemed by no point. Its confessions have no real beauty behind them." This about-face served to confuse and embitter the dramatist and ultimately resulted in his complete withdrawal from the theater.

When Clurman rejected *The Time of Your Life,* Saroyan sold it to Eddie Dowling, the actor-producer, who saw in it a fine leading part for himself. Dowling worked out a coproduction deal with the Theatre Guild, and I was again assigned as director. This was to be my first time away from home (the Group), and my initial flight as a fledgling in the world of commercial management.

Lawrence Langner, his wife, Armina Marshall, and Terry Helburn (the most professional theater mind of the three) met in the Guild office with me for casting conferences over lunch, which Lawrence had ordered in advance. The lunch consisted of portions of cottage cheese, only one of which had fruit on it. A good deal of time was spent placating Lawrence, who was always annoyed at my grabbing the one with the fruit. "This one isn't mine," he'd sulk, looking balefully at his naked cottage cheese. "Bobby's got mine again." With admitted ill-grace I'd switch cottage cheeses, resenting the class discrimination between producer and director, even though it was only expressed by canned fruit at that point.

My next shock was the Theatre Guild's manner of casting the parts. They kept a large loose-leaf book with all actors and actresses categorized; not, however, according to type or ability, but according to price. Next to each actor's name was his salary. When a certain part in the play was being discussed, Lawrence would look at his budget and check out how much that part paid; let's say it was two hundred dollars. He'd pick up his casting book, run his finger down the right side of the page until he came to two hundred dollars. Then he'd follow his finger over to the left to see what the actor's name was. It was the way parsimonious people read a menu. Down the prices you go; ah, there it is, $1.75; move to the left—uh, oh, hamburger.

As the rehearsals of *The Time of Your Life* got underway, I was delighted to receive from Saroyan a letter dated September 16, 1939, from San Francisco, concurring with the heightening and musicalizing I again had in mind to match the particular poetic style of his writing. (One of Saroyan's alternate titles for the play was *Sunset Sonata.*) Bill wrote, "Dear Bobby: I'm delighted you're directing *The Time of Your Life.* I know you'll do a great job. You'll have to. We're both at stake, as it were, and if that's the expression. The play is a great play. I'm convinced of that. Objectively. Apart from who the hell the writer is. It is something miraculous, even for me. I know you will see all its values, and exploit them. The gadgets involved are important. The sounds they make are important. The telephone. The marble game. Take pains to get the kind of marble game I have written about. See that the dialing of the telephone is loud and ga-ga, as it truly is. The ringing of the telephone bell the same. Stylize the ringing . . . Joe's mechanical toy. Big and ridiculous and wonderful. In motion, apochryphal. Costumes, sizes of players, voice variation, stance, posture, personal rhythm, idiosyncrasies, get 'em all. Be a poet." And so on.

In full agreement with this approach, I chose the highly imaginative Boris Aronson as designer, who sketched a wild marble game as well as settings and costumes that were indeed "ridiculous and wonderful." The talented Lehman Engel agreed to compose the music and choose the sounds.

Early in the rehearsal period, I got my first view of the kind of death dance that would accompany my work on this production. One day Aronson brought his costume sketches to rehearsal for the approval of the leading lady, Julie Haydon. It was no secret that Julie had been put forward for her part by George Jean Nathan, her particular friend. This wasn't "show biz" gossip, but a state of affairs confirmed by Miss Haydon herself in her biography at the back of the theater program. This was peculiarly honest of her, since most theater people try to keep their patrons' names secret.

I now learned that in the Broadway set up it was possible for someone in Haydon's position to have approval of Boris Aronson's designs before he could go ahead. Not to discuss, mind you, or suggest, which would be in the normal course of artists' collaborations, but to approve. Boris Aronson was not only a superb designer but a brilliant painter as well. Whenever I was lucky enough to have received a hand-made Christmas card from him, I rushed it at once to the framers and then hung it proudly on my wall. My eyes widened, therefore, as I saw this artist hand his beautiful sketches, one at a time, to Julie Haydon, only to have her carefully take each one that she didn't approve and tear it straight down the middle. "This is nice," she'd say, sweetly of one, putting it aside. "This is a bad color for my hair," she'd complain of another and rip it in two. I couldn't look at Boris's face. Even now I feel the shame of my silence. Why didn't I grab those little paintings out of her hand and throw her out of the rehearsal? I already must have developed that particular cowardice in the theater that comes from not wanting to "make waves."

What is this obsequious behavior we assume in the presence of what we ridiculously accept as the theater power structure: stars, sometimes the least talented members of the cast; producers, whose only ability may consist of assembling the backers; playwrights, who may be literary giants but know little of the precepts of theater practice; and since you are thinking it anyway, let me add: directors, who may be good traffic cops but understand little of the mechanism of acting—or designing—or writing? No, we cannot achieve a decent life in the theater without respect for, and collaboration with, *all* the contributing artists. *Control* (artistic) in the hands of the director may be necessary for a sense of unity in the production, but the flagrant exercise of sheer *power*? In anybody's hands, that is a plague to dread.

In *The Curtain Falls,* producer Joseph Verner Reed tells how his great star, my former idol, Jane Cowl, had her own idea for the set of their proposed production of *Twelfth Night.* The designer, Raymond Sovey, had another plan and he, the producers, and the director stayed up one whole night preparing a model to show Cowl for her approval. She arrived at Reed's office early in the morning, saw the model out of the corner of her eye, and started circling the room while giving orders for every department of the production. She then went deliberately to the chair where the fragile model was placed and without even looking at it, squatted on the poor thing and reduced it to rubble. "She blew us a kiss and was gone," says Reed. "After a short silence, the four of us went about our work." There it is again. Silence. Don't make waves. I once heard Oliver Smith gasp for air when Tallulah Bankhead, at a dress rehearsal, deliberately shoved her foot right through the wall of one of his sets. And we think reviewers can be rough in their criticisms.

A subtler kind of vandalism manifested itself during the rehearsals of *The Time of Your Life*. That was the refusal on the part of a performer to be part of the effort to make all the stage arts contribute to the directional concept. One of the characters in the play, Elsie, a nurse, has one short scene where she takes a boy off to bed after a cynical speech of hopelessness. Hortense Alden, who played the part, had a marvelous low, husky voice, and I devised a high soprano wail to be sung faintly offstage as she spoke, a keening counterpoint to her harsh words. The first time Hortense heard it she stopped dead and demanded, "Is *that* to be going on while I'm talking?" I attempted to reassure her, not only of the appropriateness of the effect from the point of view of the overall style of production I was working for, but that the sound actually made her scene more moving. But this was her one moment in the play and it was going to be hers alone or no dice. So the whiff of death I smelled at each chipping away of the concept began with actors. Producers and author were still to come.

During the rehearsal period, I discovered a weird managerial practice. There seemed to be some huddled figures in the rear of the theater's balcony. At first I paid no attention, thinking they might be some kids who sneaked in for a look. When I realized they came back each day, I sent the stage manager, Johnny Haggott, to find out who they were. It turned out they were possible acting replacements, and the Guild had told them to watch rehearsals. In that way, if one or another of them should be called on to step in, they would have already benefited from the original direction. I cleared the vultures out.

Lehman Engel, our music composer, testifies in his book *This Bright Day* that "Bobby directed the play with scrupulous honesty. What Saroyan had set down was carried out explicitly. I wrote all the music as nearly as possible as it had been described. Boris Aronson's set was magnificent, and it, too, adhered faithfully to the author's meticulously detailed intentions." But somehow, through inexperience, weakness, or whatever, I was allowing my orchestration of the acting, movement, scenery, lighting, music, and sounds that made up the five scenes (movements) of Saroyan's sonata to be pulled out of shape daily by the Guild's and Dowling's suggestions. By the time the production got to dress rehearsal in New Haven, and Saroyan arrived, things became chaotic. My desperation mounted as the playwright was persuaded by the Guild to scrap his poetic instructions and opt for a realistic approach. Maybe what he saw differed from the dream in his head. After all, I only found out he also had reservations about my stylization of *My Heart's in the Highlands* six years after the production played. In 1945, Harold Clurman, in *The Fervent Years* wrote, "He (Saroyan) thought of his play as virile realism, not at all as fable. He did not approve of Bobby Lewis's delicate stylization, though he did not fail to borrow from it later in his production of *The Beautiful People.*" Had I, in the fall of 1939, known those feelings of Saroyan about *Heart's*—I certainly could never have guessed them from his letters of instruction to me regarding *The Time of Your Life*—I would never have presumed to accept the offer to direct the latter play.

But I had, and now I was trapped. Acquiescing to any more of the changes Langner and Dowling wanted would further distort my directorial plan and make the show neither fish nor fowl. To keep on fighting for my concept would force a confrontation that would get me fired. (Your lawyer or agent always instructs you in these situations: "Don't quit. Let them fire you. Then they have to pay you." At this point, I had neither lawyer nor agent, but the little man inside me clearly indicated the end was near.) The Guild was famous for rewriting, recasting, and restaging plays and their troubles with other directors were fresh in my mind—and in theirs, too. The Orson Welles-Mercury-Theatre Guild *Five Kings* was a recent debacle, and John Houseman had also been given the sack from Maxwell Anderson's *Valley Forge.* Houseman was fired in the Pittsburgh hotel where Duse died. Herbert Biberman, his directorial replacement, was brought in to the final meeting with the Guild from a room down the hall where he had been kept waiting. Houseman, being a gentleman, wished him luck and walked out. Langner followed him down the hall to the elevator and asked Houseman if he wouldn't mind staying on with the production to spy on Biberman because Lawrence didn't trust the new director's taste. Houseman was to report anything he disapproved of in Biberman's work to Langner personally. And guess what? Houseman stayed on.

I was not a gentleman, however. I was a neophyte in these matters and when the Guild, with the collaboration of Dowling and Saroyan, got ready to lower the boom on me, I made a childish decision. I locked myself in my room and stayed incommunicado until I could figure out what to do. It was a foolish move but that is like saying the victim didn't behave well on the rack. All I knew was that I had to get out or suffocate. I quit and went back to New York. Lawrence Langner's last words to me were, "After you and Orson Welles, no more geniuses." I felt a little better to be associated, even in this way, with Orson, whom I admired. Tennessee Williams said Lawrence also called him a genius when the Guild produced Tennessee's embattled *Battle of Angels.* The playwright claimed that when anyone called him a genius he felt his inside pocket to be sure his wallet was still there. "Genius" was obviously a nasty word to Langner and served him as one substitute for the genuine dirty words he was afraid to enunciate. His wife, Armina Marshall, once told me that this inability of Lawrence's to use swear words when he felt the urge to do so had such a frustrating effect on him that he was forced to seek the help of a psychiatrist. One day Armina returned to their apartment and was surprised to hear unrecognizable sounds coming from the bathroom. Upon opening the door, she was shocked to see Lawrence bending over the commode spitting out one four-letter word after another. The psychiatrist had recommended this strange therapy as a cure.

In Boston, the next tryout city, Dowling and Saroyan took over the direction of *The Time of Your Life.* Most of the supporting parts were recast at once. Gene Kelly was brought in to replace Martin Ritt as a downtrodden hoofer constantly trying to get someone to pay attention to his act. I had cast Ritt precisely because he wasn't Gene Kelly, who, although not a star yet, had only to lift an arm or a leg to command attention. As Lehman Engel records, "It seems curious to me that Ritt had been engaged as an *actor*—and was replaced by a superb dancer who was *supposed* not to dance well. Logical?" It is if you're casting to sell entertainment rather than interpret the author's intention.

Boris Aronson's beautiful, "heightened" set was torn to bits (as his costume sketches were earlier), this time by the star and the producer. Lehman, whose original score was also being scrapped, witnessed the defacement of the scenery: "To my horror I observed Langner and Dowling go up on stage and physically tear down artificial flowers, uproot grass mats, and other parts of Boris Aronson's scenery, which had been stipulated expressly by Saroyan. It was the day of the butcher." Boris's set was replaced with a realistic one by Watson Barratt, a Shubert standby designer, who, without offense (but also without exaggeration), had less talent in all his paint brushes than Boris had in his little finger.

As for the lighting, John O'Malley, one of the actors in the cast who had been retained, wrote me that on opening day, in Boston, when they were relighting the show, Terry Helburn called out from her seat in the auditorium, "Bring up the blue footlights. All the poetry's gone out of this thing."

Thirty years later, Harold Clurman, remarking in his *Nation* magazine review of the revival of *The Time of Your Life* by the Lincoln Center Repertory Theatre, that the production was "conventional" and the setting as "ugly as anyone would have such a place be," goes on to make the essential point: "The play has always been staged as realism. It is real, but not 'realistic.' Its characters are painted in tender 'clown' pigments; the world they float in is delicately inebriate, harmlessly psychedelic. When Robert Lewis first attempted its direction for the Theatre Guild in 1939 he was aware of this aspect of the play and tried, with the support of a Boris Aronson setting, to embody its locale as a sort of modest dream palace, a realm apart from the main drag, an essential San Francisco in which different ethnic strains blended in the soft air of that still gracious town, as if it were all bathed in a shimmering mist. Saroyan insisted at the time that the saloon in which the action takes place be literally rendered as a drab and crumby little joint. The play came to New York in that guise, with an excellent cast but with the other elements of production indifferent—the whole sufficient to carry the play's message. Saroyan may have been right. But I have always hoped to see the play done poetically, with its fancy made visible, and with more song in its total expression.—Alas, no one has as yet had the imagination, courage, and skill to do so."

Courage to fight the Philistines: that was what I lacked in 1939, I realized, as I read this review in 1969. *The Time of Your Life* rehearsal period was the first fiery ordeal that made me understand, all too clearly, what my family doctor, Samuel Greenberg, meant by "The bastards won't let you live."

As for Saroyan, having won the Drama Critics' prize hands down this time with *The Time of Your Life,* he decided to submit his next, *Love's Old Sweet Song,* to the Guild again. This time they tried to rewrite the play at once. And Bill, supported by George Jean Nathan, fought them. "Saroyan does not believe in structure," Terry Helburn writes in her autobiographical book *A Wayward Quest,* "he has no use for technique." When *Love's Old Sweet Song* failed, Bill threw down the gauntlet: he would only sell his work to managers who'd let him direct the productions himself; no more sharing of the creative process. He didn't have a suspicion that directing is a skill separate from writing. He only knew he could no longer endure the torture of someone else interpreting his work. It takes a stable, confident, technically sure creator to maintain his balance while the interpreters grab his baby and whip it into shape, sometimes successfully, sometimes not. There aren't too many artists like that in our theater setup, but I can think of at least one in the music field. When the Group was in London with *Golden Boy* I sat in the balcony of Queen's Hall one morning with Aaron Copland, listening to Sir Adrian Boult rehearse Aaron's *El Salon Mexico.* That jaunty piece was the American entry in a program of international compositions. I not only knew the music by heart from the old Koussevitsky recording, but I'd heard Aaron play it on the piano, bouncing away, evoking the sounds of all the instruments with his ten fingers. He managed to convey the insinuating rhythms of the sleazy saloon that gave the piece its title, a bar where the customers checked their guns at the door. Now here was Sir Adrian beating out nice, square rhythms that I knew were light miles away from delivering the colors needed. I looked at Aaron. His face had a quizzical smile on it. I couldn't believe that I was upset and he wasn't. I nudged him. "Go on down there, Aaron, please, and talk to him."

"That's the way he is," said the composer. "That's the way he feels it. You can't change people's nature." He seemed genuinely interested to hear

**Aaron Copland: "That's the way he is."**

his piece done this way. And he didn't even flinch when Ernest Newman, the distinguished English music critic, in his review, complained that Aaron's American entry was the weakest of the evening and seemed no more than some Latin folk tunes strung together. I have tried ever since to profit from Aaron's attitude of normalcy and strength in these matters, but it isn't easy.

And it wasn't easy for Saroyan. His struggle with directors (Eddie Dowling, with collaboration from Saroyan, had staged *Love's Old Sweet Song*) led him to this conclusion: "The director is a conductor, not a composer." If I take his point correctly, he's saying the composer (playwright) is a creator and the conductor (director) is an interpreter. True. But there are creative interpreters and slavish interpreters. No one could accuse

Meyerhold, Piscator, or Peter Brook of not being creative or say that they didn't "compose" their productions. What he must insure—and if this is what Bill meant, I agree with him—is that the interpretation the creative director contributes has its seeds in and grows out of the composer-playwright's text and is not some smart-assed ego trip of a fancy director pasted on to the text and destroying it.

Nineteen forty-one found Saroyan staging his own play, *The Beautiful People,* at the Lyceum Theatre, and the following year he produced his own *Saroyan Theatre,* staging two of his short plays. In the Sunday *Times* drama section of August 23, 1942, Brooks Atkinson rapped Bill's knuckles for not being as creative an interpreter as he was a composer. Under the heading, "Mr. Saroyan Tosses On A Show," Atkinson wrote, "On the whole, Bill is O.K. But he knows very little about the theater. It is most apparent in his producing and staging. *The Beautiful People* was only about half-staged when he directed it at the Lyceum in 1941, and *Across the Board on Tomorrow Morning* and *Talking to You* are only about half staged now. 'If the performers are competent and know how to talk, no director in the American theater knows how to "time" speech and event,' says Mr. Saroyan. But that is where he is wrong, for a number of directors do, and a few of them also know how to create a performance out of a script. Mr. Lewis did that with *My Heart's in the Highlands.* Having had considerable practical experience in the theater, Mr. Lewis knew how to make his imagination work in terms of time, space, sound, and motion. A genuine performance of a play is not a recital; it is a living organism. Mr. Saroyan's direction is hardly more than stage managing. In his presentation of the two current plays, he has committed the unpardonable sin of being uninteresting. He is wasting his plays and our time. He is not learning anything about the theater. Although many things are wrong with it, he is not solving them nor providing workable substitutes. Bad as the theater is, it cannot be improved by incompetence."

These words might have cheered me during the purgatory of *The Time of Your Life.* Now they depressed me and could only serve to embitter Bill. He was encouraged in the beginning to be freewheeling. He was never warned of the inherent danger to the artist from neglect of form. Like so many other meteoric talents in the theater, he seemed to have been set up only to be knocked down. Sadly, another fine literary artist got lost in the jungle of the theater.

CHAPTER 9

# Prelude to Hollywood 1940-42

AFTER *THE TIME of Your Life* crash, I thought I'd better fly again, immediately. In the second Group Theatre summer, Harold Clurman had turned down Albert Bein's play about hoboes, *Heavenly Express.* Now, eight years later, with my one-word part in *Thunder Rock* hardly sufficient therapy for my recent wounds, and no role for me in the next production, *Night Music* by Odets, Harold encouraged Kermit Bloomgarden, the Group's business manager, who liked *Heavenly Express,* to produce it independently and use me as director. I jumped at the idea because the play, a fantasy, although short on plot and psychology, offered marvelous opportunities for directorial strokes. Seeing it as a sort of comic miracle play, I hastened once more to get Boris Aronson as designer. His beautiful opening setting was a mysterious, star-filled sky backing up some hoboes huddled around a little fire in a discarded automobile fender. Crosslike telegraph poles diminished into the horizon. The effect was tinselly religious, like a marvelous Christmas card.

I resuscitated another victim of *The Time of Your Life,* Lehman Engel, and asked him to compose a musical score. The newly passed union rule (no more doubling of instruments by the same musician as we had done in *My Heart's in the Highlands*) made the cost of the kind of score I wanted prohibitive. Making a virtue out of the new decree, I commissioned a choral score (singers were another union) which we recorded and played during the show. The overture was "The Wayfaring Stranger," sung by Burl Ives, who was in the cast. This became Burl's identifying number over the years. In other roles Phil Loeb, Art Smith, Richard Conte, and Harry Bratsburg, all of whom had been in *My Heart's in the Highlands,* together with Russell Collins of the Group Theatre Company, made up my security blanket. For the lead character, The Overland Kid, a combination of hobo and child was needed. Off I went to California to lure back from the films

John Garfield in *Heavenly Express*: "A combination of hobo and child."

my old Group buddy and pupil, John Garfield. He accepted enthusiastically, and while I was there I picked up Harry Carey, a character actor from the movies, for the part of the freight train engineer.

I wrote down three names to interview for the crucial role of the boardinghouse keeper. Since one always starts at the top, I listed three of the great actresses of the day: Pauline Lord, Laurette Taylor, and Aline MacMahon, who actually played the part. Pauline Lord turned me down graciously, and although I tried, I couldn't pick her brains much about her acting secrets. But the hesitant way she spoke her unfinished sentences, her acute vulnerability, the sudden swells of feeling, the constant dropping of her purse, her handkerchief, her cigarettes—all so reminiscent of her stage characters—were present in our interview, and it was hard for me to tear myself away and leave her to her desired privacy.

Laurette Taylor seemed more accessible, and we talked about Garfield, whom she admired. But she, too, excused herself from tackling the part of "Granny" in *Heavenly Express.* I seized my opportunity, however, to launch into a series of questions about her acting, which was the supreme example of the art of concealing art. I was puzzled when I heard her describe how she worked. She insisted she devised and "set" every last move, gesture, look, and line-reading in rehearsal and then faithfully executed them all religiously on stage. I could only surmise that if, indeed, that were so, she certainly seemed to forget them all once she came on. For no one had more of a sense of "the first time" and less of a studied look than Laurette Taylor. I remember her arriving (she never "made an entrance") in the bar of the ship in *Outward Bound,* looking like all of the Hundred Neediest Cases, seeming not to know where she was, who all those people were, and what was going on. I sat forward in my seat and wanted to cry out, "Don't worry, honey, it's only that you're dead." Now, mind you, once she was in the scene she found out whatever she needed to know, but it all happened completely spontaneously and seemed to have no sense of anticipatory preparation. I surmised that, with performing artists, what they say they do, and what they actually do may be quite dissimilar.

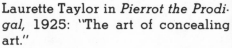

Laurette Taylor in *Pierrot the Prodigal,* 1925: "The art of concealing art."

The critical reception that greeted the premiere of *Heavenly Express* was instructive. Although the production was praised, the critics dismissed the script out of hand, with the exception of Brooks Atkinson. After saying "Bob Lewis, who directed *My Heart's in the Highlands,* has recaptured the same magic in his staging of this tall tale of God's special devotion to the tramp brotherhood. . . . For once the theater is truly imaginative," Atkinson had this comment on the script: "To say that *Heavenly Express* is too long, too sprawling, and underdeveloped in detail would doubtless be a sage observation, worthy of the dignity of criticism. But matters of that sort are of academic interest only." They interested the other critics, though, and the ticket buyers, too, since the play had a short run. People wouldn't pay to see a production, no matter how praiseworthy, if they were told it's of a bad play.

I was becoming more and more convinced that the further away a playwright gets from the realistic style, the more stringent his discipline must be in creating the form, no matter how free, that defines poetic expression. I was unable to help the author, Albert Bein, cut and organize his script on the pre-Broadway tour, which might have improved it somewhat, although not enough to cure the weaknesses in the writing itself. I was not a good enough dramaturge, and Bein was too emotionally involved in the material of the play, having himself lost a leg when a brakeman threw him from a train on which he was freight-hopping.

Directors, like actors, get typed in the theater, and I was beginning to be known as a director of "fantasy," a dirty word on Broadway. So when, early in 1941, a writer with the unlikely name of Lucille B. Prumbs submitted a knockabout comedy, called *Five Alarm Waltz,* about a freewheeling, Saroyanesque playwright named Adam Boguris, I asked Gadget Kazan if he'd like to play the role. When he agreed I went to work, and Walter Winchell went to press with the hot item that L. B. Prumbs was really Bill Saroyan. Bill replied, "Poor Winchell is mistaken again. . . . The character which is supposed to be Saroyan is in reality Walter Winchell. . . . When I am the author of a play it is never a secret." Saroyan held out little hope for the play's success. He was right. The critics and audience didn't have nearly as much fun watching the play as Gadget and I had rehearsing it.

But neither Kazan nor myself, brought up in the "home" of the Group Theatre, could have been fully happy at that time, even if our play had been a success. We would never again be fulfilled with the hit or flop life of the Broadway theater. We were seeking some place to "settle in" and develop the ideas that were infused in us by the recently deceased Group. We began to talk of starting our own theater, which, of course, would retain all the virtues of the Group with none of its shortcomings. Knowing that the cheaper seats to the Group's shows always sold well, even when the orchestra ones went begging, we set about finding a house large enough to

Elia Kazan in *Five Alarm Waltz*: "A freewheeling, Saroyanesque playwright."

be able to sell all seats for a dollar. Seasoned theater practitioners thought we were mad. Lee Shubert, to whom I had gone for a theater, said our plan was ridiculous because "if the play is no good, no one will come to see it, and if it is good, you should get $3.30 out of it." I made the mistake of mentioning the Federal Theatre, which had packed houses, continuously, at low prices for all kinds of plays. "The Federal Theatre," he fumed, "was set up to give an opportunity to a large number of people to steal money from the government."

Kazan had to go to Hollywood to act in a film for the summer; therefore he would tackle playwrights and money people on the West Coast while I held down the fort in New York, ably assisted by Molly Day Thacher, Gadget's wife. Joseph Burstyn, the foreign film impresario, agreed to be our business manager, and we actually gathered finished scripts by Irwin Shaw, Victor Wolfson, and Hy Kraft and promises from Clifford Odets and Paul Green, two Group stalwarts. From out West came word from Kazan that John Steinbeck was also working on a play for us.

As for the all important problem of raising money, Gadget had as little success in movieland as I had in the East. Pledges amounted roughly to

$20,000, but actual investments in our stock only came to about $5,000, half of which was from a pupil in one of my classes, the torch singer Libby Holman. This was, unfortunately, not nearly enough to get started as the proposed opening date of October 1941 loomed up. Also, America's involvement in the ongoing Second World War made each budget obsolete as we drew it up. Just in time, Joe Burstyn saved our lives by getting us to throw in the towel as we were on the verge of signing a long-term lease on the 1,434-seat Adelphi Theatre. Kazan and I set about returning the raised money and releasing the acquired plays. What was left was my personal financial debt to Kazan, who had sent me eating money out of his Hollywood lucre during the summer siege and batches of printed stationery which the two of us had used for the lengthiest coast-to-coast correspondence, full of high hopes, since the communications of Stanislavski and Nemirovich-Danchenko; or Strasberg and Clurman. For years afterward, Gadget and I used the fine stationery, crossing out the letterhead proclaiming our smashed dream: "The Dollar Top Theatre."

Since the end of the Group, it had become increasingly clear to me that eating could be a sometime thing in the theater unless you hit it big. Fortunately, I had developed my teaching abilities during the thirties, and by the end of that decade I began to establish my reputation as an acting coach. Having already taught courses in Bronxville at Sarah Lawrence College in 1936 and 1937, I now took a job in the New York City school run by Tamara Daykarhanova, a former Moscow Art Theatre actress. My meager earnings at her school were supplemented with private classes that, ten years later, would lead to my own theater workshop, still in existence today. At that time, I got five dollars a week for two, two-hour sessions weekly from each private pupil, and I put the bills carefully in a budget filing envelope I kept, with compartments marked rent, food, telephone, and so on. In 1942, I also did my first of many stints as a professor at the Yale School of Drama, under Dean Allardyce Nicoll. Robert Brustein, who attended my classes there in the fifties, was the dean when, after thirty-five years of giving sporadic semesters in between directorial assignments, I finally retired from the Drama School. By that time I had become, under Brustein, Chairman of the Acting and Directing departments.

One day, Ralph Holmes, an actor in one of my early private classes, asked if he might bring his wife to the next session. And that is how I had met the Dollar Top's chief benefactor, Libby Holman. She'd been co-starred in the musical revues *The Little Show* and *Three's a Crowd,* both times with Clifton Webb and Fred Allen. Her rich tones and impressive stage poise led John Mason Brown to dub her "the Flagstad of the Blues." Elspeth Holzman (the name she was born with in Cincinnati, Ohio) had married the tobacco heir, Smith Reynolds, of North Carolina. The next year, Libby was accused of shooting her husband dead during a weekend party. When it was discovered she was carrying Reynolds's child, the charge was mysteriously changed from first to second degree murder and finally dropped altogether. Much litigation followed the birth of Christopher, called Topper. Libby was ultimately awarded a sizable sum and Topper a huge trust fund.

Tragedy continued to stalk Libby's life forever after. At the outbreak of the Second World War, her boyfriend, Phillips Holmes (whom I had directed in the Chicago company of *Golden Boy*) joined the air force and asked his brother Ralph to take care of Libby. He did; he married her. Phillips was subsequently killed in a plane crash. By 1945, Ralph had committed suicide, as had Libby's wealthy sister in Cincinnati. Then Topper, aged seventeen, fell off California's Mount Whitney during a climb and was killed. The entire estate went to Libby. Her last appearance on the stage was in Denver, Colorado, in *Yerma* by Federico Garcia Lorca. Yerma, a woman whose husband refuses to give her a child, chokes him to death at the end of the play, crying "I have killed my son myself!" Libby's own end came in 1971 when she was found dead of carbon monoxide poisoning in the locked garage of "Treetops," her Connecticut estate, slumped over the steering wheel of her Rolls-Royce.

The first scene Libby brought to class for my inspection was a light comedy bit which she tossed off with ease, using her husband, Ralph, as her partner. When it was over I remarked that, although she performed well, the scene didn't really challenge her too much. After all, I maintained, an acting class should be used to stretch one's self, to work in difficult areas that would present interesting challenges. "For example," I suggested, "why don't you do a really dramatic scene, one that will tap a deeper part of you, maybe from a play about a wife killing her husband." The second the words crossed my lips, I realized what I had said. A low gasp emanated from some of the actors. Something inside me warned, "Don't panic. Keep talking." So I continued. "You might try the Jeanne Eagels part in *The Letter,* for instance, when the woman kills her lover, insisting he was trying to rape her, when actually it was because he had a Chinese mistress and . . ."

"All right, all right," said Libby, rescuing me quite affably, "I'll do it."

When she brought the scene in, I warned myself to be extremely careful how I chose my words of criticism. But, having worried so much about putting my foot in it again, I found myself saying things like, "Your shooting of the lover wasn't quite believable." I actually got up to show her how to hold the gun more convincingly.

Libby was not only gracious during my repeated gaffes, she even invited me to the first of what were to be many weekends at "Treetops." She understood why the Dollar Top Theatre died aborning and wondered if it were not possible to do something less elaborate. We spoke of the possibility of taking a small theater away from the center of commercial activity and working on a single play as a starter. There was not a great off-Broadway movement in 1942. The Living Theatre was more than a decade away. Once more I set about looking for a theater and making lists of plays and actors.

We decided to start with *Mexican Mural,* a script I had read when it was submitted to a Group Theatre contest for playwrights under twenty-five years of age. Tennessee Williams had won one hundred dollars for three one-act plays, but the top prize of five hundred dollars went to Ramon Naya for *Mexican Mural.* Settling on a tiny auditorium on the fiftieth floor of the Chanin Building on Forty-second Street, thanks to another assist from Libby, I cast the play, choosing for some of the twenty parts Monty Clift, Libby, Kevin McCarthy, and Mira Rostova, all four of whom became fast friends during this production.

Mira had been in my acting class at Daykarhanova's, having been brought to my attention by Aline MacMahon. Aline was on a committee to find employment for refugees from Hitler and showed me a scrapbook of clippings from German newspapers. "Read these reviews of this young actress," said Aline, "I just can't place her in some glove factory." After reading such quotes as "a young Duse" and "Duse-like," I interviewed Mira immediately. Her story was a history of the refugee movement. Her father, a Russian businessman, fled the Soviets with his family and settled in Germany where Mira grew up and learned her second language. With the advent of Hitler, she was forced to pursue her blossoming stage career in a ghetto theater. A lucky break came in an offer to appear in a Hungarian play in Vienna, and Mira grabbed the opportunity. With the Anschluss breathing down her neck, she soon took off for France, and then to England, where she mastered still another tongue. To get a passport to America, Mira was willing to stand up in an arranged marriage (cost: two hundred pounds). Rosovskaya, her own name, was soon changed for America, to Rostova.

I told Mira that if I could get Mme. Daykarhanova to give her free diction lessons, I'd take her on as a scholarship student in my acting class. Madame did and I did. We agreed she'd work first on some roles she knew in Germany. In that way she could concentrate on her American speech problems. In that season I witnessed from Mira some of the most luminous acting, both comic and serious, I had ever seen. At the end-of-the-year demonstration, Mira did the death scene from Margaret Kennedy's *The Constant Nymph* so movingly that everyone in the audience went limp. I was happy to ask her to play a fake witch doctor in *Mexican Mural,* which she turned into a hilarious gadfly.

Monty and Mira hit it off immediately and when, a few years later, he went off to the movies, she went along with him and coached him in all his film roles.

Mira Rostova in *Mexican Mural*: "A hilarious gadfly."

For the Naya play I once more conceived a poetic production that would have color, dance, music—all the elements that would create the festival life of Vera Cruz on Ash Wednesday. I went back to Herbert Andrews, who had designed *My Heart's in the Highlands,* for the décor and chose, with Ramon Naya, a couple of beautiful Mexican songs for Libby to sing.

*Mexican Mural* opened on April 25, 1942, for a few special performances. Broadway critics were not used to covering such off-Broadway productions in those days, even though mine was only two blocks off Broadway. My old friend Burns Mantle, who had clobbered me for *My Heart's in the Highlands,* said he wouldn't come "until I read what the other boys say." Brooks Atkinson came but tried to leave after the first act. He ran smack into me guarding the down elevator on the fiftieth floor and slunk back to his seat, a captive critic. In his review he gave Clift a rave and concluded with, "*Mexican Mural* deserves to have its few evenings of mortality in the fiftieth floor of a modern skyscraper in Gotham." Although the play got a generally poor reception and barely survived its few scheduled performances, I was relieved to see that my particular directorial approach, in regard to style, was noted. John Gassner, dramatic critic as well as scholarly editor of many highly useful technical books on the theater, and Professor of Playwrighting at the Yale School of Drama, wrote that "Robert Lewis directed the proceedings with a magnificent sense of color, a musician's feeling for rhythm and mood, and a theatrician's aptitude for

Libby Holman and Kevin McCarthy in *Mexican Mural*: "Deserves to have its few evenings of mortality."

emphasis." Gassner reminded me of my lack of expertise in revising scripts that needed help: "If he had worked as effectively on the revision of the script, *Mexican Mural* would have worked its spell more strongly on both critics and audiences, though neither (with the exception of Brooks Atkinson and Stark Young) can be exonerated for a certain obtuseness with respect to the genuine creativeness of this enterprise. There is still power in our theater, and sources of regeneration are at hand."

Long after, *The New York Times* magazine section published a feature that posed the following question to a number of celebrities: "What production that you have seen would you like to have revived?" Tennessee Williams voted for *Mexican Mural,* and when the newspaper called me, I dug up a fine photograph that Monty Clift had taken during one of the rehearsals and sent it along to accompany the citation.

It was, oddly enough, a letter from Tennessee that I received in June 1942, two months after the opening of *Mexican Mural,* that helped me make up my mind to leave the East for awhile. He had borrowed thirty dollars for bus fare in order to get out of New York, he said, and was now stranded in Macon, Georgia, without a cent. Having wanted me to direct his early short plays, he now promised to include in the deal some new one-acters he was writing if only I could get up some option money. With the wipe out of *Mexican Mural,* I just couldn't. No prospective backers I went to had yet heard of Williams, and an evening of one-act plays was too tough for me to sell. History shows that Tennessee made it back to New York, in the fall of 1942, with a couple of long plays.

I took stock of my own situation. From April 1939, and my life-giving success with *My Heart's in the Highlands,* to April 1942, I had attempted the following: an abortive production with the Theatre Guild; an unsuccessful fantasy with Julie Garfield; a commercial flop featuring my friend Kazan; a popular-priced theater, again with Kazan, that never got off the ground, and an art production in a tiny off-Broadway theater that lasted but a few performances. Although I'd learned a hell of a lot, the money I could earn teaching was not sufficient to pay back my debts incurred in the pursuit of the kind of experimentation I needed to develop my theatrical ideas. I decided to solve the problem of existence first. Gadget had been excited by the whole idea of filmmaking, and I could certainly get myself on my feet by acting in the movies for a short time and then come back to conquer the big city. I didn't dream that short time would last four years. Libby, my Lady Bountiful, came through one final time with the train fare, and on June 26, 1942, I struck out for the West Coast to join my other Group colleagues already out there. I made a vow I would not let California become my artistic graveyard.

CHAPTER 10

# Hollywood 1942-46

THE *HOLLYWOOD REPORTER*'S announcement of my arrival in movieland proclaimed that practically every former Group Theatre member was now working in town, among them Harold Clurman, Clifford Odets, Franchot Tone, Michael Gordon, Harry Morgan, J. Edward Bromberg, Art Smith, Roman Bohnen, John Garfield, Morris Carnovsky, and Lee J. Cobb. When the William Morris office got me a dialogue director's job at Twentieth Century-Fox, the *Los Angeles News* was quick to point out that with three "full-fledged college professors" (Monty Woolley and myself from Yale and Thomas Loring from the University of Nebraska) working on the lot the atmosphere was "thick with learning and erudition." My interest was in learning camera technique, and I was lucky to be assigned to John Brahm, a solid, German-trained film director who was working on a little number called *The Undying Monster*. Brahm didn't make many important films but he planned his shots—positions and movements of characters, camera angles, cuts, etc.—with great care, and I assiduously studied his handling of the actors and crew. His script was marked so meticulously that it made Bertolt Brecht's famous, detailed director's book for *Mother Courage* look sloppy by comparison.

Ultimately, Brahm also used me as an actor in one of his films. The part was a French collaborationist, and I made myself up to look like Laval, the foreign minister in the Vichy government. The picture was called *Tonight We Raid Calais* and had a cast including Annabella, Beulah Bondi, Blanche Yurka, Marcel Dalio, Howard da Silva, and Lee J. Cobb. Since the United States had entered World War II, Hollywood films concentrated on Nazis, Japanese, and collaborators. In the next picture, also about the German occupation of France, *Paris After Dark,* I was promoted to a Nazi colonel with the unlikely name of Pirosh. This one starred George Sanders who, with his clipped British delivery, naturally played the leader of the

**George Sanders and Robert Lewis in *Paris After Dark,* 20th Century-Fox film: "I say, old boy, what *are* piroshes, anyway?"**

French underground. Too bored to read his dull material in advance, Sanders hardly knew the plot of the picture. He'd doze happily in his dressing room until they called him for a "take." "What do I say, luv?" he'd ask the script girl. After checking his lines, he'd deliver them in that charming, vague way that couldn't possibly disturb whatever meaning the speech might have. This Sanders Method kept him working successfully in films, without a pause, for years.

At one point in our picture, the character I was playing had been shot and was dying. The Germans were holding fifty Frenchmen as hostages, threatening to kill them if my assassin didn't surrender. George said his line as given him by the script girl: "It's monstrous. Fifty Frenchmen's lives hanging on Pirosh's." "Fine. Print it," called the director. As he passed me, walking back to his dressing room, George asked, "I say, old boy, what *are* piroshes, anyway?"

"They're those gibbets, George," I answered, "on which they hang the enemies' bodies."

"Oh, yes, of course," said George as he left to resume his day-long nap.

Sanders was amusing to everyone but himself. Still bored at sixty-five, saying he'd lived long enough, George took a sufficient number of pills on April 25, 1972, for the long sleep.

Back in New York, the draft board had dubbed me deferred. Therefore when I got to Los Angeles, in order to contribute to the war effort, I worked at whatever defense jobs I could manage: busboy at the Hollywood Canteen and director of two shows featuring the workers at the Lockheed aircraft plant—*The Eve of St. Mark* by Maxwell Anderson, and *Jason* by Samson Raphaelson. To keep my franchise as a mover in experimental groups, I directed a production of Andre Obey's *Noah* at the Actor's Lab, a West Coast attempt to keep the spirit of the Group Theatre alive, presided over by the Group's own Roman Bohnen. Lee J. Cobb played Noah, Ruth Nelson his wife, and others in the cast were Larry Parks, Constance Dowling, Helen Craig, and Ruth Ford as the second lamb.

Meantime, an opportunity to get out the eye-pieces and resume my old profession of impersonating Orientals came along with MGM's announcement that they were about to embark on Pearl Buck's *Dragon Seed.* My agent managed to spring me from Fox and get me signed to an acting-directing contract at Metro. Playing the Japanese villain I was cast for in the picture held out no great challenge in characterization for me since I had an uncanny way of looking genuinely Oriental on the screen—even when I wasn't supposed to. In Fox's *Paris After Dark,* I had taken special precautions to be a believable German army colonel. To my Hitlerian moustache and thick eyeglasses I added a perfect imitation of Otto Preminger's "Cherman occent." Sitting at the preview of the picture in Westwood, I was appalled to hear the woman next to me turn to her friend as I made my first entrance on the screen and ask, "What's that Chinese man doing in that German uniform?"

It was natural for me, therefore, to be back at my Oriental stand at Metro. Now that I was officially a film director, too, I made tests of other applicants for parts and coached them in Oriental accents and behavior. Even Keye Luke, the well-known MGM actor who was a genuine Oriental, but specialized in sympathetic roles, asked me in the commissary for help in playing an Oriental villain.

One day when working in the makeup department, checking up on the women they were preparing to test, as to type, for the tiny part in *Dragon Seed* of the old Chinese grandmother who gets raped by a gang of Japanese soldiers, I recognized the face of a woman standing outside in the hall waiting her turn to be made up. My heart stopped as I realized it was the great Metropolitan Opera House star, Margarete Matzenauer, who had thrilled audiences on both sides of the Atlantic for years with her luscious contralto voice and superb musicianship. Her American debut, in 1911, was an unforgettable opening night at the Metropolitan: she sang Amneris in *Aida* with Caruso, Emmy Destinn, and Pasquale Amato in the cast. Arturo Toscanini conducted. Now, at sixty-four, she stood at the end of the line awaiting a makeup test for a bit in a movie. I dashed over to her, brought her to a seat, and babbled about the joy her recordings had given me through the years. She was at first startled at being recognized—then pleased. I tended her all through her test in a vain attempt to make it bearable for her, although all she was required to do was face front for the camera, then turn to the right, and left. I don't know whether it was a blessing or a hardship that she was ultimately turned down for the part. It went to some woman whose features accepted the makeup more believably.

The other faces in the film that were easy to Orientalize (outside of my own) belonged to Akim Tamiroff and Turhan Bey. The main stars—Walter Huston, Katharine Hepburn, Aline MacMahon, and Agnes Moorehead looked more like Abraham Lincoln, and family, with eyepieces. Of course, there were hundreds of real Orientals bused in daily from downtown Los Angeles, but they were the extras. To create genuine atmosphere, a complete Chinese village was built in a place called Calabasas, a two-hour drive from Hollywood that was to be our location for six months.

The first thing the cameraman, Sidney Wagner, did was look through his finder only to discover that the distant mountains blended into the sky and therefore had no definition. Jack Conway, the director (he died during the picture's shooting) sent back to Hollywood for help. Soon, dozens of workmen arrived with huge buckets, went up into the hills and insanely sloshed black paint in lines across the mountains to create furrows. Wagner looked through his finder again. "We might as well have stayed on the studio lot," he wailed. "Now it looks like a painted backdrop." Katharine Hepburn, sitting on the ground waiting, remarked, "Well, Bobby, at least I'm the only girl in America who's laid a five-million-dollar Chinese egg."

Actually, she played certain emotional scenes in the film with a great sense of truth. I was only sorry she found it inadvisable to retain, in the shooting of the film, the characterization she had experimented with in her screen test. I did that test with her, standing in for Turhan Bey, who had not yet arrived at the studio. It was both delightful and thrilling to witness a complete transformation, in terms of voice and movement, on Hepburn's part that resulted in a believable Chinese girl. A breakthrough, I thought; the star with the most recognizable physical characteristics in the world was submerging herself completely in a role. But, alas, the preservation of that recognition factor thought so necessary to the maintenance of stardom in America won out when the shooting began and she fell back on the old safe crutches of personality performing once more. In England, Laurence Olivier doesn't mind transforming himself physically, as well as psychologically, into a character; in fact it is a badge of his artistry.

Bobby and Turhan Bey on the set of *Dragon Seed,* with Katharine Hepburn: "The only girl in America who's laid a five-million-dollar Chinese egg."

Akim Tamiroff played a Chinese collaborator in *Dragon Seed,* and when we had a scene together (I was a Japanese general) we looked like an Oriental version of Tweedledum and Tweedledee. The director who followed Jack Conway had been a cutter, and while he knew something of film technique, he knew nothing about acting. Therefore, he relied on the safe bet of all such directors: "Go faster." I had traced one possible origin of this ploy when I was at Fox. Bryan (called Brynie) Foy, known as "the King of the 'B's" was a producer there. His pictures may not have been of high quality, but they were real fast, and they sold well. In addition to the rapid pace of the acting on which he insisted, the cuts from one shot to another were so close that often words would be spliced in half as the film switched to the next shot. You never had time to worry if what you saw was good or bad—it didn't stay there long enough for you to decide. I was determined to track down the genesis of this particular producer's success.

Brynie was the youngest son of the great vaudevillian, Eddie Foy, whose famous act was known as "Eddie Foy and the Seven Little Foys." Brynie was the littlest, and the worst, dancer of the lot. Old Eddie would stand in the wings and watch a tap routine the kids were executing and, as always, there was little Brynie out of step. One day the father called this kid into the dressing room. "Listen Brynie," he said, "you're the rottenest dancer in the lot. I'll tell you what to do. When you get out there, don't try to keep in step—you can't anyway—don't even bother to listen to the music. You just dance as fast as you can. Tap any old way, but go like a whirlwind." Well, of course, who do you think the audience looked at after that? Who do you think they laughed at? Who became the hit of the number? Little Brynie, of

Akim Tamiroff and Robert Lewis in *Dragon Seed*: "Wild horses were not going to disrupt us."

course. "I never forgot that," Brynie told me. "When you're stinking up the joint, be sure you go real fast. It's saved me ever since."

So now when the day came that Akim and I had our big confrontation scene to shoot, we met early in the makeup room to plan our strategy. We had rehearsed carefully together. Our acting intentions were clear. We related to each other. All pauses were justified by our thinking. We had the scene licked. We decided that wild horses would not disrupt us. Sure enough, after running through the first rehearsal for our director, he called out, "That was fine, boys, only it's much too slow. Let's shoot it, but go ten times faster."

Now Tamiroff and I went into our big act. I turned to him accusingly. "It's your fault, Akim, you don't pick up your cues fast enough."

"*I* don't pick up?" he screamed. "You could drive a truck through *your* pauses."

"All right, boys, calm down," the director said, trying to keep this from developing into a brawl. "Never mind who's fault it is. Just do the scene a little faster." After a few more dirty looks at each other, Akim and I went through the scene again for the camera exactly as we had done it previously—just the way we'd rehearsed it. "Cut," called the director when we had finished. "There, you see, it is much better that way. Print it."

After my stint as actor, test director, and dialogue coach on *Dragon Seed,* I began to wonder if, and when, I'd get a picture of my own to direct. Meantime, my sanity was being preserved in large part as the result of an introduction to Katherine Anne Porter, provided me by Libby Holman. There were many impressive literary names neatly painted on the office doors of the writers' building at MGM in the early forties, including William Faulkner, Aldous Huxley, and Katherine Anne Porter. However, very few of their words ever ended up in the stuff being shot on the sound stages. From Katherine Anne Porter I gleaned at least one explanation.

Libby had met Porter when they both served on a Roosevelt-for-President committee. Dorothy Parker, another member, struck by the resemblance of Miss Porter to a well-known beautiful society leader, had remarked, "She looks just like Mrs. Harrison Williams, if Mrs. Harrison Williams could read and write." Katherine Anne and I gradually latched on to each other. Trying to avoid the staggering boredom of our movie lives, we had dinner at each other's house or drove up along the Pacific ocean to a restaurant. Then we'd rush back to her place in Santa Monica, or mine in Westwood, to listen to our rapidly growing phonograph record collections. We both admired the pure soprano voice of Isobel Baillie in Purcell and Handel airs and vied with each other in amassing more and more of her recordings.

Katherine Anne was in Sidney Franklin's "unit" at MGM and she defined it this way: "He could just as well have put a monkey wrench, a cheese sandwich, a live frog, a ball of twine, a copy of *PM,* and a bottle of

**Katherine Anne Porter: "I can do almost anything except invent a way to have Queen Elizabeth show her gams."**

Florida Water in a paper bag and called *that* a unit." But Katherine Anne was pleased when she was assigned to do a treatment for a projected film about the first Elizabeth of England, to star Greer Garson. Enamored of the period, Miss Porter did all her homework, checking books and letters of the time. Finally she submitted her outline. Franklin called her in and told her it was fine but couldn't she find a place in the story where Queen Elizabeth might show her legs, as Greer Garson had such "lovely gams." "I can do almost anything," said Katherine Anne Porter, "except invent a way to have Queen Elizabeth show her gams." End of Porter script.

My switch from the Pandro S. Berman unit, which had produced *Dragon Seed,* to the Arthur Freed unit, was purely accidental. I was sitting one day with Vincente Minnelli, goofing off on the set of *The Ziegfeld Follies,* which he was directing for Freed. I had known Vincente on Broadway where he was a scene designer. Fred Astaire, in his perfectionist way, was going over his steps with Lucille Bremer for an atmospheric dance version of "The Limehouse Blues." Vincente, who had seen my Oriental doings in *Dragon Seed,* got the idea of including me in a prologue and epilogue to the number. I could use my leftover yellow makeup and eyepieces. "Go on down to wardrobe, Bobby, pick out something a rich Oriental would wear and come back. We'll try some things." And that, film buffs, is how I got to be in a ballet with Fred Astaire—and incidentally, into the Freed unit.

Watching Astaire work took me back to the time Laurette Taylor told me

Robert Lewis, Fred Astaire, and Lucille Bremer in *Ziegfeld Follies*: "Purely accidental."

how she prepared her roles. Although he was meticulous in his rehearsing of every step, every gesture, every look, the moment the cameras turned over for the shot, although nothing was altered, he *seemed* to be improvising. I had known actors who prepared their parts with the same care as Fred and delivered the result so faithfully that the audience could sit back, certain that the performance would go off well. But the feeling that they were looking in on a life being lived at that moment was absent. Then there were those who, in order to achieve spontaneity, stretched or contracted their timing, injected little sounds and pauses, or even changed the dialogue—a big price to pay for personal freedom. Fred Astaire, however, by drilling the "form" into his system so thoroughly in rehearsal was able, somehow, to dive into the performance, muscularly relaxed, secure in the knowledge that the pattern was in his bones. He met each moment as though it were a welcome stranger. At last I understood the true meaning of the phrase "the quality of the first time."

At lunch in the commissary one day, Irene Sharaff, the costume designer for Freed—she had also worked at the Civic Repertory Theatre when I was there—tried to coach me in the procedures by which I might get a film to direct at MGM. All these matters, she told me, were involved with social doings, and I must learn to mix more with top guys like Arthur Freed, who was, after all, the head of the most flourishing musical comedy unit at MGM and a "close friend of L.B." (Mayer, of course). Dubious though I was, I ran up a nice little Saturday night supper at my house in Westwood and invited some of the Freed unit. In addition to the boss himself, I asked his assistant Roger Edens, Minnelli, Judy Garland, and, of course, my mentor, Irene Sharaff. For topping I got up enough courage to call Charlie Chaplin, whom I had known since the thirties, when Clifford Odets introduced us. As the members of the Freed unit arrived, I caught Irene's eye when Freed, casing my little house, cracked, "Well, I guess I'm gonna have to give you a big picture to direct so you can keep up a fine place like this." Happy, protesting laughter from Irene and me. Then Chaplin walked in. Every smile froze like illustrative expressions on a Delsarte chart.

Why did so many Hollywood folk hate Chaplin? They couldn't seriously have believed he was a communist just because of some political remarks he made. Charlie, chameleonlike, simply took on the color of whatever radicals whose company he might have been in, just as he sounded like a capitalist when complaining to Sam Goldwyn about the unions. The movie worthies certainly couldn't object to his fooling around with young girls, since they were all fooling around with young girls. Not a citizen? Well, many of the Hollywood British contingent never took out citizenship papers and still retained respectability. It had to be that they couldn't stand his being a genius—and worse, a genius who wouldn't play their game. Charlie never "socialized" for business reasons, as I was doing that night. For one thing, he didn't need to. When the great in any field arrived on the West Coast and were asked whom they'd like to meet, they invariably said, "Chaplin." If he wished, he'd entertain them in his own home and didn't even bother to invite Hedda Hopper.

As my party's conversation fizzled out, I tried to ward off disaster with that famous beast-soother, music. "How about some records?" I suggested, trying to make it sound as if that could be real fun for this musical unit. Pressing my personal record catalogue into Judy Garland's hand, I begged, "Pick something. Anything." Judy flipped the pages of the catalogue casually to the *G*'s. Her eyes widened as she realized there were at least eighty-five Galli-Curcis and only one Garland. Modestly foregoing "The Trolley Song" as her request, Judy was desperately trying to choose between Galli-Curci's "O luce di quest' anima," from Gaetano Donizetti's *Linda di Chamounix* or her "Carceleras," from Ruperto Chapí's zarzuela, *Las Hijas del Zebedeo.* Charlie saved the day.

"Do you have Caruso singing that *Pagliacci* aria?" he asked. "I love that bitter laugh he gives after the high note."

"Do I ever?" I sang with relief. "Several versions."

This was that selfsame aria I had used in my rapturous pantomime act when I was a kid, and it was going to serve me again. Rushing to my cabinet, I grabbed the record as though it were blood for an emergency transfusion. I turned the volume up nice and high, and the famous golden voice filled every corner of the house. Charlie was in heaven, I was in hell,

Caruso as Canio: "*Pagliacci* was off and running again."

and the distinguished members of the Freed unit eyed each other with that unmistakable "How-can-we-get out of here" look. How can Caruso be a flop, I wondered? But at my Hollywood party he certainly was. I grabbed the record off the turntable the second the great Italian's sobbing died away. Quickly I reached for "The Trolley Song."

"God, that was beautiful," moaned Charlie. "Please—please play it again." Defiant glares from the Freed unit. Misty eyes from Chaplin. Although I knew I was going to my cinematic grave, *Pagliacci* was off and running again. At the downbeat of the encore, all the guests, except Chaplin, hit the buffet in the next room. At about the thirty-second bar, the entire musical unit, as though on cue, made a beeline for their cars, still chewing.

Instead of being drummed out of town, as I expected to be, I was stunned to get my obligatory return invitation for a party Freed was giving the next Saturday night, in honor of his wife's birthday. Thinking that a bit of ass-kissing mightn't be amiss after my fiasco, I called Roger Edens and told him I'd like to bring along a little present. I then learned my next big lesson, which is that in Hollywood there's no such thing as a *bit* of ass-kissing. "What does Mrs. Freed like?" I asked. "Gold," he answered, simply.

In those grandiose Hollywood days, you didn't just give a dinner party. You produced it. It had to have a "motif," and the theme of this one at Arthur Freed's was "Russia, our wartime ally." As I entered the house, two huge cossacks, complete with shiny boots and Russian blouses, greeted me. A yellow-braided, comrade maidservant in native dress took my coat. Although simple, peasant borscht and black bread would undoubtedly be served, it was clear to me at once that I was the only one there who didn't make five grand or more a week. I could sense that Freed was hard put to find a way to introduce me around. The only credit of mine he knew was my direction of *My Heart's in the Highlands.* Vincente Minnelli had told him I had had an "artistic success" with it, about as dirty a jab as you can get on the gold coast. Or on Broadway, for that matter. As Freed maneuvered me gingerly toward Tallulah Bankhead, I could see his face screwing up in an apologetic smile.

"Tallulah, this is Bobby Lewis. You know he directed that Saroyan play." Miracle of miracles, she had actually seen it.

"Darling, you're a poet," she growled, grabbing my arm. With this she backed me out of the room onto the terrace and pinned me to the stone wall.

> So are you to my thoughts as food to life,
> Or as sweet-season'd showers are to the ground,

she began in the well-known, husky voice and went on to the end of the sonnet without dropping a syllable. Though sufficiently convinced we

"Little did I know the power of poetry."

were both poetic, I was also cold, and I started back into the warm room, hungrily eyeing the canapés, the drinks, and the famous personages who were going to spin me to the top of the Hollywood heap. Little did I know the power of poetry, or of Tallulah. Fully revved up now, she laid a second sonnet on me and then a third and a fourth. Standing in the chill night air, frozen with admiration at how many of the poems she knew, I was also panicked with the realization that Shakespeare had written over one hundred and fifty of these little masterpieces. I screamed over her rendering of

> O thou, my lovely boy, who in thy power
> Dost hold time's fickle glass

that, if I wasn't to die of pneumonia, I had better have a glass with some liquor in it, fast. This suggestion brought her magically back to a more prosaic state of mind, and I darted indoors.

It was well known that Tallulah was having a long ride on one of her famous "wagons," this one having to do with her abstinence from alcohol until her beloved England would have won the war. I was present, later, in her Pound Ridge house, during the time when Bankhead swore she would never take a drink again until Adlai Stevenson became president—a long drought that would have been unless you understand what she meant by "on the wagon." She meant you weren't to make her a drink; but that didn't stop her from taking a good gulp from yours, his, hers, anyone's. It was also apparently OK for her to imbibe some witch's brew concocted of Coca-Cola and spirits of ammonia. For an additional high, she popped and sniffed some odd capsules that her sister Eugenia insisted were used to revive horses that slipped and fell on the winter ice. Tallulah always said of her sister, "She's the witty one, I'm the pretty one." (One night, during this Adlai Stevenson no-drink-for-Tallulah period, our heroine was, as usual, loudly defending the Democratic party, to which her Speaker of the House father and Senator uncle belonged, against the staunch Republicanism of her friend, theatrical agent Edie van Cleve. At one point, to support the logic of her position, Tallulah delivered Edie a huge kick in the ass. Sister Eugenia, next to me on the couch, stopped the passing butler. "Sylvester," she said, "will you please find out what it is that Miss Bankhead isn't drinking and bring me one of those.")

Cut back, as we say in the movies, to the Arthur Freed party. As I reentered the living room where everyone was having cocktails, I was surprised to hear Tallulah, following behind me, call out, "I want to propose a toast, darlings." Although the war was not quite over, it was clear that Tallulah was ready to acknowledge victory for the Allies. Her drink was brought, and she raised her glass high. "To Franklin Delano Roosevelt, commander in chief of the armed forces of the United States of America!" With that, she downed the drink and—whoosh—dashed her glass into the fireplace. Now when I say glass, you understand I'm not talking about those inexpensive tumblers you get out when you're having a big party. I'm talking about a gold-rimmed number that Mrs. Freed had had engraved at Tiffany's. Both Freeds stared into the hearth at their shattered treasure. Moving away, thanking God that the toast was over, the Freeds were halted by the actress's next booming order: "I'll have another." This, too, was brought. "Winston Churchill, bulldog of the British Empire!" Gulp—and whoosh—down went the second glass into the fireplace. The Freeds looked at each other in horror, mentally counting up the Heads of State on our side. Tallulah went through them all, concluding with Chiang Kai-shek. She didn't even skip her hated Stalin. The ceremony seemingly over, everyone started a hasty retreat from the mound of broken glass in the fireplace. "I'll have another," commanded Tallulah. I racked my brains trying to figure which Allied Head of State she'd overlooked. "Field Marshal Montgomery!" she cried. An agonized groan emerged from Freed as everyone realized she was preparing to go through every five-star general, as well as those with only four, three, two, or one star—and most likely to continue on to and through the privates. Somewhat less patriotic than Tallulah, our host tiptoed gracelessly away, leading the rest of the guests to the various tables set up in the dining room.

The meal that followed made Alice's mad tea party seem like a quiet dinner at Emily Post's. Finding herself alone, a condition she couldn't endure for ten seconds, Tallulah came loping into the dining room and plopped down at the extra bridge table in the corner, to which I had been relegated. She wouldn't eat anything. Tallulah was religious about not mixing food and liquor, not even stooping to contaminate her drink with a bit of nourishing lemon peel. As a matter of sad fact, when she was rushed to the hospital for what turned out to be her final illness, I was told that she hadn't eaten any food for five days.

The Slavic dinner having begun with some very special caviar, the serfs arrived with the hot borscht and piroshki. As a blonde-plaited maid came over to our table with a couple of steaming plates of the soup, Tallulah, in a sudden rush of comradely affection, enveloped the poor girl in a Russian bearhug. Borscht and piroshki went flying over heads and into laps. At the other end of the room, where he had hoped he was safely settled, Mr. Freed, rising ever so slightly, stared at our battlefield with a kasha-under-the-nose expression but didn't dare approach the formidable enemy.

The second skirmish began with the arrival of the shashlik. These were held high on huge flaming swords by the cossack waiters. As Tallulah, smiling a maniacal challenge at the flames, rose and advanced, the terrified servants danced around the tables trying to avoid her. By now the more prudent guests were scurrying out of their seats and fleeing the inevitable scorched earth of the dining area back to the living room.

As soon as the retreat had been accomplished, Tallulah, flushed with victory, sailed in and took up her post at the fireplace, the scene of her earlier triumph. As she glowered contemputuously at the entire cowardly assemblage, Arthur Freed did what any normal host would do on finding he had a loaded tigress in his living room. He turned to Judy Garland and said, "Won't you sing something?" In a split second, Roger Edens, not head of the music department of the Freed unit for nothing, was banging out an introduction at the piano. Judy, terrified, hung onto the curve of the piano, glazed eyes down. Her famous tremolo rapidly growing to a wobble, she sang, "The last time I saw Paris, her heart was young and . . ." She never got to "gay" for, from the fireplace, looking under and up from her tremulous eyelashes, Tallulah, unwilling to relinquish her generalship for more than a couple of bars, slowly growled, in her lowest contrabass, "I—hate—young—people." Ominous silence followed. The only movement in the room was the smoke pouring from the patrician Bankhead nostrils. How would our brave host manage the perilous generation gap between the two stars? He did the only thing possible—unless you are crazy enough to suppose that with the help of fifteen or twenty of the strongest male guests, plus cossacks, he could simply have tossed Tallulah out. Wearing the most pathetic, pleading expression since the little match girl, Freed gently placed a forefinger to his trembling lips, which he pursed silently, into a "shh" position. To this mildest of reprimands, Tallulah reacted as though a volley of cannon shot had been fired at her. She swooped down on Freed, grabbed that offender by his collar, and pulling his face ignominiously up against hers, barked, "How dare you shush me, you—you—*songwriter*!" A triumph of the art of acting made this noble profession sound as if it were the lowest perversion. Eyeballs rolling back, Judy, our shaking chanteuse, slowly started sinking to the rug. The lightning manner in which Vincente Minnelli gathered up the stricken singer and helped her to a couch made it clear he'd be, as indeed he was, the next man in Judy's life.

Now all hell broke loose. Some joined the resuscitation of Judy. Others expressed hushed disapproval of the hurricane called Tallulah. Still, nobody dared come near her physically. Nobody, that is, except one white-haired gentleman who approached her and said, quietly, "Miss Bankhead, I would like to hear the song."

"Who the hell are you?" was Tallulah's witty rejoinder.

"My name is Jerome Kern. I wrote it."

The virago dissolved at once. Tears streaming down her face, Tallulah flung her limp body on poor Mr. Kern. "I know every song you ever wrote," she sobbed and promptly began with "Who—o—o stole my heart away, Who—o—o . . ." Without missing a note, and just as she had done with me earlier in the evening, she backed Kern out of the room, this time down the hall and into a study, closing the door behind them. Seizing on this lull in the battle, the guests all flew out of the house in a magical Disney-like exit. As I passed the room where Bankhead was treating Kern to what was surely going to be an all-night, captive musical feast, I could hear the basso profondo version of "Why do I love you?" just getting under way.

My first glamorous night out in Hollywood was over. A week later, Armistice Day, on a Manhattan street, Jerome Kern collapsed and, soon after, died.

All my feeble attempts at playing the game didn't get me an offer to direct a decent picture at MGM. Odd jobs, such as supervising the dubbing into English of a Mexican film, *Maria Candelaria,* with Dolores del Rio, or directing the screen tests of Cyd Charisse, Linda Christian, and others were hardly enough to relieve the boredom of living in Hollywood in those days. It has been repeated many times, but I believe Lulla Adler was the first to describe the Hollywood of that time as the place where no matter how hot it got in the daytime there was no place to go at night. I tried to improve each shining hour with a variety of activities.

Alla Nazimova in *Hedda Gabler*: "One of those Isben plays."

At MGM I'd check in every morning and go immediately over to the little office the studio heads reserved for Buster Keaton. He had a workbench at which he devised and constructed all sorts of unusual props to be used in various pictures. His imaginative inventions and the silent, craftsmanlike concentration he employed as he worked were a never-ending treat for me. The office was a lifetime reward for the glorious pictures and barrels of money he had made for the studio. But no one would dream of giving him a decent part to act or, God forbid, a film to direct.

One happy break was the presence in Hollywood of Alla Nazimova, whom I hadn't seen since the Civic Rep days. I visited the actress often in the single room bequeathed to her in the Garden of Allah, a hotel on Sunset Boulevard that had been her own home when she was a silent film star. Going with her to such concerts, operas, or dance recitals as there were, then, in Hollywood was a joy. Her outlook was consistently youthful, with no nostalgic lingering on her past. She had great wit and told me stories of theater encounters with everyone from Stanislavski to Lee Shubert, who, when she was starring under his management in *Hedda Gabler, Ghosts,* and *The Doll's House,* asked her one day, "Why do you always want to do those *Isben* plays?"

I got to know Tyrone Power when his wife, Annabella, took me back to their house after we'd completed a day's shooting at Fox. Thereafter, my Sunday mornings were taken care of playing croquet. Since Tyrone was the best player, and I was the worst, we were teamed together for balance opposite Cesar (Butch) Romero and Annie, Annabella's daughter by a previous marriage. On Tuesday nights, Annabella and Edie Goetz, Louis B. Mayer's daughter, went off to dance with the soldiers at the Canteen. Tyrone always arranged to have that evening at home with some friends. After dinner, we'd sit on the living room floor and look at a Johnny Mack Brown movie, the object of the game being to guess, and say aloud, the corny lines just *before* the actors in the film did. Sammy (Laird) Cregar was so good at this, rattling the exact dialogue along seconds ahead of the actors, that I often suspected him of having run the film in the afternoon to memorize the script.

Having been invited to dinner at the Powers' one Christmas Eve, I brought along my former acting student, Constance Dowling. Connie and I were driving along Sunset Boulevard on the way to the dinner party in a heavy rain storm, a dangerous time for Hollywood motorists. The fellow in the car in front of me suddenly stopped short. I plowed into his rear end, and Connie's face and mine smashed through the windshield. The guy in back of me then rammed into us, whipping our gashed heads backward. Blood flowing freely down our faces, we staggered out of the wreck and stood on the side of the road in the downpour until a police car came along and got us to some medical attention, not an easy task on Christmas Eve.

When we finally were bandaged up, I called Tyrone to say we couldn't make dinner. "I know," he said, "I passed you on Sunset Boulevard on my way home and saw what happened." Now before you pounce on Ty, remember that big stars were always advised not to get involved in messy situations with police cars and all that. It did make me meditate, though, on the constraints of friendship in the City of Angels.

Charles Laughton had seen my production of *Noah* at the Actors' Lab and professed an interest in doing some stage work there. He was considered very special in the Group Theatre days. Strasberg was always pointing out Laughton's ingenious use of an animal characterization in *Henry the Eighth* when, as the aging monarch, he held his food in ferretlike paws and nibbled away, eyes darting from side to side. In the Hollywood studios, of course, Laughton's acting techniques were looked upon with suspicion, especially since he flaunted them with some abandon. He'd bring framed oil paintings from his great private collection and place them around his dressing room so he could draw on them for ideas of characterization. He was inclined, in describing his approach to a certain part, to express himself floridly: "Beethoven, not Tchaikovsky. The Seventh, of course—allegretto movement." In the commissary one day, a producer, himself heavy with affectation but without the towering talent that justified Laughton's behavior, was mocking the actor. After listing Charles's various pretentions, the producer concluded, "Ah, but he does have God's telephone number!"

We rehearsed Gorki's *Lower Depths* at the Actors' Lab, with Laughton reading a superb Luka, the old philosophical optimist. As director, I surrounded Charles with the best actors I could round up. No public performances were ever scheduled due to the wildly conflicting obligations of the cast. However, it was fascinating to work with such an inventive actor as Laughton, just as it was riveting to listen to him at his Pacific Palisades home illustrating a pet theory of his regarding the soliloquies in Shakespeare. He felt the Bard meant them all addressed to the audience, rather than to be done in an introspective way. To hear him use this technique on "To be or not to be" was a revelation.

Sunday afternoons on Maberry Road, near Laughton's house in Pacific Palisades, was the weekly high point of my life in Hollywood, in the early forties. If you were lucky enough to be asked, you would find yourself in the salon of one of the supreme hostesses in the world—Salka Viertel. Her husband, Berthold, was a well-known German poet, dramatist, and stage director whom I knew during the Group Theatre years. One of her sons, Peter, is the writer now married to Deborah Kerr and who lives in Switzerland, where Salka died in 1978. Salka, herself, had been an actress with Reinhardt earlier on. Now, in the forties, she was Garbo's friend, confidante, business adviser, and collaborator in the writing of many of the

Swedish star's films. On a typical Sunday at Salka's I got to rub shoulders with the likes of Thomas Mann, Heinrich Mann, Arnold Schoenberg, Lion Feuchtwanger, Bertolt Brecht, Hanns Eisler, Donald Ogden Stewart, and Charlie Chaplin—to drop but a few names.

Salka was Polish-born, but her wit and her food were strictly Viennese, and the talk at her salon was always heady. And where else could you witness a birthday surprise for Hanns Eisler that consisted of a four-part canon composed on a sheet of music paper for the occasion by Arnold Schoenberg, which, when played upside down, came out the same as right side up? The parade of refugees from Hitler, in every phase of artistic life, that moved through Salka Viertel's house was enough to constitute a Florentine Renaissance in Hollywood, if only Hollywood had known who they were. As it was, they gradually drifted back home in the years following the war.

Meanwhile, back at the studio, I was unsuccessfully trying to get my agent, Nat C. Goldstone (if you say it fast it comes out Nazi Goldstone), to get me out of my acting-directing contract since, one, I was not getting a picture to direct, two, I became fed up with acting uninteresting parts, and three, I had amassed enough phonograph records of dead singers to last me the rest of my life. I mentioned this last point to Mr. Mayer in one of my conferences, begging him to set me free. "You can't confine the human spirit," I cried. "I'm just going to walk out of the studio and go back to New York. But I'll always think of you when I play my records." I meant I had gotten enough money from him to afford my collection. He took my meaning to be that every time I listened to music I'd think of him. His eyes filled with tears. "I'll never let you go," he said. "You're too intelligent." I made a beeline for the door, which turned out to be a closet. He led me gently to the correct exit, purring, "You'd better learn the right door. You'll be using it a lot now." When nothing happened for a long time, I tried to get Mr. Mayer on the phone. No luck. He was out. He just left. He'd be in soon. After diligently making three calls a day, at different times, for one solid month, I was finally rewarded. They cast me in the role of a German officer, supporting Lassie, one of the big MGM stars, in *Son of Lassie.*

When I say Lassie was the star, I mean that on the way to our location in Patricia Bay, British Columbia, Canada, Lassie got the one bedroom on the train while Peter Lawford, Lassie's co-star, and I, a mere featured player, were relegated to lower and upper berths, in that order. When the script required the three of us to play a scene in the icy waters of Patricia Bay, the first one to be pulled out at the end of the shot was Lassie, who was immediately wrapped in towels and placed in front of an electric heater. Peter and I, left to fend for our shivering selves, downed several fingers of Scotch that a charitable electrician gave us in order to ward off pneumonia.

But, at least, I had an opportunity to study the remarkable acting technique of Lassie. He was the complete Stanislavskiite. Requiring an emotional memory exercise to get to a fever pitch high enough to make the

**Lassie and Bobby in *Son of Lassie,* an M.G.M. film: "The complete Stanislavskiite."**

dog bare his teeth and snarl at the enemy (me), Rudd Weatherwax, Lassie's personal trainer and Method coach, had only to "rev up" a motorcycle.

Suddenly, as if in answer to my prayers, I was sprung from my bondage. There was some sort of workmen's strike at Metro, and a number of employees were fired. By a mistake I did not stop to investigate, my name got mixed in with theirs. I didn't say a word to anyone, but immediately put my house up for sale. It was disposed of in one day by a suave real estate agent, Rod la Rocque, former film star of the twenties. I then rushed over to Chaplin's studio where he was shooting *Monsieur Verdoux.* Charlie had already offered me the choice of a couple of parts in the picture, but MGM had refused to loan me out, even though they could have made money on the deal. They simply wouldn't do anything for Chaplin. When I told Charlie I was free for about ten days while my house deal was in escrow, he immediately assigned me the role of a pharmacist whose scenes he was about to shoot.

I naturally didn't say goodbye to Mr. Mayer. The next time I saw him was more than a year later when his daughter, Edie, who was a good friend of Alan Lerner's, brought her father backstage after the premiere of *Brigadoon* in New Haven. "How wonderful you have a successful show, Bobby," said Mr. Mayer. "Now I can give you a good picture to direct." He didn't even know I was no longer employed at MGM.

# CHAPTER 11

# Chaplin 1946

IT WAS EASY to define the position held by Charlie Chaplin in the making of *Monsieur Verdoux.* He was everything—writer, star, director, producer, and casting director, as well as supervisor of all other departments: costumes, scenery, makeup, lighting, shooting schedules, camera setups, and the musical score. He also crawled around the set with a knife, scraping up bits of old chewing gum stuck to the floor. For good measure, he'd entertain the troops between shots with hilarious imitations, such as William Gillette's inanimate underplaying in *Sherlock Holmes,* a Kabuki actor pounding his feet into the floor and crossing his eyes in pain, or Maurice Schwartz, the Yiddish actor, intoning a speech while twirling an imaginary beard that went clear to the floor.

My favorite was an imitation of a gigantic advertising billboard that was in Times Square at the time, depicting the enormous round face of a man blowing cigarette smoke rings. Charlie would reproduce the rumbling windup sound of the complicated cacaphonous machinery behind the sign. Then, face reddened and eyes popping, he'd open his mouth to emit a tiny, ineffectual puff of smoke. It was a one minute condensation of *Modern Times.*

One day, having eaten his lunch of a single tomato, and while waiting for the others to return to work—he could never understand why the crew needed a whole hour for lunch when he only took a couple of minutes—Charlie told me a story that, in part, explained his need to control the entire production of a film. His grandfather was a shoemaker, and Charlie's grandmother had a tendency to dally with blokes other than her husband. Charlie would notice how, when marital depression overcame him, the old man would sit down to his cobbler's bench, pick up a sharp knife, and start to cut leather. He wouldn't stop until he made a whole shoe. As he surveyed his beautiful creation, a satisfied, peaceful look would come over his face.

No one could take away from him the joy he experienced from his creative act. Charlie felt that, as an artist, this responsibility for the whole was an indispensable source of strength for him. He had already illustrated in *Modern Times* how the impersonality of the endless conveyor belt system created nervous wrecks. There could be no splitting up of work operations for Charlie. He had to make the whole shoe.

An example of the hopelessness of artistic collaboration with Charlie occurred one night in the late thirties at Clifford Odets's house. Hanns Eisler was there, and Charlie remarked how wonderfully ironic it would be if the German composer would contribute the music for *The Great Dictator,* which Chaplin was preparing, the leading character of which, Adolph Hitler, was responsible for Eisler's exile from his homeland. Hanns bowed and said it would be an honor to work with such a film master.

Charlie moved to the piano. "For instance, here's a tune I've been working on," he said, and with one finger he picked out a simple, pleasant melody. "What would you do with that?" Rushing to the piano stool, Eisler went to work. "We might arrange something like this," said Hanns. He then built the tune into a charming little piece with marvelously original harmonies.

"That's fine, Hanns," said Charlie, reclaiming the piano seat, "but what I meant was more in this vein." He then repeated his original few simple bars, exactly as he had played them the first time.

"Ah, I see what you mean," said Hanns with all the ingratiation he could summon. "Let me give you another approach." This time he improvised a completely unadorned, but still enchanting, version of the tune.

"That's beautiful," Charlie assured Hanns, "but actually what I need is something like this." Again he picked out his same original notes. It was clear that even Bach, Beethoven, or Mozart couldn't shake Charlie from what he heard in his head. The credits of *The Great Dictator* ultimately listed Meredith Willson as "musical director." Brahms also helped with his fifth Hungarian Dance in the famous shaving scene.

Charlie was equally impervious to criticism. After *The Great Dictator* opened, Boris Aronson asked him (once again at Odets's house) why the Jews in the film had to be so all-fired good and holy. Charlie, turning to talk to Clifford, made no reply. Why, Boris persisted, couldn't Chaplin have made them good *and* bad, holy *and* unholy and still show the evil of Hitler's persecution? Charlie went on with what he was saying, pretending not to hear Boris. Boris moved closer and repeated the question. Charlie continued on his subject. He obviously had no intention of ever hearing, much less answering, the potent question.

Charlie's healthy ego somehow seemed acceptable not only on the grounds that he was a creative genius, but because it expressed itself so naturally. In describing a certain effect he arrived at, he was apt to remark, "That's rather Chaplinesque, don't you think?" He was also secure enough to treat all persons without a trace of discrimination. If, on his way out of the studio, the doorman complimented him on a scene he'd just shot, Charlie would stop and carefully explain what he had been working for, going into the particular technical aspects of the setup, lighting, conception of character, and so on, with the same fervor he'd use with some fellow artist.

All members of the cast received equal respect and attention from Chaplin, the director. In *Monsieur Verdoux* there was a scene with an infant-in-arms so young that, at short intervals, a different baby had to be substituted as the previous one would tire. After one take that he didn't like, Charlie came out from behind the camera, stalked up to the startled infant and scolded, "You're anticipating again!"

Chaplin shot all screen tests himself and was as scrupulous making them as he was with the film itself. I was with him throughout the entire day's shooting of Edna Purviance's test for *Monsieur Verdoux*. He hadn't seen her for a couple of decades, but she had been his leading lady, as well as his sweetheart for a while, in the silent film era. Chaplin had kept her on his weekly payroll even after she stopped making films. When he subsequently shut his Hollywood studio and gave all his employees their severance pay, Charlie still continued Purviance's weekly salary until her death.

His courtesy in handling her throughout the test was exemplary. She arrived at his combination office and dressing room in the morning, looking ideal for the part she was to test for, Mme Grosnay, one of the rich ladies Verdoux does in to get needed money to support his own little family during the depression. Outside of this Bluebeard-like activity, Verdoux was a typical bourgeois husband, seen at first trimming his rose bushes, being careful not to squash a caterpillar near an incinerator where one of his victims was going up in smoke.

Miss Purviance was still an extremely handsome woman, and she was faultlessly turned out from head to foot. Removing her gloves, she picked up her test scene, and the two old friends started to read through their parts. She did very well, talking simply and intelligently and, in fact, she hardly needed to look at her script, having memorized the lines quite thoroughly.

Charlie then explained that, to keep the exchange from being too static, she would have to be serving tea during the dialogue. He set up an improvised tea service for her to work with. Then the trouble began. Miss Purviance would say a few lines, stop talking to pour some tea in a cup, say a few more lines, stop talking again to add a couple of lumps of sugar, and so on. She would never talk while performing the business of serving the tea and seemed unable to work with the props while she was delivering the lines. Charlie pointed out that this procedure might hold the scene up a bit. Miss Purviance tried again but couldn't manage her two tasks simultaneously. In the silent movies she had been used to illustrating points with movement and talking became an intrusion that was clearly upsetting her.

"What do you want me to do, Charlie," she pleaded at one point, "act or talk?"

Charlie was a monument of patience, continually encouraging her and going through the scene again and again. Finally, he said she'd probably feel better on the set in front of the camera and suggested she go to wardrobe and get into her costume.

On the test stage things were no better. Miss Purviance was lovely to look at, spoke well but couldn't seem to coordinate the movement with the dialogue. Charlie never betrayed a single sign of displeasure as they went through countless takes. Later, he invited her back to his office for a light snack, thanked her, and bid her a cordial goodbye. The moment the door was closed he turned to me and said, "Wasn't that agonizing? I knew early this morning that she'd never make it." When he had to notify her of her rejection for the role, Charlie told Miss Purviance she had been fine, lacking only a certain "Europeanness" that was needed.

A different side of Chaplin, the director, was revealed when he came to shoot a certain scene with Marilyn Nash. She played the young prostitute Verdoux takes to his apartment in order to test a poison on her that is supposed to kill without leaving any evidence. When she tells him of her husband having died from a wound suffered in the Spanish Civil War, Verdoux, moved by her tears, decides to spare her. Chaplin knew the limitations of Miss Nash's acting experience. He had chosen her, as he had some other ingenues in previous pictures, for the proper quality he needed, rather than for her performing experience. Chaplin knew there were directorial tricks that could be used in films to get emotional results. This practice is useless in the theater where the actor has to be able to recreate that feeling himself eight times a week.

The day before he was to shoot Miss Nash's crying scene, Charlie began his strategy. He expressed such dissatisfaction with everything she did during the dialogue leading into her crying close-up, that Marilyn was completely shaken by the end of the day's shooting. As they were wrapping up, Charlie made it pretty clear, with remarks she could easily overhear, that if things didn't go better the next day, he'd have to reconsider his choice for the part.

The next morning, Miss Nash arrived on the set, still red eyed from what had obviously been a sleepless night of many tears. Her emotional state wasn't helped much when, as she sat down in the set to rehearse the scene, she observed, standing quite innocently near the camera, a beautiful young girl of her same type who had obviously slept very well. That did it. Tears filled Marilyn's eyes. Seeing that she was close to the breaking point, Charlie approached the camera and ordered her to start the dialogue. Falteringly, she pronounced her first words about her dead husband: "That's why I loved him. He needed me."

"Oh, come on," said Charlie, annoyed. "This will never do. Begin again, and this time try to get it right." Marilyn broke down and started to cry. "Go on talk, just talk, never mind anything, keep talking," Charlie yelled, surreptitiously signalling the cameraman to "roll 'em." Egged on now by Chaplin/Svengali, Marilyn sobbed through the entire scene.

"Cut. Print it," called Charlie. The decoy girl disappeared, Chaplin moved on, businesslike, to the next setup, and Marilyn Nash sat there, stunned and bewildered at having contributed a most moving moment to the art of the cinema.

My character in *Monsieur Verdoux,* Maurice Bottello, was a pharmacist to whom Charlie comes for the perfect poison that he wants to try out on Marilyn Nash. I found Chaplin, as a director, to be an actor's dream. In my short film career I had been afflicted with all the usual types of directors, plain and fancy. The latter talk too much. Before you get going, they fill your head with so much background of the character, behavior of the character, and feelings of the character that by the time you add a possible idea or two of your own you have built up quite a mishmash. Others instruct you too little. After you've finished rehearsing a scene, they stare at you for a long time with a look that could only come from acute stomach distress. Finally they come up with "Try it again, Bobby."

But what Charlie, a superb actor himself, said was just enough and immediately useful. He gave me one direction: "He's the kind of bore who doesn't talk. He lectures." That was all I needed. I dwelt on and enjoyed the precise enunciation of the Latin medical terms in my dialogue. I rounded up a conservative dark suit and wore scholarly eyeglasses. In other words, I could start building a character, inside and out, from the one apt image Charlie gave me.

In April of 1947, one month after the opening of *Brigadoon,* which I directed when I returned from Hollywood, *Monsieur Verdoux* had its New York première. I went with my sister. The response of the movie audience, and the party afterward at "21," made a sickening evening for us both. Chaplin's awareness of his atrocious publicity resulting from a paternity case he was involved in, as well as from his much misunderstood political statements, prepared him somewhat for the frosty and, at times, frightening reception of some organized, hostile members of the audience. Worried about the possibility of demonstrations, Charlie had flanked himself with his wife, Oona, on one side, and Mary Pickford, America's old-time sweetheart, on the other, when he entered the theater.

As the film unfolded, insane booing greeted such lines as, "Millions are starving and unemployed. It is not easy for a man of my age." Agonized groans greeted Verdoux's reply to his little child who asks him what sort of a man Santa Claus is: "Very kind—to the rich." But the angriest response was to the scene in the death house where a priest visits the doomed Verdoux in his cell just before his execution. "Have you no remorse for your sins?" the priest asks Verdoux, who comes back with, "What would

**Charlie Chaplin and Robert Lewis in *Monsieur Verdoux*: "He lectures."**

you be doing without sin?" The demonstrators weren't too thrilled with Charlie's reply to the priest's "May the Lord have mercy on your soul" either. "Why not?" said Verdoux, "After all it belongs to Him."

A particularly beautiful moment followed this scene as Verdoux is handed his last drink. Being a model breadwinner and husband, a teetotaler in fact, he refuses at first. Then he has a sudden change of mind. "Just a minute," he says. "I've never tasted rum." After taking a sip of the liquor, a supremely telling look comes over Charlie's face, as if to say "Maybe I missed something. Maybe I was overly virtuous." The righteous members of the Legion of Decency in the audience probably missed the point.

After the premiere, at the party upstairs at "21," Charlie, surrounded by ill-wishers, downed a couple of drinks at once, which was a rare thing for him. Only a few of his friends—Donald Ogden Stewart for one—complimented him on the film. Stewart, in addition to being a well-known playwright, was the president of the Hollywood anti-Nazi League. The other celebrities there didn't even mention the picture. They simply took over the party. After supper, entertainers got up, one after the other, and did their numbers. While Ethel Merman sang, I watched Louella Parsons, dressed in black, sitting in a corner, her disapproving eyes glued on Chaplin. She looked like some predator waiting for him to do or say something that might be used against him in her column.

Finally, in a desperate attempt to recapture his own party, Charlie leapt up to perform himself. It couldn't have been easy to be funny under the circumstances, but he launched determinedly into his hilarious bullfight act where he plays both the matador and the bull. It was an exquisite pantomime, executed brilliantly, but apparently it was not enough to get much response from that crowd. Charlie had once told me of a terrifying, recurrent nightmare from which he suffered all his life. He'd be performing a comedy act in front of a large audience, and no one would be laughing. He'd always leap awake in a cold sweat. Now his nightmare had become a reality.

Oona had left the party early. Don Stewart came over to me and suggested we get Charlie away from there. I agreed, and within minutes we stepped into the waiting limousine and started back to the hotel where the Chaplins were staying. It was easy to see that Charlie, although a bit tight, was genuinely shaken, not only by the awful party, but by the antagonism of the movie audience to what he felt was a truthful, as well as entertaining, expression of the times. Don and I helped Charlie undress. In his shorts, sitting on the side of his bed, the twentieth century's mighty performing artist sniffled like a little boy. "They couldn't take it, could they?" he kept repeating, "I kicked them in the balls, didn't I? I hit them where it hurt."

CHAPTER 12

# Brigadoon 1947

IF *MY HEART'S in the Highlands* was my first artistic success as a director, *Brigadoon* was the first commercial hit. Of all my productions, it has been revived the most. I never wanted to direct any of the revivals because, once a show was conceived and presented, I felt little desire to repeat the process years later. It seemed like going back, or worse, standing still. Exceptions to this rule were English companies of New York productions. They came soon after the original ones, and recreating them for the English audience constituted a new experience. I had this pleasure with *Teahouse of the August Moon,* as well as with *Brigadoon.* I also redid the opera *Regina* four years after its premiere, but that was because it was presented in the wrong place the first time (on Broadway), and I wanted to do it in its rightful home (the opera house). And finally, twenty-three years after I directed *The Sea Gull* at the end of the first year of the Actors Studio, I did it again at the Center Stage, in Baltimore. It had only been shown for one performance the first time, just for Studio members.

Because *Brigadoon* was a big success, some critics, and I suppose the public as well, assumed that my direction must have been on a higher level than it was for shows that didn't make it. Yet, artistically speaking, there was more worthy creative work in *My Heart's in the Highlands,* which had a limited acceptance, than in any of my commercial successes. When you have a hit, the theater world assumes you're a genius. When you have a failure, the assumption is that somehow you've turned into a bum. This inability to evaluate intrinsic worth, wherever it occurs, plagues the other arts, too, I'm sure. But nowhere is it as virulent as in the theater.

While critics may insist that my directorial results were more successful in one case than in the other, you must believe me when I tell you that, in each case, I employed the same professional approach and exerted my same talents to the full. I got up each morning, studied my script, prepared my staging, went to rehearsal on time, devoted myself all day to the actors, designers, musicians, lighting designers, whatever, and gave of my best creative juices right through the opening night. Some plays and productions obviously enjoy easy acceptance. Some don't. Therefore, it seems idiotic to assume that, if a show is a success, the playwright, director, designers, and actors are great talents at the top of their form, and that, if a production is a flop, all these same people are cretins who should be soundly whipped and tossed onto the garbage heap.

Where was I? Oh, yes, *Brigadoon.*

Alan Jay Lerner had concocted a whimsical tale of a confused young American called Tommy who, finding himself unable to settle on marriage with his fiancée because "everything seems wrong," takes a trip to the Scottish Highlands in search of some answers. There he witnesses a completely populated two-hundred-year-old village coming alive (it does, this one day, every hundred years). Naturally Tommy falls in love with a village maiden named Fiona and, in the end, follows her back into the village as it vanishes for another hundred years, thus solving his problems for awhile at least.

Alan had based his libretto on a nineteenth-century German tale, by Friedrich Wilhelm Gerstäcker, called *Germelshausen.* No one seemed to notice this—no one, that is, but George Jean Nathan. Cheryl Crawford, my friend from the Group Theatre days, was the producer, and by the time she chose me as director, Agnes de Mille had been set for the choreography and Oliver Smith for the scenery.

Agnes and I were old colleagues since I had loused up the Queen Elizabeth number in her dance recital a decade earlier. The first thing I did after reading the script of *Brigadoon* was to sit down in a quiet bar with Agnes, order a couple of martinis—it turned out to be a couple for each of us—and face up to the problem of how to neutralize the operettalike goo in the story. The question we asked ourselves was, "How do we set about killing Jeannette MacDonald?" Oliver Smith told me that he stopped reading the script when he came to the reply of the Scottish dominie to the American Tommy's question, "So you're all perfectly happy living here in this little town?" The old man answers: "Of course, lad. After all, sunshine can peep through a small hole." Said Oliver, "If I had read any further I'd never have been able to design the show."

By the time Agnes and I finished our analysis of the original script, the inherent whimsy in the story was alleviated by the addition of a violent chase, a stately sword dance, and a powerful funeral. This last was always resented by the composer, Fritz Loewe, probably because the musical accompaniment was an existing, authentic Scottish funeral dirge played on bagpipes that emitted a sound offensive to his Viennese ears.

Agnes and I developed a fine director/choreographer relationship. We became such a close team that, at one moment, when Agnes was on one side

Agnes DeMille and Bobby Lewis, *Brigadoon*: "How do we set about killing Jeannette MacDonald?"

(below) Marion Bell, David Brooks, George Keane, and William Hansen in *Brigadoon*: "Sunshine can peep through a small hole."

of the rehearsal stage suggesting a line-reading to one of the actors, I found myself telling a dancer on the other side to be sure to flex his knees as he descended from his jump. Although the integration of book, songs, and dances in musicals had been established by the time we did *Brigadoon,* Agnes and I collaborated on techniques to remove the intruding "seams" that come in the transitions from music to dialogue and vice versa. For example, when a number ends, often with a good "finish," the spoken dialogue that picks up then, being dynamically much lower, always invites a spate of coughing in the audience until ears become adjusted. So at the start of the dialogue after a number (and applause?), I'd give the actors some strong intention to execute that would immediately grab the audience's attention, and then let the performers gradually slip into the ordinary dynamics of talking. Similarly, when going into a song, I would think up some justification for lifting the actors' speech dynamics as the music cue approached, then have them half-talk the early words of the song and glide easily into singing. There'd be no apparent break in the dynamics. Agnes, for her part, was a master at starting dances with movements that grew out of walking, or any lifelike activities, and then allowing them to formalize into dance patterns.

Now the moment I have said this, I can think of possible exceptions to the rule, for that's in the nature of the artistic beast. There are occasions where you *want* a dynamic shock going from one discipline to another. Simple. Just forget the above instructions.

I could hardly wait for the magical time of dress rehearsal in the Shubert Theatre of New Haven, when all the elements of the production would be brought together—acting, singing, dancing, sets, costumes, lights, and the full orchestra. Shows closed on Saturday night at the Shubert, and the next one opened on Thursday, played three nights and one matinée and then were off to Boston. Well, by the time the production before *Brigadoon* was moved out, our scenery moved in and set up, the lights hung and focused, we had had a technical rehearsal without the actors ("dry tech"), and we finished setting our last few light cues, it was 8:15 P.M. Thursday, and the opening night audience was milling about in the lobby. Turning to Cheryl I said, "We can't open. We haven't had our dress rehearsal with the performers."

"Too late to postpone now," said Cheryl. "People have come up from New York. Open the doors and let them in." And so it was that the dress rehearsal and the world premiere of *Brigadoon* turned out to be one and the same thing. And guess what? The evening went off without a hitch.

The New Haven premiere might have been a breeze, but the Boston opening at the Colonial Theatre, the following Tuesday night, was a cataclysm. With less time to set up, anything might go wrong. And it did, in spades. Agnes and I were standing in the back of the orchestra watching the first short dialogue scene of the American, in a forest setting, discussing his problems with a cynical friend who had accompanied him on his trip to Scotland. The scene went smoothly. Then it happened. As the front "tab" curtains closed in, a few villagers of Brigadoon, waking up after their hundred-year sleep, started to cross the stage in front of the curtain from right to left, singing. During this short cross-over scene, the stage hands were busily setting up MacConnachy Square behind the curtain, and the rest of the villagers were assembling in it. At a certain cue, with no pause in the music ("Come ye, all ye, ev'rywhere to the fair"), the curtains were supposed to part, and those crossing in front were to blend with the villagers behind, and then we'd be into the first big song and dance chorus number, "MacConnachy Square." The cue "ev'rywhere to the fair" came, and no curtain parted. I smiled foolishly at Agnes as if to say, "It's a bit late, isn't it?" and turned back to the stage. We could hear the merry villagers behind the curtain singing and dancing up a storm, but all we could see were the hapless choristers stuck in front trying to decide what to do since they clearly couldn't blend through the curtain. Glancing right and left for the closest exit, they all quickly disappeared. Still the curtains didn't part. Franz Allers continued conducting the music—what else could he do?—as Agnes and I grabbed each other and pasted ourselves against the back wall of the theater, both experiencing the drowning sensation that comes from witnessing months of painful effort going down the drain. Suddenly, near the very end of the orchestral recital of the number, the curtains, with a violent jerk, were pulled open, revealing the following amazing scene: a few of the singers were bravely trying to carry on, while most of them were just standing around trying to figure out how they got into this business anyway; some of the dancers were halfheartedly going through their steps, while the rest sat on the floor, some in Degas-like positions, and some in just positions. In addition to all this chaos, for reasons never uncovered, at the same moment the front curtain parted, the backdrop on which was painted the entire MacConnachy Square decided to go up, revealing the singularly un-Scottish back wall of the Colonial Theatre of Boston. At this catastrophic moment, David Ffolkes, the costume designer, rushed up to me, exclaiming, "Bunty Kelley's got the wrong socks on again!" That, lads and lassies, is specialization.

I've survived some pretty insane pre-Broadway road tours of musicals but, by and large, *Brigadoon* was not one of them. Of course, we rehearsed and tried to improve the show wherever possible. Alan Lerner and I would sit up night after night trying to think up jokes that would relieve the obligatory plot scene in an American bar toward the end of the show. We never succeeded but we did laugh a lot.

One bone of contention was the ending of the show. It was a quiet finale with the dominie leading Tommy off into the misty light to join his Scottish love in the disappearing Brigadoon. Many people, Fritz Loewe among them, felt this was too downbeat an ending, and we should somehow contrive to get the villagers back for a rousing finale, so beloved of musical comedies. Standing in the back of the theater one night during the Boston tryout, I heard Harriet Ames, one of the musical's most important backers, whisper to Cheryl Crawford, "The show's great but when are you going to change that awful ending?"

"Over my dead body," replied Cheryl. It was this uncompromising attitude that made it possible to bring *Brigadoon* into New York with the integrity of the production intact—no mean feat in the history of musicals. The New York Drama Critics Circle, of which John Mason Brown was the president in 1947, awarded *Brigadoon* the following special citation: "Because it is an altogether original and inventive blending of words, music, and dance; because its taste, discretion, and thoughtful beauty mark a high note in any season; and because it finds the lyric theater at its best."

I sailed on the *Queen Mary* in January of 1949 to stage the London production of *Brigadoon* at His Majesty's Theatre. (By the time I did *Teahouse* in the same theater five years later, it had changed its sex to Her Majesty's). Being aware that England is closer to Scotland than Broadway was, I was determined to make all things Scottish—accents, costumes, and so on—as authentic as possible. I fortified myself with a production assistant, Ian Wallace, the son of a Scottish MP and a superb singing actor himself. The first news Ian brought me after reading our script was that if I were serious about authenticity, I couldn't do the show at all. The main scenes, he said, took place two hundred years ago. That would be 1749, smack in the middle of the period when kilts were banned in Scotland. *Brigadoon* with no kilts? No way.

I contacted Alan Lerner at once, and we came up with a solution. Toward the end of the play, in that contemporary scene in the American bar where Tommy tells his fiancée he can't go through with the marriage plans, we set the time as 1935 by dressing the girl friend à la thirties and noting the year in the program. That made our *Brigadoon* date 1735 and we were home free.

The next problem arose when Ian examined the costume sketches. He found that we had put Royal Stuart tartans on the peasants. Why no one—not even the costume designer—ever pointed that out to us in America I'll never know. *That* boner was corrected instantly.

The biggest contribution Wallace made was in the area of authentic Scottish accents. He not only monitored the principal actors but coached the chorus, too. Hearing the ensembles sung with the proper Highland brogue added beauty to their expression and much enjoyment for the British audience.

A typical managerial ploy of that day involved the Oliver Smith sets. In an attempt to reproduce, without payments, the American scenery for the London production, Cheryl had mailed blueprints and photographs to the

English producer, Prince Littler. Parenthetically, I may say that since this was also before the Society of Stage Directors and Choreographers, my direction of the original production—physical staging as well as instructions to the actors—was compiled in a script that was rented out to anyone directing the many subsequent companies of *Brigadoon* with no compensation to me. When I arrived in London, the entire set was finished and installed in the rear of the huge stage of the Drury Lane Theatre. We were to rehearse there. I took one look at the scenery and let out a yell that was heard all the way to the Stage Designers' Union in New York. First of all, the blueprints that Oliver had cleverly left with the producer were his original ones, before the many corrections derived from the planning and rehearsal of the show had been given to the builder and thus incorporated in the construction of the finished scenery. Secondly, the photographs the English scene painters tried to copy were the color pictures from a *Life* magazine layout. With all due respect to *Life*'s printers, the colors, as they came out in the magazine, didn't even approximate the originals. They were all garish and completely unacceptable. I immediately relayed the disastrous news to Cheryl in New York and, you may be sure, I phoned Oliver at once. The upshot was that the whole mess had to be done over, and Oliver, after supplying the proper sketches and plans, was paid for the reproduction of his work.

The English press on *Brigadoon* was as enthusiastic as the American had been. But what was particularly rewarding was to have the English critics notice the care taken to make the show authentic to Scottish tradition. The *Manchester Guardian,* at the premiere, noted at once that "The Scots should have no complaint against *Brigadoon.*" This was followed, after the London opening, by the *Times*'s pointing out that "Mr. Robert Lewis, the director, has in fact treated the fantasy, such as it is, with the scrupulous, imaginative respect which English producers give as a matter of course to a 'straight' play but are apt to think just a waste of mental energy in the light musical theater, which is for them a place where a jumble of oddly assorted traditions must be allowed a free-for-all."

Back home, I had celebrated the success of the Broadway *Brigadoon* by buying a house in Westchester's Pound Ridge. The place was about a mile from "Windows," Tallulah's home, and I could hear her clearly if the wind was right. When Marlon Brando learned I knew Tallulah and lived close to her, he asked me if he could stop by my house on his way to her's, where he was to have an interview that would decide whether he'd play opposite her in her forthcoming vehicle, Cocteau's *The Eagle Has Two Heads.* Tallulah was under the impression she was to audition Marlon (this was months before *Streetcar* made him a household name), but it was Marlon who was unsure that he could cope with Tallulah and it was advice on this point that he wanted from me.

My travel directions to Marlon were specific. He was to go to Grand Central Station, take the 11:30 A.M. train for Stamford, Connecticut, and I'd pick him up at 12:15. It was a twenty minute drive to my house in Pound Ridge, and I figured we'd be safe to sit down to lunch at one o'clock. And I didn't mean 1:02. This was because of Hajima, an Oriental perfectionist who was my houseman and by whose meal announcements you could set your watch. After innumerable disasters with housekeepers of all sizes, sexes, and nationalities I had finally landed Hajima. He was half Chinese and half Japanese and covered the tempestuous emotional war going on inside him with a dignified facade. I felt sure Marlon, with his predilection for exotics, would sympathize.

Hajima had been employed in houses far grander than mine and changed his jacket going from the kitchen to the rest of the house, never seeming to notice that I wore the same blue jeans in every room. At night, after turning down my bed, he'd come downstairs, stop in front of me and deliver a speech, full of feeling, on the honor it was for him to work for me. Then he'd bow from the waist and go to bed. I was touched, not so much by the flattery, but because I knew how he always died a little inside when there were guests and I hadn't provided the correct silver serving fork for this or that vegetable. He was worried that the people might think *he* didn't know which fork to offer. His pride in his profession was deep.

And now Marlon was coming to lunch. I let Hajima know that Brando was a talented young actor who would, undoubtedly, go straight to the top of his profession. I even hinted that Marlon's sudden, unpredictable emotional outbursts in his acting style were not unlike certain Kabuki effects.

As I left for the station, Hajima, who had set Marlon's place and mine neatly on the dining room table, was in the kitchen getting the hot things hot and the cold things cold. When Marlon didn't get off the train, my heart sank. I ran up and down the station platform looking in the train windows, thinking he might have fallen asleep. No Marlon. I called Hajima to find out if Marlon had telephoned. No. Assuming he had to be on the next train, I waited around for an hour or so. When he was not on that one either, I drove home wondering how I could ever find a housekeeper as good as Hajima again.

When I got back, long past lunch time, Hajima, who at one o'clock had brought himself up to curtain-time readiness, was suicidal. I thought, insanely, that I didn't even have a proper hara-kiri knife. Suddenly the phone rang. It was Marlon.

"Where the hell are you?" I yelled.

"Bedford Hills."

"But I told you Stamford, Connecticut. That doesn't even sound remotely like Bedford Hills, which is in New York State. You've taken the wrong railroad line to the wrong state."

"Oh." Marlon's voice brightened. "Stamford. That was the name I couldn't think of. I told the ticket man your phone exchange was Bedford Village and the closest he had to that was Bedford Hills. How do I get to Stamford from here?"

"Don't you dare move, Marlon," I warned him. "Stay right there until I come and get you."

After driving the eight miles to Bedford Hills, I noticed, in the center of this tidy little village, a crowd milling around a truck in the square. I knew at once that our boy must be in the middle of the melée. He seemed to be winning a four-letter word battle with the truck driver. I tried to pull Marlon toward my car.

"Just a minute," he said. I could see he'd forgotten something as he ambled into the drugstore. I followed him in, and there he was at the soda fountain, standing next to a girl who was obviously studying to be the first hippie. I had a feeling she might be related to that Charles Addams character with the dead white face, dank hair, and with her dress ending in a pool of blood on the floor.

"This is Blossom Plum," said Marlon, as easily as though her presence and her name were the two most natural things in the world. My mind flashed back to Hajima who, at that moment, was reheating only two plates and re-cooling only two wine glasses.

"Come on," I whimpered. "Pile into the car." Off we went—Marlon Brando, Blossom Plum, and I.

On our arrival home, Marlon wanted me to take him and Blossom on a tour of the house and grounds, but I forced them into the dining room chairs as we were already hours late. Balefully staring at Miss Plum, Hajima stretched the ruined food three ways, a catastrophe for a culinary artist.

The pathetic lunch was only one of the day's disasters. The next was called: Trying to keep the house from burning down. After lunch we repaired to the upstairs terrace for a smoke and to talk about Tallulah. To enjoy the sun, Marlon and Blossom stopped on the way and stripped to their briefs. I wondered about Blossom's manner of undressing when, days later, I pulled down the bedroom window-screen and one of her silk stockings unfurled from it.

Hajima had provided a huge ashtray on the terrace, and I warned the smokers that it was the dry season, that the ground below was full of flammable leaves, and the danger of forest fires was great. I pointed to, and clearly identified, the ashtray. But as one or the other of them finished a cigarette, the ashtray would be forgotten and the still-lighted butt tossed over the side of the terrace into the dry leaves. I flew down the stairs, plowed through the leaves and stamped out the butt. While going back up through the house I gathered up every ashtray I could find. On the way, noticing a burning cigarette on the wooden cabinet in the john, I put that out, too. I now made a complete circle of ashtrays around the two smokers so that they could see and reach a tray from any angle. No use. Some altercation had developed between them, and it grew so heated that a mere forest fire seemed the least of their worries. Returning to the terrace after one of my fire-prevention trips to the ground, I noticed that Blossom had disappeared from the house. Marlon didn't seem perturbed and, since she was his guest, I didn't give it another thought.

We then discussed the possible problems Marlon would have acting with Tallulah. Since they employed widely different methods of work, and since they both had unshakable independence of spirit, a clash of personalities was a distinct possibility. With this in mind, I suggested he ask for a contract with a two-week notice clause in it. If things got impossible on the road tryout, he could leave the play. I then deposited him at "Windows" and rushed back home to see what state Hajima was in. He was locked in his room, and although he was too dignified to complain, I got no speech of thanks that night.

The confrontation of Bankhead and Brando did not find either of them at their noblest. Marlon greeted her with, "Are you an alcoholic?" to which she cracked, "No, darling, just a heavy drinker." The weirdest part of the interview, Marlon recounted later, took place on a sofa when Tallulah's hand started up Marlon's trouser leg. "What did you do?" I asked him. "Well," he said, "I was interested, from an engineering point of view, to see if it was possible for her to gain her objective through that difficult route. You know," he marveled, "it was."

Marlon took the part in the play, and when it opened on the road, my advice about the two-week clause turned out to be unnecessary. Tallulah, for all her fiery talent, clung to the old tradition of certain stage stars, namely that when they are holding forth in a scene, everyone for miles around should be immobilized. They count any move or reaction from the other actors as distractions. Marlon, on stage, is the kind of actor who has a continuous life going for him, a life which results in scenes rather than star arias surrounded by accompanying robots. Tallulah even placed spies out in the audience to report to her if Marlon was acting behind her back in sections where she couldn't keep an eye on him. Finally, his irrepressible sense of truth unnerved her and she had him fired. Marlon Brando was replaced by Helmut Dantine, who stood still.

In addition to the Pound Ridge house, another *Brigadoon* dividend was getting to know Billy Rose, who owned the Ziegfeld Theatre where the show played. Billy had a grand office (formerly Mr. Ziegfeld's) on the top of the theater with a fine kidney-shaped desk and a view, through a window, of the great stage of the theater where he could check the show. Along the hall outside his office, Billy kept a battery of writers, in cubbyhole offices, knocking out a daily newspaper column that appeared under his by-line in the *Herald Tribune*. Billy, seeking a larger audience, obtained a fifteen-minute spot on radio station WOR where, once a week, he was to read the best of his column material. Thinking he needed a bit of coaching in his vocal delivery, Billy invited me to a meal in his office one evening and asked me if I'd eat dinner with him regularly before he had to do the broadcast, listen to him read his script, and offer any advice I might have. I wasn't sure I could be much help, but I told Billy I'd try. The dinners, prepared and served by his houseman, were fine, starting inevitably with cold madrilene soup topped with a thin layer of sour cream and caviar. The rehearsals were less rewarding.

Reading through the first broadcast, Billy came upon the words "orange juice." Leaving the large issues of his delivery for later, I thought I'd test his ability to take direction with something modest for a start.

"Billy," I began, emulating my first diction-conscious director, Jane Kerley, "that was just fine. But you said 'oranjuice.' It's 'orange juice.'"

"That's what I said," Billy replied, looking at me with surprise. "Oran-juice."

"No, Billy," I persisted. "What you are saying is 'oranjuice.' There are two 'J' sounds in there, one at the end of 'orange' and one at the beginning of 'juice.' It's not very important, since everyone will know what you mean, anyway. But as long as I'm here, I thought I'd mention that it sounds like you're saying 'oran' instead of 'orange,'"

"No, I'm not. I'm saying 'orange.'" Billy was getting testy.

"Then 'juice' is coming out 'uice,'" I went on, mesmerized, "because we're only getting one 'J' sound in there, and we want two, don't we?"

Billy stared at me as though I were nuts. I was, because he could never hear the difference, couldn't care less anyway, and wasn't going to do anything about it in any case.

The next week, I tried to get out of the arrangement by assuring Billy he was doing just fine and didn't need me. He insisted he did. In the next few sessions we gradually dropped the formality of reading the script aloud. We just ate dinner. It took me a while to wean myself away from Billy because I was never quite sure whether I wasn't an antidote for loneliness.

Of the movie proposals I received after *Brigadoon,* one was in an intriguing call from Harry Cohn, the head of Columbia Pictures, asking me if I'd read a certain film script he was interested in having me direct. I said sure and gave him my mailing address. "No, no," he said, "I'd like you to come out to California to read it. We'll put you up in a cottage at the Beverly Hills Hotel."

"But, Mr. Cohn," I protested. "Suppose I don't like the script. You'll only have to send me right home. Wouldn't it be cheaper just to mail it?"

There was a long pause after this while Mr. Cohn was obviously trying to figure how I could possibly not like a script he was offering me. "Look," he said. "You'll like it. And if there is anything wrong with it, we'll fix it. I can't mail you the script."

"If you'll send me right home in case I don't feel it's for me, fixed or not, I'll come out to read it," I said, thinking this was a hell of a good chance to get a nice short vacation and visit my old Hollywood pals. And who knows, I thought, the script might even be interesting.

I was given the full VIP treatment on my arrival in California. The chauffeured limousine from Columbia Pictures picked me up at the Pasadena railroad stop so I wouldn't have to endure the milling crowd at the downtown Los Angeles station. I was whisked away to the Beverly Hills Hotel to get ready for a meeting with a welcoming committee headed by Jerry Wald, Mr. Cohn's deputy. This meeting was to take place in a house a block away from the hotel. I emerged from my bungalow freshened up and ready to walk down the block. The chauffeur who was waiting grabbed my arm to save me from the dangerous consequences of being seen walking on a Beverly Hills street. We drove safely the one block to the meeting. After many pleasantries, the precious script was placed in my hands and was driven, with me, back down the street to the hotel.

I called a movie-writer friend to have dinner, and he warned that if I even opened the cover of the script to sneak a peak before at least ten days of pleasuring myself in the pool, the executives would think I was a shnook and would have no respect for me.

After one fine dinner, the check for which I signed with a flourish, and an invigorating swim the next morning, my curiosity got the better of me. I cracked the script. It was clear after a few pages that not only would I not direct it, I wouldn't go to see it.

I called Mr. Cohn's secretary at Columbia and got an appointment. When I told him what I thought of the script, he was patient. "That's fine," he said. "We'll fix it. We'll put the best writers on it. Who would you suggest?" I suggested that whoever worked on it, the subject matter didn't interest me enough to want to be connected with the project, and please, could I just go home? The next hour revealed Harry Cohn's performing range all the way from pleading to threatening and made Louis B. Mayer seem like an amateur actor.

Finally, Mr. Cohn was forced to accept the fact that I was standing pat on my deal that if I didn't want to do the picture, he'd send me home. With consummate rage, he ordered me to be taken to the downtown Los Angeles station. In an old Chevrolet. My punishment was complete and ignominious.

More important than the fun I enjoyed as a result of my first commercial success was the realization that, since I could breathe easily for awhile about the problem of employment that continually haunts life in the theater, there was at last a chance to resume my profession of serious theater craftsman.

The abortive enterprise of the Dollar Top Theatre had been an attempt by Gadget Kazan and myself to set up a home where we not only could direct plays but expand the boundaries of our craft. Now that we both were established as directors, we might at least aim for some sort of laboratory like the studio we ran in the Group Theatre. There we could work with talented actors in an experimental way, without the pressures of an opening night curtain limiting exploratory work. It was, in fact, an attempt to keep our franchises as artists while pursuing our careers as working theater practitioners.

On a beautiful day in the spring of 1947, only a couple of months after the New York premiere of *Brigadoon,* Kazan and I took a long walk through Central Park and planned an Actors Studio.

CHAPTER 13

# The Actors Studio 1947

MEMORIES OF EXACTLY how the idea of the Studio was born depend, as in *Rashomon,* on who's doing the remembering. Harold Clurman recalled giving the idea to Kazan. Gadget doesn't remember that at all. I remember a walk with Harold and Gadget some time before the specific idea of the Studio was considered when I suggested that it was a few years since the Group ended, the three of us were pursuing our individual careers profitably, and we should pool our energies to establish a new theater where the ideas and idealism of the Group could be reborn. I exhorted the other two so enthusiastically that Harold turned to Gadget and remarked, "Bobby sounds like a young man I knew in the thirties called Harold Clurman."

An unprecedented reunion at the thirtieth anniversary of the Actors Studio.

Cheryl Crawford remembers a Greek restaurant as the place where she first put the idea of the Studio into Gadget's mind. Gadget doesn't remember the talk or the restaurant. He says, "I remember talking to Bobby first. And then I remember going up to Cheryl's office and proposing it to her there and she, of course, went for it."

What Gadget and I both recall in detail is that walk in Central Park where we spent a whole spring day talking. We even remember extraneous events of the day like Moss Hart passing by and joining us on a park bench for a short chat.

The common emotional base for the long talk between Gadget and me was the yearning we felt for something like the "home" we had had in the Group Theatre—a place where we could explore and expand our theatrical ideas. There is never time for this kind of activity when you're rehearsing a play and have an opening night deadline. I'm sure that Gadget, for his part, also wanted a place to train talented actors for the kind of plays and films he would direct. He told Michel Ciment, the French film critic and historian (in *Kazan on Kazan*), "The Group Theatre had meant a lot to me and I missed it personally and professionally . . . I missed it, not as a memory or as something of the past, but as a place where I could find new actors, where I could work myself on things of an experimental nature."

I, too, needed a setup where I could further develop the change of emphasis on certain aspects of the Stanislavski System that had first been brought to light by Stella Adler after her return from working with the Russian director. I also wanted a place where I could pursue my continuing interest in problems of style for the actor.

Gadget and I decided that, this time, we didn't want to start another theater (we still had that Dollar Top stationery to use up). We wanted a workshop. And we knew that many talented actors yearned for a place to get together and practice their craft—much as good soloists meet to play chamber music for themselves. It was also decided that no money would be involved in the project as far as fees from the actors or payment for us was concerned. We would raise from friends whatever was needed for the basic expenses: rent, heat, telephone, etc. In that way, talent would be the sole criterion as to who would be chosen for membership.

This agreed, Kazan and I next appraised each other to decide how we would divide up the teaching chores. Gadget liked to work with the younger actors, and so it was decided he would concentrate on technique exercises with them and on developing the tools of the actor's craft. For my part, I would take the older actors—well, not old, but those with more experience. My group would rehearse scenes in all styles, with particular emphasis on the process of "inner action" or "intention" (subtext), plus a healthy discouragement of working for emotion for the actors' own sake rather than for its relevance to the character and play.

To prevent any muddying of our objectives, Gadget and I decided there would be no acting teachers aside from the two of us. We would ask our Group Theatre colleague, Cheryl Crawford, if she would join us in the venture as administrator. Remembering the invaluable inspiration it always was when Harold Clurman spoke on any theater subject, we determined to get him to talk to our actors whenever possible. The next important decision we took that day in the park concerned Lee Strasberg. Kazan and I deferred to no one in our respect and admiration for his contribution in establishing, and slaving for, the Group Theatre in the thirties—an achievement for which he would have been knighted in a civilized theatrical world. But we both agreed that, valuable as his contribution was in starting us all off in the Group, his manner of dealing with young actors was light miles away from what we now planned, and therefore, he would not be considered for the acting faculty. Cheryl, always faithful to Lee, tried to soften Gadget's attitude to Lee during the ensuing summer, and Gadge, in California, finally agreed with her to let Lee work with a beginners group. When I reminded Gadget of what he had expressed to me about Lee and the teaching of young people, Gadget wrote me a letter on Twentieth Century-Fox Film Corporation stationery (he was shooting *Gentleman's Agreement* then) saying that what he meant to convey to Cheryl was that Lee was the most qualified person in the world to instruct actors on the *history* of their craft. I couldn't have agreed with him more and, in fact, had suggested on our Central Park walk a weekly lecture in the Studio, by Lee, on the tradition of acting. Gadget had vetoed even that involvement with Lee. So you can imagine my surprise when I read an article in *The New York Times* written by Gadget sometime after I had left the Studio, and he had chosen Lee Strasberg to be its artistic head. Gadget said in this article that Strasberg was not only the best acting teacher around, but he couldn't understand how Lee wasn't in the Studio from the beginning.

At the end of the summer, on Gadget's return from Hollywood, we settled the roster of actors for our two classes in what we called the Actors Studio—using the word "studio" as we had when we named our workshop in the Group, the Group Theatre Studio. Kazan's people met twice a week and included, among others, Julie Harris, Jocelyn Brando, Cloris Leachman, James Whitmore, Joan Copeland, Steven Hill, Lou Gilbert, Rudy Bond, Anne Hegira, Peg Hillias, Lenka Peterson, Edward Binns, and Tom Avera. My group, meeting three times a week, consisted of Marlon Brando, Montgomery Clift, Maureen Stapleton, Eli Wallach, Mildred Dunnock, Jerome Robbins, Herbert Berghof, Tom Ewell, John Forsythe, Anne Jackson, Sidney Lumet, Kevin McCarthy, Karl Malden, E. G. Marshall, Patricia Neal, Beatrice Straight, David Wayne, and—well, I don't want to drop names, so I'll stop there. In all, there were about fifty. The class was so large, in fact, that Gadget and I pruned it after the Christmas break, with loud protestations from all, pruned and unpruned alike.

Two famous alumni of my 1947 Actors Studio class: Montgomery Clift and Marlon Brando. (upper left) Monty as a child model. (left) Monty in his dressing room during the shooting of *The Misfits,* 1961. (above) Marlon "stretching" into a Habsburg prince.

The early sessions were held on West Forty-eighth Street in an abandoned church. After the Christmas holidays, we moved for a few months to a dance studio on Fifty-fourth Street, ending that first season in fairly good headquarters at 1697 Broadway. This last place was a gift from a generous art patron, Mrs. Dorothy Willard.

Gadget concentrated on technique exercises with his group: sensory recall, imagination, improvisation, etc. I delivered the downbeat of my class with a talk on the nature and importance of Intention. Scenes were then chosen. We analyzed the complete plays, described the character elements of the parts being studied, broke down the chosen scenes into sections, and staged them. Two aspects dominated the work: emphasizing Intention and developing a sense of form. Also, scenes of a nonrealistic nature were encouraged. For example, Jane Hoffman and Tom Ewell (who was in *John Loves Mary* on Broadway at the time) tackled Elmer Rice's expressionist play *The Adding Machine*. E. G. Marshall and Herbert Berghof worked on Kafka's *The Trial*.

Another aspect of my approach was to encourage the actors to stretch themselves by trying roles they would not usually be cast in. There was never a question of teaching acting to the likes of the people in my group, as they were all highly talented actors. But here was an opportunity to work on characterizations that might open up new areas of performing for them. It was with this principle in mind that I assigned Marlon Brando the role of the Archduke Rudolf Maximilian von Habsburg in Robert Sherwood's *Reunion in Vienna*.

"I want a complete physical characterization, Marlon," I said. "The works—full uniform, including a sword, mustache and monocle, long cigarette holder, accent, Habsburg lip, and waltz music offstage." Marlon was horrified. But, with Joan Chandler chosen as Elena, the woman whose love he wanted to rekindle, he reluctantly began to rehearse. Each week I'd call for the scene to be performed, but Marlon always had some excuse: he forgot the phonograph record for the waltz music, he didn't have some article of costume, or his monocle wouldn't stay screwed in his eye. Finally, convinced I was never going to give up, Marlon presented the scene. He came onstage and slowly circled his Elena. Then in that unpredictable way that was to become his trademark, Marlon suddenly slapped her, grabbed her, kissed her passionately and then murmured, "How long has it been since you were kissed like that?" The roar of approval that this evoked from his fellow students (well known as the toughest audience in the world) spurred Marlon on to give a hilarious light comedy performance that is still remembered by all who were there that day.

The converse of Marlon's problem was that of Jerry Robbins. I wanted to stretch Marlon into areas far removed from his natural behavior. Jerry's performing experience was rooted in a sense of form. He was a superb young dancer, now wishing to explore what the difference was in the source of expression for acting as opposed to dancing. We chose a completely realistic scene for him from Odets's *Waiting For Lefty,* with Jerry playing the young Jewish intern, a victim of anti-Semitism in a large hospital. I still remember the look on the future choreographer's face when, in my critical remarks after the scene, I complained that, fine as his emotional quality was, his physical movement was a bit awkward.

It has long been considered one of the democratic rights of actors in classrooms to express their opinions of scenes performed by fellow students. Usually the floor is thrown open to these remarks immediately after the performance of the scene. Thereafter, the instructor gives his criticism. I've always suspected this system is based on the idea that, by the time everyone has torn the actors apart, the teacher has enough ammunition to sum up what has been said and emerge as either a benign Solomon mediating an artistic debate or a Simon Legree whipping not only the performers of the scene but also the poor shnooks who thought *they* knew better than he what was wrong.

In my class that first season at the Actors Studio, I tried to minimize this sort of free-for-all, which more often than not, is a form of bloodletting. I still do discourage it on principle, although a certain amount of input by the class *after* the scene has been criticized by the teacher can be permitted as long as it remains constructive and pertinent. It is a misuse of rehearsals or classes—where the creative process of work between actors and directors (or teachers) is taking place—to turn them into "democratic" forums for the expression of equal artistic rights. Can you imagine a dance student at the end of an étude in one of Balanchine's or Martha Graham's classes proclaiming, "I didn't like the way Shura extended her left foot."

There is the story of the time Julie Harris completed a beautifully played emotional scene at the Actors Studio in one of Strasberg's classes. "Does anyone have anything to say?" inquired Lee. "I do," piped up some guy who couldn't shine Julie's shoes, artistically speaking. "When she drank that coffee I didn't believe it was really hot." "That did it," said Julie and walked out of the Studio before she had to listen to anymore of what I call the hot-and-cold school of acting.

To actors, then and now, who maintain that my attitude on this subject is authoritarian, I agree. But without central control in dance groups, orchestras, or theater activities being in the hands of choreographers, conductors, or directors the result can be chaos. I am not talking of abusive power but artistic leadership. Even the few times I've attended conductorless orchestra concerts, I couldn't help noticing the concert master tilting his violin a bit to signal the downbeat to his colleagues.

Other than this difference of opinion on the part of some Studio members in my class on the degree and amount of participation in the criticism of their colleagues and a congenital intolerance on my part toward absenteeism, the season progressed serenely and productively.

In the spring semester, Gadget and I decided on two plays we'd present in the Studio to wind up our inaugural season. He chose a first play by the novelist Bessie Breuer, *Sundown Beach,* which had lots of parts for the actors in his class. I picked Chekhov's *The Sea Gull* and, for a while, used the class sessions to illustrate how, in the rehearsal process of a complete production, we could apply the principles of the scene work we did all year. In the last few weeks before presenting the play, we proceeded on a regular daily rehearsal schedule.

I cast Monty Clift as Treplev, the poet, and he balked immediately. He was sick and tired of playing "sensitive" parts, he said, and wanted to break the image he had created in his Broadway roles. I walked him around the block a few times and tried to convince him that in Treplev he had the chance to find elements of character other than sensitivity, and also, that he should solve his problem by facing up to it. I even pointed out that in the premiere of *The Sea Gull* in the Moscow Art Theatre, Meyerhold, a notoriously rebellious theater artist, played Treplev. Monty replied that America wasn't turn-of-the-century Russia. His solution was to accept a Hollywood offer in a John Wayne film, *Red River,* and play a cowboy role where he would get to ride a horse. "The problem that is giving you concern, Monty," I told him, "is never going to be resolved by riding a horse."

Monty was adamant; so I cast Henry Barnard as Treplev. Maureen Stapleton was Masha, and the others were Joan Chandler (Nina), Thelma Schnee (Arkadina), David Wayne (Medvedenko), George Keane (Trigorin), William Hansen (Sorin)—these last two were in *Brigadoon*—Herbert Berghof (Dr. Dorn), Mildred Dunnock (Paulina), and Michael Strong (Shamraev).

The day we put on *The Sea Gull* there were only a few friends in the audience, in addition to those Studio members not in the cast. There naturally were no reviews, but Cheryl Crawford sent me a dazzling letter that included the following evaluation of the performance:

"Your production of *The Sea Gull* has haunted me. I've seen the Moscow Art Chekhov, the Old Vic, the Civic Rep with Alla (Nazimova) and the (Margaret) Webster production. But for the first time, that Friday, I felt I had seen the real Chekhov with the depth of his understanding, tenderness, and compassion for all human beings. The whole production was fragrant with his incredible sweetness and truth. And you unfolded it, not slowly and grimly but with vitality and buoyancy."

The elation I felt at such praise from my colleague was tempered by the fact that I had just turned in my resignation from the Studio. These are the circumstances that brought about that decision on my part. Cheryl had acquired the musical play *Love Life* for production. The music was by Kurt Weill, and Alan Jay Lerner, our *Brigadoon* author, had written the book and lyrics. Cheryl asked me to get on board again as director. After reading the script I had many doubts about it and gave it to Gadget for his opinion. He, too, thought it needed major revisions and told me his wife, the former Group Theatre play reader, Molly Day Thacher, "hated it." Gadget advised me to stay away from the project unless I were sure I could get those revisions done. I felt he was right and after being convinced the setup was such that I couldn't succeed in getting major rewrites, I turned down Cheryl's offer to do the show. She immediately submitted it to Gadget.

When he knew I heard he had been offered the show, Gadget kept telling me he was too busy to do the production, that he told Cheryl and the writers that, but they wouldn't take no for an answer, kept "pestering" him to listen to an audition, etc., etc. Then one day Gadget went off to Florida and asked Cheryl to call me and give me the news that he was doing the show. I felt sorry for her, as I could hear her voice trembling on the telephone. It was Gadget who was gambling with my friendship, but Cheryl had to be the messenger with the news.

These things happen all the time in show business. But what staggered me was the *way* Gadget did it. In our classes we always stressed the point that, at a given moment in a part, an actor asks himself three questions regarding the behavior of his character: *What, Why,* and *How*. In his accepting the assignment to direct *Love Life,* I understood completely *what* Gadget was doing and *why* he was doing it and I would have given him my blessing if it were not for *how* he did it.

Jimmy Proctor, a theater publicist close to Gadget and me, had this same problem of the *how*—only his referred to behavior involving Kazan and Arthur Miller. According to Victor Navasky's *Naming Names,* Arthur visited his friend, Proctor, early on the morning Jimmy was to testify before the House Committee on Un-American Activities. Miller wanted to help bolster Proctor's morale. Proctor had previously been named by Kazan before the committee. Proctor was understandably shocked, therefore, when Miller, who had not wavered in his resolve not to name names, later turned over his play *After the Fall* to Kazan to direct. (The play involves Quentin, a former communist, who breaks with a friend because he is about to turn informer before a congressional committee.) Proctor didn't talk to Miller for a couple of years after that, just as Miller earlier stopped talking to Kazan for the same act. Proctor, Navasky says, summed up his feeling this way: "I've always believed that *Why* a person behaved as he did was a proper subject for medical study, but *How* he behaved was a proper basis for judging a person." Proctor, incidentally, is the name of the protagonist who refuses to confess to witchcraft in Miller's *The Crucible*.

It seemed to me then, as it does now years later when Kazan and I are friends again, that something like the following should have occurred in view of our extremely close friendship, our long collaborative work together, and the history of the *Love Life* project up to the moment Gadget accepted the job of director (I wrote him this opinion in my letter of resignation from the Studio on June 15, 1948): Gadget should have spoken to *me* when he decided to do the show, telling me he liked the music, that he now felt he could fix the book, and if I still didn't want to do it, would I mind if he did? Then all would have been in the open. I would have wished him well and that would have been that.

Gadget replied this way: "Perhaps I should have called you but you were out of it so long, and from your attitude, so well out of it, that it simply never occurred to me. I'd say I was at fault there. I am careless about these things, but Christ, Bobby, your demands on people are certainly absolute!" He finished his letter with "I think you're the best teacher for young actors in the city today, not excluding myself. I think you need Cheryl and me. I think you need the Studio."

In that letter of Cheryl's after *The Sea Gull,* she also tried to explain the handling of the *Love Life* matter. "If I seem to you remiss in friendship and not quite worthy of your trust, it's not through lack of feeling or interest, but those damn human defects I'm still working at, tho' I sometimes think they should have improved more with forty-five years under the belt."

Taken point by point, I can now understand Cheryl and Gadget's protestations. Gadget's remark on my needing the Studio also has validity because, if I had stayed with it, my teaching work and my emphasis on the problems of style for the American actor might have had a more concentrated forum. (Actors Studio stalwart Shelley Winters on meeting me always asks, "Bobby, when are you coming back to teach us *sty-ull*?" As soon as you can pronounce it in one syllable, Shelley.) Maybe I was too demanding of my longtime colleagues in considering it a betrayal of friendship not to be open and honest with me about *Love Life.* Maybe I was not critical enough of my own admitted fault of hypersensitivity. But damn it, the lack of ethics I've continually encountered in the theater world must, in the end, be faced up to, especially in important relationships. I could not then, and cannot now, reconcile a situation where education of students in theater craft, based on the search for truth, can be carried on honestly if there is dissembling leadership at the top. I would rewrite that Gordon Craig remark, "After we've reformed the art of the Theatre, we must remake the life of the Theatre," to read, "We *cannot* reform the art of the Theatre *unless* we remake the life of the Theatre."

I think that "careless" was too simple a word for Gadget to use in describing his behavior. It's true that many, including myself, are "survivors" in our profession. Gadget, in his answers to Michel Ciment in *Kazan on Kazan,* refers to himself as "a person who wants to survive, by any means!" (He will survive this chapter.) What I suspect is that Gadget's feeling of guilt was the root cause of his unacceptable behavior. He told Ciment, speaking of why he named colleagues in his testimony before the House Un-American Activities Committee: "I also have to admit, and I've never denied, that there was a personal element in it, which is that I was very angry, humiliated, and disturbed—furious, I guess—at the way they booted me out of the Party. . . . I had behaved secretly for a long time. Our behavior in the Group Theatre was conspiratorial and, I thought, disgusting: our cell would discuss what we were going to do, then we would go to Group Theatre meetings or Actors' Equity meetings and pretend we were there with open minds. The whole thing was a way of taking over power."

I am in no way equating the disastrous effect of destroying employment opportunities for people named in the HUAC sessions with my resignation from the Studio. But I do believe friendship is a covenant, too—more important, even, than political allegiance. The work an artist tries to do is affected by the world he has to live in and the agonizing road of the American theater artist becomes recognizable by its pile of heads either stepped over or stepped on.

A suffocating feeling lay on my heart all during the last weeks of *The Sea Gull* rehearsals. I wanted the actors to have a good finish to their season, so I said nothing. I resigned as soon as the performance was over in order to be able to breathe freely again in my work.

The first problem that Kazan faced after my departure from the Studio was finding someone to mind the store. He could always teach some classes himself, but with his Broadway and Hollywood commitments, Gadget needed a codirector who would be in charge and hold the Studio together. It took from the spring of 1948, when I resigned, to the fall of 1951 for Kazan to turn the artistic leadership of the Studio over to Strasberg, where it remained until Lee's death. In the three year interim, Gadget approached many teachers, starting with an offer to Harold Clurman to direct a play at the Studio. Harold refused. For an average of a couple of months at a time, various theater people who were recruited by Kazan took over the acting sessions. Among them were Josh Logan, Sandy Meisner, Daniel Mann, David Pressman, David Alexander, and reluctantly, Lee Strasberg, still smarting from being excluded from the Studio in the beginning.

Realizing he'd better focus on a single method of instruction to avoid chaos, Gadget, with nudges from Cheryl, finally capitulated and tried to accommodate his mind to the idea that was, in the years to come, to be accepted by the faithful: that Lee Strasberg was the great acting teacher of America. When I say accommodate, I mean in public. Gadget was never, I say never, reconciled to Lee's artistic approach to teaching acting, feeling that Strasberg's overemphasis on emotion, at the expense of other elements of the craft, had a limiting effect on the style of much American acting. When Gadget (and his codirector Bob Whitehead) asked me to take over the training program of the proposed Lincoln Center Repertory Theatre in 1962 (Gadge resigned from the Studio then to avoid conflicts of interests, since the Studio also planned an acting company), he again reviewed the two major differences from Lee's approach that he wanted me to emphasize with the Lincoln Center group: one, to accent Intention as the most important element in the craft, rather than belabor emotional recall; two, to pay strict attention to problems of style.

Meanwhile, back at the Studio, in 1951, with Lee now the sole artistic director, it was business as usual: private moments, affective memory exercises, and only lip service to the various theatrical forms other than purely realistic. In the sixties, months after his resignation from the Studio, and as head of the Lincoln Center Repertory Company, Gadget wrote an article for *The New York Times* expressing his disappointment with the work of the actors at the Studio with its "preoccupation with the purely psychological side of acting." He went on, "there have been days when I felt like I would swap them all for a gang of wandering players, who could dance and sing, and who were, above all else, entertainers."

I would add: above all else, masters of theatrical styles necessary to interpret the world literature of plays required by the proliferation of regional, university, and repertory theaters that depend on classics and revivals, as well as avant-garde plays, to survive. Your average Studio freak, these days, is recognizable by one style alone—the style into which he has distorted the Stanislavski System: a bogus Stanley Kowalski stance and a

The Actors Studio Mafia: "Lewis going for Strasberg's neck, Crawford getting Lee's finger in her eye, Kazan dubious about it all."

speech pattern that makes Brando, as Stanley, sound like John Gielgud. Dialogue is distorted with endless hemmings and hawings, repetitions of words, interpolations, and a general mangling of rhythms. No wonder we've lost the ball to English actors.

Listen to the late British stage director Tyrone Guthrie on "Style" in acting: "Style . . . is an alarming word to American actors. They think of it as something assumed, something 'fancy' and affected, something connected with being more elegant and flossy that anyone has a right to be in private life.

"It is hard to convince them that style in acting, as in dress, is concerned with appropriateness, with suitability to environment, and does not necessarily involve a great deal of elaborate mannerisms and posturing. It sometimes escapes notice that a style of speech or deportment suitable for one environment is entirely unsuitable for another. But both styles may be equally 'natural.'"

When the Group Theatre actors were first exposed to Stanislavski, our idols of truthful acting were Alfred Lunt, Pauline Lord, and Laurette Taylor, all of whom spoke English. After all, language is a major element in a dramatic performance, and the ability to use it, control it, and distort it, if necessary, for character is a prime requisite of the fine actor. Some modern American performers dread language other than what falls naturally from their lazy tongues. I remember going over Tennessee Williams and Donald Windham's *You Touched Me* with Monty Clift and trying to keep him from cutting every speech of his that was longer than a grunt. "I can't say all those words," he kept complaining. It's no wonder he never became the great American Hamlet we all hoped he would be.

For admission to the Studio when Strasberg took over, a five-minute audition scene was suggested. David Garfield, in his book on The Actors Studio, *A Players Place,* tells us, "A contemporary piece was suggested, something the actor could do simply and easily, featuring a character close to himself in age, type, and experience. He was told that the judges would try to estimate his native talent, his use of himself in a part he felt close to, *and not his verbal or physical skills as an actor.* He should therefore avoid the special complexities of Shakespeare or 'period' drama."

Contrast this with the audition demands of every serious theater enterprise that's not stuck in the rut of the thirties. In addition to a realistic scene, the applicant is always asked to perform a period piece, preferably in verse. In this way, aptitude in both realistic and poetic theater can be ascertained. It's too late, after you accept someone who was very impressive in that park-bench scene from Odets's *Golden Boy,* to discover he goes all to pieces when faced with problems of verse, period, and so on.

In the tape-recorded sessions, *Strasberg at the Actors Studio* (edited by Robert H. Hethmon), we hear Lee saying to Actor X, "You have set yourself very deliberately and correctly the problem of moving away from the localized way of speaking that you have. As a problem that is perfectly plausible, but it is not an acting problem. It is a speech problem and is, therefore, correctly worked on as a purely technical problem in a speech class. As soon as you make an acting problem of it, you double the difficulty: You have to work on the scene and, at the same time, keep the speech less close to your natural speech.

"External skill becomes a matter of aesthetic principle only when it is disassociated from inner technique."

There it is in a nutshell. In acting training we *cannot* separate the means of expression from the inner content. Indeed one must derive from the other. You learn how to behave and speak from studying the psychology of the character, and you glean the thoughts, sensations, and emotions of characters from an understanding—no, a practicing—of their behavior and speech. And they must be worked on together. You cannot "paste on" a speech pattern you've learned in a diction class after you've conquered the "insides." It's precisely this practice that discourages present-day Methodists from solving the problems of speech and movement. They claim it "felt" so much better ("truer") when they spoke and moved as they do in life. When they try to add on the correct style of speech and movement they have studied, "a purely technical problem," as Strasberg said, their sense of truth is rocked. Which do you suppose they're going to slough off? Their true feeling or their correct speech? You guessed it.

When I became chairman of the Acting and Directing departments of the Yale School of Drama, we had a weekly workshop every Friday supervised by the acting, voice-speech, and movement teachers. During the week, we all did our own special exercises training the three disciplines. In the Friday session, after a couple of students did a Shakespeare scene, for instance, I would turn to the voice and speech teacher and ask for corrections in that department. After some necessary technical work—opening a closed throat, unscrambling mangled verse rhythms, or whatever, I advised the actors, as they repeated the scene, to think only of the points they were making and not of their throats or diction. We then could see at once how the technical results just adhered to and became part of the playing out of the scene. The same process was followed with problems of period movement or any other behavioral expression. Each time a stance or gesture or walk was corrected, the actor went right back to the scene and again concentrated on his acting problem. But the "inside" and the "outside" were being trained in the same laboratory at the same session. The "compleat" actor of today (Meryl Streep is a shining example) emerged from this training approach. She is not "alarmed," as Sir Tyrone put it, by style. She embraces all forms of acting. This attitude is the hope of the future American actor.

Strasberg, in one of his countless nostalgic paeans to Eleanora Duse, told the Studio members, "Duse achieved a fusion of the inner and the external which we have not arrived at in our theater. The emphasis in the theater today seems to be on one or the other. The work in the Studio has tended to be on the inner phase of this work. It has not encompassed the actor's sense of the external as part of the creative process, wherein the external elements themselves become heightened, and the human being thereby becomes a more wonderful instrument of expression and therefore responds, like a rare violin, more deeply and truly to the dictates of the inner technique. The theater will require the next hundred years to deal with what Duse represented in this area." I don't know. As Irina says in *The Three Sisters,* "We must work." We don't have to wait a hundred years to tackle total acting.

Speaking of *The Three Sisters,* the Actors Studio production of the play, directed by Strasberg, revealed the results of the system of concentrating on full feeling for the actors with no attention as to how this emotion is expressed in terms of the language of a particular play. Peter Roberts in *Plays and Players* tried to analyze the formula for the particular sound of the Actors Studio diction in *The Three Sisters* production when it played London: "First . . . you tack on an 'er' to every second or third word. Between every fourth and fifth, you insert an 'um,' or more occasionally, an 'ah,' and every now and again you repeat a phrase once or twice. In moments of stress, you string along the trivial and the important things altogether and let them out in one hell of a rush. So much the better if you can pull up right in the middle of this flood of words . . . you stop dead in your tracks, pause for a few seconds and let the rest of the speech fall out of the side of your mouth like a piece of mouldy chocolate." Penelope Gilliatt in *The Observer*: "(They) plough up the lines and trundle backwards and forwards over the same words in a sort of heavy agricultural backstitch." The London *Sunday Times*'s Harold Hobson: "This production has no rhythm and no orchestration . . . the men talk as if straight from the Fulton Fish Market." And in case you think it might be just a problem relating to English ears, back home, the American Vincent Canby, reviewing the filming of the stage version of *The Three Sisters* in *The New York Times* was saying, "The accents don't match, some are out of Topeka, Kansas, some out of Broadway, and some out of the Yiddish theater."

How far we have come from the Constantin Stanislavski, whose spirit guided us in the Group Theatre days. In his *Building a Character* he discusses diction (Tortsov is the name Stanislavski uses in the book to designate himself as Director of the Moscow Art Theatre and school):

"'Stym ta'ope nwy dor t'yawn p'ness!'

"These were the unexpected sounds that issued from Tortsov's lips as he came into class today. We looked at him and at each other in astonishment.

"'Don't you understand it?' he asked after a short wait.

"'Not a word of it,' we admitted. 'What do the scolding words mean?'

"'It is time to open wide the door to your own happiness.' The actor who pronounced them in a certain play had a good, big voice, audible in all parts of the theater, nevertheless we could not understand them any better than you could, and we too thought, as you did, that he was scolding us,' explained Tortsov.

"After many years of acting and directing experience, I arrived at a full realization, intellectual and emotional, that every actor must be in possession of excellent diction and pronunciation, that he must feel not only phrases and words, but also each syllable, each letter.

"We do not feel our own language, the phrases, syllables, letters, and that is why it is so easy for us to distort it. Add to this lisping, guttural, nasal, and other ugly distortions of good speech!

"The dropping of individual letters or syllables make as glaring defects for me now as a missing eye or tooth, a cauliflower ear, or any other physical deformity.

"Lack of rhythm in speech, which makes a phrase start off slowly, spurt suddenly in the middle, and just as abruptly slide in a gateway, reminds me of the way a drunkard walks, and the rapid fire speech of someone with St. Vitus' dance.

"Poor speech creates one misunderstanding after another. It clutters up, befogs, or even conceals the thought, the essence and even the very plot of the play."

A clear clue to the basic reasons for the stylistic failures of the Actors Studio came when I attended a performance there of the first act of Verdi's *La Traviata.* If the Moscow Art Theatre could have a Musical Studio, why not the Actors Studio, too? I didn't expect the singing actors to have legitimate operatic voices and was prepared for an emphasis on the problems of acting while they were singing. What I found was no understanding that the source of the acting content (intentions, emotion, etc.) must derive not only from the words but from the music as well which, in opera, is the major portion of the complete text. You cannot perform the sections of your part according to your feeling of the situations and allow the music (or, in plays, the verse) to be twisted out of shape by *your* personal rhythms and pauses. For an example: In the well-known duet from the second act of *Traviata* (which they never got to at the Studio) "Dite alla giovine" ("Tell your young daughter"), Alfredo's father, Giorgio Germont, finally extracts a promise from Violetta to give up her lover to avoid disgracing the Germont family, whose daughter is about to be married. Now, if you study the notes, in addition to the words, you'll find that Verdi precedes the actual melody with a held note (B flat) on the sound "Ah!" The way that B flat then drops into the first note of "Dite alla giovine" (G) is all you need to understand that Violetta's acting intention is "to capitulate to the old man's painful request." And for further emotional fuel, only a stone could remain unmoved by the holding back and the falling into tempo of the beautiful melody.

I understood that day the failure of so many practitioners of the Americanized Stanislavski System with Shakespeare's plays and other poetic dramas. They first solve the acting problems by psychology alone; then they try to add what might have been gleaned in their voice and speech classes. It does not occur to them to arrive at their psychological results by conquering the stylistic problems of the text as well as through an analysis of motivation. As with Verdi's music, they would be helped to arrive at that motivation through an appreciative study of the sounds, rhythms, and sentiments of the playwrighting language, whether it be verse, poetic realism, or any other style.

Unless this problem of fusing the "insides" and the "outsides" of the acting mechanism into a totality is faced and solved, chances of a fine repertory theatre of American actors capable of playing the world literature are slim. A goodly number of our most talented actors have already been grounded in the thirties. Since the Actors Studio grew naturally out of the Group Theatre, it worried Harold Clurman in the last days of his life (1980) that the Actors Studio was not moving with the repertory demands made on actors by the growth of regional theaters all over the country, to say nothing of the requirements of the new playwrighting. He feared the Studio actors were becoming—and this is his word—"ghettoized."

On the twentieth anniversary of the Actors Studio in 1967, I was asked, as one of the founders, to write a statement for a brochure that was being prepared. I sent in the following: "One afternoon in 1947, Elia Kazan and I walked through Central Park planning the Actors Studio. The park wasn't safe in those days either." To their credit the members of the Studio board printed it, and it's reported that even Lee Strasberg smiled when he read it.

CHAPTER 14

# Opera

ON MY RETURN from the launching of *Brigadoon* in London, I eagerly signed the contract Cheryl Crawford handed me to direct Marc Blitzstein's *Regina,* his musical version of Lillian Hellman's *The Little Foxes,* because it put me back in the world of my first love—opera. Although in my young days I could only worship operatic gods with phonograph records or from a seat in the balcony, one of the dividends of having become a director was the privilege it gave me of meeting two members of the top royalty in the world of opera—Titta Ruffo and Rosa Ponselle.

Walking along a street in Florence in 1951, I stopped to admire a beautiful, carved front door of an elegant apartment house. A glance at the ornate brass name plates at the side of the door revealed the legend: *Titta Ruffo.* If you are an opera buff, you will believe that my heart skipped a beat just at the sight of the name. The early decades of our century hailed as unchallenged a triumvirate of front-rank male opera stars: the tenor Caruso, the bass Chaliapin, and the baritone, Titta Ruffo. Many were the operatic binges I enjoyed, intoxicated by the sound of their recorded voices. Now here was Ruffo, living out his final years (he died in 1953), behind that door. Turning to my companions, Felicia Montealegre, the actress who was to become Mrs. Leonard Bernstein, and Paolo Vaccarino, a Florentine sculptor friend, I speculated on the possibility of visiting the great man. Paolo rang the bell, and we all went in. A housekeeper came to the apartment door. After identifying us all, Paolo assured her that we wanted nothing more than to pay our respects to the artist.

"Momento," said the housekeeper and disappeared inside. When she returned we were informed that if we came back the next afternoon, Signor Ruffo would receive us.

Titta Ruffo as Hamlet: "Why wasn't a movie made of his life?"

Upon being ushered into the apartment by the housekeeper the following day, we understood at once why the singer needed a full day to prepare for our visit. He not only had arranged photographs of himself in his famous roles all around the room, but there were pictures of his favorite colleagues, each warmly inscribed. On the piano was the fencing foil he had used in *Hamlet,* and other characteristic props from his roles were scattered about. Pieces of several costumes were carefully laid out on the couch. And, standing tall, in the center of all this history was the seventy-four-year-old Ruffo, magnificent in a cape and loose, flowing black silk tie.

After a guided tour through all the precious operatic artifacts, the singer invited us to have refreshments and a chat. Paolo translated for Felicia and me. Ruffo wanted to know at once if his records were being played in America. When I assured him that all collectors of fine opera singing did still enjoy his voice, he demanded to know why he wasn't receiving any royalties. To bolster his case, he dug out a dusty contract, signed by him, with the Victor Talking Machine Company and waved it in front of me. I said I was a director and not a lawyer, but maybe the date on the contract (1908) had something to do with the problem. Well, if I was a director, said Ruffo, why wasn't a movie made of his life? I asked him if he had seen the film of the life of his beloved colleague, Enrico Caruso. He had not. Well, I said, if he had, he might not be too anxious to be immortalized in that way. Paolo's Italian translation of my words seemed to mollify Ruffo, and hoping to steer the conversation away from commerce and over to art, I asked the singer if any one of his recordings actually represented his live voice faithfully and, if so, which one? With no hesitation, he named the great aria of Hamlet, over the body of the dead Ophelia, in the last act of Ambroise Thomas's opera of the Shakespearean play. He had recorded "Come il romito fior" in 1908 when he was thirty-one years old and at the height of his vocal glory. What happened next in that room was unforgettable. The baritone went to a cabinet, brought out the very record, and placed it on one of those old table model windup Victrolas, inserting a new needle in the tone arm. Standing next to the machine as the glorious, youthful baritone sound poured forth, he suddenly closed his eyes and started to sing along with the record in still sweet though veiled tones. When he held his mouth open wide on the high F sharp toward the end, and no sound came from his throat as he, as well as we, experienced the thrill of the ineffably beautiful note pouring out of the phonograph, Felicia and I spouted tears, helplessly. We were barely able to pull ourselves together, to thank Titta Ruffo and get to the street. Up until her untimely death, whenever Felicia and I would meet, we had only to look at each other to relive that excruciatingly moving experience.

"Here comes Rosa Ponselle."

If you think the Ruffo episode was an emotional opera bath, here comes Rosa Ponselle. One of the dividends I hoped for when I accepted the job of directing two Harold Pinter one-act plays at the Center Stage in Baltimore, in 1971, was the chance that I might get to meet Ponselle. Until her death in 1981, she lived out her retirement in Stevenson, a suburb of Baltimore, in a house she called Villa Pace. "Pace, pace, mio Dio" was the aria from *La Forza del Destino* in which she made her Metropolitan début with Caruso in 1918, at the age of twenty-two. Two years later, she was to appear in *La Juive,* again with Caruso, in what would be his last stage appearance.

On my arrival in Baltimore, before I even unpacked my bags, I was on the phone to members of the Center Stage executive board trying to find out who might know Ponselle, or at least who might be able to get me an introduction to her. This was soon arranged, and I prepared myself to meet the singer who was considered, as a soprano, to be the equal of the tenor, Caruso. In fact, Ponselle was often referred to as "the female Caruso." The taxi dropped me on time at her imposing house, and I rang the doorbell. A secretary led the way through several rooms, finally depositing me on a couch in a large parlor with heavy drapes hung over the windows and French doors that apparently led to a patio. A large table in the center was loaded with mouthwatering foods of all kinds: various cheeses, choice meats, a huge basket of fruit, and dozens of Italian pastries—enough for the whole chorus of *Aida*. "Damn," I thought. "I wanted her all to myself. I didn't expect a party." As it turned out the whole banquet was laid out just for me; that is, if I could have consumed a morsel of it considering the emotional state building up in me.

Suddenly, I was propelled to my feet by the startling entrance of the star. She had obviously been waiting in the wings (the patio) and now, when the moment came, she whipped apart the drapes that were over the French doors and stood there, arms outstretched, for all the world like Bertha Kalich on her entrance in *Magda* that had thrilled me as a kid. I was in love again.

The singer then sat down on the couch and gestured for me to join her. Knowing I was a stage director not only of plays but musicals and operas, too, she launched into her ideas on acting in opera, taking as an example her performance of Violetta in *La Traviata.* In 1930, when Ponselle knew she was to sing the part for the first time, she traveled to Europe to study the role with Gemma Bellincioni (1864-1950) who had actually worked with Verdi himself. Ponselle, lying back on the couch, started from the top of the last act in Violetta's bedroom to delineate her every move and—this is what's important—her every thought, moment by moment, phrase by phrase. In the middle of reading the elder Germont's letter, she leapt up. Rushing to her record player, she whipped out a recording of one of her live performances of *Traviata* at a Saturday matinée (January 5, 1935) at the Met. As the whole last act unfolded, she sang along with the record, starting with the "Addio del passato." She "used" me as a partner for all the other characters, including her lover, Alfredo, and as her voice was still in unbelievably good condition, I was, of course, as close to being in heaven as a mortal opera lover can be. Her emotion as she sang, composed as it was of memories both of the part and of her life, spilled over and culminated in a death scene with Alfredo that had her crying and exhausted and me, with my head in her lap, sobbing uncontrollably. We stayed in this orgiastic state for some minutes. No conversation could follow this. She arose, took the three LP copies of the opera performance air checks and autographed each one: "To Bob—Love, Rosa," "To Bob—Happy Remembrance of your first visit to Villa Pace," and "To Bob Lewis—Lest we forget. Love, Rosa."

Don't worry, Rosa, I won't.

To segue now into Jane Pickens as Regina may shake up some opera purists. In point of fact, Jane Pickens, although famous as one of the vaudeville trio, the Pickens Sisters, was also the possessor of a good mezzo-soprano voice and had studied with none other than Marcella Sembrich, the soprano who graced the Metropolitan Opera stage during its opening week in 1883.

While I was in London staging *Brigadoon,* Marc Blitzstein finished composing the score of *Regina* in my Pound Ridge house. Since it was to be presented on Broadway, we hesitated calling *Regina* an opera, but that's what it was. Broadway audiences weren't apt to flock to a grand opera, and opera fans weren't too thrilled with Broadway musicals. As a result, *Regina* didn't find its true home until its revival in 1953, by the New York City Opera Company, at the City Center. Still, even on Broadway we needed operatic voices. Risë Stevens and Blanche Thebom, both comely American mezzos, respectfully declined the role of Regina. The thought of eight operatic performances a week sent shivers up their spines. Finally, when Jane Pickens auditioned, we settled. She was tall, handsome, Southern, and musicianly. We surrounded her with a fine cast that included the superb operatic actress, Brenda Lewis, as Birdie, and William Wilderman, with his beautiful bass voice, as Regina's husband, Horace.

When Tallulah heard I was going to direct *Regina,* which was the role in which she made her biggest American success, she asked who was going to play her part. When I said, "Jane Pickens," she cried, "Darling, I didn't even like her when she was one of the Andrews Sisters."

Libby Holman had expressed keen interest in playing Regina when she heard Marc and I, two of her best friends, were preparing a musical based on *The Little Foxes.* Both of us assured her that although she could manage the acting of the role, musically it was way out of her vocal range. She refused to believe us. Therefore, when she heard the news that Jane Pickens was selected, she felt betrayed. Marc and I were banned from her court, and she set about planning revenge. So sure was she that Pickens would have a disaster that Libby bought out the entire first row of the Shubert Theatre in New Haven for the world première on October 6, 1949, and filled the seats with her retinue. Marc, Cheryl, and I stood at the back of the orchestra, apprehensive as to what Libby and her cohorts might be up to. The curtain rose on the two black servants, Cal and Addie, singing a spiritual in front of the Giddens' house with Regina's daughter, Alexandra, joining in. A street band entered and played a jazz counterpoint to the spiritual, the whole thing building up in volume to Regina's entrance. For this, I had arranged an upstairs bedroom window, split down the middle, that opened from the inside when pushed with both hands. Regina's dressing gown had long hanging sleeves to it so that when she opened the two sides of the window and the sleeves hung down, she'd appear to be some huge, predatory bird. Well, the moment came. The music rose. Cal, Addie, and Alexandra were singing and dancing to the stage band, the window burst open, and Jane Pickens as Regina yelled down, "Alexandra!"

Seemingly on cue, a huge groan emerged from Libby Holman's throat. "This is too much," I whispered to Cheryl, and we rushed to get the house manager. Libby had fallen to the floor and was then carried up the aisle by her friends. An ambulance was summoned and she was taken to the New Haven hospital with a ruptured ulcer. She had actually "busted a gut."

The first task I set myself in the *Regina* rehearsals, facing a whole cast of opera singers, was how to dispel the prevailing notion that opera acting consists of lurching from one position on the stage to another while emitting sounds—even beautiful sounds—that come from the throat rather than from thought and feeling. I was determined to prove that the mere act of producing a singing tone didn't automatically shut off the workings of the brain and the heart. Pierre Boulez, in discussing the state of opera, topped Eleanora Duse's famous remark. In order to save the theater she had maintained, "The actors and actresses must all die of the plague." Boulez, for opera, with one crashing chord, proclaimed, "Bomb the opera houses!"

For decades, the Metropolitan Opera Company, for one example, has had a training program for young singers (the Kathryn Turney Long Courses). The curriculum consists of music coaching, language studies, body work, and instruction in stage deportment. You will notice that the references to acting all have to do with external movement, not even a word about the *source* of movement: thought and feeling. Maralin Niska, the lovely prima donna I directed in Carlisle Floyd's *Susannah* at the New York City Opera in 1971, would probably have liked to work on the "inner line" of her part, if we had had the time. Instead, in a sweet note of thanks after the performance, she said she loved my "blocking" (of her positions on stage). Martina Arroyo, the Metropolitan opera soprano, tells of practicing at home by walking around her living room *working out her movements,* while a tape recorder plays her singing of the part. In *Regina* I was determined to get more than movements out of my singers.

The first thing that was in my favor was time. I had five weeks, the allotted period for a Broadway musical. The rehearsal schedule of a working opera house is not in terms of weeks, or sometimes even of days. "You can have the prima donna on Tuesday for two hours, but she can't sing because she has a performance that evening," Sir Rudolf Bing told me when we had an interview, during which I was to decide whether I'd follow director Margaret Webster into the Met as the second recruit from the legitimate theater. The opera offered me was *Die Fledermaus.* "Will there be any other possible reason she cannot sing at rehearsal?" I asked. "Oh, yes," replied Sir Rudolf, "if she has sung the night before." I then asked him, "In what language do you plan to do *Die Fledermaus*?" "English, of course," said Bing. "Will anyone understand Madame if she sings in English?" I asked. "Not a word," said Bing. "Then why bother?" I queried. "What?" exclaimed Bing in mock horror. "A Broadway director, and you don't want opera in English?" A really funny guy, Sir Rudolf. I carefully crept away from the Met.

Now here I was on Broadway, with five weeks and willing opera actors. My first step was to rehearse the cast in the dialogue just as if we were to perform the play without music. Actually, the text was not too different from that in Hellman's play, *The Little Foxes.* When the inner line—the subtext (intentions)—was firmly set, I then called in the piano accompanist. Now, with the pianist playing the score, the actors still spoke the dialogue, but this time fitting it to the special requirements of the music. As an example, let's take the scene where Horace comes home from the hospital and his wife, Regina, confronts him for the first time in five months. She needs him to help her in a deal she wants to make with her brothers. Regina first "tries to break the ice" (her intention):

> *Regina*: Well.
> *Horace*: Well.
> *Regina*: Well, here we are. It's been a long time . . .

In the reading of the dialogue without the piano, Regina had picked up her cue from Horace's "Well" and had gone on immediately to "Well, here we are . . ." *But,* with the music playing, it turned out that there were four bars of rubato, cogitating-like music between Horace's "Well" and Regina's "Well, here we are." It now obliged the performer to fill in those four bars with the appropriate thinking; in this case, "to figure out the best way to deal with him since he's sick, and she needs action immediately." I had her maneuver herself around the back of him, while playing this intention during those four bars, so he could not see her plotting eyes. If the actress didn't account in her *thinking* for those four bars, she would have been left with one of the two options usually employed in opera during orchestral interludes, one, standing there trying to look generally interested, or two, making some physical move or cross simply to fill in the time.

The final step for the singing-actor was to add the vocal line—the notes. In opera houses, the learning of the music is usually done with an assistant conductor coaching the singers privately in the music. The performers are then turned over to the director who "blocks" the movement. Even if he drops some hint about the interpretation of the words, the singing (words plus music) has been so firmly drilled into the artist that the most that can be expected in the way of meaning is the use of appropriate, indicated facial expressions. But if the inner line of thinking has been set before, or along with, the learning of the music, you can forget working your face. It will work itself.

This method of rehearsal delivered double dividends. First, the result was a *sung play,* with clear characterizations and confrontations. Second, the problem of opera in English was automatically dealt with. I always suspected that the difficulty of understanding sung English had to do, not with diction alone, but with the lack of clear thinking. If you know what the actor's *objective* is, it goes a long way toward understanding what he's saying—in any language.

In a Donal Henahan *Sunday Times* piece, where he refers to opera in English as "one of the most overexplained and under-understood subjects in all of music," Mr. Henahan maintains that when an American singer "delivers the familiar lines of a Mozart comedy in his own language . . . we hear the singer inflecting phrases and touching them with subtle meanings rather than merely shaping them in elemental musical ways." So far, so good. But it must be pointed out that these "subtle meanings" are not to be found in the words alone, but in the *intention* behind those words. This is uncovered by an analysis of the subtext, as well as the text, plus the meanings derived from the music itself. Acting derives not only from the literal sense of the words but by what is intended to be *conveyed* by them. It is this all-important element in the craft of acting that suffers almost total neglect in the training of singing actors and in the preparation of opera roles.

The five rehearsal weeks I had for the Broadway production of *Regina* gave me a good chance to work on the singers' "insides" as well as their "outsides." It would be a big step forward if the opera houses and music schools would begin to think about including this aspect of training *before* the singers have to face up to the problem in performance. Alan Rich, in *New York* magazine, made this pathetic plea: "Could the Met, or the City Opera, broaden its base of operation so that a singer is trained in the internals, as well as being prepared in the externals, of his performance? Don't ask me if the money for something like this could be found, but wouldn't it be wonderful if it could?" Don't hold your breath, Alan. I've tried to sell this point to the Met and other opera houses and to Juilliard and other schools. No luck, so far.

Certain specific points made in the critics' review of *Regina* confirmed the efficacy of the rehearsal procedure we adopted. Mr. Atkinson in *The New York Times* summed it up: "Since *Regina* is in the operatic form, the cast has to be chosen for the ability to sing. Let it be said, at once, that they are all good singers, with excellent voices, and knowledge of vocal music. But that is less remarkable than the fact that, under Mr. Lewis's direction, they act with complete understanding of the characters they are playing and with ability to project and move and express points of view. On theatrical terms, the performance is exciting. The characters are developed from the inside out; and the operatic form in which most of the dialogue is sung does not seem artificial."

Arthur Pollock of the *Compass* put it this way: "The actors not only sing and act like singers who are actors and actors who happen at the same time to be singers, but they do it superbly, like actors who, though these are not, are products of long experience in this kind of fusion of drama and music.

"The direction of such a production must, you would guess, have demanded a kind of director that does not exist. But there is, obviously, one, Robert Lewis, who has learned, somewhere in parts unknown, just how music and drama may be made to speak as one."

Between the New Haven première and the Broadway opening, *Regina* played a Boston engagement at the Colonial Theatre. One night, after the performance, Mike Todd and his then wife, Joan Blondell, came backstage to see me. Mike began, "I want a pup out of you." "A what?" I asked, not knowing what the hell he was talking about. (He seemed like a good-looking Billy Rose.) I turned to Blondell for a translation. All she came up with was, "Isn't he a card?"

"I saw your show tonight," Mike went on, "and now you're going to do one for me. I'm producing *My Darlin' Aida,* and it has the greatest book and score in history." "If the music is still Verdi's," I said, "I can agree with you about the score. But how's the book? I'd like to read it." "You don't have to read it," said Mike, "I'm telling you, it's the greatest." "Isn't he a card?" asked Joan. "Well, Mr. Todd," I said, "if you say so, I'm sure it's great, but since I do have to read it sometime, I'd really prefer reading it before I direct it. Besides, I've already signed a contract with Rodgers and Hammerstein to do a play called *The Happy Time,* after *Regina* opens in New York." Mike leveled a look at me. "You don't have a con*tract,* Bobby, you have a con*flict.*" I looked to Joan for her comment. She obliged.

Well, Mike did send me the book. It took the *Aida* story, laid in Egypt during the reign of the pharoahs, which was written by an Italian, Ghislanzoni, from the French of Camille du Locle, after a sketch by an Egyptologist, Mariette Bey, and plunked it down in the American South, at the time of the Civil War. After ploughing through a dozen pages, I returned the script to Todd with, "Thanks, but no thanks," and awaited the arrival of a couple of guys who would undoubtedly drop me into a cement mixer. Nothing happened, though, and I attributed that to dear Joan Blondell, who probably told Mike to go easy on me. Recently, I learned from S. J. Perelman's unfinished autobiography that he had a similar experience with Todd. The humorist was roughly threatened by Mike after Sid turned down the offer to make a screenplay of Cervantes's *Don Quixote* saying, "The truth is, Mike, no matter how many times I've tried to read *Don Quixote,* I've never been able to get beyond page six." Since I made page twelve of Mike's *My Darlin' Aida,* I feel I paid my dues, and then some.

As predicted, the opera *Regina* didn't survive the rigors of Broadway more than a couple of months, although it had its enthusiastic partisans. There was a demonstration in front of the Forty-sixth Street Theatre on closing night, with picket signs reading "*Regina* has been stabbed." By 1952, these partisans had grown to such a number that when we put on a concert version of the opera at the Ninety-second Street "Y" with the original cast, literally thousands of people were turned away.

I arranged the concert with a semicircle of chairs for the artists who would arise as their solos, duets, or whatever, came up, step down front center to perform and then return to their seats. On stage right was the orchestra, led by Maurice Levine, and in an armchair on the left, sat Lillian Hellman, who read the connectives between the numbers. Only the week before, Lillian had made her celebrated appearance before the House Un-American Activities Committee. After her entrance applause at the "Y" had died down, and before she read her introduction, Lillian adlibbed, "This seat is a lot more comfortable than the one I've been sitting in lately." The evening was off to a good start.

The following spring, the success of the "Y" concert version led to the booking of the piece by the New York City Opera at the old Mecca Temple on West Fifty-fifth Street. This time, Brenda Lewis replaced Jane Pickens as Regina, Marc having revised the role slightly for a dramatic soprano instead of a mezzo. William Wilderman, making his New York City Opera début, again sang Horace, Regina's husband, as he did in the Broadway production. The opera company could afford to schedule three performances that season, since the *Regina* scenery from the original production had, fortunately, been stashed away by Cheryl Crawford in a horse barn on the Pound Ridge property of her associate producer in the Broadway version, Clinton Wilder. Mysteriously, two large props were missing however. One was the beautiful chandelier, which had hung over the Giddens's living room, designed by Horace Armistead. (The room's wallpaper pattern, evoking the jungle metaphor of the predatory family, featured trees and branches laced with bloody red streaks, causing Agnes de Mille to remark, "I loved that set with the old family placenta on the walls.") The City Opera Company could only afford to replace the chandelier with a cardboard cutout. But it didn't look too bad due to the tactful lighting of the late, great Jean Rosenthal.

The other important absent prop was one of those little blackamoor statues that horses used to be hitched up to. William Dillard had a number called "Chinky-pin," in which he used the little statue as the partner he sang to, so it was an important prop. I asked Aline Bernstein, our costume designer, what we could do on our limited budget. "Come with me," she said, and off we went to the "21" Club on Fifty-second Street. Aline had white hair, a beautiful face and she could flirt like a young girl. Approaching "21" owner, Jack Kriendler, she turned her big eyes on him and told him our plight. He couldn't resist her. One of the famous statues that adorn the steps in front of the restaurant was ripped from its moorings, placed in a cab with Aline and me, and taken to its place on the set of *Regina*. "21" had finally made up for its refusal of a table to Saroyan and me on the opening night of *My Heart's in the Highlands*.

*Regina:* "The old family placenta on the walls."

Now that *Regina* was in an opera house, the music critics took over from their theater brethren. The production was praised again, but this time the composer, Marc Blitzstein, got his due. Howard Taubman, in *The New York Times,* called *Regina* "one of the best operas any American has written." The point about opera singers acting was covered by Arthur Berger, music critic of the *New York Herald-Tribune*: "Robert Lewis, who directed the Cheryl Crawford production, was on hand again to direct this one, and when it comes to making singers really act, he seems to me to have been more successful than any director I can recall who has worked in any of our local opera houses."

I recently uncovered an interesting sidelight on *Regina* by reading in the *Metropolitan Opera News* of a production of the opera in Houston, in the spring of 1980. The article stated, "Maralin Niska, in preparation for an April production of Blitzstein's *Regina* with the Houston Opera, discussed the heroine with Jane Pickens, who originated the part on Broadway, in 1949. From this meeting grew the Niska concept that Regina is not vicious, but the victim of male domination, driven to outwit brothers who have suppressed her—an early libber." (Are you listening, Lillian?)

I was hard put to understand how the greedy Regina was going to be transformed into Gloria Steinem, until I read the review of the performance in a subsequent *Opera News,* which explained, "Regina did not goad Horace into a heart seizure and then refuse to fetch his pills; she caused his death by negligence rather than intent, taking some of the sting out of Blitzstein's and Hellman's message." Suddenly, it was all clear to me. When I directed Jane Pickens in 1949, I felt she had a reluctance, as so many performers do, of appearing unsympathetic on the stage. Also, she was a Christian Scientist, and not only made herself concentrate on "good" thoughts all the time but tried to get the vixenish Regina to do the same. (Marc once thought of calling his musicalization of *The Little Foxes, The Vixen.*) My job was to toughen up Jane's insides without her feeling she was playing a bad girl. I therefore explained every wicked thing Regina had to do as being necessary and "good" for her, her daughter, her family, etc. When we came to Horace's death scene, any charge of murderous complicity on Regina's part was kept a deep secret from Jane. But my staging made it crystal clear that Regina, facing away from Horace, hears Horace's bottle of heart medicine drop to the floor and break, hears Horace say, "The other bottle, upstairs," hears Horace go to the stairs himself when he realizes she is not going to move, hears Horace collapse on the stairs, and *then* she gets up, goes over to Horace and, making sure he's dead, calls for help. It was not too easy for me to convince Jane that Regina was thinking of something else all during this and didn't know what was happening, so she could feel innocent of contributing to Horace's death. But Jane believed me, passed on *her* understanding of the character of Regina to Maralin Niska, and that's how operatic "traditions" are born.

When Julius Rudel, who had conducted the City Center *Regina* so expertly, was made General Director of the New York City Opera at Lincoln Center, he offered me productions to direct several times. The first opera was a new one, but I didn't like the libretto. The second was *Traviata,* but the rehearsal time conflicted with a play I was planning to direct. Finally, in 1971, he sent me *Susannah* by Carlisle Floyd, which had been done several times by the New York City Opera Company under several different stage directors. I hesitated to accept because I knew that as many times as people maintain, "we want a new approach," they always end up saying, "but when we did it before we . . ." Moreover, the leading male role of the evangelist, Olin Blitch, had always been played by the wonderful singing-actor, Norman Treigle, and the part had, by now, become his personal property. Any further exploration of it might not be looked on too favorably by him.

Ultimately, I overcame my disinclination to accept Julius's offer, mainly because of my wish to work in an opera house that would be more receptive to the problem of acting than the Met was. Unfortunately, the experience turned out to be one of those "slow deaths" that cured me forever of wanting to direct in an opera house.

When Peter Hall was named to succeed Laurence Olivier as Director of Britain's National Theatre, he wrote an article for the Sunday *New York Times* (Oct. 29, 1972) in which he spoke of his experiences directing opera: "The drama's problem in opera is not singers, or the demands of conductors, or the vagaries of individual managements, but the worldwide system for churning out the maximum amount of opera with the minimum amount of rehearsal." The Metropolitan Opera's manner of preparing a performance caused Margaret Webster to refer to that place as "Heartbreak House." The New York City Opera's sausage-factory approach at that time led me to dub it "Heartburn House."

The problem with rehearsing an opera is not only that the allotted time is inadequate, but that it is so sporadic. On different days you get this or that principal for a bit, and the chorus for a few hours in all. One day Maralin Niska (Susannah) couldn't show because she was singing in Houston. Another time, Treigle would be playing Mefistofele. And always, other operas are being prepared at the same time as yours with the same singers. There can be no cumulative results of the work, only patching things together. It is a miracle when any good productions emerge.

One day in the rehearsal room, I had run through a number with David Hall, the young singer who was playing a sort of mentally retarded character called "Little Bat." At the end of the piece he exited through the door and kept going. I yelled at him to come back as we had only gone through the section once, and I had quite a few corrections to give him. "I can't stay," he called back. "I have a rehearsal of *Cosi Fan Tutte.* I must go down the hall." Stanislavski had always said an actor should know where he was coming from when he entered a scene, and where he was going when he exited. This kid was going into another show.

Next: the chorus. Having been brought up in the Group Theatre where we were taught that no part, however small, could be performed with less devotion to truthful detail than the leading parts, I always insisted that each member of a crowd, or a chorus, have an identity and create an individual characterization. If the chorus behave as a mass of unidentifiable bodies, the principals have to live in a phony world, and *their* believability is threatened in turn. Since I didn't have nearly enough rehearsal time to work with individual members of the *Susannah* chorus, you can imagine my delight when I noticed one of them beginning to develop a characterization of her own. I immediately made her the lone "secret" friend of Susannah in the village, unable to stand up for her friend openly against the stern elders and the bigoted women. Her wish, however frustrated, to side with Susannah, helped dramatize the conflict.

Then it began. The first objection to any such humanizing of even one member of the crowd was manifested by disdainful sniffs from the other chorus members. "Julie Harris" they dubbed her, although it was never clear to me how that name could possibly be thought a term of opprobrium. But while the other chorus members of AGMA merely considered this creative girl uppity (the fact that, try as I will, I cannot remember her name is testimony to her chorus status in the hierarchy of the operatic firmament) the bigwigs were definitely worried. Julius Rudel, who was not only to conduct the work, but was the boss of the City Opera, took a look. When I explained that I was trying to keep the village from being just black and white—all evil (the Preacher and the mountain folk) or all-virtuous (Susannah)—and thus avoid accenting the inherent melodrama of the story, Julius did not say "no" to the effort to create one live character in the amorphous chorus group. What he did, instead, was to ask me to excise just a couple of little moves that he felt might call too much attention to the girl. I complied. The next time he saw the crowd scene, he'd take away another tiny bit until the part was whittled down to meaninglessness. Finally, Julius said it: "Get rid of that girl." I didn't, but I removed the last tiny vestiges of her character so they wouldn't look like mistakes. As each idea of my production concept went down the drain, I began to smell that poison gas that stifles creativity so effectively in the theater.

Why, you might ask, wasn't it possible for the director to have charge of the direction and the conductor take charge of the conducting? It isn't possible when the conductor is the general director of the opera company too. It would be equally unthinkable for me to tell Julius he was playing too loud. Actually, he was. One of the many things Donal Henahan objected to in his *Times* review was that "Much of the night, the orchestra sounded as if it were going at 'Die Walküre' rather than Mr. Floyd's musically flimsy opera."

Now we come to the late Mr. Treigle. I had hoped to get together with this great singing actor in an attempt to remove any possible traces of conventional villain from the part. To avoid the cliché (Reverend Davidson in *Rain*), I prepared suggestions for humanizing the part of the evangelist to make believable what could easily become pure melodrama. However, I never got to communicate any of my ideas to Treigle and certainly never worked on them in what few rehearsals we had. He arrived from New Orleans too late for any individual sessions. And in his rehearsals with the company, in the crucial revival scene particularly, he never did more than "mark" his part (walk through it). Not ever being sure what the preacher was going to do made it difficult for me to set the reactions of the crowd. I had asked one old woman at what was supposed to be the height of the reverend's passionate sermon on hell, to drop her head back in an ecstatic fainting spell. Treigle, in the classic tradition of stars who think in terms of *my* scene instead of *the* scene, was quite categoric: "If she does that, I'm not staying on the stage."

*Susannah:* Norman Treigle and Maralin Niska: "The question of the black suit."

Then there was the question of the black suit Treigle had always worn in this part. Patton Campbell, the costume designer, and I, felt a sort of tan summer suit would be less of a cliché and finally persuaded Treigle to accept the idea. Frank Corsaro had split with Treigle on the issue of the suit, too, when Corsaro directed *Susannah* in an earlier production. So when Treigle agreed to drop the conventional black suit, Bonnie Leuders, Corsaro's wife, who played one of the village women in the production, whispered to me, "You don't know what a hero you are around here for getting Treigle to wear that tan suit." Little did she know, and little did I know. During the intermission on the opening night, I went backstage to Treigle's dressing room, where he was sitting in his dressing gown, to congratulate him on his introductory scene in the first act. Believe it or not, even though I was the director, I witnessed his actual acting of the part for the first time from my seat in the audience at the opening performance. I wished Treigle good luck on his big revival scene in the church, which was to come up in the second act and went back out front. Treigle had worn the tan suit in his short opening scene, but when the lights came up on the big revival scene, there was Reverend Olin Blitch in his old black suit. I would never understand how a superb artist like Treigle could lean toward a stereotype.

The *Times,* in its poor review of my production by Donal Henahan, referred to the direction as "melodramatic," the one word I had tried so assiduously, all through rehearsals, to avoid. I know the *Times* music review is from the true Bible, but *Susannah* is an Apocryphal tale, so perhaps I'll be forgiven if I quote a contradictory opinion from the more mythic *New York Post.* Harriet Johnson, remembering the previous productions of *Susannah,* maintained that this version "projects the work even more humanly as drama and with more subtle currents and cross currents expressed through the characterizations . . . Lewis has directed Miss Niska and Treigle to be searingly real through making their sequences of movements logical as the inevitability of a Beethoven development section."

It takes a powerful effort on the part of the recipient to refute such praise. But, by then, my own embittered feelings were more sympathetic than shocked when one of the stagehands I happened to know from the legitimate theater greeted me backstage on the opening performance of the opera with, "Hope you find something good on Broadway soon—not this crap."

CHAPTER 15

# The Fifties

AS FAR AS my personal output was concerned, they really were the "fabulous fifties." In addition to the two *Regina* revivals already mentioned—the concert version at the Ninety-second Street "Y" (1952) and the one at the City Center Opera (1953)—I directed the following stage productions during the decade:

1950: *The Happy Time* (a Rodgers and Hammerstein production—New York and touring companies)
*Enemy of the People* (Arthur Miller's version of Ibsen's play with Fredric March)
1952: *The Grass Harp* (Truman Capote's first play)
1953: *The Teahouse of the August Moon* (Maurice Evans production—Broadway and London versions)
1954: *Witness for the Prosecution* (Gilbert Miller, producer—New York and touring companies)
1955: *Reuben Reuben* (Cheryl Crawford production)
1956: *Mister Johnson* (directed and co-produced with Cheryl Crawford)
1957: *The Hidden River* (by Ruth and Augustus Goetz)
*Jamaica* (Lena Horne in a David Merrick musical)
1958: *Handful of Fire* (David Susskind, producer)
1959: *Candide* (London production of Leonard Bernstein's musical)
*Chéri* (by Colette, directed and co-produced with the Playwrights' Company)
*Juniper and the Pagans* (by *Teahouse* author John Patrick)

In 1955, I also went west to direct a film musical for Paramount Pictures—*Anything Goes*—with an all-star cast headed by Bing Crosby, and a new book, but the original Cole Porter score.

My teaching chores continued too, in between productions, throughout the decade. I returned to the Yale School of Drama for a couple of stints in 1950 and 1951 and established my own Robert Lewis Theatre Workshop in 1952, which continues to this day. By far the most important "happening" of the decade, as far as my role as a teacher is concerned, was a 1957 series of lectures I gave at the old Playhouse Theatre, for eight Monday nights at 11:30 P.M., to which I invited all professional actors. The series was called "Method—or Madness?" and was an attempt to clear the air of the confusion surrounding the Stanislavski System. These lectures were published the following year by Samuel French, and again, in 1960 in an edition for England, published by Heinemann, Ltd. Two years later, the book was translated into Portuguese by Barbara Heliodora in Brazil.

It was a period of highs and lows. Commercially, *The Teahouse of the August Moon* was the most successful play I directed, while *Reuben Reuben* and *Juniper and the Pagans* both closed out of town. From the artistic point of view, the distance went all the way from the satisfaction of the "Method—or Madness?" lectures to the depths of an agonizing stint as the film director of *Anything Goes.*

My first stage play in the fifties contradicted the old theatrical saw that happy rehearsal periods end in disastrous openings and vice versa. Samuel Taylor's *The Happy Time,* produced by Rodgers and Hammerstein, was a joy to rehearse and came in a hit. The first order of business was the casting, and on Broadway, with casting comes the bugbear—auditioning. No one likes being on trial, and for certain sensitive actors, exposing themselves to these merciless tests is impossible. Such a one was Maureen Stapleton. Knowing her extraordinary talent from classes, I would ask her any time I was casting a play that had a part even remotely in her range. Getting her in to audition for the author and producer was something else again.

I desperately wanted Maureen for the mother (Maman) of the freewheeling French-Canadian family of *The Happy Time.* We had had no luck with the many actresses that had been sent in to try out for the part. I explained to Dick Rodgers and Oscar Hammerstein about Maureen's fear of auditions, and they were sympathetic. "We believe you about her talent as an actress, Bobby," said Dick, "but wouldn't it be nice if she'd just walk on to the stage and let us meet her—not to do a scene—but at least to give the author a chance to see what one of his leading characters looks like?" "Seems reasonable," I said. "I'll ask her."

"No, no, no," pleaded Maureen on hearing the producers' cruel request. "I could never go out there and face them."

"Look," I said. "There's nothing to be afraid of. You don't have to read. They're all nice guys who just want to meet you."

*The Happy Time:* The director (Lewis) flanked by the producers (Rodgers, right, and Hammerstein, left), with the playwright (Sam Taylor) standing. "A joy to rehearse."

"What will I have to do?"

"Nothing. They'll probably say 'hello.' And then you'll say 'hello,' and it'll all be over in a jiffy."

"I'll try," said Maureen. "But I have my doubts."

"Just put on a simple dress, comb your hair, be as beautiful as you are, get the part, and then we'll have loads of fun in rehearsal," I promised.

Well, the great day came. Dick and Oscar, Sam Taylor, and I sat about half way back in the orchestra of the Plymouth Theatre listening to actors auditioning for one or another of the characters in the play, when Johnny Fearnley, our stage manager, stepped out and announced, "Miss Maureen Stapleton."

Pause. Then a creature, about half the height of the Maureen I knew and loved so well, crept out of the wings and landed about a quarter of the way on to the stage. Terrified, Maureen seemed to be sucking in her cheeks to the disappearing point and smiling maniacally at the same time. It's not easy.

Those of you lucky enough to have seen Maureen later in *The Rose Tattoo* will remember the scene where Serafina hopefully awaits the arrival of her new friend, Mangiacavallo, who has attracted her because on his chest he has a tattoo of a rose, just like her dear dead husband's. Maureen sat stiffly on the edge of the sofa, hardly able to breathe for having gotten herself gussied up and corsetted within an inch of her life for the great event. That picture was similar to what greeted the startled eyes of Rodgers and Hammerstein.

Oscar leaned toward me. "Is she sick?" he asked. "Well, not exactly," I replied. "Then what's she doing?" demanded Dick.

"I think she's being pretty for you," I offered, defeated, knowing we were all still looking for our Maman.

Leora Dana eventually was cast in the part, but getting her to the audition was an even crazier experience than the one with Maureen. Only this time the fault was mine. I had seen a play the previous summer (1949) at the Westport Country Playhouse called *A Story for a Sunday Evening*, by and with Paul Crabtree. There were also two women in the cast, Cloris Leachman, whom I knew as a member of Gadget's class in the Actors Studio, and Leora Dana. When Dick Rodgers suggested that Leora try out for Maman, I thought he was balmy. You see, as he mentioned the name of the part he saw Leora play in Westport, I was firmly convinced he was referring to Cloris. (I still don't believe it wasn't a misprint in the program, with the names of the two actresses reversed in the cast list.)

Anyway, with Cloris's look and demeanor in that play firmly in my mind, I peered at Dick pityingly and assured him she was not at all what we were looking for. Being a good producer, he was not going to force someone on me that I was convinced was wrong for what was needed. However, after each fruitless day of seeing prospective Mamans, Dick would gently suggest that since we were auditioning practically every available actress in Equity, perhaps we might read Leora Dana, too. Finally, just to end it by proving how wrong his suggestion was, I agreed to hear her. (Can you believe these directors?)

Next day, Johnny Fearnley stepped on the stage and announced, "Leora Dana." Out walked the girl who in my mind was Cloris Leachman. What do you think I said? "You're not Leora Dana!" Looking genuinely confused (and if you knew her, you'll believe this), Leora replied, "I'm not?"

"No," I persisted. "You're Cloris Leachman."

"I am?" asked Leora.

Well, the upshot was that after reading only a few minutes, she had the part. This time it was the director who shrunk to half his size. Dick Rodgers never said a word.

The irony of the story, as I now look back on it, is that the very real Cloris Leachman, who went on to sweep up every acting award since, could undoubtedly have played the part just fine, too. So much for the omniscience of directors.

The whole business of the French-Canadian accents in *The Happy Time* was taken out of my hands by the playwright's instructions on the first page of the script under the list of characters: "It is not the author's intention that they speak with an accent." Well, nobody did. That is, nobody spoke with a French-Canadian accent. But we ended up with nearly everything else. Claude Dauphin, who played Papa, had a fine, pronounced Parisian accent. Edgar Stehli, the Grandpère, although born in France, spoke rather British English. Kurt Kasznar, Uncle Louis, was Viennese, with plenty of whipped cream in his consonants. The Americans in the cast threw doubt on their presumed French-Canadian heritage when confronted with such jawbreaking French expressions as "C'est possible" or "Mais oui."

Talking of "mais oui," there was Eva Gabor making her dramatic debut on Broadway as the maid, Mignonette. Everyone who owns a television tube knows Eva has parlayed her pronunciation of "v" for "w" into a major ingredient of her long career. When she had to utter the monosyllabic French word "oui" in the play, it came out "vee."

"Eva," I pleaded, "if you can't say a simple word like 'oui' correctly, no one is going to believe you're French-Canadian."

"Vot should I say, dolling?" she asked.

"Oui," I said.

"Dot's vot I'm saying, dolling. Vee."

"Look. Forget we're talking French, Eva. Say the following English sentence 'We are there.'"

"We are there."

"Good. Great!" I clapped my hands in admiration. "Now leave off the last word 'there.'"

"We are," said Eva. We both applauded.

"Now—leave off the 'are.'" I held my breath.

"Vee."

"All right," I said, realizing there were a couple of other things I had to rehearse in the production, "when Papa brings you into the house, and Maman asks, 'What does she do?' instead of replying, 'She is an acrobat,' Papa will simply say, 'She's a Hungarian acrobat.'"

Whatever their accents, *The Happy Time* company was a truly happy one, all through rehearsals and during the long run. On matinée days, most of the actors stayed in the theater between shows and had company teas with sandwiches and cookies they'd brought along. Not only did the usual intramural romantic attachments develop, but Leora Dana and Kurt Kasznar actually got married. Thereafter, most of the company repaired nightly to their Eighth Avenue apartment near the theater for refreshments. I had not witnessed such camaraderie among actors since the days of the Group Theatre.

There was but a single incident that disturbed the usually calm atmosphere of *The Happy Time* and that one occurred January 24, 1950, on the opening night in New York. I had finished visiting the actors in their dressing rooms and taken my seat in the orchestra of the Plymouth Theatre, waiting for the first curtain to go up. Suddenly, I saw the pass door from the auditorium to the stage open, and Johnny Fearnley came through and made straight for me.

"Please come backstage immediately," he whispered. I followed him, inquiring what the trouble was.

"Kurt says he can't go on."

"What?" I yelled in disbelief, as I made a beeline for Kasznar's dressing room. There the poor fellow sat at his makeup table, shaking with terror and dripping perspiration. I recognized a classic case of stage fright. Kurt had had but one other part in a previous Broadway production, and then he only played the piano onstage in a scene. I had to think fast.

"Why do you suppose you can't go on?" I asked him. "What do you feel will happen if you do?"

"I just know I'll faint if I do," he pleaded.

"Oh," I said, acting relieved. "Is that all? Well, I happen to know something about that. It's a scientific fact, and you can check this with any doctor, that it is psychologically impossible to faint while you're out there. The adrenalin that's being pumped into your system when you're in front of an audience prevents the blood being drawn from your head. So you can't faint onstage." I was improvising madly. "Now, of course, as soon as you come off, you'll probably faint in the wings." I had to promise him something.

"I will try," said Kurt, buying my medical prognosis somewhat reluctantly.

"I'm not worried at all," I lied, as I went back to my seat.

It was hard for me to concentrate on the first scene because Uncle Louis

Kurt Kasznar as Uncle Louis in *The Happy Time*: "He forgot to faint."

wasn't in it. But in the second scene, when Kurt arrived onstage, screaming at his wife, drinking from his wine-filled water-cooler carried under his arm, he got his first good laugh from the audience, and that was the adrenalin I had promised him. He was fine from then on and even forgot to faint when he came offstage.

Pleasant as the success of *The Happy Time* was, a nagging sense of guilt that I ought to retreat from show business and exercise my heavier creative muscles persisted. Although high-minded culture watchers could easily criticize my riding the seesaw of artistic enterprise on the one hand, and simple entertainment on the other, I wish they would tell me how else I could have worked continuously in the American theater for well over half a century.

The Actors Studio *Sea Gull* may have been painful to rehearse because of my situation with Gadget, but the result on the stage gave me deep satisfaction, whereas putting on *The Happy Time* was a lark but didn't quite satisfy that critical little man watching inside me.

Chekhov and Ibsen being two of my favorite world playwrights, I was lucky to be able to follow the Russian with the powerful Norwegian. I turned to *An Enemy of the People*. Fredric March and his wife, Florence Eldridge, had been asked to play Dr. Stockmann and his wife by a Scandinavian producer named Lars Nordenson. The translation that the Marches

*An Enemy of the People:* rehearsal shot. Morris Carnovsky, Fredric March, Florence Eldridge, and the director.

sent me with a view to my assuming the direction was by an Englishman, and I didn't like it at all. I said I'd do the play if a new and proper version could be made.

Translation of the work of great authors is a notoriously tricky business. Too much faithfulness to the original words can make the new language seem "unspeakable" for the stage. Too much intrusion by the translator into the playwright's creation, in the guise of "adaptation," can wreck the original. What is needed is a writer who can preserve the meaning of the text but reproduce it in its new form with such freshness that it will seem to have been written in the language of the translation. But how to find a playwright sensitive enough to accomplish this and willing to devote his time and creative energies to someone else's baby?

The first thing I wanted to know was exactly what Ibsen had written in Norwegian. I asked Nordenson, who had a copy of the director's script of the original production, to go through the play speech by speech and tell me, literally, what the Norwegian words meant. When he'd stop and give me two or three possible meanings in English of certain key words, I realized how much had been missed in previous translations of the play. Arthur Miller was in my mind as first choice for translator, but I worried that I couldn't convince him to spend his time on another's work, even Ibsen's, Arthur's ideal as a playwright of ideas. *Death of a Salesman* had gathered up all the awards a little over a year before, and Miller had his own exciting writing career to pursue. But I knew there was a chance if Arthur could hear Lars Nordenson's literal translation of Ibsen's Norwegian. He did and was intrigued by the challenge. But—and it was a big but—Arthur found himself disturbed by two major points in the play. One was Stockmann's insistence that the majority is always wrong. The other was Ibsen's use of the word "aristocrats" for revolutionary thinkers.

The first objection was easy to overcome as Arthur could, upon examination, embrace the "majority" statement as a cry to protect political minorities in critical times. The second point, about aristocracy, sent me scurrying to do some research at the Theatre Collection of the New York Public Library on Forty-second Street, then under the capable direction of the late George Freedley. (The Lincoln Center Theatre Library was more than a decade away.) I came up with a speech to a club of workers that Ibsen had made after *An Enemy of the People* opened. He explained his use of aristocracy this way: "Of course, I do not mean the aristocracy of birth, or of the purse, or even the aristocracy of the intellect. I mean the aristocracy of character, of will, of mind—that alone can free us." No reason for Arthur not to buy that, and we were on our way.

In addition to Freddie and Florence March, I cast two former Group Theatre colleagues in leading roles, Art Smith as Mrs. Stockmann's father and Morris Carnovsky as Stockmann's brother, the Mayor of the town. In various other parts were a generous sampling of Actors Studio members, the final name in the list of the crowd of townspeople being Rod Steiger. Surrounding oneself this way with familiar faces may seem a form of nepotism. Actually, it's an attempt to create even for a single production, a sense of a smooth-working ensemble. A common approach makes the process of rehearsal more rewarding.

One episode marred the preparation of the production. In the play, Mrs. Stockmann's sense of protecting her family, even though standing by her husband's battle for the truth, called for a quality of simple practicality, which was tough to get into Florence Eldridge's performance. She had a touch of the disease that afflicts the work of some talented American leading actresses: the need to be "sympathetic." Arthur sensed this wish of Florence's to be loved by the audience. Blowing his top in the middle of a scene one day at a run-through, Arthur yelled up to Mrs. March, "Why must you be so fucking noble?" It was a correct acting note, but it came in the wrong form, at the wrong time, from the wrong person. There is often a moment when the playwright feels the director is never going to get a result they both know must be achieved. Sometimes they're right. But, right or wrong this time, Arthur had unleashed an atomic bomb. Florence flew off the stage and into her dressing room, followed by her equally anguished husband. The Marches insisted neither of them would return to the production until Arthur apologized in front of the company. The playwright compromised by offering a private apology, and the Marches finally accepted that. The rehearsals continued.

Fredric March, in the opinion of all knowledgeable theater people, gave

*An Enemy of the People:* onstage party. Standing: Lars Nordenson, producer. Sitting left to right: R. Lewis, director, A. Miller, playwright, F. March, star. On March's lap: Mrs. March. On Miller's lap: the first Mrs. Miller.

the best stage performance of his life as Dr. Stockmann. The daily critics agreed with *Newsweek,* which maintained, "March gives a performance that builds in power to a climax that packs more sheer theatrical force than any to be seen currently on the New York stage." Louis Sheaffer called it "probably the finest performance of his distinguished career."

When Arthur Miller autographed my copy of the published play, he probably was thinking of the fact that, although his version of *An Enemy of the People* received good notices in the newspapers, the public only bought thirty-six performances. In March of 1951, the playwright wrote on the flyleaf:

> Dear Bob:
>
> The God of the Theatre is the old God—the last incarnation of Jehovah, and his ways are crazy, his wrath insane, and his son did come from the North to lead us.
>
> Whatever else is to be said, we bucked the time, and stood for Man—and that is more than a little to have done.
>
> Good luck.
>
> Art Miller

The lesson I learned preparing Truman Capote's *The Grass Harp* for the stage was that it doesn't necessarily help to be a successful and elegant writer of stories, short and long, when brought face to face with the theater's inelegant, but inexorable, laws (vide Henry James). My own initial mistake was to agree to direct the play as a result of enthusiasm generated after reading only the first half. I found what I read to be charming, fanciful, funny, and moving. While waiting for Truman to finish the second half of the play, which he was adapting from his own story, we proceeded with the casting. Virgil Thomson was assigned the job of composing an incidental musical score, and Truman chose his friend Cecil Beaton to design the sets and costumes. I wrote a long letter to Beaton, who was in England, apprising him of my plans for the first half of the play and my guesses for the second half.

In the novel of *The Grass Harp* there was a character called Sister Ida who had fifteen children "and no sign of a husband!" Sensing that fifteen kids on the stage might prove unwieldy, Truman invented a different character for the second act of the play to replace Sister Ida. She was called Miss Baby Love Dallas, purveyor of "Sweetheart Cosmetics." Her scene was a capricious vaudeville turn, having nothing to do with the rest of the play, and out of style with it. This fault was compounded by the casting of Alice Pearce in the part of Baby Love. She, too, was a dear friend of Capote's and a favorite cult comic of small but swank nightclubs. I tried to warn Truman that everything that was good in Alice as an eccentric entertainer would only serve to make this section of the play seem even more of an interpolated number.

"Tell y' what," said Tru. "You have to hear it, not read it. If it doesn't work in rehearsal, I'll change it. That's what rehearsals are for, aren't they?"

At the first run-through, I conveyed to Truman my conviction, which was agreed with by Annie Laurie Williams, his bright literary agent who was present, that the first act seemed to work fine, but the overall mood and style of the performance was interrupted by Baby Love's cavortings in the second half, and the play never got back on its tracks again.

"Tell y' what," said Tru. "It needs an audience. If it doesn't work in Boston, I'll change it. That's why we go on the road, isn't it?"

Well, on March 13, 1952, we opened at the Colonial Theatre, and Elinor Hughes in the *Boston Herald* hit the nail squarely on the head: "Miss Pearce had about as much to do with the play as a passing butterfly lighting on Mr. Beaton's tree."

I confronted Truman. "Well, what now?"

"Tell y' what," said Tru. "Miss Baby Love Dallas is really New York humor. Wait, you'll see."

"Alice Pearce," wrote Walter Kerr, in the *New York Herald-Tribune,* "as a cosmetic saleswoman, plays what is practically a short revue sketch with fierce, and very funny, intensity."

Maybe it was New York humor, but it was not *Grass Harp* humor, and the fragile play, in my view, instead of building steadily to its rightful, moving denouement, slowly went down the drain.

Truman once said I had tried to tell him what his play was about and he knew that better than anyone. (Samuel Beckett said if he knew who Godot was he wouldn't have had to write the play.) Well, I didn't attempt to tell Capote what his play was about. But I was trying to tell him something of what I felt the theater is about, which was that you can't lead an audience along one road for half an evening, then pull them into an entirely foreign atmosphere, and, finally, try to drag them back home as though nothing had happened. The spine of the play had been broken.

A spine I apparently straightened out was that of *Brigadoon,* as graciously acknowledged by the writer Alan Jay Lerner in his book *The Street Where I Live*: "When Cheryl Crawford, the producer of *Brigadoon,* sent Bobby Lewis the script with the hope that he would direct it, Bobby came to see me and asked me what I thought I had written. I was startled. It was the first time anyone had ever asked me that. I said, rather glibly, that I had written a fantasy about a town in Scotland that returns to life one day every one hundred years. . . .

"'No,' said Bobby, 'that's not what you have written at all. What you have written is the story of a romantic who is searching, and a cynic who has given up. . . . In the end cynicism is proven wrong.' The moment he said it, I realized he was right. And after having struggled with the imperfections in the script for many months, I was able to complete the final draft within a week."

What Alan, as the writer, recounted was the story of the play. As the director, I was searching for the theme.

Another thing *The Grass Harp* taught me was to beware of overpowering scenery that gets a huge round of applause on its own before the audience can suspect that the set is going to smother the actors instead of complement them. I call in an expert witness on this case. Virgil Thomson, who is not only an artist, but a prestigious critic as well, in his autobiography called, for good reason, simply *Virgil Thomson,* wrote the following: "*The Grass Harp,* by Truman Capote, was a fragile play sunk by scenery. An interior by Cecil Beaton, full of bric-a-brac and china, a treehouse and a tree that filled the stage, were beautiful, all too beautiful. . . . Because we were opening in Boston, and the tree was tremendous, we held no dress rehearsal in New York. We gave, however, to an invited group of some two hundred Broadway professionals, a last run-through in street clothes, on a bare stage with only worklights. The play was touching; everybody wept. After we had got into our scenery in Boston, nobody out front ever wept again."

If you're still wondering why the director doesn't exercise more control over every department of the production, you should. I remember one day trying, and failing, to prevent Cecil Beaton from creating an interminable "entrance" for the tree, by starting his lighting of it with a silhouette effect and then a long, slow rising of front lights, revealing first one, then another, beautiful limb of the goddamn tree, ending in a blazing, fully lit revelation of the scenic star. The whole long dim-up was accompanied by appropriate music. It always got a deafening round of applause in performance. At the lighting rehearsal, I went down to where Cecil was feeding his cues into his talk-back phone to the electrician and said, "Cecil, this is not a play about a tree." That probably sounded cutting, but was mild compared to what I was feeling. A haughty stare from the designer gave me the distinct impression that he wasn't sure who I was. My complaint to the producer, Saint Subber, got me nowhere for two reasons.

First, the hierarchy in the Broadway theater is not built on artistic principles but on a power base. Theatrical logic expects that the director should be responsible for the overall concept of the production and that all departments—acting, designing, music—should contribute to the central theme. How can there be a sense of unity otherwise? What often happens in practice, however, is that the person with the most clout emerges triumphant, even if the play doesn't. This person can be a star, a choreographer, a designer, anyone.

Second, Cecil was British. You aren't Broadway-minded if you don't

**Mildred Natwick and Johnny Stewart in Truman Capote's *The Grass Harp*: "This is not a play about a tree."**

know that an English accent as upper-upper class as Cecil's automatically confers the status of royalty on the owner. Speaking what I can only guess is mid-Atlantic English, I didn't stand a chance.

When Truman offered me just the first act of his next script, the musical *House of Flowers,* and even sang me the "Bee Song" himself, with the composer Harold Arlen at the piano, I was not going to be sucked in, even by such juicy bait, without clapping my eyes on the second half of the show. I demurred. Stung, Truman flew off to London and hired Peter Brook. Even Peter, plus Pearl Bailey, didn't help.

So Truman Capote, whose novels and stories sparkle with lively dialogue, has not yet conquered the impenetrable mass of vegetation waiting to trip up some of the staunchest literary adventurers in the theater.

I cannot leave *The Grass Harp* without remarking on the high professionalism of Virgil Thomson. No fancy talk from him. What a pleasure it was to be able to say, "Virgil, I need a bit of music here to cover this change." "How many bars?" he'd ask. "Oh, about sixteen," I'd say. "Fast or slow?" "Fast," I'd reply, certain that he would know from that that the music should presage the next action rather than conclude the bit before. No need for a lot of palaver. And every bar he wrote was not only beautiful, it was apt.

In spite of two unqualified raves from Brooks Atkinson in the daily and Sunday *New York Times,* the show, like *An Enemy of the People,* also ran for only thirty-six performances, which indicated that although the *Times* may be able to break a show, it can't always make one. It also indicated that thirty-six performances was a rut to get out of—fast.

I did. On October 15, 1953, *The Teahouse of the August Moon* opened on Broadway. As the house lights came on at the intermission, Henry Hewes, the drama critic of the *Saturday Review,* stopped at my seat as he came up the aisle to say, "Bobby, you're going to be rich." Indeed, *Teahouse* was the most financially successful of all the plays I directed. To get the vulgar details over with fast (why do I feel guilty?) there were five companies under my direction. There were productions on Broadway, in Chicago, on tour in the United States, a London company, and a British touring one. In addition to the fees and a percentage of the box office receipts, I now had a share of the profits, too, and *Teahouse* played all over the world, from the Habimah Theatre in Israel to Mexico, where Sakini, the leading male role, was undertaken by a woman.

*Teahouse* also marked the acquisition on my part of Judd Mathison, a paragon of directorial assistants, and he is with me to this day. The reason Judd is the best is that he doesn't think of himself as a "second" anything, but by being creative in his job, he becomes the "first" of assistants. Whatever he does—conduct understudy rehearsals, run my theater workshop, whatever—he approaches the task with the devotion of an artist. At present he is steadying my wavering English construction in this volume. (Don't touch this paragraph, Judd.)

The first script of *Teahouse* that Maurice Evans, the producer, sent me I returned, saying I couldn't direct it. All the native Okinawans spoke a kind of gibberish to indicate they were talking Japanese. It went like this: "*Matamoto, Matamoto, Matamoto.*" I maintained it was too cutesy-pie an idea to last a whole evening since all the natives, including the lead, Sakini, would be *Matamoto*ing from the beginning of the play to the end. More importantly, the device would turn the whole business into a long vaudeville turn and kill any chance of believability. The playwright, John Patrick, said the device was necessary because even if the original cast could learn all the Japanese dialogue necessary to communicate with each other in the scenes, the stock rights would be ruined, as actors in those companies would never have the time to master the Japanese. I suggested that when the play was published, two versions should be made: one with the Japanese as we would use it, and a stock edition where they could *Matamoto* to their heart's content, as long as I didn't have to hear it.

When Maurice Evans and John Patrick arrived at my house in Pound Ridge with the revised, *Matamoto*less script in hand, they brought along the designer of the show, Peter Larkin, who had already been set. Not only

David Wayne, John Forsythe, and Larry Gates in *The Teahouse of the August Moon*: "You yourself might get occupied."

was he signed before the director, but Peter had in his hand a completed model of the scenery for *Teahouse*.

"What do you think?" Maurice asked me as he proudly displayed the set. As I had not yet even perused the corrected script of the play and had done no work on it whatever, I hardly knew what to think. I said it was very pretty, which it was, and allowed as to how maybe, after I had some idea as to my approach to the production, Peter and I could meet and talk in more detail.

Having eliminated the cuteness of the gibberish Japanese, I now set about trying to incorporate in the set some point about the whole idea of the occupation of Okinawa. The script was funny enough, but I wanted to hang the comedy onto some theme. In the script, while the Orientals were slowly adapting to American ways, from manufacturing and selling liquor to singing "Deep in the Heart of Texas," the army lieutenant and psychiatrist were shedding their uniforms and putting on robes and kimonos. I explained to Peter that I'd like to get across the idea of the idiocy of trying to "occupy" a country and force an alien culture on the people—you yourself might get "occupied"—and that I'd like the set to reflect this. From this conversation came the idea of taking the pretty Oriental arch that graced the center of the stage in the original model and replacing it with an arch constructed of the tail of a downed American plane propped up by a pole of local bamboo. (See illustration.)

There was no question that a proper search would turn up enough Orientals to play the various Okinawans in *Teahouse*. The one problem would be the leading role, Sakini. The part carried the show and required an actor of great experience, as well as real charm. Sakini not only had every kind of scene within the context of the play but was also required to address the audience all evening in the manner of a master of ceremonies. No one could think of any Asian stage actor, at that time, who might have had the opportunity to gain the kind of experience for such a leading role. After auditioning all available Oriental actors for the part, we invaded other fields in the hope that in the United Nations, the professions, wherever, we might unearth some treasure who could be trained. The closest we came was Sho Onodera. Although it turned out he couldn't really hold the stage in the manner required by Sakini, he was able to become our valued translator, language coach, and technical adviser in all matters Okinawan.

The main problem in casting was that I wanted to play all the Oriental parts myself. I had to be restrained, physically. During rehearsal, my desire to demonstrate how each part should be played was overwhelming. David Wayne, who was finally selected to play Sakini, would constantly frustrate me in rehearsal by yelling, "Don't show me, Bobby. Just tell me."

The pre-Broadway road tour of *Teahouse* presented but one main problem: the removal of the little laughs that were fuzzing the big ones. I set about this cleanup work with a prayer that I should always have this kind of trouble.

The night of the preview, just before the New York opening at the Martin Beck Theatre, was a benefit for a Jewish organization that has, by buying out whole houses, been one of the chief supporters of theatrical productions. But, as on many such occasions, there was as much performing in the audience as on the stage. People were surrounded by their friends and took the occasion to wave to them, call to them, and visit with them in the aisles. The *Teahouse* actors had had such unqualified success in New Haven and Boston that this disruptive audience in New York was a real depressant. When I came backstage to David Wayne's dressing room after the show, he looked at me with a sad twinkle in his eye and confessed, "Bobby, I'm sorry. I've fought it all my life but tonight I feel anti-Semitic." "Don't worry about it, David," I said, "I'm Jewish, and tonight I do, too." I got on the 11:35 train at Grand Central to go home to Pound Ridge and sat in the last car, as usual, with the other theatrical commuters. Eileen Heckart rushed up to me and asked, "How did it go, Bobby?" "I don't understand it, Hecky," I said. "It went so well on the road, but it was a disaster tonight. They wouldn't listen to it. I guess it's just not a New York show."

The next night, the opening, when David came onstage at the beginning of the play and delivered his first monologue, you could feel the waves of love from the audience break over him. I could detect in David's eyes a return to his natural affection for all the races of mankind.

After the curtain fell on the premiere, the thrifty Maurice Evans having arranged no opening celebration, John Patrick threw a champagne party in the lobby of the Martin Beck for the cast, as much to celebrate the occasion as to point up what he felt was Maurice's obsessive frugality. The week before, the playwright had blown his top in Boston's Ritz Hotel when he discovered Evans had deducted Pat's impressive liquor bill from the hotel tab, which was paid by the company. As a result, Maurice was persona non grata at Pat's party. *Dial 'M' for Murder* was playing down the street at the Plymouth Theatre, and since Maurice was starring in it, he couldn't be at our opening but rushed over to the Martin Beck the moment the curtain fell on his performance in order to see how *Teahouse* had gone over. He didn't find out at once though, since the moment he stuck his head in the lobby of the Beck, Pat, having drunk too many toasts already, went berserk. As soon as he spotted Maurice starting up the lobby stairs to the mezzanine landing where the actors were gathered, Pat announced, "I'm going to kill him." Then, placing his champagne glass carefully on a nonexistent table, he aimed his body at Maurice and lunged down the stairs. Maurice, with proper English reserve, stood frozen for a split second as the Irish avalanche roared toward him, then turned and zoomed back through the lobby door with the playwright snapping at his heels. Pat chased Maurice all the way down Forty-fifth Street and back into the stage door of the Plymouth. It was one opening night reception Maurice Evans would not soon forget.

*Teahouse* won unanimous raves from the eight newspaper reviewers, and the lines were steady at the box office starting early the next morning after the opening. A Mr. Anton Aghomburg wrote from Luxembourg for two seats, enclosing fifteen cents extra for an air mail stamp, and two members of the Pulitzer Prize Committee couldn't get tickets until Maurice sprung his house seats. Good thing, too, because on May 3, 1954, *Teahouse* won the Pulitzer Prize. It also copped, among other honors, the Drama Critics Award, which I also won for my direction. The production was in the black after six and one-half weeks.

*Teahouse*'s financial success was not lost on the musicians' union. When Evans sent the show on the road, it replayed the Shubert Theatre in Boston, the same house it tried out in originally. Only this time the musicians' union, cocking a new ear at our incidental score of Japanese gongs, woodblocks, etc., classified *Teahouse* as a musical. Their timing was meticulously musical, too—they announced the new classification about ten minutes before the first curtain on the opening night. The unheeded and unwanted orchestra members' salaries swelled the show's payroll considerably.

Although Seymour Peck referred to me as "the hottest director in town," in a Sunday *Times* piece, I had tried to explain to him that the inner satisfaction felt in the work I had done on *My Heart's in the Highlands, Regina,* and *An Enemy of the People,* all prestige failures in terms of Broadway, was by no means less important to me simply because those productions didn't have the commercial appeal of a *Brigadoon* or a *Teahouse.*

Obeisance to popular success was responsible for at least one artistic shock I had during the first year of the run of *Teahouse.* Mariko Niki, the beautiful Tokyo-born actress who played the leading feminine part, Lotus Blossom, in the play, was out on sick leave for a few weeks. When she returned to the cast, I saw that, in an attempt to have more American commercial appeal, she had had a nose job. One of the reasons I had picked her was because of her lovely oval face, the kind you see in classic Japanese prints. Now with her once delicate slender nose bobbed, she looked like any conventionally pretty co-ed in Berkeley. I could have killed her. If she thought she was preparing to be more saleable for a movie career in America, the new nose apparently didn't help. It did help, however, to warn me of the inherent danger of bobbing my artistic nose in an attempt to court easy success.

As it came close to the time when David Wayne would take a well-earned vacation, we started to look for a Sakini who could replace David and then head up a road company of the show. One of the actors sent in was James Dean, whose behavior at his audition for *Teahouse* made Maureen Stapleton's for *The Happy Time* seem spartan.

Jimmy had impressed me with his talent the year before in a small part in a play called *See the Jaguar.* I was not worried about his acting, but the author and the producer had to be sure Jimmy could successfully manage the Japanese manner and accent. It was, therefore, no more unreasonable to insist on an audition than it would be if he were asked to prove he could tap dance, if that special talent were required in an acting role.

Jimmy was paralyzed with fear when I told him to prepare a few lines of Sakini's opening monologue. "Look," I said. "I've assured them about your acting ability. They just want to be certain you'll be a convincing Oriental." Reluctantly, he agreed to try.

When the audition day arrived, John Patrick, Maurice Evans, and I sat in the orchestra of the Martin Beck Theatre as James Dean, soon to be the film idol of his generation, shuffled out to the center of stage. "Lovely ladies, kind gentlemen," he began. "Please to introduce myself. Sakini by name."

That's as far as he got. He started to smirk, then to giggle, then to laugh, then to guffaw, and finally ran offstage in a paroxysm of pealing laughter.

"Just a minute," I said to my startled colleagues. "I'll be right back."

I found Jimmy collapsed in the alley still howling. "Listen, Jimmy," I begged him, "You only had a few more lines to go. You were doing fine. Just get this bloody audition over with, and then we can get to work on this fun part."

"It's all so embarrassing," Jimmy pleaded.

"I agree with you," I said. "But there are lots of uncomfortable things we must put up with in our work. Now pull yourself together and get this job."

"OK. I'll try once more," Jimmy promised.

"Good boy," I said and ran happily back to my seat in the theater.

Out shuffled Jimmy once more. He started. "Lovely ladies, kind gentlemen." That was all that came out before he broke down again in crazy laughter. This time when he ran off the stage, he kept going. Burgess Meredith, more professional and less neurotic, eventually filled in during Wayne's vacation and subsequently took the show on the road.

The casting of Sakini for the London production was a problem, too. I wanted to take Eli Wallach over with me even though Eli had turned me down for the original production. He had read the script and found it patronizing to the natives. I worried about that, too, and of course it could have been. But, by careful avoidance of stage cuteness in the Okinawans, and a clear delineation of the fatuousness of our Army brass in their handling of the occupation, we eliminated all sense of condescension. When Eli saw the play onstage in New York, he was sorry he did not do Sakini, and now here was his chance to create it in England. But British Equity balked. Since Sakini was an Oriental, not an American, why shouldn't an English actor get the plum part?

A script was sent to John Mills, who I agreed would be able to fill the bill with distinction. Mills accepted and tried to get his producer, "Binky" Beaumont, to release him from the run of *Charley's Aunt* Mills was playing in at the time. That play was scheduled to close shortly after *Teahouse* was scheduled to open. Mills would have to be replaced for the last weeks of his production. While hopeful negotiations for this were going on, the rest of our casting was accomplished. We were close to the first day of rehearsal when Binky gave his final word. It was "no." Too late to start a search for a suitable substitution for John Mills in a part of such special requirements, we appealed to Equity to permit Eli to come over; otherwise the whole project might have to be abandoned. Equity finally relented, and Eli packed his things, including a tape recording of all the Japanese dialogue generously provided him by David Wayne.

The next big casting difficulty in London was the goat. First of all, the

Lord Chamberlain, who at that time had to pass on all scripts before production, objected to the goat's name in the play: Lady Astor. The viscountess was still alive at that time, and no goat was going to be named after the first woman member of the British Parliament, not by any Irish-American playwright, anyway. We suggested Elsa Maxwell and that seemed to make the Lord Chamberlain very happy. One of the biggest laughs in the performance was earned by the goat, who was used as a guinea pig in the second act, by having it test a concoction supposed to be homemade brandy that the Okinawans made from sweet potatoes and that the GIs hoped to sell to other army posts in order to bring needed money to the village. In the New York production, the goat used to stick its head into an army helmet with some Coca-Cola in it and lap it up. Then came the animal's big moment. As the GIs looked on expectantly for the goat's reaction, our Lady Astor in New York would peer straight out at the audience and lick her lips ecstatically from one side of her mouth to the other, bringing shouts of joy from the GIs and applause from the audience. I used to brag that I taught the goat to use a Stanislavskian "sense memory" of good brandy.

**The London production of *The Teahouse of the August Moon*: Eli Wallach restraining "Elsa Maxwell": "The English goat was obviously anti-American."**

The damn English goat, though, this Elsa Maxwell, was obviously anti-American. One sniff of the Coca-Cola and she turned her head away in disdain. We next tried plain sugar. The goat condescended to lap that up, but no lip-licking resulted. Finally, Prince Littler, the possessor of a large farm of animals, as well as owner of Her Majesty's Theatre where we were to play, came up with the exotic answer. "Try a mixture of beer—warm, of course, this being an English goat—and cigarette butts." That did it. The goat licked his chops so rapturously that I had to have him turned upstage after he got his laugh. I didn't want the English audience to think he was milking it.

The casting of the pompous colonel brought double trouble: political and artistic. Drew Middleton in his *New York Times Teahouse* dispatch from London of May 2, 1954, remarked that "an intelligent Briton, reading the London dailies, gets the idea that somewhere between the mental gyrations of Senator Joseph R. McCarthy and the rambling polemics of Secretary of State John Foster Dulles, Americans had lost their ability to laugh at themselves." W. A. Darlington, London theater critic, gave the answer in his review of *Teahouse* in *The New York Times* of June 13, 1954. "The ability to laugh at one's self and one's most cherished institutions is a quality by which the Englishman sets great store. He values it in himself and welcomes it in other peoples, and he is flocking in the thousands to Her Majesty's to see with what gentle, good temper America can mock at herself."

The key to all this lay in the casting of the part of Colonel Purdy, owner of the Purdy Paper Box Company of Pottawattamie, Michigan. The dyspeptic Colonel's great ambition was to get his promotion to general. He said his job in Okinawa is "to teach these natives the meaning of democracy, and they're going to learn democracy if I have to shoot every one of them." In New York, the part was ideally cast with a comic personality called Paul Ford, who subsequently made a career of playing similar parts.

Try as I did, I found no counterpart among the actors available in London who could manage to sound typically American and be funny in that unconsciously pompous manner of Paul Ford. I finally had to settle for a competent character actor who could be a believable colonel of the U.S. Army but just was not funny enough. When Captain Fisby, on being interviewed for a job in the Colonel's outfit, offers to learn the native dialect, Purdy says "No need. We won the war." When Paul Ford said that he always got his laugh. But our more sober Colonel in London drew a gasp of resentment from the rest of the English cast the first time he uttered the words in rehearsal. I knew I was in trouble if I couldn't get over the idea that these sort of remarks were not to be taken "straight." I came up with this solution. Each time the Colonel uttered something that was supposed to be pompously funny, I'd have the Captain, or whomever he was talking to, react with openmouthed shock that anyone could be so fatuous. That got the laugh and took the curse off what the English might think a rude comment.

When Louis B. Mayer's nephew, Jack Cummings, the designated producer of the film version of *Teahouse,* asked me if I'd be interested in directing it with Marlon Brando as Sakini, I was tempted to break my rule of not going back to reconstruct past productions in other mediums. But with Marlon in the picture? Well, I'd think about it.

The first thing I thought was that just as David Wayne was no Brando, Brando was no Wayne, either. Physically, as well as internally, Marlon was "heavier" than David and difficult to transform into this particular Oriental. I'd have to come up with some different approach to make Brando believable as a gadfly of an Okinawan. I decided that Marlon could convincingly play the MC part as a sort of Eurasian student with eyeglasses, the kind you might find on a university campus. Then he'd "act" the native role for the GIs' benefit and sprinkle it with a touch of "Uncle Tom" in order to get what he wanted from the Americans. We'd be inclined to accept him that way.

I visited Marlon in his Hollywood Hills home and laid it all out for him. He seemed genuinely interested in the possibilities. Then the movie script arrived on my desk. I felt the play had been blown up and somewhat vulgarized, with more geishas around than you could shake a fan at. I said, "No, thanks."

I didn't go to see the film, but Bosley Crowther in *The New York Times,* speaking of Marlon, said, "As for Mr. Brando's appearance as Sakini, the amiable Okinawan who engineers the confusion and subversion of the American Army's aims, it is broad and bounding, shot through with grimaces and japes, but somehow it lacks the warmth and candor that are called for in the role.

"In the first place, Mr. Brando looks synthetic. A conspicuous makeup of his eyes and a shiny black wig do not imbue him with an Oriental cast. And his manner of speaking broken English, as though he had a wad of chewing gum clenched between his teeth, is not only disconcerting but also makes him hard to understand.

"More than this, Mr. Brando is too elaborate, too consciously cute. His Sakini is less a charming rascal than a calculated clown."

I quote the above fully because in the *Herald-Tribune* William K. Zinsser, although excoriating the rest of the film, maintained that Marlon was "the only truly Oriental thing" about the movie of *Teahouse*: "The real Marlon is hidden behind oblique eyes, a crooked smile, and some descending strands of black hair.

"In his stylized hand gestures, his splayfooted walk, and his way of coming to rest on his haunches, as if it were the most natural position in the world, he is every inch an Okinawan. And his accent is just right—not the absurd dialect that usually emerges when actors enter the tricky realm of pidgin.

"All of this may be a disappointment to the millions of girls who revere Brando as the rough and tough American boy. But it is a triumph of acting.

For Brando has caught the character of Sakini, the interpreter, in all its subtle humor and deceptively simple wisdom. This amiable rogue stands for the eternal ability of Eastern people to temper their brash conquerors from the West."

I knew the late Mr. Crowther, and I know Mr. Zinsser, and I give each a favorable review as to his qualities of intelligence, charm, and gentlemanliness. But, come on, they couldn't both have seen the same Brando film performance.

I cannot leave *Teahouse* without reflecting once more on the pernicious habit Broadway has of equating professional worth with financial success. John Patrick, moved by the gold mine his play had become, presented me with an inscribed copy of the printed version of the play. Trying hard to restrain himself, Pat could only come up with this: "To Bobby—with admiration, affection, gratitude, warmth, respect, devotion, esteem, deference, homage, appreciation, friendship, fondness, felicity, and eudemonia, man! Pat." I had to look up "eudemonia." It was natural then, when Patrick, in 1959, wrote his next play, *Juniper and the Pagans,* that he'd ask me to direct it. Although this time David Merrick was the producer instead of Maurice Evans, Pat and I tried to keep the lucky *Teahouse* team together by hiring David Wayne for the lead in *Juniper.* I prepared my director's script with the same care I applied to *Teahouse.* David and I worked as diligently as we did for *Teahouse.* But the play never got far enough off the ground and collapsed in Philadelphia.

No eudemonia this time, man. No nothin'. And when, in 1970, *Tea-*

Bobby and Pat (John Patrick, *Teahouse* playwright): "Eudemonia, man!"

*house* was produced as a musical, I was not asked to direct it. As it turned out, that was one of my luckier breaks.

Upon returning from staging *Teahouse* in England, I was not too thrilled to be offered *Witness for the Prosecution* as my next production. Mystery plays, in general, never excited me much as I really couldn't care less "who done it." *Witness* had been playing in London when I was there, but although I attended the theater often, I had failed to see it.

When the Agatha Christie script arrived, I was in bed with a cold and asked my assistant, Judd, to read it for me. He recommended it so highly that I finished it in a single reading, convinced it must be one of the best of its genre. It also seemed challenging to try to bring off something that had so little opportunity for colorful staging as in *Teahouse, Brigadoon,* or some of my other efforts. Here, with mostly question-and-answer courtroom dialogue, I would have to maintain interest and suspense with solid acting and precious little help from theatrical effects. I accepted the challenge in the same way a symphonic composer might decide he'd like to write a good march.

To start the casting, I met with Peter Saunders (now Sir Peter), Agatha Christie's agent and the producer of her plays in London. He had been dispatched to New York to coproduce, with Gilbert Miller, the American version of *Witness.* Most of the character parts were cast from the stable of good English actors living in America. The female lead, Patricia Jessel, was imported from the London production, in which she had made a notable success.

The part of the young man who, in the startling finale of the play, turns out to have been the murderer, proved the toughest to fill. It was essential that no one in the audience believe he could have hit that nice old lady on the head with a "cosh" and killed her. After auditioning many applicants, it came down to two talented young actors: Will Hare and Gene Lyons. Now if such a thing could be measured, Will may have had a touch more pure acting talent than Gene. But I chose Gene. Why? Well, there was something a little too intelligent, too knowing, in Will's countenance and general manner that seemed difficult to erase. The audience might just feel this kid could dream up such a murder and execute it. But Gene—well, Gene had an absolutely open, innocent look. Although, by dint of excellent acting, Will subsequently succeeded in the part in the road company, Gene's innate guileless quality contributed a good deal toward establishing the play's success in the original New York company.

Mrs. Gilbert Miller—Kitty—famous as a party hostess, was the official costume supervisor of her husband's production. The part of the secretary to the defense counsel was an adenoidal character, sloppy enough in her typing to leave out the word "not" in a report of a "not guilty" verdict. Mrs. Miller outfitted the actress, Mary Barclay, in a stunning beige suit, silk blouse, and spike-heeled shoes and then whisked her off to Kitty's own chic hairdresser for a teased-up coiffure. I flipped when I saw my slovenly secretary turned into Ginger Rogers. Getting rid of the jacket to the suit immediately, I went on to pull the blouse out of the waistband on one side and ordered Mary to wear her own flat rehearsal shoes. Then I unteased her hair and stuck a pencil in it. Kitty Miller objected strenuously.

"That girl doesn't look neat," she complained.

"I know, Mrs. Miller," I said, "I thought that would help define her character."

"Oh," said Kitty, "Mr. Miller's opening night guests will never understand why one of his actresses' hair and clothes are untidy."

Truth to tell, Mr. Miller's overwhelming interest did seem to be in inviting his hundreds of friends, all outfitted in obligatory Rolls-Royces, to the premiere. This so exhausted him that on the rise of the curtain the producer, having lowered his ample frame into his aisle seat, he immediately fell asleep and remained so until the final curtain.

The Millers hosted only one party for the cast of *Witness* and that was the occasion of the first yearly anniversary of the play's run. They took over Sardi's Upstairs and generously invited the entire crew as well as the cast. They also asked Henry Fonda and his beautiful Italian contessa, in order to

*Witness for the Prosecution:* (left to right) Francis L. Sullivan, Ernest Clarke, Gene Lyons, Patricia Jessell, Robert Lewis: "Material for an Agatha Christie mystery."

dress up the Miller table. (Fonda was later to admit, "She wasn't any more a contessa than my flannel shirt.") In the middle of the meal, Kitty Miller, in a spurt of democratic emotion, rose from her seat and toured the room to greet the show people. Stopping at the table where Gene Lyons, who had played the lead in the play for a year, sat, Mrs. Miller greeted him with, "And you, young man, are you one of the stage crew?"

The universally favorable press *Witness* received assured a long life to the production. This was not true of a goodly number of the company. Starting with the suicide of one of the cast members and the death of the wardrobe mistress, over half a dozen of the actors died during the run of the play or shortly thereafter. It was material for an Agatha Christie mystery.

Looking back to 1955 from the eighties, it is hard for me to understand why I followed two big commercial theater successes with a commercial picture in Hollywood, instead of tackling some meritorious play, on or off Broadway. I must have felt that with the all-star cast I was offered, it was a safe bet to practice film directing under favorable circumstances and to decide if I wanted to add that to my other activities. The picture was Paramount's *Anything Goes,* with the great Cole Porter score. It starred Bing Crosby, Donald O'Connor, Zizi Jeanmaire, Mitzi Gaynor, Phil Harris and, as a friendly reminder of the New York stage, my old friend Kurt Kasznar. I was even assigned a special camera expert to instruct me in the technical aspect of setting up film shots.

Robert Emmett (Bobby) Dolan, Bing's producer on *White Christmas,* came to New York with a breakdown of a brand new book by Sidney Sheldon that was to serve the original musical score. All that was left of the regular *Anything Goes* story was the ship on which the action unfolded. Dolan assured me that once I got to Hollywood he, Sidney Sheldon, and I would have story conferences that would develop the shooting script. I figured with that cast and that score at least the many musical numbers had to turn out fine. And so they did—especially Zizi's two: a lovely ballet and "I Get a Kick Out of You," both with expert choreography by her husband, Roland Petit.

We shot all the musical numbers first, and when finished, they were shown to the elder statesman of Paramount, Adolph Zukor, who said, "Don't let anyone see these numbers. They'll steal them. Put them in a vault!" That day, at lunch in the commissary, Danny Kaye passed my table. "You look terrible, Bobby," he said. "Shooting all those big musical numbers has exhausted you. Well, don't worry. Next week you'll be directing the book. Then you'll eat your heart out." I laughed, but how right he was. The book remained leaden enough to sink our ship.

Life as a director in Hollywood proved much more cataclysmic for me than my stint as an actor there did in the forties. First of all, Paramount wanted me to sign a contract that had a clause in it assuring them that I was not, and had never been, a communist. This was still the so-called McCarthy period. I refused, saying I would not countenance my political opinions being a condition of employment. They persisted, but when they realized I was adamant they took me anyway, proving what I suspected all along: that they'd have hired Stalin if they thought he would have been good box office.

The next pains in the ass were the endless conferences. You didn't ask anyone for a glass of water. You had a conference about it. One of the favorite phrases used at all conferences was "Let me tell it back to you." That meant repeating your suggestion in such a way as to render it unrecognizable. For example, I remember a costume conference with the picture's designer, Edith Head, and Dolan, the producer, where I suggested that, in one of her dances, Zizi wear a derby hat with her little black pants suit.

"Let me tell it back to you," said Bobby Dolan. "You mean—" and here my heart sank because I didn't mean anything. I just thought Zizi would look better if her costume included a derby. "You mean," Dolan continued, "that she would display more of a *gamine* quality"—he stressed *gamine* and we were all duly impressed that he knew the feminine form of *gamin*—"if she wore a beret." I didn't even have time to object to the more cliché beret, because my popping eyes caught Edith Head's practiced hand sketching Zizi Jeanmaire's head with a rakish *fedora* perched on top.

The expertise of Hollywood technicians was not only impressive, it could be frightening. Just before one shot that took place in the huge ship's dining room with about a hundred tables set for dinner, I reached in to remove a tall glass that was blocking Zizi's face at the front table. By the time I climbed up to my perch on the camera to call "action," I noticed that *all* the crystal had magically disappeared from *all* the tables.

Zizi, by the way, was pregnant during the shooting of the film, and although she wasn't the kind of girl to blab it to Hedda Hopper, she had to tell me. There was a scene in the ship's gymnasium where I planned some shots of Zizi being bounced up and down on a mechanical exercise horse. That would not have been too beneficial for her forthcoming daughter, subsequently called Valentine.

Did you know that hopeless, crushing boredom can also swell your stomach? Well, it can. When it hit me that I would be working on this pedestrian story for months, I began to develop a painful distension of my abdomen. When the agony became continuous and beyond endurance, I started my trek to specialists in every medical category. My trouble was hard to locate in materia medica, however. It was a strictly Hollywood disease. To compound my misery, the social life in Hollywood, after a long day of shooting and a discouraging visit to still another doctor, was nonexistent. I found no Katherine Anne Porter this time. There were mostly nightly immersions in bathtubs full of boiling hot water, the only remedy I discovered that gave me any relief. The burning of my skin helped disguise the internal pain.

Finally the purgatory was over, the last shot was shot, I couldn't have cared less that the studio picked up my option and the trade papers loved the film. Don Hartman, Studio Head of Paramount Pictures, wrote me on June 17, 1955, "I really think it is the best musical in the history of Paramount, and one of the best shows in the history of the industry in taste, entertainment, and showmanship. I am very proud of you for your enormous contribution." Now why can't we get *him* on *The New York Times*? Even three and a half stars in the *Daily News* couldn't persuade me that the film wasn't kitsch. I also had determined that film directing was dangerous to my health. I didn't like making movies as much as Gadget did—at any rate, not enough to take all the crap that went with the studio setup.

I was happy to get out of Hollywood and back to the stage. I had promised Cheryl Crawford I would direct Marc Blitzstein's musical *Reuben Reuben* and follow it with Norman Rosten's *Mister Johnson,* agreeing to coproduce that one with her. While still in Hollywood, I had been offered the direction of *My Fair Lady* several times by its producer, Herman Levin. I had to turn that down because the dates conflicted with *Mister Johnson.* Levin couldn't wait, and I wouldn't go back on my word to Cheryl. Besides, I felt *Mister Johnson* was a good play on an important subject. Telling this story in her autobiography, *One Naked Individual,* Cheryl states that I behaved like "an honorable gentleman." Be that as it may, I didn't feel too bad because, while I may have lost *My Fair Lady,* I also lost my swollen belly.

CHAPTER 16

# The Fifties-Continued

*REUBEN REUBEN* WAS made up of the best and the worst of Marc Blitzstein's artistry, from the ineffably beautiful melody "The Hills of Amalfi," to the confused libretto about a soldier released from the army with a medical discharge; he is left with a serious inability to communicate with others. The only trouble was that this plot about noncommunication never communicated itself to the audience. The early scenes of exposition did not make it clear why he could talk some times and not others; why he could talk to some people and not others; and finally, why, if he was so tongue-tied, he could sing up a storm.

Psychiatrists in the audience understood, of course, and the best reviews we got were contained in letters from them. The medical answer was simple enough. Tensions brought on by confrontation, violence, and hatred activated Reuben's wartime traumas and tied his tongue. Love and fine feeling released it.

The main trouble with the book was that these basic points were never made clear to the members of the lay audience in the early scenes of the show, and the resultant confusion prevented them from enjoying the good stuff that came after. And that stuff was very good: "The Rose Song," a number about a gutter Romeo and Juliet, performed exquisitely by Sondra Lee and Timmy Everett and prophetic of *West Side Story*; "Sleep," sung by Evelyn Lear, who was "introduced" in this show and whose lovely soprano was later to delight opera audiences around the world; a scene in a ward of an insane asylum representing the best of Hanya Holm's choreographic talent. There were many other beautiful musical numbers, not the least of which was the aforementioned "The Hills of Amalfi," which reduced Eddie Albert, who played Reuben, to tears when he first heard it in rehearsal sung by Enzo Stuarti and our chorus. The cast also included Kaye Ballard, at the top of her form. The chorus was distinguished by the (above) Evelyn Lear and Eddie Albert in *Reuben Reuben*: "It never communicated itself to the audience."

(below) Timmy Everett and Sondra Lee in the "Rose Song" number from *Reuben Reuben*: "A gutter Romeo and Juliet."

presence of Miss Lear's husband, Tom Stewart, who also went on to become a global opera star. Never has so much lovely material and so much superb talent gone down the drain for faults in a libretto, which could have been fixed. Oddly enough, so impressed were we all by the beauty of the material we were working on that the weaknesses inherent in the exposition didn't bother us at all. In fact, the small audience invited to the dress rehearsal, about 300 in all, laughed and applauded in all the right places. We were completely unprepared for the disaster that overtook us at the out-of-town opening.

The review of the premiere in the *Boston Record* of October 12, 1955 (which I quote in its entirety), served as an obituary: "It took the opening night audience no more than ten minutes to decide that *Reuben Reuben* had nothing to offer but the toil of its creators. Then, more in sorrow than in anger, they began to leave the theater. The exodus was stealthy at first. Many took advantage of the intermission to slake an overpowering thirst. Others drowned their sorrow at subsequent points. None of the escapees returned to the Shubert to find out how it all ended. For the files, let it be chronicled that Marc Blitzstein wrote both words and music for *Reuben Reuben,* that Cheryl Crawford produced it at great expense and in loving care, that Eddie Albert gave a virtuoso performance in the star part, and that everybody else responded to Robert Lewis' meticulous stage direction with commendable skill." Mr. Gaffney, the critic, erred on only a single point. At least one theatergoer did leave in anger. When he got to the back of the orchestra he saw Marc Blitzstein leaning against the wall. "Did you have anything to do with this?" inquired the patron. "I wrote it," confessed Marc. Whereupon the guy hauled off and socked Marc squarely on the jaw.

Marc then retired to his room in the Ritz Carlton to try to rework the show. Eddie Albert took a verbal beating from the audience at each performance. When, in the ward of the insane asylum, Reuben confesses he "musta been crazy," someone invariably would yell up at the stage, "No, Eddie, we're crazy for coming here."

On the fourth day in Boston, Marc appeared at rehearsal. Eddie eagerly held out his hand for the desperately needed clarifying revisions. Marc gave him a sheaf of music paper. Eddie studied it for a few minutes and then asked, "Where are the changes?" Marc pointed out that in the quartet of the opening scene Eddie would now sing the melody line instead of the harmony. Eddie gasped in disbelief and then cried, "We waited three days for this? I'm being murdered out there every night, and he changes some notes."

Finally, Marc agreed to Cheryl's request to get help. But who? No one mentioned was either available or acceptable to Marc. At a meeting, Cheryl at last came up with the happy news that she could get Tennessee Williams to come to Boston and try his hand at straightening out the exposition. We all lit up at this possibility of salvation. All, that is, except Marc. He admired Tennessee, he said, but the Williams style, philosophy, and so on, were out of kilter with the essence of *Reuben.* We all knew the jig was up. We would never get to New York.

In 1963, I was happy to learn that Blitzstein, on a grant from the Ford Foundation, was at work on an opera based on the Sacco-Vanzetti case and was salvaging my favorite, "The Hills of Amalfi," for use in it. Tragically, though, on January 22, 1964, while vacationing in Martinique, Marc was attacked by three men and savagely beaten. He died twenty-four hours later. At a memorial concert in Blitzstein's honor, Leonard Bernstein conducted some sections of the unfinished Sacco-Vanzetti opera. Referring to the aria containing "The Hills of Amalfi," the music critic Irving Kolodin said Marc "had penetrated to the heart of his subject." It was too late.

*Mister Johnson* (1956), Norman Rosten's dramatization of Joyce Cary's novel about Nigeria, was the first of three productions with predominately black casts that I directed. The play also served as my first foray into producing, with Cheryl Crawford as my partner. I was not too proficient in the money raising department but succeeded in attracting some investors with a series of readings of the play in elegant living rooms. Earle Hyman would read the title role he was to assume, and I read all the other parts. Marilyn Monroe, a good friend of Norman Rosten's, would always enter and slither through the room, after we were well into the first act, and settle down close to where Earle and I were acting our hearts out. Not many eyes were trained on us after Marilyn arrived, but we didn't mind too much, as she was the very best shill for prospective backers one could wish for.

Later we'd go back to Norman Rosten's Brooklyn house for some food. Arthur Miller, a Brooklynite friend of Norman's, would be there carrying forward his courtship of Marilyn. After dinner, we helped with the dishes. I washed and Marilyn dried. Although she had a way with a dish towel, this talent figured only marginally in Arthur's ultimate wiving of Marilyn.

*Mister Johnson* boasted many theatrical treasures, not the least of which was a stunning wedding ceremony choreographed by Pearl Primus. But the crowning achievement was the shattering performance of Earle Hyman as Mr. Johnson. Every critic agreed about that even though each carped a bit about the construction of the script. Kenneth Tynan went home to London after seeing *Mister Johnson* in New York and wrote in the *Observer,* "One of the Broadway plays is at least two jumps ahead of London, where it properly belongs." Of the acting Tynan said: "Earle Hyman as the clerk, and Josephine Premice as his haughty native bride, are giving performances of which London must not long be deprived."

We never got to London, and even New York audiences were deprived after forty-four performances. Mr. Atkinson in the Sunday *New York Times* of April 8, 1956, issued what he called "a minority report." "Most of

**Earle Hyman in the last scene of *Mister Johnson*: A performance "of which London must not long be deprived."**

the newspaper reviews range from jubilant to appreciative," he wrote.. "But this department regards Mr. Rosten's drama as a bright-colored, well-acted show that never comes to the point." Although there was an unusual amount of letters to the editor disagreeing with Mr. Atkinson, this damning with faint praise from the powerful *New York Times,* plus the possibility that an African play may well have been ahead of its time, and further, the feeling on the part of the black community then that they weren't all that welcome in Broadway theaters, sealed poor *Mister Johnson*'s doom. Earle cannot forget, to this day, how his fellow actors in other productions tried to save *Mister Johnson*'s life. In an unprecedented gesture, they called their audience's special attention to Earle's performance in *Mister Johnson* at their own curtain calls and urged playgoers not to miss it. Among the pleaders were Shelley Winters in *Hatful of Rain,* Sammy Davis, Jr., in *Mr. Wonderful,* Patricia Jessel in *Witness for the Prosecution,* Uta Hagen in *A Month in the Country,* and Charles Bowden, producer of *Fallen Angels.*

An interesting sidelight of the production of *Mister Johnson* was a suit that Actors' Equity Association brought against Cheryl Crawford and me as producers of the play. Pearl Primus had invited any actors who were cast in *Mister Johnson* to her classes in African dancing. Since nearly everyone in the play was in the wedding scene, she thought they might like to limber up for the ceremonial dancing required. Pearl offered her instruction free, and some of the actors took advantage of her generosity by starting in the classes a couple of weeks before rehearsals began. Equity contended those actors should be compensated for what the union called rehearsal time, since some of the African movements they learned in the dance classes turned up in the choreography. I pointed out in the arbitration hearing that, with that kind of reasoning, if an actor went to a speech coach in preparation for his appearance as Hamlet and used the "To be or not to be" soliloquy for an exercise, the management of the Shakespearean play would have to pay him rehearsal pay from the first fricatives and vowels in which he was coached. The union's allegation was disproved and a unanimous decision in favor of the producers was voted by the arbitration board consisting of Tom Ewell (actor), Herman Levin (producer), and Milton Rubin (businessman).

If *Mister Johnson* was before its time, theatrically speaking, *The Hidden River* was after its time. This play, laid in the Loire Valley, France, about the poisonous hangover of World War II, was a dramatization by Ruth and Augustus Goetz of a novel by Storm Jameson. Its producers were the actor Martin Gabel and the restaurateur (Chambord) Henry Margolis. I agreed to direct it because, although I suspected that by 1957 the audience had had it with films and plays about Nazis, collaborators, and the like, I was attracted by the authors' theme "about the many kinds of morality and rationalizing that men practice as the result of the unlovely acts that they sometimes commit."

The cast consisted of many good actors including Robert Preston, Lili Darvas, and Dennis King. The latter played a wreck of a civilized French intellectual who had been accused and found guilty of collaboration with the occupying enemy. He had been sent to prison and now after many years was coming home, a broken and dying man. Dennis was a famous and highly attractive personality who had been a successful star for years. He had no patience with any "newfangled" attempts to analyze, or even discuss, the theme of the play, the character he was playing or, heaven forfend, the subtext of a scene. All that sort of carrying on he considered amateurism. He was the sort of elegant, oldtime star who boasted that the only method was to "say your lines clearly and not bump into the furniture." He'd repeat the so-called professionals' dictum that "the motivation behind your speeches is your salary."

It always interested me that certain old-fashioned stars who derided any mention of technique in the craft of acting had a bushelful of "tricks" of their own that constituted a solid mountain of technical effects. One of Dennis's most spectacular feats was the way in which he was able to make the audience believe it was his partner's fault when Dennis forgot his lines.

Instead of fumbling himself, he would glare questioningly at the other actor as if to say, "Damn it, why don't you say your line?" I once saw him, in performance, even point an accusing finger directly at poor Lili Darvas when it was actually Dennis's turn to speak.

Since King was not about to sit around with the whole cast in the early rehearsals when we would read through the entire play and plan production ideas, he'd only join us for his scenes and then disappear. This practice led to a weird occurrence. The character Dennis played died in the second act of the play, after which event, in rehearsals, Dennis would go home. At the first run-through of the entire play, he prepared, as usual, to leave after his death scene. Instead of going out the stage door this time, he ambled through the theater and was about to exit from the front of the house when something caught his attention: his fellow actors walking about on the stage saying lines. He paused at the door, listened for a few minutes, and then found it interesting enough to take a seat in the auditorium and watch. Presently he approached me and asked what they were doing. "The third act," I answered, simply. Now you're not going to believe this, but either Dennis had by now forgotten that there was a third act or he never knew. Clearly miffed, he left the theater. Next day, the producers received a call from his agent informing them that there was a third act to the play and Dennis, who was one of the stars, wasn't in it. When told that these facts came as no surprise to us, the agent insisted that Mr. King be written into the last act. The authors, talented though they were, confessed that would be difficult since his character was already dead. Some way, the agent insisted, he would have to be brought back or Mr. King would be too unhappy to stay in the show. Sadly, nothing could be done, and Dennis, who had a run-of-the-play contract, had to stay in the show but was, indeed, decidedly unhappy.

So, too, were we all unhappy, but for another reason. In spite of a universally enthusiastic press—this time Mr. Atkinson joined his brethren, concluding his review with "the writing is skillful and the performance is superb"—the timing of the production obviously was wrong enough to insure a run of only a couple of months in New York. The fact that the producers did virtually nothing to promote the unanimous favorable press *The Hidden River* received (seven out of seven newspaper reviews), didn't help, either.

It is easy for me to remember why I accepted the assignment to direct the musical *Jamaica* for David Merrick, even though the book, once more, was far from ready. The reason was Lena Horne. She and I had tried to find something to do together for some time. *Jamaica* had actually been designed for a male star, Harry Belafonte. When he dropped out, the creators of the show, Harold Arlen, Yip Harburg, and Fred Saidy, promised Lena that if she agreed to head up the cast, they would rewrite the book and

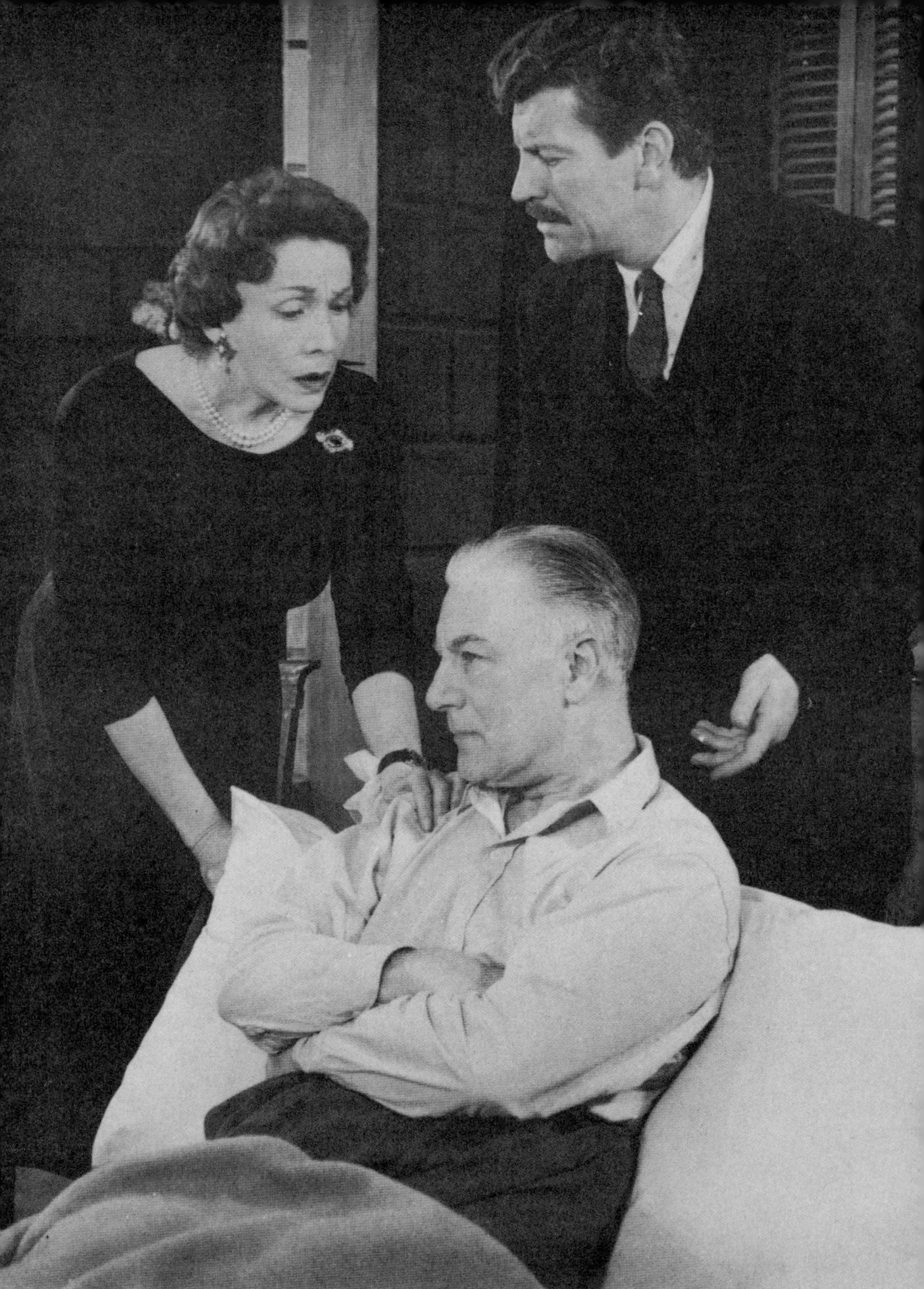

*The Hidden River:* Lili Darvas, Robert Preston, standing, Dennis King, seated. "Damn it, why don't you say your line?"

the score and throw the weight of the material in her direction. Cautiously, she and I each signed a contract containing the stipulation that its validity depended on the presence of the other party in the setup.

The casting of a co-star for Lena presented a problem. He had to be a strong actor since this was Lena's first time at bat in an acting (as well as singing and dancing) part in a Broadway musical, and I wanted her to have solid support. The man playing opposite her had to have charm, looks, and a vivid personality that would not be washed out next to Lena's exciting luminosity. Oh, yes, he had to act and sing and dance, too. The few casting suggestions quickly narrowed down to one name: Ricardo Montalban. Merrick and I flew out to Las Vegas where Lena was appearing at the Sands Hotel, and Ricardo came from Los Angeles to join us. Soon after they met, it was clear that Lena Horne and Ricardo Montalban were a fascinating team, and Ricardo was signed. Oliver Smith, Miles White, and Jean Rosenthal were put in charge of sets, costumes, and lighting, and that mostly unsung genius of the dance, Jack Cole, filled the chorus with top flight people like Alvin Ailey, Billy Wilson, Charles Moore, and Claude Thompson, all choreographers themselves now.

David Merrick, although he wouldn't want to be accused of having more interest in the art of the theater than a paramecium, turned out to be a powerful producer, commercially speaking, wily enough to read the small print in all the theatrical union contracts. Chorus Equity, for example, passed a ruling that their members could no longer be asked to pick up dancing shoes at Capezio's on their lunch hour or have their measurements taken during breaks in rehearsal. All these activities were to be counted as rehearsal time. Well, when we were auditioning dancers and singers for the chorus I noticed, at the next-to-the-last callback, a little man stopping people in the wings after they finished their auditions. It turned out he was getting their complete measurements. No one could object as they were not yet employed, and it seemed a hopeful sign to the performers that someone was interested enough in them to take their measurements. By the time the final chorus was set, everyone was measured for everything. I must say, in passing, that I always enjoyed working for Merrick since it was invariably clear exactly where he stood in any situation. The tough producers for me were those who would discuss artistic matters forever in the theater or rehearsal hall, while at the same time making management decisions in their offices that precluded any morsel of art from seeing the light of day.

The book of *Jamaica* being what it was, I was sure my friend Oliver Smith would never get through it. I told him what he needed to know of the story and advised him to let me see his sketches before presenting them to Merrick. Good thing I did, too, because Oliver had made a lovely sketch of the Grandmother's house, the only trouble being there was no Grandmother's house in the show. I handed that sketch back to Oliver quickly before anyone guessed he hadn't read the book.

Some attempts were made to fashion the show for Lena. Harold Arlen wrote a couple of new numbers for her; but it was not enough. Although the dialogue of the man's part remained better than Lena's, she never complained, ploughing into her work like an enthusiastic acting student. She herself had said, "I never talked before on the stage. I never even announced my songs." Everyone knew her songs would be no problem, but the surprise was how quickly she molded a completely engaging speaking character, even mastering a fine West Indian accent. Everyone also knows by now that Lena not only announces her songs in her exciting concert program but talks up a storm.

Lena always kidded me about my being an opera buff. When I'd say "orchestra rehearsal at ten tomorrow morning, Lena," she'd reply, "Well, that's fine, but when's the band call?" She had heard me refer to my favorite old opera singers I'd listen to on my record player as my "dead singers." One day Harold Arlen brought in to rehearsal a lovely tune he wrote for her called "Cocoanut Sweet." He played it once for us on the piano, and then Lena sang it through so beautifully that I exclaimed, "Lena, you sang that just like a dead singer." Clapping her hands she cried, "Oh, great. Now I know you really like me. I'm right up there with Tetrazzini!"

By the time the *Jamaica* rehearsal period wound down, it was clear we had great dances (and dancers), great Lena Horne (although still with not enough songs), and big book trouble. The Philadelphia and Boston critics agreed, and then the fun began.

There was a show-biz prayer that Hitler should have been sent out-of-town with a musical. And it should have been *Jamaica.* The sedate Ritz Carlton hotel in Boston was rife with wild meetings, screaming resignations, and indiscriminate threats of replacements. If only we would have gotten some of that excitement into the story that unfolded, like dough, on the stage of the Shubert Theatre. Harold Arlen took to his bed, and when I telephoned to find out if he could provide us with some needed music, Mrs. Arlen informed me that he was dying and "only had about four more bars left in him." Arlen was particularly upset because he wanted to replace Jay Blackton, our conductor, with his own brother, Jerry Arlen. Lena and her husband, Lennie Hayton, who acted as her musical arranger, advisor, and conductor, wouldn't hear of it. No one, of course, would think of using Lennie as conductor—too sensible. Lehman Engel was eventually called in as a compromise candidate everyone could accept.

Josephine Premice, comedienne of the show, got one bad review on the road, and Merrick called for her immediate replacement. Lena and I fought that idea, and New York eventually enjoyed Jo's classy, comic contributions.

Now about the book. The problem was simpler to state than to solve. The writers had been working on the material since the old Harry Belafonte days and had apparently exhausted their store of ideas. The produc-

*Jamaica:* **Lena with Bobby in the recording studio: "I'm right up there with Tetrazzini."**

er's choices were to get help, take a chance in New York with what we had, or close the show out-of-town. But the strongest contract in the production setup is the writers'. The Dramatist Guild gives the playwright the last word, not only on the script, but on casting, scenery, direction—the lot. Therefore, when the writers were immovable on the proposal to bring in a play-doctor, Merrick announced he was closing the show in Boston. That did it. In no time at all Joseph Stein, coauthor of *Mr. Wonderful* and *Plain and Fancy*, was dispatched to Boston, cut huge chunks out of the dialogue, and tinkered with what was left. He couldn't transform the book into a masterpiece, but at least we were able to bring Lena front and center and give the customers what, after all, they wanted to see. Lena, single-handedly, kept the show going for a whole season at the Imperial Theatre in New York. Mr. Atkinson of *The New York Times* helped, too, with, "*Jamaica* is a beautiful, jovial, old-fashioned musical comedy that has been produced and staged with taste and style," and on Sunday, after remarking that "the book of *Jamaica* is not notably intellectual," focused properly on Lena who, he said, was "a woman of pride and grace who can pour feeling into a song without sacrificing her good manners."

N. Richard Nash's *Handful of Fire* was one of those Purity versus

Corruption morality plays laid in a Mexican border town. If you think *Handful of Fire* is a lousy title how about these ten—a mere sampling of more than half a hundred that were endlessly discussed and finally discarded:

*Doves of Fire*
*Unto the Pure*
*Mad with Much Loving*
*The Hot Lands*
*The Lover's Touch*
*Pocket Full of Pesos*
*My Love, My Caballero*
*Six Strings of Love*
*Plaza for Pleasure*
*Mangoes Are Murderous*

The production did boast a stirring performance by Roddy McDowall in the leading role of Pepe, a street photographer (pure).

The interesting problem of accents was raised by John Lardner in his review of the play on October 11, 1958. He wondered why Pepe, a Mexican, spoke in a dialect when presumably talking in his own language to other characters who were also Mexican. Logically, of course, Lardner had a point, and I worried about it at the time. However, theatrically, there were problems to be faced. First, accents gave local color to the Mexican characters and differentiated them from Kay Medford, who used straight English as an American-born madam of the town. Then, too, how could Pepe avoid an accent when calling out, "Eh, lady, I take your picture?" And try shutting someone up in these words without a bit of plebeian singsong: "You keep your mouth."

When an English actor uses a cockney accent for a character residing in London's East End in a Shaw play, it's obviously OK. But when an English actor does a play in England or America about French people in France and uses a Cockney accent to indicate a lower-class Frenchman, it's hard to escape the feeling that the character isn't from London rather than Paris. The matter of proper accents can get so complicated that the director is finally left with only one sensible choice: do whatever works. The best answer to the problem was once given me by Tennessee Williams. I was in Chicago when *The Glass Menagerie* first opened there. Not being able to pinpoint the accent Laurette Taylor was employing for the mother in the play, I asked Tennessee from what southern state Laurette's mode of speech emanated.

"I don't know what the particular state is, Bobby," said Tennessee with

Roddy McDowall, Louis Guss, and Leonardo Cimino in *Handful of Fire*: "You keep your mouth."

his Mississippi drawl, "but I do know this. Somewhere in the South there's a woman who talks just like that."

*Candide* was a hybrid. It was not in the strictest sense an opera, an operetta, or a musical. "What's wrong with that?" I said to myself. "It's itself, and a giant step up the cultural ladder from *Handful of Fire.*" I jumped at the chance to direct it for a British production in 1959. Four years earlier, Lillian Hellman had phoned me when I was in Hollywood and asked me to direct the New York production. I had to turn it down then for the same reason I gave Herman Levin on his offer of *My Fair Lady*: My commitment to Cheryl Crawford to do *Reuben Reuben* and *Mister Johnson.* Sir Tyrone Guthrie put it on in New York, and in a sort of lend-lease arrangement, I was now shipped to London.

In 1956, the American production only had a run of a couple of months but attracted vociferous partisans. The very same outcome awaited it in London. After breaking the house record at the Saville Theatre in its opening weeks, it ran out of London supporters in a similar amount of time. My English friends advised me that their opera enthusiasts simply did not go to musicals, and musical fans did not go to operas. It was the *Regina* syndrome again. The only time *Candide* broke its box-office jinx was in 1974, when Lillian Hellman's book was replaced by Hugh Wheeler's, and the show enjoyed Harold Prince's inventive staging. The superb

*Candide* in London. The Gambling Ballet, Jack Cole, choreography: "*Candide* was a hybrid."

Leonard Bernstein score on that occasion was rearranged by Hershy Kay for a small ensemble. I, for one, missed the sound of the original orchestration that Lenny himself had done with Hershy.

With *Regina,* the only other work of Lillian Hellman's I staged, Marc Blitzstein, the composer and lyricist, had followed *The Little Foxes* play faithfully, and Lillian didn't turn up until the dress rehearsal. With *Candide* I wanted much more input from Lillian, especially her suggestions of what she'd like to correct from the Broadway version. A weekend meeting on Martha's Vineyard in July 1958, with Lillian and Lenny Bernstein, resulted in my going home with a packet marked "Notes on *Candide* for the London Production." Either in a burst of generosity or because she was reluctant to do any more writing on *Candide,* Lillian agreed to let Michael Stewart do the book revisions. Michael was soon to gain fame as the author of *Bye Bye Birdie,* and if you can understand his choice then as the hopeful improver of Lillian Hellman's dialogue and the guardian of Voltaire's savage satire, you are on the way to passing your test as a student of theater logic.

Another weird story involving Lillian and a different playwright may be one of the definitive show business stories. She told it to me herself. In 1963, in the course of one of her dinner parties, Lillian's maid came up behind her and whispered in her ear, "Miss Hellman, a gentleman wants you on the telephone."

"You know I can't go now," said Lillian. "Get his number and tell him I'll call him back."

"But," the maid insisted, "this gentleman says he must talk to you immediately. He seems very upset."

Lillian excused herself from the table and went to the kitchen phone. "Yes, who is it?" she asked.

"Oh, Miss Hellman." The voice at the other end sounded urgent. "This is William Inge. I'm in trouble, and you're the only one who can help me."

"Well," Lillian said, "I *am* at dinner, but what is it?"

"I go into rehearsal this week with my new play, *Natural Affection,* and I have written two possible third acts. I can't make up my mind which to use. You are such a great constructionist, I'm sure if you'd read them both, you could advise me. I'd trust you."

"Now, Bobby, you understand I hardly knew Inge," Lillian reported. "I may have met him at a party, but that's all."

"Look, Mr. Inge," said Lillian, continuing her story. "I have to go back to my guests now and, anyway, I'd like to think about this. Give me your number and I'll call you back in the morning."

"Oh, thank you. You are very kind." Inge gave Lillian his number and hung up. Back to the dining room went the hostess and put the matter out of her mind for the time being.

Later, after all the dinner guests had gone home, Lillian went to her bedroom and began to think of the unusual telephone conversation she had had with William Inge. As she started to get ready for bed, she thought to herself, "I'm not going to get mixed up in this. I'm busy with my own writing and this little job will require reading two versions of his play. Then I'll probably have to make some kind of breakdown and analysis of the scenes. I'll have to meet with him and give him the reasons for my decision after I make it. It'll get me way off the track of my own work. No, I'm going to tell him I can't do it." And she got into bed.

Lying there, she thought, "Oh, Lillian, you're just thinking of yourself. This poor man is obviously desperate or he wouldn't have called you. Why he hardly knows you. He's a colleague in bad trouble, and you must help him. It might take some time from your own work, but you can get back on your tracks again. You must agree to help him."

These warm, comradely thoughts almost lulled her to sleep when another idea bolted her upright in bed. "My God, suppose the thing turns out to be a flop. He'll blame me. He'll say he did what I told him to do and look what happened. No, I mustn't get involved in this business. I'll just have to find some way to turn him down." And so, on and on into the night, Lillian tossed from yea to nay and back again.

By morning, the battle between the strictly professional and the strictly human side of Lillian was finally over. Human Lillian had won, but just barely. Groggy from lack of sleep, she staggered to the kitchen phone to get the number she'd written down the night before. Seeing it was only eight o'clock, she thought, "I can't call that poor man this early. He's probably had a worse night than I did. After all it's *his* play that's in trouble." She made some needed coffee and downed it. Then she went through the entire *New York Times*. She got dressed. Finally it was ten o'clock.

"Damn it, he's slept long enough," Lillian said to herself and dialed the number.

"Hello," moaned the sleepy voice at the other end. Lillian felt a pang of guilt at having wakened the stricken author.

"This is Lillian Hellman," said Lillian Hellman.

"Who?"

"Hellman, Lillian Hellman, you called me last night about helping you with your play."

"Oh, yes." The voice was finally waking up. "It's sweet of you to call back but you needn't have bothered. You see after I hung up on you, an actor friend of mine, Mendy Wager, came by, and he told me which act to use."

Lillian has said that her disillusionment with theater started with the New York production of *Candide*—"all that business of not having enough money on the road to fix things," and so on. She hits the mark, however, when she confesses that she's just not a collaborator. "I'm happiest with the theater," she says, "when I'm alone in my room writing." There it is. In no way can an author's play become a living thing in the theater without the contributions of actors, directors, designers, composers, producers, etc. Lillian's feeling about all these interlopers has soured her over the years to the point where she no longer uses her writing talent for the theater but sticks to autobiographical books.

The successes of some far from "well-made" plays in recent years may also have contributed to Lillian's retirement from playwrighting. One actor she does admire is John Gielgud, so I took her to the opening of *Home* by David Storey, in which Sir John starred with Sir Ralph Richardson. As each of these old knights tossed abstruse, truncated verbal ejaculations at each other, Lillian stole glances at the other theater patrons to see how they were enduring this kind of dialogue. To her growing horror she observed that they were not only absorbed but genuinely moved. After the show, as we strolled down the street to a restaurant, I could see Lillian was deeply depressed. But with that greatest of all her personal attributes, her wicked sense of humor, she revived herself with, "Hell, I don't care. I've already written a play about two old ladies." (*Toys in the Attic.*)

Lillian stayed away from the British production of *Candide* until our pre-London stop, Liverpool. She arrived just in time for this road opening on April 17, 1959. I had not called a rehearsal that day, but to give the company a chance to meet their author, I assembled them in the theater's lounge. Among them were Denis Quilley (Candide), Laurence Naismith (Pangloss), Mary Costa (Cunégonde), Victor Spinetti (Marquis), Ron Moody (Governor), and Edith Coates (Old Lady). Osbert Lancaster had done the sets and costumes, and the producer was Geoffrey Russell. Jack Cole again scored as choreographer. Immediately after the introductions to the cast were over, Lillian launched into a detailed description of each character, laying down firmly her ideas as to interpretation. These performers had been playing the piece a certain way eight times a week in Oxford and Bristol (after more than a month of rehearsals), and now, a few hours before their Liverpool opening night, they were receiving directions from the playwright, who had not seen the show yet. Even if they could absorb her instructions, it was unlikely they would be able to do anything about them before the curtain went up. My favorite reaction from the startled cast members was that of Edith Coates, a campy contralto in the last days of her distinguished career as an operatic star of Covent Garden. Edith had a habit of smiling and commenting, "Lahvely," on every occasion from a tea party to a funeral. When Lillian finished her interpretive remarks, not one word of which meant anything to the contralto whose acting I had extracted by constant illustration, Edith asked Lillian, "Have you ever had any of your other plays done in London, Miss Hellman?"

"Yes," growled Lillian, "two—and they were both flops."

"Lahvely," gushed Edith.

*Chéri* was the second play I coproduced. I also directed it. My coproducer this time was Roger Stevens and the Playwrights' Company. I was in London with *Candide* when I read that my *Chéri* partner-to-be, Roger Stevens, had purchased the Empire State Building. Cabling at once, I demanded to know if, due to our partnership, I owned half. Roger said no.

As with *An Enemy of the People,* the question of a proper adaptation of *Chéri* was the first order of business. It was a particularly delicate problem this time since the adaptor not only had to be a fine dramatist, but more importantly, he had to preserve the special fragrance of Colette's writing. Her *Chéri* story had been done on the French stage, but I wanted to add Colette's follow-up novella *The Last of Chéri* as a third act.

Three possible playwrighting choices came to mind: Thornton Wilder, who had often expressed his great admiration for Colette; Terence Rattigan, a good constructionist and European; and Anita Loos who, in the 1950-51 season, had done the successful dramatization of Colette's *Gigi.* It turned out that both Wilder and Rattigan were out of the question as they had conflicting assignments, so we went with Anita.

The casting of the difficult part of the captivating Chéri turned out to be easier than one would have thought. Both Anita and I happened to have seen a German film version of Thomas Mann's *Felix Krull.* If Horst Buchholz, the young actor who played the title role, could speak English,

*Chéri*: Anita Loos, Horst Buchholz, and Bobby Lewis. Horst "learned to speak English through studying American movies."

we felt he would be ideal casting for the role of Chéri. I arranged to meet Horst in London while I was there and discovered he spoke idiomatic English with practically no trace of accent—just a flavor of the European in his inflection that colored his speech. He told me he had learned to speak English through studying American movies and English-language broadcasts during the Second World War. Horst was indeed the perfect type for Chéri, and the machinery to sign him up for his American stage debut was begun at once.

The big casting problem turned out to be Léa who, at forty-nine, was, according to Colette, "nearing the end of a successful career as a richly kept courtesan." Everyone agreed that we should try for an international star to play this difficult and glamorous role. Scripts were dispatched to Marlene Dietrich, Simone Signoret, Irene Worth, and Edwige Feuillère with the hope that none of them would find out we were approaching the others—always a dangerous business. They all turned the part down for a variety of reasons, Marlene's being the most pithy. I excerpt a few remarks from her long letter to me in London on March 24, 1959, mailed from her Park Avenue apartment:

> Dearest,
>
> I wish I wouldn't have to write to you—and could talk to you instead. My original lukewarm feeling towards *Chéri* has not changed. Not that the script is the reason. I think it is very good—and faithful to Colette.
>
> I still feel that the story, the problem, the characters are "démodés". . . . It is, maybe, a "chimère" that I trust I will find a part with guts or balls or passion or whatever you want to call it, but at any rate, alive—concerning a subject or problem which regards everybody. . . . Today there is a tinge of the ridiculous in Léa, double in this country where youth is God. This, naturally, is my own humble opinion, not as far as the success of the play is concerned—only my craving to be part of it is absent. And I know you would not want me halfheartedly.
>
> Mille tendresses,
>
> Marlene

The only American actress I had considered along with the others was Kim Stanley. (I know that Irene Worth was born in Nebraska. But she got her training in England, acted there for years, and played all over the world, including Persepolis in Iran with Peter Brook's Company. That's why I put her in the international category, whereas Kim was, theatrically, completely homegrown.) When Paris, France's Simone Signoret ultimately came to see Tularosa, New Mexico's Kim Stanley as Léa at the Morosco Theatre, she came backstage after the performance to say, "I could have done the part in the movies. But I never could have approached what Kim Stanley did on that stage."

Kim herself was worried that when Maurice Goudeket, Colette's husband, saw the play he would say, "Get that Irish girl out of here." Instead, Goudeket assured Kim that, "Colette would have thought of you as her own child." And that distinguished and sensitive theater critic, Mr. Stark Young, wrote of Kim, "I can think of few actors in our country who could have so completely created on the stage this kind of woman so well-known to the French, a woman, that is to say, whose love turns not to a man but to essentially a boy, toward whom she carries, at times, also the depth of a mother's feeling."

For me, the most vivid memories of the production of *Chéri* will always be centered around Kim Stanley. She was the most gifted acting artist I ever worked with. She didn't need the usual direction—only a bit of editing here and there. "What you do with the mirror in that spot is very good, Kim," I might say, "but it's a little like what happens in the previous act." "All right, I'll find something else," she'd agree. And she would. "I'll find something" was her refrain all through rehearsals. By "something" she not only meant a piece of "business" or a movement. It could be a thought or a feeling—some personal emotional reference that would change a particular moment from something understood to something experienced. This was her art. By the time she was finished there wasn't a single passage in her performance that didn't ring completely true.

Did I say finished? She was never finished. She worked creatively on her part throughout the run until the closing night curtain fell. Between matinée and evening shows, I'd find her stretched out on a couch in her dressing room thinking about her part. "I've found something for the moment where Chéri says to Léa so-and-so and so-and-so," Kim would announce. "I'll try it tonight." Thus her performances not only had the "quality of the first time," but they improved daily.

What parts, you might ask, has this paragon of an actress played on the stage in recent years? None, so far, is the answer. This is what Kim says happened. Five years after *Chéri,* she was one of the prime movers in getting Lee Strasberg to stage Chekhov's *The Three Sisters* as an Actors Studio Production on Broadway. It took her three of those five years to persuade Lee, who had always wanted to direct *The Three Sisters,* to turn his wish into action.

I've already discussed the peculiarities of the Actors Studio diction as it related, or didn't relate, to the Chekhovian characters in *The Three Sisters.* The lack of a sense of period style applied equally to the staging and the characterizations. Only Tamara Daykarhanova as Anfisa, the old nurse, seemed to belong in Mother Russia. It wasn't too hard for her, however, since she was actually from the homeland. In spite of everything, *Newsweek,* in a generally unfavorable review of the production, broke down and called Kim Stanley "our greatest actress."

After the New York run when the Studio approached Kim to appear in a proposed London engagement of *The Three Sisters* (which would also include James Baldwin's *Blues for Mister Charlie*) at the Aldwych Theatre for the annual World Theatre Festival, she refused at once. No love had been lost between Kim and Kevin McCarthy (Vershinin) during the rehearsals and performances of the play on Broadway, and Kim was not about to go through all that again. Also, Kim had cooled to Lee, too, as a result of the New York experience. She didn't appreciate his trying to get her to approximate his memory of the Masha in the Moscow Art Theatre production he had seen, even playing a recording of the Russian actors' performance for the cast to hear. Kim also resented Lee's constant bullying of Shirley Knight, the Irina, to the point where members of the cast, Kim included, rose up and put a stop to it. She advised Lee to yell at *her* saying, "*I'm* the one you want to yell at." But Lee couldn't. He was, as one cast member put it, "scared shitless of Kim."

To get her to say "yes" to the London appearance, the Studio heads put pressure on Kim, telling her they'd have to call it all off if Kim didn't go, since hers was the most important performance in the cast. Without *The Three Sisters,* America would have no representation at the World Theatre Festival and, finally, her refusal would deal a mortal blow to the Studio. Kim, against her better judgment, capitulated. But Shirley Knight refused to be punished again and was replaced by Sandy Dennis. Geraldine Page got pregnant, and Nan Martin took her part of Olga. When Kim made a new Vershinin one of her demands if she agreed to go, Lee, after a fight, reluctantly replaced Kevin with George C. Scott.

Kim wouldn't fly and so arrived days after rehearsals had begun in London. The company couldn't get on the Aldwych stage until the opening day. When they did, they discovered that the stage was steeply raked. Upon requesting the upstage legs of the furniture be cut down so the props wouldn't fall off and onto the floor, the Studio was told they were rented antique pieces and there would be no sawing off of legs. What with the difference in English lighting boards and the costumes not ready, the actors never got through a dress rehearsal. The opening night was the first complete run-through—and it was a major disaster. The actors, as well as the furniture, tilted on the raked stage. Aging Tamara Daykarhanova, at one point, fell and fractured her arm. The endless intermissions and the slow tempo of the acting added more than an hour to the length of the evening.

The audience was in a foul mood to begin with. Lee had been quoted as calling the English theater "stultifying" and the first production of the Studio's contribution of two plays to the Festival, *Blues for Mister Charlie,* had had a bad reception. Worse, Lee, in a press conference following the poor notices of the Jimmy Baldwin play, had disavowed it, saying those actors were not Studio members. This pleased neither the actors nor the English sense of fair play. The critics were waiting with poison pens in hand for *The Three Sisters*. The opening night audience booed the actors, calling out, "Yankees go home," and when Sandy Dennis said her line, "It's been a terrible evening," someone yelled, "It sure has been," and broke up the audience.

The critical reviews of the Actors Studio production of *The Three Sisters* in London, and the cruel personal remarks about Kim, were mostly too savage to repeat at this point. Pénelope Gilliatt summed up the evening as "the suicide of the Actors Studio." Lee ultimately blamed the actors, saying that Sandy Dennis did "her junk," "was just stupid," and he complained of "her nervous tics." Sandy countered with the advice that she hadn't had a bowel movement in two weeks and had to go to a hospital. She wailed, "I can truly say Lee Strasberg was the cause of my first major constipation."

Strasberg also blamed George C. Scott for causing Kim to slow up, "like she was drugged," completely destroying her performance. Cindy Adams, in her book on Strasberg, quotes Lee as saying, "I don't to this day know what happened because I never spoke to her afterwards. Kim's not a person you talk to easily." And at a meeting called the morning after the London notices, Lee told the actors the reviewers were right in their criticisms. George C. Scott, who always referred to Strasberg as "Lee pardon-the-expression Strasberg," stood up in a rage and advanced on Lee, threatening him with bodily injury for maintaining that it was the actors who were lousy and that the fiasco was their fault. As he did when Ruth Nelson threatened to kill him at the *Gold Eagle Guy* dress rehearsal in the thirties, Lee opted to turn and walk out. Scott didn't show at the second night's performance. Someone walked through his part reading his dialogue from a script.

Lee claimed, "I will never forget what Kim did to me by dictating to me it would be her way or she wouldn't go to London. I may forgive her but I won't forget." Kim doesn't forget or forgive. Some say the nervous breakdown she suffered after her terrible experience in London was the result of feeling guilty at being the one who forced Lee to turn his dream of *The Three Sisters* into a reality. This is what Kim said to me on her return to America: "When I was making a film and something went wrong, I could always say, 'Oh, come on, Kim, it's only a movie.' When I did a TV show and was unhappy I'd say, 'Oh, come on, Kim, you're only doing it to make money.' But when I entered the Cathedral and found *that* to be corrupt, well, there was no where else to go. Bobby, I'm never going to act on the stage again." "Please, Kim," I said, "time is what you need. Even in the jungle of the theater, time eventually heals. You'll be back." "No, Bobby," she said, in a very quiet voice, "I'm never going to act on the stage again."

As of this writing, Kim Stanley has fulfilled that terrible promise.

CHAPTER 17

# The Yale School of Drama

THE DECADE OF the fifties closed ignominiously with John Patrick's *Juniper and the Pagans,* which I have disposed of in an earlier chapter. If I had been occupied solely with the various hits and flops of those ten years, I would have considered that I had succeeded only in becoming a routine, busy Broadway director. But I managed to hang on to my franchise as a theater craftsman by filling in the time between shows with teaching and lecturing.

Although I have done teaching stints in universities all over the country at one time or another, for thirty-five years (1941-1976) I kept returning to the Yale School of Drama for short or long periods, depending on my availability. The first dean I worked for there was the Glasgow-born scholar, Allardyce Nicoll. Two memories of that initial period on the Yale faculty remain with me. One is a Drama School production of the full-length *Hamlet,* interesting enough to seem shorter than the usual cut version. The other is Professor Nicoll's particular speech pattern. He had a way of lovingly hanging on to the letter "M" before releasing it to a waiting world. The title of one of his famous books became a veritable choir of humming birds in his mouth: "MMMMasks, MMMMimes, and MMMMiracles."

1948 to 1951 found me lecturing on and off at the Drama School, this time under the dean who followed Nicoll, Boyd Smith. Present in one of my seminars was a bright student by the name of Bob Brustein who was to turn up at Yale again later on. From 1967 to my retirement from Yale in 1976, by which time I had become the Chairman of the Acting and Directing departments of the Drama School, Robert Brustein was my dean.

Not being as expert a critic as Brustein, let me tip my hand at the outset of this review of his tenure at Yale. If I can somehow convey my opinion of him as a theater man right off, my recounting of the Brustein years at Yale might be kept in better perspective. One of the strangest conceits in the world of theater is that proficiency in one field of the craft automatically confers authoritative knowledge of every other artistic discipline on the possessor of that proficiency. For some reason, Clifford Odets's talent as a writer made him certain he was an expert musicologist. Saroyan, having achieved success as a playwright, immediately assumed that directing would be a breeze for him. As for the Bru himself—forgive this seemingly hideous familiarity, but I must tell you that whatever differences there may be in our artistic opinions, Robert Brustein was, is, and I hope, will be, my close friend—there is no doubt in my mind that he is a first rate critic of plays, and a superb lecturer on the history of drama, classical and contemporary. Whenever I could, I used to attend his courses and marveled at the way he related the plays and playwrights he was discussing to the life of their times. Expert as he is in these fields, when it comes to the practical crafts of acting and directing, he has the attitude of a high-minded amateur. His theory of "conceptual" play direction has resulted in slapping metaphors onto the works of his own revered playwrights, mangling them in the process. His own acting, with one notable exception, has that rigidity that results from a brilliant mind sending intelligent line readings directly from his brain to his voice box. A good actor takes a longer route—from his mind (thinking), down through his heart (true feeling that comes from thought being sifted through experience), and then up and out of his mouth. The audience feels it is looking in on a life being lived, not just having one described to it. Only once, sitting in the audience at a Brustein portrayal, did I get the thrill that comes to the spectator when, suspending his disbelief, he is captured by stage truth. In a revue put on by the Yale Repertory Theatre called *Watergate Classics,* Brustein appeared in the final sketch as Richard Nixon in a Philip Roth parody of a presidential Address to the Nation. As Nixon promised to safeguard all American citizens, members of the National Guard and other armed forces entered, with guns drawn, from all the doors of the theater and surrounded the audience. Bob delivered this address with such quiet artistry that it froze one's blood. He had found his part.

As a director and the producer of the Yale Repertory Company, Brustein was a self-confessed irritant. I once asked him if the consequence of many of the Rep's productions provoking the audience was intentional. Decidedly, he maintained, and cited the analogy of the oyster which, when containing a foreign particle rubbing against it causing friction, works the intruder over until a pearl results. Like so many analogies, it sounds better than it works out in practice. Some of Brustein's productions may have been oysters but, although irritating, they didn't all deliver pearls.

The whole idea of "conceptual" theater, as promoted by Brustein, has gotten way out of hand recently. Instead of the style of the production emanating from the context of the material, it seems as if trendy directors, upon reading *King Lear,* ask themselves, "Now what can I do with this mother? Peter Brook has already come up with a Samuel Beckett *Lear.* How about a punk rock one?" Meyerhold warned, "The greatest danger for a director is to yield to caprice."

The simple truth of the matter is that no artist worthy of the name creates without some concept, even if it's unconscious. It is the definition of an artist. It is what he sees in the material that the ordinary person doesn't that gives him the right to be called an artist in the first place. He then sets about using the technique of his craft to create his image. What comes out, in the end, is some version of what he saw in the material in the first place, or his concept, as Orson Welles saw those hundreds of skulls in *Danton's Death.*

Soon after the opening of *Bingo* by Edward Bond, beautifully directed for the Yale Rep by Ron Daniels, a colloquy about the production was held in the Drama School with the students and the director present. Brustein started things off with a question to Daniels: "What was your concept for *Bingo*?" Ron thought for awhile. Then he began. "Well, I tried to do the first scene as well as I could. Then I went on to the second scene and tried to do that as well as I could. And so on. I suppose if you put them all together, that was my concept." It sure cleared up the sinuses in the Drama School for awhile. It called to mind a student who was studying composition with Dimitri Shostakovich and complained that he couldn't find a theme for his second movement. "You shouldn't be looking for a theme," the composer cautioned him, "you should be writing the second movement."

For one example of Brustein's coming a cropper as a result of superimposing a concept on a play—his notorious "camera-lens" version of *The Wild Duck* was another—let's take his direction of Molière's *Don Juan.* Bob saw in it the image of a Black Mass. When the audience arrived, they found themselves in a theater that had been transformed into a church, complete with altar, pulpit, and stained glass windows. Since the theater had previously *been* a church, it was being born again. The exquisite Carmen de Lavallade, completely covered in a black robe, accompanied by several other performers, was already conducting some sort of ritual, seemingly sacrificing a goat on the altar. It was not clear how long these celebrants had been there, but they kept it up during the arrival of all the patrons and up to the start of the play proper. The gloom engendered by this prologue permeated the whole production, and the continual hammering home of the concept of a black mass (Don Juan's father—played by John Cromwell—delivered one of his speeches from the pulpit) obscured the flashes of wit in the author's dialogue. Brustein's shadow totally eclipsed Molière.

When I assumed the chairmanship of the Acting and Directing departments of the School of Drama in 1974, I read my prospectus for a directors' and actors' workshop to the Yale students, setting forth my attitude on conceptual theater. After outlining the approach for the actors to achieve a "total" effect by monitoring both their internal truth and their external expression of that truth so that the one would flow from the other, I turned to the problem of the director: "In the field of directing, it is to be hoped that the wedding of form and content would make an artistic whole. The stylistic conception of a script, no matter how freewheeling, that derives from and grows out of the material, is apt to have a more harmonious result than an idea leapt on for its own clever sake and grafted on to the play with an attendant sense of distortion. On the other hand, there are no limits to the interpretive possibilities of a script if they are rooted somewhere in its nature. Let Thomas Carlyle speak: 'It is meritorious to insist on forms. Religion and all else clothes itself in forms. . . . All substances clothe themselves in forms; but there are suitable true forms, and then there are untrue, unsuitable. As the briefest definition one might say, forms which *grow* round a substance, if we rightly understand that, will correspond to the real nature and purport of it, will be true, good; forms which are consciously *put* round a substance, bad. I invite you to reflect on this. It distinguishes true from false in Ceremonial Form, earnest solemnity from empty pageant, in all human things.'"*

When I finished my presentation, Bob congratulated me and referred particularly to my quote from Carlyle, calling it "beautiful." I was discovering again that the distance between what one subscribes to in art, and what one practices, can be infinite.

On February 5, 1966, shortly after accepting the post of Dean of the Yale School of Drama, Brustein had asked me if I would consider teaching at the University again, full time or visiting, but what with my own theater workshop going and commitments to other universities, I had enough teaching hours on my schedule. By the time Bob's second year rolled around, I was able to accept his offer of Professor of Acting and Directing and devote half of the week to the Drama School.

The happiest memories of my Yale years, under Brustein, are of the pleasure in working with so many talented students. They were chosen from auditions held all over the country every season. There was, as always in student drama classes, a fair percentage of duds. But even a partial list of my pupils from Yale who have gone on to successful, professional careers is impressive: Meryl Streep, Ken Howard, Sigourney Weaver, Jill Eikenberry, James Naughton, Henry Winkler, Joyce Fideor, Ben Halley, Jr., Alma Cuervo, Christine Estabrook, David Marshall Grant. Among the Yale Repertory Theatre's professional actors who came to class, too, were: Elizabeth Parrish, David Ackroyd, David Clennon, Joan Pape, Louis Plante, and Norma Brustein, the Dean's wife, who also acted as my expert

---

**The Hero As King*—last one (May 22, 1840) of six Carlyle lectures ("On Heroes, Hero-Worship, and the Heroic in History").

assistant. The directing seminars I held were attended by what sounds like a roll call of the bright young directors of today: A. J. Antoon, Peter Mark Schifter, Michael Posnick, Jeff Bleckner, Stephen Rudnicki, Walton Jones, Tom Bullard, Alan Mokler, Tom Moore.

It sounds fatuous to say I learned from them as they learned from me. But it's true. When someone asks me how I could still be teaching after so many decades I say, "Where else would I learn?" The fact is that every time an actor gets up to do a scene, some new aspect of the work gets revealed. In isolating a particular problem and trying to solve it, I learn something new myself. If students ever started making the same mistakes in the same way, I'd probably quit out of boredom.

There are certain generalities that can be observed after a lifetime of teaching. One is that whole classes tend to develop recognizable personalities of their own. If there are a few really brilliant students in the group, the tendency of the others is to try to stretch themselves in the direction of the good ones. And, lo and behold, you find yourself with "a good class." Conversely, if there are a number of goof-offs, or plea-coppers, a sort of poison gradually seeps through the group and you are stuck with "a bad class."

Another generality I feel safe in making (then I'll stop) is this: those students whose acting doesn't satisfy always do a little more less fully; whereas the good ones always do a little less more fully. Meryl Streep was one of the latter. As I watched her in whatever part she presented in scene class (she could play anything from a mewling babe to an octogenarian in those days, too), I always held a secret wish for the playwright to be present, since he would never again see his character so imaginatively realized.

Henry Winkler doesn't like me to refer to him as the Fonz, hoping that I, his teacher, will at least keep the flag of his artistic purity flying until he's milked the last buck out of his TV triumph and returns to his old profes-

Meryl Streep in class, Yale Drama School: "Everything from a mewling babe to an octogenarian."

sion of good actor. And good actor he was, too, in his *Merchant of Venice* scene in class, and with his creation of an étude based on a painting by Delacroix in my style class. In going over my assessments of the Yale acting students, I notice next to Henry's name, "Has to be funny, but works hard." After Henry had parlayed his deft TV characterization of the Fonz into a colossal fortune, he returned one day to the Drama School in one of my last semesters there to address the current students. In introducing him I said, "Do you remember, Henry, how, when you were in class, I used to say to you, 'Henry, don't always try to be funny. Play the character. If it's a funny scene, you'll be funny. But don't you try to *act funny* all the time. You see, Henry, if you had only listened to me, you'd be a pauper now.'"

Stress was the operative word for the condition that permeated the entire Drama School during the Brustein regime. I found out that it was also a medical term at the end of a particularly stormy semester during my tenure as Chairman of the Acting and Directing departments. I had a massive heart attack. When I asked the doctor what some of the warning symptoms might have been, he mentioned high blood pressure, high blood cholesterol, and stress. I had normal blood pressure and low cholesterol.

When Brustein wrote the story of his Yale years *(Making Scenes),* I advised him that since Harold Clurman's review of the Group Theatre's stormy decade in the thirties was titled *The Fervent Years,* Bob's should be

Dean Brustein, *The Ferment Years.*

called *The Ferment Years.* The two adjectives also describe the difference between the two theater men. While working at the Drama School, particular stresses I felt seemed at the time to be the result of this or that pressure emanating from the student body or the faculty. In hindsight, I know they were all due to waffling at the top. This uncertainty on the part of Brustein as to which training procedures were best for the kind of actors he wanted to train haunted the dean all through his regime at the Drama School. He listened to contradictory advice from many sources and this practice took its toll in such disasters as the loss of his best teacher, Stella Adler. Norma Brustein had studied with Stella, and Bob believed in the great coach's worth. But when she resisted the idea of pupils who were still learning their ABCs appearing in Rep productions, Bob was persuaded by some trendy faculty members, and a few student directors sowing their wild oats, that Stella was a thirties product, therefore old-fashioned. That epithet was also hurled at me when I resisted the throw-them-in-the-water-and-they'll-learn-to-swim method of training performing artists.

The notion that truthfully experienced acting (which is all Stella and I were ever talking about) could be tagged old-fashioned is hogwash. So is the notion that Brechtian alienation acting, for example, is avant-garde. Acting is good or bad. The choices you make are what lead to a particular style. Ekkehard Schall, who I saw play Brecht's *Arturo Ui* and is now, after Brecht's death, holding down the fort at the Berliner Ensemble (he also married into the family—Brecht's daughter, Barbara, is his wife), maintains that no special acting approach is required for Brecht. He says he performs everything "the same way." I saw four Berliner Ensemble productions personally directed by Brecht, and I can testify that when Helene Weigel and Ernst Busch, two of the leading actors in the company, acted, they played like great actors anywhere—fully, and according to the character, the situation, the moment, etc. The only thing that gave them that cool "Brechtian" quality was their acting choices—all nonsentimental.

As for being "old-fashioned": When my friend Boris Aronson, the acerbic scene designer, was hit with the same accusation, he shot back with, "A tree is old-fashioned, Mozart is old-fashioned, sexual intercourse is old-fashioned. So what?" At the time I directed *My Heart's in the Highlands,* which happened to be nonrealistic, here are some of the epithets hurled at the production by the critics: "cubist," "surrealist," "weird," "crackpot," "experimental," "madcap," and "screwy." Not an "old-fashioned" in the lot. By the way, how do you defend yourself against such charges without sounding defensive? Never mind.

My approach to training (and Stella's) is based on an idea of the normal growth of a student actor's technique: start with a complete set of exercises to prepare the actor's performing instrument; go on to the analysis of scripts and roles and the preparation of realistic scenes; and finally, tackle special problems of style—the Greeks, Shakespeare, Restoration, Molière,

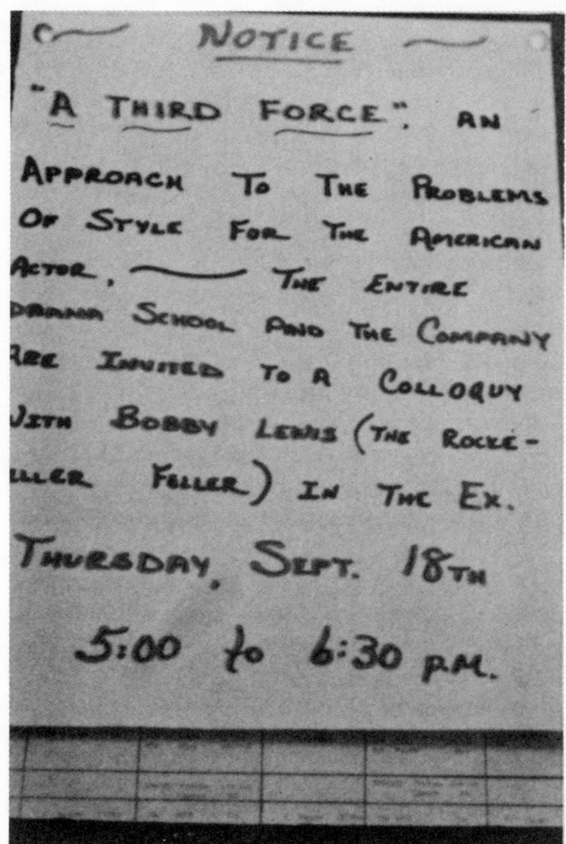


Poster in the Yale Drama School Green Room: "Finally, tackle the problems of style."

avant-garde, and so on. When I first agreed to teach under Brustein at the Drama School, I found that Jeremy Geidt, an English actor and a member of the Repertory Company, was catapulting his first-year students straight into Shakespeare. It wasn't easy to reverse this trend but I succeeded; not, however, without experiencing my first bout with stress. Brustein's "spine," to use a Stanislavski term, was enunciated by him in his book, *Making Scenes*: "Tragedy with a twist of cabaret, that is what I wanted to show the acting students." OK. But this stylistic concept can be achieved only after you have learned to act. Otherwise you end up with that all-too-familiar look of "play-acting." A solid technique will prepare the acting student for whatever flights of stylistic expression he, his playwright, or his director might require.

These are the aims I discussed during many an evening at the Brusteins, who graciously invited me to fine dinners. Having picked Bob up at his office at five in the afternoon and talked to him in the car to his house, over drinks, during dinner, and after the brandy, it was a good seven hours before I went home at midnight. I'd go to bed happy, feeling that I'd gotten my message through. The next morning, Bob would poke his head out of his office as I went by and assure me that he now knew exactly what had to be done. A couple of days later some procedure would be announced to the school that was light years away from what we had discussed. At first I couldn't understand. Ultimately I caught on. After Bob had his meeting with me, someone else on the faculty—Richard Gilman maybe, or Gordon Rogoff—would capture his imagination with suggestions for some other plan. That is one example of what I meant when I referred to Bob's "attitude of an amateur."

About Rogoff, Brustein ultimately fired him in 1969, and Gordon, agreeing with those who maintained that Yale Rep practices were interfering with student training said, "The question is, does the theater serve the school or is the school in servitude to the theater?" At about the same time, Arnold Weinstein, professor of playwrighting, submitted his resignation but, having been a close friend of Brustein's, when asked by the press why he quit, would only deliver this mind-boggling reply: "The whole situation is too complex to brave the epistemological vicissitudes of journalism." How's that for tragedy with a twist of cabaret?

One example of how the Yale Repertory Theatre took advantage of the Yale School of Drama was with the acquisition of a solid repertory actor by the name of Tom Hill. Ostensibly to encourage the idea of students being apprenticed to the professional actors, which was one of Brustein's long time principles, Hill was assigned to teach a class in the school. Now some actors may very well be good teachers. Alvin Epstein, for example, was a fine actor in the Rep Company and an inventive director, as well as a delightful teacher. Tom Hill was an actor, period. I suspected that the teaching salary he got, added to what the Yale Rep budget could afford to pay him, made up the amount needed to keep him in the acting company.

When the students started to complain to me (as Chairman of the Acting Department) about Hill's teaching methods, I dropped in on his classes for a look-see. Now, Tom Hill had a mannerism in his acting which always startled me. When it was necessary for him to turn from someone he was addressing on his left to someone on his right, his head, as it revolved around, always paused for one split second in its orbit to "connect" with the audience. When I visited his class, I discovered this was not just a mannerism. It was a conscious technique that he was instructing the students to emulate. They were resisting like mad. After class I talked it over with Hill. He insisted that the glance directed at the audience was a way of bringing it into the experience being generated on the stage. What to do? I told the class that here they had a good chance to deal with a problem they'd have to face sooner or later in their careers: how to preserve your own artistic integrity while working with directors of all kinds, including some who were pushing you in areas counter to your sense of truth. It didn't help. The stand-off between the students and the instructor remained unshakable. I called a meeting with Brustein and Howard Stein, the Dean of Faculty, and gave them my opinion: Tom Hill should stop teaching. A terrific flare-up ensued. A list of people who had been removed from the faculty since my appointment as Chairman was thrust at me. It included the names of the fellow they had replaced with me, as well as changes in the dance and speech departments Brustein had agreed were necessary for the new approach the department was to take. He had also obviously forgotten the clean sweep he had made of the staff when he became dean. I threw the list back at him and suggested he add my name to it and walked out. The upshot, though, was that the students were relieved of Tom Hill and the need to practice any more audience-glances. But I had been dealt another serious psychological (and physical) blow. I felt I was walking in quicksand and dreamed of the time I would get out.

By 1977, a year after I was gone from the Drama School, I had recovered enough to get a good laugh out of Erika Munk's review of Brecht's *Mister Puntila,* presented by the Yale Repertory Company. Of Tom Hill in the title role, the avant-garde critic said, "He has an irritating way of addressing the audience: Is that the vaudeville motif, or a twenty-five-word-or-less notion of alienation techniques?"

My directing jobs at Yale had one salutary effect on me. By choosing plays I had always wanted to direct on Broadway but couldn't get the backing for, I was able to satisfy frustrated desires. *Little Eyolf* by Ibsen was one such choice. A new translation by Michael Meyer shed interesting light on this neglected work. I informed Brustein I would like to direct it at the Yale Repertory Theatre since he had agreed I could do one play there during the 1969-1970 season, in addition to my work at the Drama School. I asked for Beatrice Straight to play the leading female role and started, during the summer, to study the play and prepare my director's script. What with Brustein's doubts about making a commitment to Straight and his wondering if I wouldn't rather do Ibsen's *When We Dead Awaken* instead, my creative juices had a tough time flowing smoothly as I tackled the text of *Little Eyolf.* I finally dispatched a letter on July 2 to Bob, at Martha's Vineyard, starting with this sentence: "I have the old faucet syndrome again—that sense of being turned on and off." I suggested that he, who was such a good critic of theater art, ought to try to understand the inner workings of theater people. Back came a sincere letter of apology and a go-ahead sign for *Little Eyolf* and Beatrice Straight.

The play is about a woman of means, Rita, who has been described as a sort of Hedda Gabler with money and a child. Her husband, Alfred, a writer, is rendered impotent by a sense of guilt brought about when the couple's baby is crippled by a fall from a table, where the husband and wife left him to make love in the next room. When the child is nine, he is drowned. The removal of the object of the parents' guilt does not bring them closer together, but instead, the child's wide open, questioning eyes under the surface of the water adds a more horrible sense of guilt onto the parents. I shipped the script off to my friend Beatrice Straight, with an assurance of her suitability for the role of the mother.

I was preoccupied with something quite different from *Little Eyolf* a week or so later, when suddenly I let out a moan and hit my forehead with my fist. A flash of memory reminded me that Beatrice's own baby had been tragically drowned in the family's swimming pool at their country home. I was stricken with remorse at what would have to seem to my friend as a monumental piece of insensitivity on my part. I ran the few blocks from my apartment in Manhattan to her town house and pressed her doorbell. She was in. Before I could begin my explanations this gracious lady, perceiving my torment at once, said "Please don't worry, Bobby. I knew that if you had remembered about my child, you would never have sent the play."

As it turned out, Beatrice was fascinated by the script itself and would have accepted the part if she had not already committed herself, for the same time slot, to play Blanche in *A Streetcar Named Desire,* a production to be directed by her husband, Peter Cookson.

After a disappointing search for someone good enough (and available) to replace Beatrice in *Little Eyolf,* I finally had to give up, and Brustein and I settled on Strindberg's *Crimes and Crimes.* There were parts in that interesting play for the other actors I had lined up for *Little Eyolf*: Alvin Epstein, Mildred Dunnock, and David Ackroyd. For the exotic Henriette, I was lucky to have Carmen de Lavallade on hand. This would be her first leading role in a straight play. Carmen was a joy to direct, mostly because dancers have a more disciplined approach to their work than most straight actors. When shown a step or a combination a dancer tries it and, through *doing* it, finds out about it—how it works, what needs adjusting, and so on. Too many actors, when given a suggestion, have a way of cogitating on it, analyzing it, questioning it, anything but doing it. For it is out of the doing that the real questions arise, not in the speculation. Too often surprising effects remain lost because, by the time they are debated, all possibility of surprise is gone.

Of the plays I directed for the Yale Drama School, T. S. Eliot's *The Family Reunion* gave me an opportunity to work out the interesting problem of choral speech for contemporary characters, while Christopher Durang's *Death Comes to Us All, Mary Agnes* was a foray into avant-garde black comedy. My favorite student production, though, was Sean O'Casey's *Cock-a-doodle Dandy,* produced in the University Theatre in the spring of 1974. I had been trying to get the play on somewhere since 1950.

Whenever I was in England I'd spend a weekend with the O'Caseys in Devon, the first one being in the summer of 1951. Sean was on the fifth

Strindberg's *Crimes and Crimes,* Yale Repertory Theatre. Alvin Epstein, Carmen de Lavallade, Mildred Dunnock, and David Ackroyd: "Carmen was a joy to direct."

volume of his autobiography, and times were lean. He said that the year before, all his work combined brought him thirty pounds of royalties in England. "Some years, less," he added. Once the bailiff came to remove furniture from the O'Casey house because of unpaid taxes. "I had a devil of a time persuading the fool not take my typewriter," Sean said, "since without it I couldn't earn the money he was looking for."

Down the road in the Civic Hall, a local theater company played. I wondered what the group of actors in this sleepy English hamlet thought of the fiery Irish rebel in their midst.

"Do you ever let them have one of your plays, Sean?" I asked.

"No," said O'Casey, "I wouldn't want to embarrass them."

The Protestant Sean O'Casey managed to become a good friend of the local Catholic priest, Father Russell. At first it was a bit rocky. "We had Father Russell over to the house for a quiet evening," said O'Casey. "My wife, Eileen, poured some paraffin in the fireplace to encourage the fire, and an enormous flame shot up into the parlor and nearly consumed us all, and there was poor Father Russell blowing on the flame trying to put it out."

Eileen, in her book *Sean,* claims that it was difficult to raise the money for a Broadway production of *Cock-a-doodle Dandy* because prospective backers didn't know who O'Casey was. Since I was the one trying to raise the money, I can attest to the fact that it was precisely because they *did* know who he was that made it tough. The most prominent backer of plays

**A stroll in Devon. Bobby to Sean O'Casey: "Did you ever let them have one of your plays, Sean?"**

in New York at that time, Peggy Cullman, turned the play down because she felt it was anti-Catholic. Once she was out of it, all her friends who usually went along with her backed away from the project, too.

The closest I came to getting the play on in New York was when Herman Levin took an option on it. Oliver Smith got busy designing the sets, and I gave readings of the play for investors, assuring them that it was an adult, comic, fairy tale about the conflict between the forces of life exemplified by the proud, prancing Cock and the forces of death manifested by people's reliance on prejudice, illusion, rumor, and superstition. A Texas backer by the name of Tad Adoue was so moved by the play and its message, that he promised to send fifteen thousand dollars as soon as he got home. Herman and I immediately indulged in a bit of harmony, parodying the old song, "Smile the while I kiss you sad adieu." Only we sang "Tad Adoue." We had only raised twelve thousand dollars up to then and felt our luck would turn when we got his check, which we then could go around waving under the noses of the doubtful. After a few weeks of silence, I wrote Adoue and suggested politely that maybe his check had gotten lost in the mail. He replied that he had addressed it wrong and when the Post Office returned it to him, he took that as a "sign" not to invest. Superstition won out again. Levin and I gave up, and the only glimmer of pleasure I got out of the whole effort was the knowledge that at least the advance received was important to Sean and Eileen.

I was sorry Sean, who had died ten years earlier, could not know that I finally got *Cock-a-doodle Dandy* up on the Yale University stage, since we had discussed it in such detail so many times, in person and through the mails. He would have loved to see Meryl Streep as Loreleen, whom the playwright describes as "a handsome, gay, and intelligent woman—with an air of her own." Just as with Kim Stanley, even when Meryl was still a student, it was not necessary to direct her, but only to edit the wealth of material she brought to her characterization as a result of translating the overall production ideas into choices for her own creation.

I worked so hard on *Cock-a-doodle Dandy* in an attempt to achieve all I remembered about the details outlined by O'Casey, that someone wrote me an anonymous letter protesting the rehearsal hours. It said, "Dear Mr. Lewis: As a friend and supporter of the Yale Drama School, it is my duty to remind you with respect that *Cock-a-doodle Dandy* is a comedy. The number of presently planned rehearsals and run-throughs, therefore, seems not only excessive, but also detrimental to the spontaneity that a production of this sort requires. Please take this humbly offered point of view with the same generosity of spirit in which it is offered. Best wishes, A Friend." I posted the letter on the green room billboard with my reply: "Dear Friend—Now that I know it's a comedy, I may have to call more rehearsals. Having directed that master comedian, Bert Lahr, I know how many agonizing hours he spent perfecting his spontaneous comedy effects. Your friend, Bobby Lewis."

Nineteen seventy-four was the year when Brustein fired the Chairman of the Acting and Directing departments of the Drama School and put me in the spot. I almost said "on the spot," because it turned out to be a pressure cooker that forced me into a state of extreme stress. I didn't mind the extra amount of work added to my own teaching chores: faculty meetings, scheduling, monitoring of other teachers' classes, dropping in on rehearsals of student productions, and office meetings with students and faculty members with axes to grind. What I did mind was the fact that in the Kingdom of Brustein, the Monarch had always to be right. In *Making Scenes,* Bob confesses, "At times, I felt like Ibsen's Brand, sacrificing my family, friends, and personal happiness for an unrealizable ideal." If, as a leader, he could have led, instead of driven, his group, maybe that ideal wouldn't have been so elusive. Wickedly, I dubbed him *Brand-X*.

There was also the problem of the understandable difficulty a few teachers and some students had of transferring their sense of loyalty from the deposed department head to the new one. Particularly resistant was a hard-core cell buried in my second-year acting class. Their first-year teacher had been my predecessor as chairman of the department, and they were going to submit me to a tough trial period. Coming as I did from the professional theater, which, in their minds, meant "commercial," made me suspect. How much did I know of the new styles of theater to which they paid so much lip service? Grotowski and his "poor theatre?" The Theatre of Political Shock? The Theatre of Revolt? The Theatre of the Absurd? I did learn a lot about the Theatre of Cruelty from them.

Although these students were a minority—another of my classes welcomed me by wearing T-shirts imprinted with my bald, bespectacled countenance—the sinking feeling in my gut, which I always experienced from exhibitions I suspected were basically anti-art, made me greet with relief the midterm Christmas holidays after the first disturbing semester. I felt quite recovered as I went to a New Year's Eve dinner party at a neighbor's house with my sister. Back in my own living room at 1:15 A.M., on the first day of the New Year of 1975, my heart blew a gasket. The reason I introduce this personal note into an otherwise theatrical memoir is because of the clear connection between the heart attack and the stresses of the Yale School of Drama. In *Making Scenes,* Brustein acknowledges, "The stressful pressures of the first semester had taken their toll on Bobby."

Throughout that first night in the intensive care unit of the Phelps Memorial Hospital in Tarrytown, I went in and out of consciousness, and each time I slept I had this recurrent nightmare: the entire avant-garde acting troupe known as the Ontological-Hysteric Theatre was being forcibly shoved through a long tube.

In a couple of days, even though it was school vacation time, and although I was allowed no physical movement, being wired from all my orifices like that character in the Living Theatre's *Frankenstein,* I was impelled to summon my sister to my hospital bedside and to dictate a letter to Brustein on Martha's Vineyard. I described my condition, estimated my hospital stay, and my period of recuperation at home, promised to be back in school in March for the auditions of the next year's students, and to begin my rehearsals of the Chris Durang play. For fear that the schedule I had set when I assumed the chairmanship of the department might get fouled up, I promised to send Bob my suggestions for procedures during my absence. This I did on January 7, and my sister also read that dictated letter over the phone to Brustein's secretary, including my wish that Alvin Epstein take over my first-year class and Norma Brustein the second year. She had been my able assistant in that troublesome class in the first semester and knew the work at first hand. In addition to assisting me, Norma had also acted in class scenes.

When the few smart-asses in that class heard Norma was going to be their substitute teacher during my absence, all hell broke loose. The *Yale Daily News,* always happy to shaft the Dean, joined the *Yale Graduate Professional* in quoting the objections of some of the pupils to being taught by "another student." The class dispatched a long, snide, complaining telegram to me, ending with a "hope for a speedy recovery." I answered them and the "Yalie Daily," recounting all of the superb critiques Norma had dispensed in the class and of her professional qualifications. As for her performing scenes in class I called that "a tribute to her industry, intelligence, and humility."

I was back in school, as promised, in March, but I had pretty much had it by then. The following year was my time for mandatory age retirement from Yale, anyway. Brustein asked me to stay on and, if I did, he would pay me through the Yale Rep. In a euphoric way, he described his new five-year plan for the Drama School to me. The first year students would participate in the Yale Rep productions. The second year would have short-term guest instructors in special subjects—Brecht, etc. There would be no master teachers. The master teacher of the third year would be the acting company of the Repertory Theatre itself. (Remember Tom Hill?) All these procedures had previously failed at Yale. In addition, I would be expected to furnish "ground work" for all this. I said, "No, thanks." Of course, Bob never got around to testing his new plan for a long enough period because the new president of Yale, A. Bartlett Giamatti, was lurking around the corner with his first order of business on assuming the presidency: the firing of Dean Brustein. Bob took his Repertory Theatre to Cambridge, and Lloyd Richards became the new Dean of the Yale School of Drama.

As a prime example of the difference between theory and practice in theater people, Brustein, in his welcoming speech to the new students on September 9, 1969, had wisely said, "The great innovators in the theater always served their apprenticeship before venturing into new territory, if only to learn thoroughly what it was they were opposed to and wished to change: Meyerhold formed his own theater in opposition to Stanislavski realism, but only after he worked for years with the Moscow Art Theatre. For that reason, we are going to ask all of you theater people to learn your craft thoroughly before seeking to revolutionize it." But when he witnessed Stella and me (and others, too) trying to put into practical application that very principle of artistic growth in the school, he became impatient with it and threw irritating roadblocks in the way. Again, no pearl.

When, in 1966, Brustein first wrote and asked me to return to Yale to teach under his new deanery, he recalled the time he had been in class as a student when I lectured there in the fifties: "The only stimulating moments I ever had there were spent listening to you." I return the compliment, Bob. It was certainly stimulating for me to work under you, too. You say in your book reviewing the Yale years that you grind your teeth at night. If I've aggravated that symptom in you, I'm sorry. But not to worry. You're a critic; you'll always have the last word.

CHAPTER 18

# Method—or Madness?

BY 1957, TEN years had passed since Kazan and I took our walk in Central Park and planned the Actors Studio. I had left it in 1948 and formed my own Workshop a couple of years after that. Meantime, the Stanislavski System, as introduced to us in the Group Theatre, was slowly being distorted into the American "Method." What had been a compilation of the technical elements that are present when a good actor is acting well was becoming rigidified into a style. The "Method Actor" was born. I have never been able to find out precisely what that meant but, depending on which camp you're in, you hate him or you worship him. Dubbing someone a Method Actor makes as much sense as referring to Horowitz as a scales and arpeggios pianist. Poor Stanislavski's half century of devotion to exploring the inner and outer workings of the actor had been reduced to a fetish. There was much confusion and infighting about his system. I decided to try to do something about it.

Judd Mathison, my assistant, and I knew the Playhouse Theatre on West Forty-eighth Street was dark. We went to the manager of the house, Abe Enklewitz, and asked him if I could have it for eight Monday nights, at 11:30 P.M., to give a series of free lectures on the "Method" to theater people. He said yes, provided I paid for the doorman and cleaning people that would be required. I agreed, announced the dates of the lectures to be called "Method—or Madness?" and printed up the tickets. One to a customer, the free ticket inscribed with the actor's name on it could be obtained by written request only. Then the fun began. I knew there was much "Method" steam stored up waiting to be let off, but I never dreamed how much. The tickets were gobbled up at once and many who had none came to the theater anyway and tried to crash. Some, turned away at the door, would go down the side alley, up the fire escape, and try to pry open the side doors of the balcony. "Method—or Madness?" lectures became known as the hottest ticket in town. When, after the final night, Judd collected all the tickets, he discovered quite a few counterfeit ones. Actors had gone to printing shops, had the tickets copied and, forging Judd's handwriting, wrote in their names.

As the first lecture got close, the stage hands union stepped in and slapped three heads of department on me. I explained that the theater was donated; that there was no admission charge; that I got no fee, indeed was already paying the bills for the front of the house; that backstage there was nothing for them to do since all I planned was to stand on the stage and talk, with the house lights on; and finally, that the whole enterprise was for the benefit of the theatrical profession. They were touched, but they were also adamant. It was too late for me to start looking for another free location so, each week, for eight weeks, I had to pay three heads of departments—carpenter, electrician, and prop man—so they could sit in the basement playing cards. My lawyer advised me to write on each check, "Paid Under Protest." I did, and you can imagine what a thrill that was for me and what a severe blow it dealt to the stage hands union. Its attitude reminded me of the story of the kid who approached the sexton at the door of the synagogue on Yom Kippur.

"I want to go in and see my mother," he begged.

**"Method—or Madness?" Lecture series, Playhouse Theatre, 1957: "The hottest ticket in town."**

"You have to have a ticket on the High Holy Days," said the sexton. "You can't go in without a ticket."

"But I just want to ask my mother a question. I'll come right out," pleaded the kid.

"All right," the sexton agreed, "you can go in for just a minute. But if I catch you *praying*—!"

The stage hands union had caught me praying.

From 11:30 P.M. to one in the morning, on eight Monday nights, here are a few of the points I tried to cover:

The so-called Method had become a Style of American acting recognizable by a distinctive slouch while standing still, a curious lope while walking, and a callous disregard of the playwright's lines, often paraphrased and sometimes thrown away altogether. All this in the name of truth. Truth, my ass. Personal comfort for the self-indulgent actor, that's all it is. How about a little truth for the material?

Next an obsessive dedication to personal emotion at the expense of other elements: characterization, style, intention, dynamics. Here I fired a sally at this onanistic school of emotion: "If crying were the sole object of acting, my Aunt Rivka would have been Duse."

On the subjects of emotion and psychological truth, I call in an expert witness. Vera Soloviova, an actress who was in the Moscow Art Theatre company at the beginning of this century, received her training in Russia from Stanislavski, Sulerzhitsky, Vachtangov, and Michael Chekhov. As a teacher of the Stanislavski System, she is in a direct line back to the master. On April 17, 1980, Soloviova taped an interview with a student from the University of Houston, who was preparing a dissertation on Vachtangov. On the subject of emotion as dealt with in Stanislavski's System as opposed to American practitioners of "The Method," here are a couple of pithy quotes from Verachka:

"Stanislavski practiced psychology; Strasberg practices psychiatry. Stanislavski's emotion came from the heart. Strasberg's comes from the kishkas."

Abuse of improvisation was the next lecture item. While useful either as a style of theater (Commedia dell 'Arte to Nichols and May), a training tool, or a rehearsal aid, there must be some sense of form in all performing, even when improvising. A jam session of jazz musicians would be cacophony if each guy simply went off on his own with no relation to the original piece. Improvisation, no matter how free, I pointed out, must be used to control, enhance, and embellish the problem at hand, not throw it out the window.

I also tried to disabuse the actors of the idea that Stanislavski's System was applicable only to realistic material. Pointing out that he himself had directed every possible kind of production from Chekhov to Gilbert and Sullivan, I read and discussed the chart of all the elements of the actor's craft that Stella Adler had brought back from her sessions with Stanislavski in the Group days. The items were equally divided between "internal" and "external."

From the response of the actors, I felt I had cleared the air of a number of Method misconceptions for the New York theater community at large, as Stella had for the Group members in the thirties. The subsequent publication of the lectures by Samuel French (and by Heinemann Ltd., in London) spread the word around and was greeted with the same sense of relief as that expressed by the actors who attended the sessions at the Playhouse. Gordon Craig said, "It's the stuff to give the troops." London's *Time and Tide*, heading its review "Sanity, At Last," concluded with, "If you feel like zipping into a pair of jeans, not washing till the first of next month, and leaving the barber to twiddle his thumbs, there are plenty of schools which will be only too pleased (for a consideration) to take you in. They will teach you how to voice-produce a mumble, demonstrate how to portray a cash register, and present you with a handsome diploma on your departure. You may, however, want to be an actor. Then this book is for you."

On this side of the Atlantic, I stared longest at this comment: "We have needed a book like this for a long time"—Lee Strasberg.

With the establishment of the Robert Lewis Theatre Workshop in 1952, I finally found the setup that permitted me the most freedom to explore training methods for actors; there was no "administration" to please. I took the training I gratefully received from Strasberg in the Group Theatre days and made it my own by keeping what I needed, discarding what I didn't, and altering all to conform with my own developing conceptions as actor, director, and teacher. So, too, I told the people studying with me that I would consider my best pupils to be those who gradually and gracefully forgot what they heard in class for the reason that what they needed had become part of their own artistic mechanism; and what they didn't had been discarded. My one fear in training was dogmatism—a sense that there is only one way to do it, and that is your way.

I also worried that I might turn out classroom actors: that is, one, actors who can only work with people who work the way they do, and, two, actors whose lax energy permits them to succeed in "getting over" to their peers sitting no more than six feet from where they're performing their scene but wash out completely on the stage of even the tiniest off-Broadway theater.

A further danger of classroom acting was inherent in the very idea of scene-study. When an actor picks a scene from a play to work on, he's not about to choose the first entrance of the character as he comes home, hangs up his hat, asks how the wife and kids are, feeds the dog, mixes a martini, and sits down to read the junk mail from the supermarket. The actor is going to pick the "big" scene—the confrontation with that wife at the end of the second act where she yells at him for not including her in the really important events of his life. (How do you like these plays I make up?) This is what happens after years of students doing scenes with the strongest situation in the play: The actor, so used to highly charged emotional acting in class—the kind that elicits the most attention from the instructor and brings forth the most interesting criticisms—is apt to overburden a part that runs through a whole evening with continuous "significance." When he hangs up his hat as he comes through the door, it has "meaning."

To avoid this all-too-prevalent disease, I tried different solutions. First, I abandoned the idea of scenes altogether and announced we would rehearse full plays and thus more closely approximate the director-actor relationship rather than the teacher-student one. Good idea. In preparing a complete role, the actor would get a sense of how to build a part from first entrance to last exit. Fine. Now we come to what play to choose. Uh-uh, we're in trouble. How many plays do you know with interesting (even if not big) parts for a group of twenty or more actors? How happy is the guy or gal going to be who has to enter periodically during weeks of fascinating rehearsals for the leads and proclaim that the carriage awaits? Even when I once put aside the last few weeks of class time of a rather large group (the Lincoln Center Training Program) to prepare the complete Murder of Gonzago scene from *Hamlet,* I was not looked on too kindly by Faye Dunaway for casting her as the Player whose one moment was to step forward and announce

For us and for our tragedy,
Here stooping to your clemency,
We beg your hearing patiently.

and then exit—forever.

The solution I came up with, and employ to this day, is a combination of scene study and a directorial analysis of the entire play. The actors work on one scene the way they would if they were preparing the whole play over a four week rehearsal period. In other words, they present their scenes four times at four strategic periods of the rehearsal span. After they've carefully read the whole play at home to familiarize themselves with the text, I witness the first reading of the scene in the workshop as it would take place on the first day of rehearsal, admonishing the actors as to what should and should not be accomplished at that first rehearsal. Then I ask them to prepare a production talk similar to one the director might give on the first or second day of rehearsal. This includes uncovering the theme of the play as they see it, the overall objectives of the characters in the text, the style of the proposed production (God help us, the concept!), elements of characterization to be aimed at, and so on. This constitutes a sort of palette of the main colors from which individual acting choices can then be made. On the day this production talk is presented, it is followed immediately by another read-through of the scene to be sure the actors are searching for and finding proof of their production ideas in the text. Nothing is more disappointing than having a director's brilliant production ideas unrealized in the actual performance.

The third time the actors present their scene is after they have broken it down into sections, with the various intentions deriving from the characters' overall objectives. In the Group Theatre we called these sections "beats," and this term is still used in some quarters. It seems that the Russian word *kuski* means "bits"—or "episodes" as Stanislavski himself called them. "Bits" was pronounced "beats" by Mme Ouspenskaya in Boleslavsky's American Laboratory Theatre, and that added one more (funny) misunderstanding of the Stanislavski System to the American Method.

The final presentation is "on the feet," the staging emerging directly out of the production ideas and the intentions of the scenes. After these four presentations based on the different plateaus of an actual rehearsal period are witnessed and criticized, if it is felt that still more can be achieved, a "final farewell" performance is scheduled. In this way, all the students work on good parts from good plays and still get a sense of the build of a characterization through all the crucial stages of a rehearsal period.

Although it is most difficult to pinpoint exactly what the term means, "character elements" is one principle in the craft of acting that I hammer away at in the workshop. In my view, the application of this approach to characterization adds a sense of style to the most naturalistic performer without diminishing his precious sense of truth. It might even enhance it. And it certainly is obligatory when tackling classics, plays of other cultures and periods, avant-garde material—in fact, all styles in addition to realism.

The tough job is how to define character elements (maybe the term is not good enough, but I never could come up with a better one). Actors often think I mean *inner* characterization: items such as nobility, brashness or shyness. These qualities may describe the "insides" of the character, but what I want to know is *how* do these qualities manifest themselves in *behavior,* yes, even in costume and makeup, and in (characteristic) props. One of the examples I give to illustrate a character element is a description of a behavioral tic of one of my favorite real-life characters from the days I worked at Twentieth-Century Fox. His name was "Lefty" Hough, and he had been the business manager of the studio for many years and during several regimes. It was fascinating to watch Lefty walk around the enormous grounds of the studio laid out with streets containing executive buildings, dressing rooms, sound stages, and commissary. Every time, but I mean *every* time, Lefty passed anyone on the street, in a corridor, wherever, he emitted a polite "Hi!" and accompanied it with a tiny military salute. Being a young director interested in human behavior, I finally got up enough courage to confront Lefty with my question: "Lefty," I asked, "I hope you won't think this is too personal, but I notice that every single time you pass anyone, you smile, say 'Hi,' and give him a little salute. I was wondering why you do that."

"Bobby," said Lefty, in surprise, as though it were the most obvious reason in the world, "you never know who's going to be head of the studio tomorrow."

He was right, of course. Rumor had it that the valet of one of the previous heads of the studio ultimately inherited his boss's mantle. Lefty's overall inner intention may have been "to survive all regimes," but that little salute to everyone was a behavioral manifestation, a physical theatricalization, of that objective. That's a character element.

Choice of a specific prop can reveal something of the "insides" of a character. A cigarette used by a modern character may just be a utilitarian prop. Inserted in the longest cigarette holder in the world it becomes a revelation of a personality. Remember Sally Bowles in *I Am a Camera*? An interesting sidelight for those who might think all this could add up to some pretty "fancy" acting is the fact that, after rehearsing for a while with a long cigarette holder and having attained the stance, the way of smoking and the attitude of foppishness required for the part, the actor may decide to lose the cigarette holder altogether. What is left, though, are elements of a physical characterization that otherwise might never have been there.

So, too, there are ways of using bits of clothes that will add to your utilitarian costume a certain revelation of character. Spats worn with a period suit may be de rigueur, but if some old gentleman makes certain to put them on when going to the back door to bring in the newspaper and the milk on the chance that a neighbor might see him, those spats are no longer a utilitarian piece of costume; it tells us something about the character of the old gentleman.

Character elements can appear in makeup, too. A blond wig of ringlets as a hairdo for an old lady who jiggles those ringlets flirtatiously at every man she encounters, in order to appear youthful, would count as a revealing bit of makeup. Here, too, maybe after the gesture that emerged from the ringlets idea was incorporated in the acting, it might be more effective if the wig was discarded, the old lady retained her white hair, and the characteristic head movement picked up from the ringlet idea remained.

This continual searching for "outside" manifestations of character, always *justified* by the inner content, I found to be a rewarding way to lead American actors away from their habit of never playing more than five minutes away from their own daily behavior patterns, as well as indispensable in an approach to the problem of Style. A consummate actor should be able not only to *play* himself but to *transform* himself.

When Laurence Olivier said he first wanted to know what his character's nose looked like (a remark that sent shock waves through the Actors

Studio) he didn't mean he was going to put on a putty nose at the first reading. He meant that if he had a vision of the "look" of his character it would help him pinpoint his inner choices. If, let's say, he saw his character with a patrician nose, he might decide that instead of choosing "to demean this person of lower birth" he was addressing, he might want "to look down his nose" at him. The resultant angle of his head, his look, all would dramatize his patrician characterization. He might, in the end, not even need to alter the actual shape of his own nose. Isn't this all Stanislavski meant by his "method of physical action," fast becoming the latest fetish of some self-appointed guardians of the system?

Another startling innovation I insisted on as soon as I got going in my own workshop was encouraging a sense of fun in the work. This may seem odd if you don't know the world the actor lives in. Theater life, in general, for most performers, students to stars, is tough. ("The bastards won't let you live.") And, as for classes, well, they aren't always a bag of fun. Teachers can be too damned omniscient, or humorless—even despotic. Students can be so cruel criticizing each other's scenes that they make John Simon appear more tender than Mary Miles Minter. Somehow, somewhere, someone should try to bring back the *joy* of acting, too.

Two attempts to lighten the approach to studying were contained in brochures I sent out when new semesters of my workshop were announced.

Here's one from 1967:

ROBERT LEWIS THEATRE WORKSHOP

Special Feature

"SURVIVAL COURSE FOR ACTORS"
(from audition through opening night)

*TRAINING IN:*

HOW TO get the part by giving an effective, but superficial, audition.

HOW TO read with an assistant stage manager who throws you a few incomprehensible cues as he looks at his watch.

HOW TO keep the part by indulging a tyrannical director.

HOW TO make the author believe he thought up that piece of business you did.

HOW TO connect on stage with actors who don't listen to you.

HOW TO enunciate with false elegance for classical plays.

HOW TO slur your words for everything else.

HOW TO carry off a costume that looks lousy on you but goes with the color scheme of the set.

HOW TO act in elaborate scenery that gets a big hand at the first curtain, but slowly sinks the play after that.

HOW TO convince your agent he got you that part for which the producer called you in.

HOW TO accept cuts and changes graciously although you know they're ruining the play.

HOW TO play a scene according to the totally different demands of the author, director, producer (and wives) and still keep your job and your sanity.

HOW TO relax when, just before the opening night curtain, friends make helpful remarks like, "You're too short for the part."

HOW TO look innocent when hearing the name "Stanislavsky."

HOW TO know when to damn and when to praise the Actors Studio.

HOW TO find the right teacher for you after having studied with Stella, Lee, Uta, Bobby, Sandy, and Mendy.

HOW TO knock repertory companies if you are not in one—or if you are.

HOW TO tell an honest commercial producer from a phony artistic one.

HOW TO vilify critics when they praise you as well as when they pan you.

HOW TO evaluate out-of-town notices as "provincial and unimportant" when bad, but "foretell New York critical reaction" when good.

HOW TO recognize your replacement in the Boston hotel lobby.

HOW TO escape from the Sardi's opening night party gracefully after *The New York Times*' review has been read aloud.

HOW TO enter Sardi's the day after your play has flopped.

HOW TO act grief-stricken when someone else's play bombs out.

The following brochure set the mood for the spring of 1971:

COURSES OFFERED IN FOLLOWING CATEGORIES
(partial list):

1. Classical Theatre
2. Avant-garde Theatre
3. Theatre of the Absurd
4. Theatre of the Ridiculous
5. Theatre in the Round
6. Theatre in the Surround
7. Theatre in the Streets
8. Theatre in the Subways
9. Conceptual Theatre
10. Theatre of Ideas
11. Theatre of Aesthetic Realism
12. Theatre of Socialist Realism
13. Theatre of Physical Shock
14. Theatre of Sexual Shock
15. Theatre of Political Shock
16. Theatre of Political Satire
17. Agit-Prop Theatre
18. Ethnic Theatre
19. Boulevard Theatre
20. Ensemble Theatre
21. Theatre of Bio-Mechanics
22. Theatre of Encounter
23. Epic Theatre
24. Musical Theatre
25. Poetic Theatre
26. Lyric Theatre
27. Stylized Theatre
28. Improvisational Theatre
29. Theatre of Social Significance
30. Repertory Theatre
31. University Theatre
32. Regional Theatre
33. Outdoor Theatre
34. Symphonic Drama
35. Period Theatre
36. Operatic Theatre
37. Transexual Theatre
38. Theatre of Nudity
39. Restoration Theatre
40. Elizabethan Theatre
41. Greek Theatre
42. Commedia dell 'arte
43. Romantic Theatre
44. Burlesque Theatre
45. Vaudeville Theatre
46. Religious Theatre
47. Puppet Theatre
48. Pantomime Theatre
49. Theatre of the Dance
50. Total Theatre
51. Delsarte Theatre
52. Music Hall Theatre
53. Living Theatre
54. Theatre of Masks
55. Theatre of the Grotesque
56. Grotowski Method
57. Stanislavski Method
58. Strasberg Method
59. Theatre of Cruelty
60. Chamber Theatre
61. Little Theatre
62. Experimental Theatre
63. Grand Guignol Theatre
64. Broadway Theatre
65. Off-Broadway Theatre
66. Off-Off-Broadway Theatre
67. Kabuki Theatre
68. Noh Theatre
69. The Third Theatre
70. The Theatre of Revolt
71. Proscenium Theatre
72. Thrust-stage Theatre

73. Provincial Theatre
74. Stock Theatre
75. Revolutionary Theatre
76. Dinner Theatre
77. Bus & Truck Theatre
78. Chautauqua Theatre
79. Theatre of Illusion
80. Mime Theatre
81. Liturgical Theatre
82. Historical Theatre
83. Comedy of Manners
84. Story Theatre
85. Farcical Theatre
86. Heroic Theatre
87. Bourgeois Theatre
88. Workers' Theatre
89. Theatre of Social Satire
90. Medieval Theatre
91. Naturalistic Theatre
92. Symbolist Theatre
93. Theatre of Neo-Romanticism
94. Fantastic Theatre
95. Sanskrit Theatre
96. Ceremonial Theatre
97. Surrealist Theatre
98. Psycho-Drama
99. Expressionistic Theatre
100. Mystery Plays (Valénciennes)
101. Mystery Plays (Agatha Christie)
102. Miracle Plays
103. Jacobean Theatre
104. Open Theatre
105. Open-air Theatres
106. Passion Plays
107. Spectacle Theatre
108. Cabaret Theatre
109. Theatre of Propaganda
110. Renaissance Theatre
111. Pastoral Drama
112. Shakespearean Theatre (indoors and out)
113. Society Comedies
114. Horse Opera
115. Soap Opera
116. Mixed Media
117. Multi-Media
118. Theatre of Alienation
119. Free Theatre
120. Ritual Theatre
121. Theatre of Commitment
122. Theatre of Myth
123. Underground Theatre
124. Verse Theatre
125. Arena Theatre
126. Poor Theatre
127. Theatre of the Über-marionette
128. Happenings
129. Games

also a couple of acting sessions.

In 1962, I interrupted the schedule of my own theater workshop to run the Lincoln Center Training Program. The unhappy history of the beginnings of the Lincoln Center Repertory Theatre has been too well documented to need review. However, since I was involved in the original setup the season before the theater actually opened, I might be able to shed some light on the seeds of the ensuing struggles.

Elia Kazan, the first artistic director of the theater (his partner was the producer Robert Whitehead), upon assuming his new position at Lincoln Center, resigned from the Actors Studio. Gadget summed up his feelings about the Studio at that time in an article in *The New York Times*: "My great disappointment with our work there has been that it always stopped at the same point, a preoccupation with the purely psychological side of acting." Lee Strasberg had supposed that Gadget would install the Studio intact in the Lincoln Center, and when he didn't, Lee was extremely angry.

After I had many lengthy discussions with Whitehead and Kazan, they offered me the job of director of the training program based on my particular approach to style in acting. Michel Saint-Denis, the French director and teacher, had also been suggested for the post, but it was felt that an American would be more compatible with the aims of a new American Company. The training program would consist of a carefully chosen group of talented actors from which a number would be selected to form the nucleus of the Lincoln Center Company. With eight months of common training behind them, they would constitute the beginning of an ensemble. Some of those picked for the training program after stringent auditions, consisting of the performance of both a contemporary and a classical scene, were Frank Langella, Mariclare Costello, Faye Dunaway, Crystal Field, Christopher Lloyd, Lawrence Pressman, Barry Primus, Clinton Kimbrough, Gail Fisher, and Austin Pendleton. Over five hundred were turned down.

The acceptees were assured that those who made it successfully through the training program would have a chance to become part of a major American repertory theater. No sacrifice, therefore, was too great for this opportunity, although some referred to it often as an eight month audition. The actors were responsible for their own support. Knowing that some of them had serious money problems, an attempt was made to line up possible evening and weekend employment for the neediest cases since attendance at classes was required mornings and afternoons, five days a

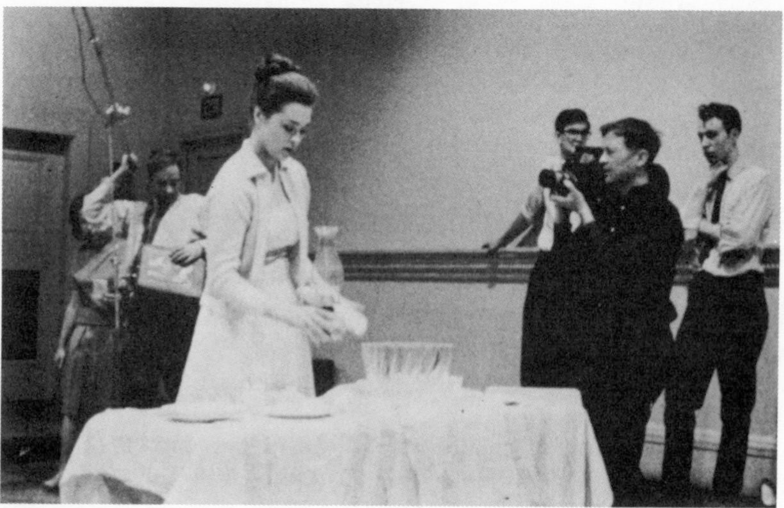

The Lincoln Center Training Program: Faye Dunaway in a classroom scene, attracting cameras.

week. Judd Mathison, who was assisting me as usual, tried to get an ushering job for Martin Sheen, one of our most talented, as well as one of our poorest, actors. The union official Judd phoned said, "Forget it. We can't keep our own people busy" and hung up. Martin then sent his wife and new baby to Ohio to live with his mother and father, and he moved into a virtual flop house. Several weeks into the program he asked Judd if he could miss his afternoon class to audition for a Broadway play. Judd had to explain the rules: auditioning for a show meant Sheen would automatically be out of the program. It was Martin's decision as to what course was best for him in his circumstances. He left at the lunch break, and the next time we saw him was as the lead in *The Subject Was Roses* on Broadway.

The actors in the program put in a full day, starting in the morning with the movement class of Anna Sokolow (accent on period movement, court dances, etc.) Then came voice and speech sessions under Arthur Lessac, who was hired by Kazan, Whitehead, and me after a nationwide search. Lessac was particularly good at correcting speech defects (he made Austin Pendleton gradually lose his stammer over the eight-month period). Lessac also coached the actors in songs of many periods and different languages. The whole afternoon was given over to an acting workshop I

The Lincoln Center Training Program. Clinton Kimbrough as Manet's *The Dead Bullfighter*: "Special emphasis on approaches to styles other than realism."

conducted, with special emphasis on approaches to styles other than realism.

The first taste of corruptive poison to sour the high-minded aspirations of the new theater had emerged during the auditions for prospective members of the program. Kazan, Whitehead, and I wanted to be absolutely sure that we would not accept anyone, no matter how talented, whose range limited them to purely contemporary material. Their approach to, and feeling for, their chosen classical scene was therefore carefully evaluated. When the acceptees were agreed on, Gadget asked me to include Barbara Loden, whom he had directed in his film *Splendor in the Grass* the year before. "But she hasn't auditioned," I protested. "She hates to audition," said Gadget, "but I've worked with her, and she's just great." Like a fool, I acquiesced. What I should have done was quit right then. I suppose I was wary of another walkout on Gadget after the Actors Studio experience. Also, this hopeful project was just beginning, and Gadget was genuinely high on Loden. In fact, in 1967 he married her.

Loden, who needed voice and speech help more than anyone in the class, resented Lessac's work almost as much as she did mine on problems of style and period. Truth to tell, she had wanted Gadget to hire her former acting teacher, Paul Mann, to head up the program.

As I faced my class for the first session, I noticed Barbara sitting directly behind someone, and I asked her if she wouldn't mind moving her chair a few inches to one side or the other because I like to see the faces of actors as I talk to them. She couldn't have been more agreeable and immediately complied. Next day she was again blocked from view, and I reminded her I'd like to see her face, and once more she graciously moved her chair. On the third day, when I began to realize she was going to do this daily, I simply asked the person in front of her to move his chair a bit so I could see Barbara. Now you're not going to believe it, but we played this game every single day for the entire eight months of the season. I asked Bob Whitehead what he thought I should do. He was sympathetic, but said that since she was Kazan's girl friend, he relied on my sense of humor to get me through. If it had been my own workshop, of course, I could have thrown her out as a disruptive influence the second day. In any case, it turned out she could never have passed the test of the classical scene. This was eventually to be demonstrated so tragically in Kazan's last production for the Lincoln Center Company, Middleton's seventeenth-century tragedy, *The Changeling*. Barbara's "little girl" voice could be well adapted to the aspirate sound of Marilyn Monroe in the part she played in Arthur Miller's *After the Fall,* but it was pitifully inadequate for the demands of the powerful Elizabethan poetry when she tackled the ill-fated Beatrice in *The Changeling.*

Barbara's talent eventually did bloom, with happy results all around when, by the end of the sixties, she turned her attention to making her own film, *Wanda*. She not only starred in it but wrote and directed it. It was a tour de force that not only used her individual personality to perfection in the leading role but revealed her as a movie maker to be reckoned with. Tragically, her death at much too young an age, cut short her directorial promise.

Barbara Loden's negative feeling about speech work and exercises in style is symptomatic of a disease of a large section of American performers brought up in a theatrical atmosphere, rooted in what they call realism. Any attempt to stretch actors' capabilities to cope with problems of voice, speech, and movement, other than their own, is frowned on as fancy, "untrue." As sound and movement get closer to their own personal patterns, they feel "truer." What a mockery of the art of acting! Some in this Lincoln Center Training Program griped about the importance put on this problem all through the season. These few listened, with obvious disdain, one day to John Gielgud, a master stylist, whom I had persuaded to give a talk on acting to the class. He later remarked on their rude attitude.

Sir John Gielgud: "A master stylist."

Others in the program, like Frank Langella and Austin Pendleton, lapped up any exercises designed to extend their ranges. Actually, Langella had such an easy, elegant approach to nonrealistic material that my whole emphasis with him was in deepening the emotional content of his work through truthful justification of his stylish characterizations.

A climactic moment illustrating this continuing problem of form and content came one day in the rehearsal of a speech of Hamlet's, as we were preparing our end-of-the-term project. Stanley Beck, a talented actor, as

**The Lincoln Center Training Program. Rehearsal shot of the "Murder of Gonzago" scene. Far right, Stanley Beck as Hamlet: "What do you want me to think of in the scene, my speech or my acting?"**

the "sweet prince," had a recurring New York sound in his speech and, as I gave my notes after the rehearsal, I reminded him again of this fault.

"What do you want me to think of in the scene, my speech or my acting?" he whined, as though they were two unrelated issues.

"Neither," I replied, "you play your situation. Your speech work, as well as your acting technique, must be second nature by the time you are into your part. If a dancer concentrated on how to point his leg, or how to hold his torso in the middle of his ballet, he might fall down. You must drill in speech class, Stanley, and never give up until your New York rhythms are gone. Then you won't have to think of them when you're wrestling with Hamlet. I assure you they'll come back, easily enough, when you get cast as that New York taxi driver."

Facing up to the problem of style (still the bête noire of American actors) was not made any easier when Kazan paid the training school one of his infrequent visits (he was busy with his film *America America*). He tried to define for the actors his feeling of what theater poetry should be. As an illustration, he summoned up all the energy and passion his own acting and directing were famous for and emitted a terrifying scream: "You cocksucker!!" "That," Gadget announced, "is what I call poetic." Well, God knows, it had made an enormous effect. And I understood what he meant. Poetry, being a heightened expression, needed fulsome emotion on the part of the actor to sustain it. But how is feeling alone, no matter how true or exalted, going to solve the problems of the *forms* of poetic speech? Isn't the truth included in the *way* in which the dramatic poet scores his text? Would Olivier's landmark stage creation of Richard III be just as good if he retained all his remarkable emotions of ambition, ruthlessness, frustration, sardonic humor, and chicanery, but spoke the verse with mangled diction in a squeaky voice?

When the training period was over, and my job completed, some of the students were absorbed into the newly formed Lincoln Center Theatre Company. Austin Pendleton was invited but said, "No, thank you." Unfortunately, only Barbara Loden succeeded in capturing any leading roles. Most of the trainees were used in small parts and as understudies the first season, while a whole new group of well-known actors was hired as the main company. All was not lost, though. A goodly number of those intrepid kids who stretched their lips and vocal cords in Lessac's class and cracked their bones under Anna Sokolow's benevolent whip, have since exhibited fine acting in many non-Lincoln Center productions. Austin Pendleton became a director in a certain moment we both remember when he presented a Hamlet-Ophelia scene in class. I was impressed with Austin's acting, but the staging and the directorial ideas were particularly inventive.

The Lincoln Center Training Program. Movement class: "Anna Sokolow's benevolent whip."

When the scene was over I said, "Austin, who directed that for you?" He was properly incensed. "What do you mean? I did, of course."

"Austin," I said, "you have the mind of a director. Not only were your acting choices original, but your staging was impressive and your interpretation of the points in the play were completely original and valid. From this moment on, you must think of yourself not only as an actor, but as a director, too."

The first administration of the Repertory Theatre of Lincoln Center, like those that followed it, failed to realize the dream of an American National Theatre. And as with those administrators who came after them, whatever problems Whitehead and Kazan may have had with the Lincoln Center Board of Directors, the fundamental failure was an artistic one. Harold Clurman had, in the thirties, defined the nature of a theater as opposed to a producing organization:

ITEM: An idea. The basic philosophy that attracts and molds a group of theater artists. I've mentioned Miss Le Gallienne's wish to provide a library of good plays of all periods at popular prices, and the Group Theatre's dedication to new American plays that reflected the life of the times. An overall theme could even be a political one, such as the Theatre Union's repertory of plays celebrating the working class. But whatever it might be, a good "spine" helps.

ITEM: The leadership. As with Balanchine in ballet, or Beverly Sills in opera, we need a theater artist who knows "the whole thing." Or a couple of artists. (No more, please—the recent Lincoln Center escapade based on the idea that five disparate directors each doing his own thing could make a cohesive theater was, obviously, self-destructive.) This leadership should chart an artistic course beyond one play or one season, be charismatic enough to attract and lead a company of gifted actors, and have an appetite, and aptitude, for all periods and all styles of plays in the dramatic literature. This has been the sine qua non of heads of great theaters everywhere, including Stanislavski's Moscow Art.

ITEM: A permanent company. While it is important for a theater to look for and train future members, the company itself, no matter how talented, should never cease "practicing." It is boring to keep repeating the analogy of Nureyev going to class every day and Isaac Stern practicing on his fiddle forever, but it can never be emphasized enough that actors who do nothing more than go to the theater, put on their makeups, go out on stage and repeat their parts night after night, tend to ossify. Continual workouts for the company members for the purpose of stretching their insides and outsides, as well as extending their ranges, is mandatory for successful artistic growth. Add in an assurance of at least a five year shakedown period, and you have a few of the basic ingredients that just might lead to an identifiable theater which, in turn, would attract a faithful audience—at Lincoln Center, or anywhere else.

# CHAPTER 19

# The Sixties

THERE WERE TWO reasons why, at the beginning of the sixties, I agreed to direct *Kwamina,* my third production that had a predominately black cast. It reunited me with Agnes de Mille who was to do the choreography, and its subject matter was unusually substantial for a musical—the problems of a small African country about to be liberated from colonial rule. Trouble was, the book writer, Robert Alan Aurthur, and the composer/lyricist, Richard Adler, bit off more than they cared to chew.

Agnes and I were carefully watched for authenticity in the dancing and staging departments by an astute technical consultant, Albert Opoku (courtesy of the government of Ghana), but the central romantic situation—the love affair between Kwamina, a tribal chief's son who studied for years in London, became a doctor, and returned to serve his people, and Eve, a white woman physician working at the local clinic—was watered down, to the detriment of the whole project. Richard Adler, the husband of Sally Ann Howes, who played the white doctor, objected to Terry Carter (Kwamina) kissing Miss Howes at any time during the action of the play. This might be understandable if there were some dramatic justification for it, but there wasn't. In the scenes where the two doctor lovers were alone, all they could do was paw one another. This idiocy was committed in a 1961 play that purported to be about the revolutionary spirit of the new emerging from the darkness of the old. It was way back in 1924 when, as a result of complaints from theatergoers patronizing *All God's Chillun Got Wings* at the Provinceton Playhouse, that New York's Mayor Hylan ordered an investigation of Eugene O'Neill's play wherein a white woman kissed the hand of her black husband (Paul Robeson). In 1943, this same Mr. Robeson, as Othello, made so bold as to kiss his wife, Desdemona, played by Uta Hagen, with no noticeable damage to the paying customers—or Miss Hagen.

When Nathan Cohen, the tough critic who covered the out-of-town premiere of *Kwamina* in Toronto, called the approach to this interracial affair "hypocritical," I couldn't have agreed with him more. Both Terry Carter and Sally Ann Howes did, too. Therefore I arranged a secret rehearsal with both of them to restage our pussyfooting love scenes. The insertion of the logical kisses in the love scenes not only made them more believable, but more moving. Suddenly, the basic situation of the play was illuminated in a human way. Without telling anyone, we planned to parade our brave osculations before the Toronto audience that night, and if no bombs were thrown, maybe Richard would let us keep them in. But—zounds and gadzooks—someone snitched on us. The back door of the O'Keefe Center of the Performing Arts was suddenly flung open during our rehearsal and there stood the outraged husband, Richard Adler, having caught us in flagrante delicto. Kwamina never got to kiss his Eve on stage in Toronto, or in Boston where Elinor Hughes wrote in the *Herald*, "The central love story does not take fire, being so cautiously handled that it never seems quite real," or in New York during all of thirty-two performances.

When the reviews came out after the Broadway opening, I was honored

*Kwamina.* **Bobby with Sally Ann Howes and Terry Carter: "Kwamina never got to kiss his Eve on stage."**

by an invitation to a ceremony held in the basement of the Fifty-fourth Street Theatre. Our African drummer and a few of his compatriots in the cast gathered to perform a voodoo ritual designed to obliterate those drama reviewers who had written unfavorable opinions about the show. I might have enjoyed the gory rites more if it weren't for the fact that I was one of those critics. During that period I had become, albeit for a short term, the drama critic for the *New Leader* magazine. Taking to task a number of escapist musicals unwilling to come to grips with their subject matter, I lit into *Kwamina,* too. (Did critic/directors Harold Clurman or Walter Kerr ever review *their* own shows? Probably not.) I concluded my obituary of *Kwamina* with, "When one aims high, the miss is more than a mile."

In spite of all, Richard Adler did write a lovely duet for Ako and Naii, two subsidiary characters in *Kwamina,* called "Nothing More to Look Forward to." Exquisite as a Schubert song, it was ravishingly sung by Ethel Ayler and Robert Guillaume in the production as well as on the cast recording. This single LP, out-of-print for so long, recently brought four hundred dollars at an auction. I'm hanging on to mine.

Ben Jonson's *Volpone* was the basis of a Klondike gold rush musical, called *Foxy,* written by Ring Lardner, Jr., and Ian McLellan Hunter, with music composed by Robert Emmett Dolan, my old boss at Paramount on *Anything Goes.* The great Johnny Mercer furnished lyrics. I directed two productions of *Foxy,* one in 1962 before the Lincoln Center Training Program and the other after it, in 1964. Bert Lahr, master comic, played the title role in both productions.

Bob Whitehead presented the first *Foxy* at Canada's Dawson City Gold

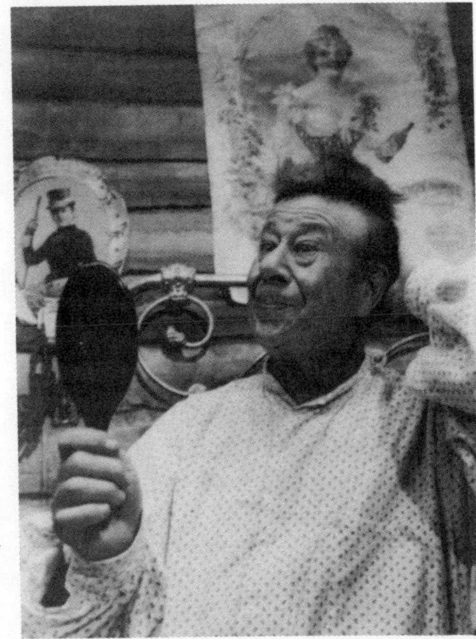

**'oxy,** in the Dawson City Gold Rush Festi-al. In the title role: Bert Lahr, "master omic."

Rush Festival, and the New York production at the Ziegfeld Theatre was produced by David Merrick. A comparison of the rehearsal atmosphere and the quality of the two productions will demonstrate a classic example of the difference between a theater attempt and the Broadway rat race. That is not to say that one show had problems and the other didn't. There is no staging of any musical without plenty of problems. But in the Yukon, *Foxy*'s altercations arose out of the material: the work to be done on text, or music, or staging. The Broadway *Foxy* was rife with disputes centering around producers' maneuverings, maintaining star status—things like that. These symptoms of show business affected the quality of the New York performance itself.

No group of prospectors in the Gold Rush of '98 could have had a more adventurous time conquering Dawson City than did our hearty band of players in the summer of 1962, led by that intrepid sourdough, Bert Lahr. Fearless though he may have been on a dog sled, Bert was a cowardly lion when it came to airplanes. This posed a bit of a problem. Dawson City was situated at the junction of Canada's Yukon and Klondike rivers, three thousand five hundred miles from New York, three thousand miles from either Los Angeles or Honolulu, four thousand miles from Tokyo, and three thousand miles from London or Moscow—convenient from just about anywhere.

At that time, I shared Bert's distrust of flying conveyances, having been traumatized by one wild, bumpy air trip from New York to Boston. Therefore, I came up with the following proposition: Why not rehearse the show on whatever land-borne or water-supported vehicles could be booked for the long trek between Broadway and the Yukon? And so it came to pass that the maddest thespian safari in history began.

Mr. and Mrs. Bert Lahr, along with a pianist, a director (me), and most of the cast of the huge musical in rehearsal left New York's Penn Station on the Broadway Limited at 6:00 P.M. on May 24, 1962, and arrived at Union Station in Chicago at 9:00 A.M. the next morning. At 3:00 P.M., we boarded the Milwaukee Road Dome Liner "City of Portland," hitting that town two days later at 9:00 A.M. A half hour after that, we all scrambled aboard a Union Pacific train and headed for Seattle, getting there at 1:30 P.M. At 2:45, the Great Northern train whisked us over the border to Vancouver where we were deposited at 6:00 P.M. on May 27. After a stay over in a hotel waiting for the next sailing of a ship to Alaska, we were all happy to trade the clickety-clack of train wheels for the sloshing of water as we boarded the steamship *Princess Louise* at Vancouver, arriving four days later at Skagway, Alaska. Once more on a train, we crossed back into Canada and rode for seven hours to Whitehorse, staying overnight. The next morning a bus left Whitehorse and dropped us all that afternoon at our theater in Dawson City.

We were now word-perfect in our *Foxy* dialogue having conducted line rehearsals in smoking-cars, studied lyrics in staterooms, and even staged some scenes in the ship's lounge. Passengers were continuously walking blithely through our acting of the scenes on their way to shuffleboard, reminding us of the shot in the Marx brothers' *A Night at the Opera* when Groucho, Harpo, and Chico are chased across the opera stage by the police during the performance and Groucho says, "Either there are cops in *Trovatore* or the jig is up."

Life in Dawson City took a bit of getting used to. There never was any night—just a momentary bit of dusk before it was bright day again. Awesome. The town itself didn't seem much different from the turn-of-the-century photos of it. The local joke held that in the next war, when the Russians come over Dawson City in a plane to bomb the town, the pilot will look down and say, "Hold it, boys—it's already *been* bombed." The Palace Grand Theatre, however, where we were to play, had been completely restored for the festival. Built in 1899, one year after the Klondike gold rush, it had been dormant for about half a century. We marched in and woke it up.

Watching Bert Lahr work on his part confirmed my belief that a true comic artist expends the same degree of effort, imagination, design, and sense of truth on his most farcical effect as the most solemn tragedian does on a powerful emotional scene. As an example, there was one moment where Foxy was chasing the pretty ingenue around the log cabin, which had one of those potbellied stoves in it. As Bert ran past the stove, he accidentally touched it. He stopped. I saw an idea germinating in his mind. Why not keep it in? Why shouldn't the blazing fire in the stove add to his growing ardor? Round he ran again, this time including the real sensation of touching the hot stove in the chase. Not good enough. Once more. This time the heat must attack his behind during the line, "Join me on the journey to ecstasy," when he pleads his burning passion of love. Wait. He was not finished yet. Next runaround found Bert trying to hit his behind on the hot stove on the particular word, "ecstasy," which would make it funnier still. Then the final polish: practicing the maneuver over and over until it became so easy that it seemed improvisational, like a happy accident. With such painstaking exercise of craft are these seemingly easy bits of comic invention born.

The opening night of *Foxy* at Arizona Charlie's restored Palace Grand Theatre on July 2, 1962, was distinguished by a blazing sun and a packed house of red-coated mounties, Indians, kilted pipers, Yukon belles in ball gowns, bearded sourdoughs in overalls, and the Governor-General of Canada. Black Mike Winage, who had been in the '98 gold rush, having trimmed his beard for the occasion and discarded his battered felt hat for a straw boater, sat in a box. The five hundred customers who packed the jewel-box of an opera house came from all over, none farther than Lady Peel, called Beatrice Lillie. Being Canadian-born, she was invited to get the

Festival under way. Miss Lillie adored Bert, having whooped it up with him in *The Seven Lively Arts* on Broadway, in 1944. When Lady Peel, in evening gown and sunglasses, met Lahr just before the opening night curtain she cried, "Bert! What on earth are you doing *here*?" She then went out on stage to kick the Festival off with a brief monologue ending with the famous trick of twirling her huge string of pearls so hard that it continued to circle her body like a sexy hula hoop as it sank slowly to the ground. It was a fine send-off for the premiere of *Foxy*.

***Foxy*** **in Dawson City. Lady Peel with "her huge string of pearls."**

Although it was well off-off Broadway, *Variety* covered the show and gave proper credit for the whole enterprise to Tom Patterson, the founder of the Stratford, Ontario, Shakespearean Festival and whose baby the Dawson City Festival was. "Patterson has built a better mousetrap than most," said *Variety*, "but just how many adventurers are going to be able to mush that far?"

The season that followed the first presentation of *Foxy* found Bert Lahr busy performing his hilarious characters in S. J. Perelman's *The Beauty Part*, while Whitehead and I were occupied with our Lincoln Center chores.

As the summer of 1963 approached, Billy Rose expressed an interest in producing *Foxy* at his Ziegfeld Theatre. The busy Bob Whitehead was willing to turn his production rights over to Billy, and then the wrangling began. I had a firm contract with Whitehead (countersigned by the authors) that assured me my usual percentage of the New York production, as a result of my doing the limited Yukon engagement for a fee and no percentage. The first thing Billy Rose did was try to cut down my percentage, he having had no involvement in the first production. I left all that financial business to my lawyer and went to confer with Rose about our relationship as producer and director.

Billy immediately announced his ideas for the complete restructuring of the script and the musical numbers, as well as changes in the sets and costumes. His suggestions were all in the direction of making it more of a "girlie" show. I began my reply by citing the inevitable objections of our most valuable comic asset, Bert Lahr. Billy was unimpressed. "I'll just tell him to play his part and shut up," he said. "How about handling the authors?" I wanted to know. "I'm the senior partner here," said Billy. "They'll have to handle me. The only one I handle is Bernard Baruch." I wondered which Klondike prospector Baruch was going to portray in the show. Anyway, it was now clear to me that I could never agree to playing Billy's stooge in such an enterprise, and I asked my lawyer to settle my contractual situation and get me out of it all. I also made a secret promise to wean myself away from all this Broadway crap and concentrate more and more on teaching; I will direct, I decided, only in situations, wherever in the world they might turn up, that aren't controlled by those "bastards who won't let you live." With only a couple of slips, I've succeeded pretty well, and although it's years since I was included in the top ten money-making directors, my stomach is in fine condition, thank you.

Bob Whitehead, on September 3, 1963, wrote a letter informing me that Billy had finally signed his contracts to produce *Foxy* and was now looking to Gower Champion as director. Said Bob: "We all wanted you very much to direct it, but I understand the principles that made you decide as you did."

When Billy ultimately dropped his plans to produce *Foxy*, it was not clear to me whether it was because Gower Champion had turned him down, or because Billy was suddenly preoccupied with his romantic life again. Having just been divorced for the second time from Joyce Matthews, he was squiring Doris Warner LeRoy Vidor, heiress to the Warner Brothers millions. Polly Rose, Billy's sister, reported that Billy had admitted, "First time I knew for sure that a gal isn't after my money. Her millions and my millions are as compatible as we are."

Enter David Merrick as the new producer. From my previous associations with David, I knew his show-business interests were concerned mainly with box-office receipts. Billy was more of a mini-Diaghilev, minus the Russian's taste. I therefore preferred working for David, and when asked, I weakened in my resolve and reentered the *Foxy* setup as the director. My first job was to reinforce the personnel of the production by two significant additions: the talented Gerald Hiken as one of the prospectors and Jack Cole as choreographer.

One of the problems that immediately started dissension in the rehearsals came from the fact that Bert Lahr and Larry Blyden who was Doc, the Mosca to Foxy-Volpone, had, for seven weeks, played their parts in Dawson City, and each had a few new ideas of what they'd like to do in the Broadway production. Since these ideas involved both the script and the staging, it fell to the authors and the director to sort them all out, try to incorporate good suggestions, and reject those that might damage the project. Bert, for instance, had a line—something about salmon swimming upstream, left over from some other show—that he wanted to insert in his part for a laugh. Ring Lardner, Jr., and Ian Hunter agreed it was funny but had to oppose it, since it bore absolutely no relation to their play. The instances of these stand-offs between the star and the writers were many and painful. Bert was a great comedy actor and knew what was funny for him; the writers were good craftsmen and knew what fit their text, granted that it was no *Waiting for Godot,* the masterpiece Lahr had appeared in, in 1956. The question always to be faced was this. Should we let Bert have his head (and all his other funny parts), or should we maintain the integrity of the script? Powerful arguments for both sides were offered in the daily battles that ensued.

The next problem was the director. Bert was famous for devouring directors. Abe Burrows, who directed Bert in *Two on the Aisle,* and Alan Schneider, the first director of Bert's *Waiting for Godot* (Herbert Berghof replaced Alan before the New York opening), had both warned me about Lahr in advance. Samuel Beckett, the author of the play, obviously agreed with Alan Schneider that it was not supposed to be Bert's *Waiting for Godot* at all, but Beckett's. The playwright later complained, "Bert Lahr, a musical hall type, dominates the play, which is not supposed to have a dominant character and is not supposed to be a vaudeville play."

Bert, on the other hand, had told me, during our Yukon honeymoon, horrendous tales of how Burrows and Schneider had tried to destroy him. I was therefore happy and proud to have left Dawson City, after that opening, still good friends with Bert. But now my time had come. Whenever I agreed with the writers on cuts or additions to the script, my stock went down a bit with Bert. And although I would hardly presume to improve on Bert's inventions, whenever I couldn't agree to his suggestions for straitjacketing his partners in scenes, my stock plummeted sharply.

That rule certain stars have adopted, that no one else on stage should move when they're doing their thing, surfaced in Bert to an alarming degree in New York. (You remember how fearful Tallulah was that Marlon Brando might move when she was talking?) It was perfectly understandable that nothing should be done to kill any of Bert's laughs, and any director would be a fool to permit such mayhem. But Bert began to insist to a ridiculous degree on everyone freezing like statues—even to their facial muscles—when he was talking or singing. Poor Jack Cole went up the wall trying to choreograph a number with Foxy and some girls. Bert sang numerous verses, which were separated by musical interludes. Jack wanted occasional slight reactions from the girls to what Bert was singing. These would not only enhance the lyrics but keep the girls from posing all during the many verses, coming to life only in their four-bar interludes. Bert was adamant, and Jack was left with a boring pattern of movement hardly commensurate with his reputation as a distinguished choreographer.

Bert got so paranoid that he stopped the rehearsal of a crowd scene one day because he "heard an actor move." It turned out to be someone in an offstage dressing room.

Everyone connected with the show grew increasingly unhappy, Bert most of all. He kept a thermometer in his pocket and at every frustrating moment he'd plop it into his mouth, wait a couple of seconds, take it out, look at it, raise his eyes to heaven, and put the thing back in his pocket till the next crisis. When things got really bad, he'd kept the thermometer in his mouth continuously, once even while munching on a sandwich.

*Foxy* was the last stage production in which this self-driven genius of a comedian played before his death. The *New Yorker* began its review of the show with this tribute: "In *Foxy* at the Ziegfeld, Bert Lahr is given every opportunity to run amuck, and he does so with all the bland and effortless ease that makes him one with the great clowns of our time."

After the Sturm und Drang of *Foxy*, I made only two more incursions into the Broadway scene before bidding it a happy farewell, for fifteen years, to concentrate on regional theaters (my own and others), opera houses, universities, and engagements abroad—from Brazil to Australia. The two New York productions were Jean Anouilh's *Traveller Without Luggage* in 1964, and, in the following year, Alan Jay Lerner and Burton Lane's *On a Clear Day You Can See Forever*.

The first play was a psychological thriller about an amnesiac, played by Ben Gazzara. His mother was portrayed by Mildred Dunnock, and Stephen Elliott acted his brother. The British designer Oliver Messel provided the interesting décor. There is not too much of historical importance to report for the purposes of this chronicle without fear of redundancy, because the production suffered the usual number of cast replacements, the usual number of threatening letters exchanged with producers about unpaid royalties, and the usual number of incidents in rehearsal, arising not from problems of the interpretation of the script but from angling for the position of top banana.

Playing an amnesiac has the same built-in trap as playing a bore. How does one do it without being boring? Ben Gazzara, loaded with talent as he was, used that talent to create a medically accurate state of amnesia which,

Mildred Dunnock and Ben Gazzara in *Traveller Without Luggage*: "Dynamic high points."

however, had the danger of acting as a soporific on the audience. I kept inserting as many dynamic high points and emotional moments as I could justify into Ben's performance, and he kept eliminating them, one by one. When an out-of-town critic called his acting "marmoreal," the producers called Ben and me in for a meeting. When asked to put back the high points, Ben refused, saying, "It's going to get more and more marmoreal. And if you persist, you'll be amazed at how quick I can get sick. I can get very sick, very quick." Thus do the terrors of the jungle make all its inhabitants run scared.

The New York notices were mixed, which meant that even the nice things were said in a way that sent too few customers scurrying to the box office; as for example, Howard Taubman in *The New York Times*: "In Robert Lewis's silken staging it moves smoothly through its chiseled obligatory encounters, pausing to chuckle at its glinting humors, to shudder at its bursts of theatricalism, and to chuckle lightly at its detached irony." Would you buy a pair of tickets?

But, *On a Clear Day—that,* my hearties, was another cup of venom. At lunch on the last day of 1964, Alan Lerner handed me a script of the musical, and later in the afternoon, Burton Lane played some of the songs he had written for the show. The next day, New Year's, I read the material Alan had given me. It told about a girl with extrasensory perception who is regressed by a doctor back to the eighteenth century (shades of *Brigadoon*). The possibilities of this subject matter, and the fine tunes of Burton Lane I had heard, persuaded me to accept the assignment as director.

The script needed clarification and cutting, lyrics had to be finished and a suitable ending devised. Although it was almost ten months before the show was scheduled to open in New York, the following October, I wasted no time. The next day found me in Alan's summer house at Shelter Island working on the script with him. From then on, right up to the Broadway opening, I pursued Alan daily, in his Manhattan town house, at Shelter Island, and for the last five weeks on his yacht in Boston's Charles River. In all that time the work was never satisfactorily completed, so it was particularly painful to be asked over and over by professionals, after the opening, "Bobby, why didn't you get Alan to fix the book?"

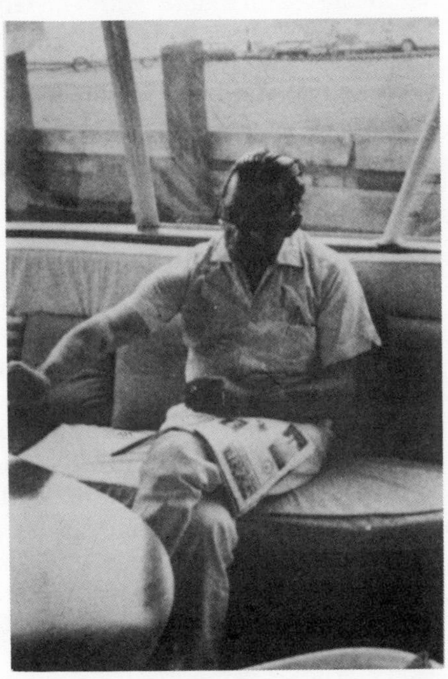

***On a Clear Day You Can See Forever.*** **Max Jacobson on Alan Lerner's yacht.**

Well, I'll tell you. It was not for lack of talent on Alan's part. He was certainly one of our best writers of musicals, with *Brigadoon* as well as *My Fair Lady* behind him. But there were two main differences in Alan's life-style since we had worked together on *Brigadoon* eighteen years earlier. The first was the penchant he had developed toward marrying every other girl he met. The second was his apparent dependence on Dr. Jacobson, known in theatrical circles as "Dr. Feelgood." Marrying and divorcing might have been distractions from the work at hand, but the never-ending ministrations of the doctor were, in my layman's opinion, what seriously impaired Alan's creative potential.

As far as his marital affairs were concerned, they would have been none of my business, if it were not for the fact that his mind, and time, were frequently distracted by myriads of lawyers, his and those of the wife he was then divorcing, herself a French lawyer. Add to this the necessary activities connected with the wooing of the current lady friend, plus daily ministrations from the doctor, and you can figure how much time was left for work on the script and lyrics.

Whatever was contained in the shots Alan was receiving daily, its effect was quite different from the beneficial result Alan described to me so euphorically. "It has done away with the necessity for sleep," said Alan. "I can now work twenty-four hours a day." Twenty-four minutes a day would move us along faster, I thought. After Alan got a shot, he really did experience a substantial "high." But some hours later, a depression would set in and another dose would be required. In his "down" periods, both Burton Lane and I had the startling experience of having Alan, while talking, fall asleep right in the middle of a sentence. Unable to waken him, we would have to leave. So much for eliminating sleep.

During the sold-out five-week tryout engagement at the Colonial Theatre in Boston, it was my sleep that was eliminated as I realized we were getting closer and closer to the New York opening, and the script was not corrected. I hadn't even been able to get Alan to cut the show, which was dangerously overlong. One evening before the performance started, I heard two older ladies talking in front of the water cooler in the lobby where Burton Lane, the choreographer Herbert Ross, Nora Kaye, his wife and helper, and I spent fruitless hours pacing up and down waiting for Alan. We couldn't complain to the producer because Alan was the producer.

"I'd love to have a drink of that water," one of those ladies said to her friend, "but I hear it's an awfully long first act."

When I pleaded with Alan to cut the show because of its unacceptable length, he said that was impossible as all his shows were one hundred pages long—the perfect length for a musical. He then kept five secretaries up all night retyping the script and brought it in the next morning. It was exactly one hundred pages—but single-spaced, with no margins. Every page was filled from top to bottom.

Also, there was that completely inconclusive last scene. What we were playing every evening was the result of some desperate improvising on the part of the cast and myself. I had said in the beginning that it was difficult for me to direct a show if I didn't know for certain how it all came out. Was it a true regression? Was it a dream? Was it a fantasy? ESP? *All* of these? Certainly if Barbara Harris, the most gifted musical theater actress one could ever work with, wasn't sure, how the hell was the audience supposed to know? One night, in my bed at the Ritz Hotel in Boston, staring at the ceiling, waiting for my execution as the dawn came up, the phone rang. It was Alan. "I've got it. The ending. Come on down to the yacht right away." Scrambling out of bed, not bothering to shave, I threw my clothes on, raced down to the street, grabbed a cab, and got out to the boat dock.

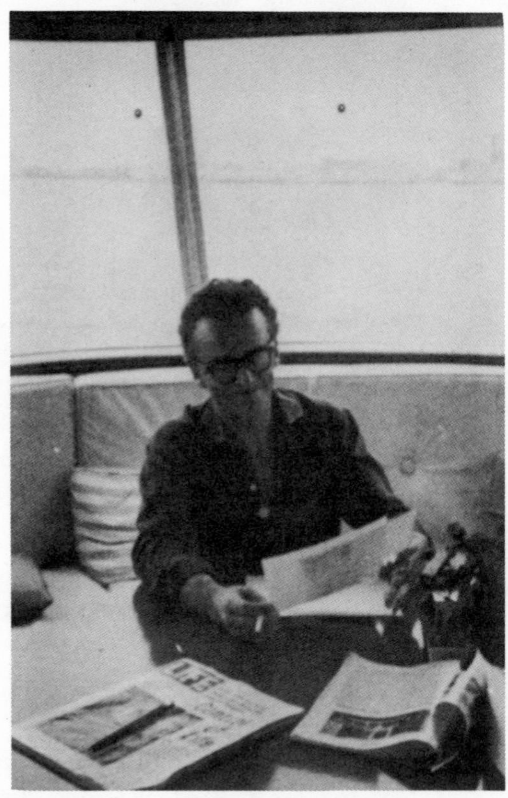

*On a Clear Day You Can See Forever.* Alan Lerner on his yacht: "I've got it."

There I sat, in the early morning fog, waiting for the yacht to come in. Finally, when it did, I raced aboard, dashed into the salon, and there was Alan, not waving the precious finale happily in the air, but just sitting there, despondent. "It was no good," he said, "I tore it up." From the time he had phoned me, he had obviously gone from a hopeful "high" feeling to a desperate "low."

After dinner one night on the yacht, Alan tried to get me to take one of the shots although I protested that there was nothing wrong with me that some much-needed dialogue couldn't fix. The doctor, egged on by Alan, started up from the table. So did I. Soon it was the second act of *Tosca* with this Scarpia-cum-Rasputin chasing me around the dining salon.

It was terrible for me to see a good, old friend like Alan taken in by practices so destructive to him. Not only did they affect his creative powers, but his personality seemed to be transformed. There was the unbelievable incident in Boston of his firing the dean of New York theater stage managers, Robert Downing. It was sad, but understandable, when our leading man, Louis Jourdan, had to be let go. Louis was giving a sensitive acting performance, but his singing voice was rather small—sweet but not effective enough to put over his numbers with the proper impact. One thing everyone agreed on was that the songs of Burton Lane were top drawer. Therefore, when the out-of-town *Variety* review bemoaned the fact that the

**Barbara Harris rehearsing a number in *On a Clear Day You Can See Forever*: "No attempt to shatter icebergs."**

score was weak, everyone agreed some action must be taken. John Cullum, who had been Richard Burton's understudy in Alan's *Camelot,* was called in, and the numbers started to go over at once.

The dismissal of Bob Downing was something else again. He was thrown out for nothing more than doing his job superbly. During the first run-through in Boston with sets, costumes, and lighting, when we came to the first scene change where the whole cast had to clear the stage as the various platforms started grinding to their new positions, Bob ordered the changeover to be executed first with the work lights on so the departing actors could see how to get off without being run down by moving scenery. As the change began, Alan called out from the auditorium, "The work lights are on." Bob stopped the change, came out on stage and carefully explained that the second time through would be in darkness, but he had to have one shot at the change in light so as to insure that there would be no broken bones. Alan claimed he had to have the change in the dark so he could study the wait from one scene to another. Bob maintained he dared not oblige. Alan insisted. Bob said, "Sorry," and proceeded to execute the change with the work light on. Alan turned to me with eyes blazing, saying, "I'm going to fire him." I couldn't believe he really would when he had time to think about it later. But he did.

The bile built up in my system from the indignities of the whole thoroughly disgraceful experience of *On a Clear Day* would have kept me from enjoying even rave notices. As it was, the New York reviews were mixed, with most of the praise rightfully going to Barbara Harris. Five years later, when reducing the film version of *On a Clear Day* to rubble, critic John Simon related that, after seeing Barbra Streisand in the movie, he went home and played the original cast album from the Broadway show featuring Barbara Harris. "Suddenly there was feeling for the words, sensitivity to the character singing them, and no attempt to shatter ice-bergs, break glasses, or pierce eardrums. After Barbara, what is missing from Barbra is not only an *a,* but everything from *b* to *z.*"

CHAPTER 20

# Retreat from the Jungle 1965-1980

AFTER THE TRAUMA of *On a Clear Day* in 1965, I set about enjoying the normal, honest pains that attend the life of a theater artist, at the same time assiduously avoiding the ignominy of being a pawn in the game of show business. Only once, in 1980, with *Harold and Maude,* did I slip—well, fall might be closer—from my state of grace. And to regain my balance I then grabbed on to a Mellon Chair at Houston's Rice University. The seesaw may haunt; but it also rescues.

I've already recorded my teaching adventures over the ten-year span of the stormy Brustein regime at Yale in the sixties and seventies. From 1965 to 1980, in addition to two twelve-week semesters a year in my own workshop, a few of the other places I conducted seminars in acting and directing were Harpur College in Binghamton, the State University of New York at Albany, the Memphis Little Theatre in Tennessee, Boston University's Playwrights' Workshop at Tanglewood, Massachusetts, the University of Houston in Texas, and I was the artistic director of the initial season of the Wolf Trap Farm Park Summer Festival in Vienna, Virginia, in 1971. Also, in one of the earliest seminars for playwrights at the Eugene O'Neill Memorial Theatre Foundation (1967), I directed staged readings of three new plays.

Places where I lectured, mostly on the problems of style for the American actor, ranged from many universities to a Dallas ladies' luncheon for a group called the Young Women in the Arts.

Nineteen seventy-six found me in Brazil, where theater people were acquainted with my book *Method—or Madness?* through a translation into Portuguese (*Método—ou Loucura?*) by Barbara Heliodora. In Rio, I conducted a seminar for professional actors and lectured at the Serviço Nacional de Teatro, as well as in São Paulo and at the Federal University of the State of Minas Gerais in Belo Horizonte. In 1979, while in Sydney,

Rio de Janeiro, 1976: "Método—ou Loucura?" Third row, furthest to the right of the picture is Fernanda Montenegro, Brazil's leading actress.

Australia, to direct *Long Day's Journey into Night,* I also had occasion to give some lectures that constituted a sort of mini-"Method—or Madness?" series, during which I tried to eliminate some germs of misunderstanding of the Stanislavski System that had infected my down under colleagues.

In none of the above activities did I encounter one lawyer, one producer, or one agent. The plays I directed in the same period were all by playwrights whose works I had longed to tackle but never could get productions for in the Broadway theater. Among those writers were Strindberg, O'Casey, T. S. Eliot, Pinter, Camus, Chekhov, and O'Neill.

Tangling with *The Sea Gull* again, a quarter of a century after I put it on at the end of the first season of the Actors Studio (1947), I departed from my belief that, theatrically speaking, you can't go home again. Although I had some good actors in the Center Stage (Baltimore) cast, the sense of ensemble playing the Studio people had developed during that year of classes, so essential to the spirit of a Chekhov production, was missing. The most interesting individual performance was given by Earle Hyman as Trigorin. At a press conference before the opening, a Baltimore newspaperman asked me how I could have cast a nonwhite actor in the role of a Russian writer at the turn of the century. Rather than go into the whole problem of blacks and whites being cast according to color instead of their aptness for the role, I came up with a short clincher based on the history of another Russian writer's racial background: "What about Pushkin?"

The summer of 1971 marked the opening of the Filene Center in the Wolf Trap Farm Park, a huge outdoor theater ideally suited to large-scale musicals, dance companies, and opera performances. The prime mover behind the enterprise was a towering patroness of the arts, Mrs. Jouett Shouse. Julius Rudel, witty Viennese, immediately tagged the theater the "Shouspielhaus."

Sixty young musical performers were chosen for training in music, dance, and acting throughout the summer, to culminate in a production produced in the new theater. It fell to me to conduct the training program and direct the production, which we called *Musical Theatre Cavalcade.* With a multimedia set by Leo Kerz, choreography by Gemze de Lappe, and musical direction by Johnny Green, the *Cavalcade* was a history of musical theater from Gay's *The Beggar's Opera* to *Hair.* The first half of the evening consisted of highlights of musical theater abroad, while the American contribution was reviewed after the intermission. Since every number chosen was an established hit of its time, it wasn't too difficult to keep up the audience's enthusiasm. The Nixons sat in a box on the opening night and then invited the cast to visit the White House.

After descending on a huge layout of food, causing it to disappear in a wink, the chorus kids rewarded Mrs. Nixon by singing a couple of numbers for her. In her thank-you speech to them she said that she hoped "you would always remember this day at the White House as you climbed the ladder of success." As I was leaving, Mrs. Nixon was gracious enough to tell me that *Brigadoon* was the favorite musical of the president and herself. She also volunteered the information that Mr. Nixon had appeared in *The Pirates of Penzance* in high school. She didn't say in what part.

In the spring of 1976, the United States was celebrating the bicentennial of its independence and I was enjoying my freedom after the long incarceration in the Yale Drama School. I started to dream of having my own theater company, where I could put into practice the approach to acting styles I had been teaching. I decided to operate in Westchester for a number of reasons. First, I lived there. Second, creative activities could proceed uncontaminated by the steamy atmosphere of Broadway, yet be close enough to New York City for actors to get back and forth. Finally, I knew that, although there were plenty of community theaters, wealthy Westchester County couldn't boast a genuinely professional permanent company.

As my golden retriever, Caesar, and I walked along our country roads, much as Gadget and I had walked through Central Park planning the Actors Studio, I kept saying, "Now, Caesar, I must do it right. I've learned a lot from the workings of other companies such as The Civic Rep, The Group, Lincoln Center, The Yale Rep. Now we must start modestly, go slowly, let it grow organically, do everything right." Caesar and I loved those dreamy walks.

Harking back to the Steinway Hall meetings prior to the formation of the Group Theatre acting company, I invited a hundred or so actors to a talk at the College of White Plains, a division of Pace University, on Sunday, June 27, 1976. Sprinkled throughout the audience were faces I recognized from the *Method—or Madness?* lectures of nineteen years earlier, and so I began with, "As I was saying . . ." Launching into a review of the growing problems besetting American actors and the need for performing proficiency in the classical repertory as well as with avant-garde playwrighting, I warned them to get ready to play characters in all styles and periods from Renaissance princes to munchkins. And, in some plays, a Renaissance prince in scene one and a munchkin in scene two.

After the talk, I threw the floor open for questions and then gave the marching orders. In September I would be back from my Brazilian safari to interview those interested in the following proposition: chosen actors would meet every week for a full season of work on études and scenes dealing with the classical and avant-garde repertory, realism having already had plenty of attention. We would then choose and rehearse a project that would demonstrate our work. Finally, we would produce it or not, as we saw fit. In this way we would gradually form ourselves into a company with a specific artistic goal.

I asked all who wanted to be considered for this project to leave their names, addresses, and phone numbers and told them they'd be contacted for interviews after Labor Day. There was a one hundred percent registration.

When I returned from Brazil I started to seek a home for our workshop, which was to be called the Westchester Laboratory Theatre. Magically, one turned up, virtually on my doorstep. Fanchon Scheier and Carolyn Zinn, two local actresses who had been in my classes, informed me there was a theater hidden in the recesses of the Irvington Town Hall. I thought they were kidding, as I had been in that building countless times visiting the public library as well as the police station, where I regularly retrieved my runaway retriever. When I asked the librarian if there really was a theater tucked away somewhere in the building, she replied, "Sure. Upstairs." "Can I get in?" I cried. "Do you have a key? Where's the entrance?" "You're standing in it," she said. "Coming up those front steps to this present library the audience used to walk through here and up two stairwells leading to either side of the orchestra. The only way up to the old theater now is a side door in the alley. Here's the key."

Through the alley door and up dusty stone steps I went and found myself in a ghostly, century-old jewel-box of a theater in complete disrepair. There were side boxes looking not unlike those of Ford's Theatre in Washington and a small balcony that was so shaky, it would undoubtedly be condemned by a building inspector. But there was a solid floor in the orchestra, some folding seats stacked up, and a small stage that was completely ill equipped for production of any sort, though serviceable enough for my laboratory work.

Researching the house, I discovered that one of my favorite "dead singers," the American operatic soprano, Lillian Nordica, had given a benefit concert there for the women's suffrage movement on March 18, 1910, when I was one year and two days old. Could I ask for more benevolent patronage?

The village fathers of Irvington agreed to let me use the theater for a season if I would pay for the maintenance: heating, and so on. Rushing over to the Westchester Council for the Arts, I persuaded them to spring for a five thousand dollar grant to cover the year's expenses. No money would be paid by the actors or received by me for the instruction. I was now ready for my interviews.

During the preceding summer, after the Pace University talk, word of the project spread through the actors' grapevine. So it turned out that I interviewed many more than the original hundred who had signed up. It was tough shaking the number down to a workable group that would be interested in, and have aptitude for, the special work on style that I planned. The actors also had to be prepared to stay with the project through the whole season. I ended up with forty talented, interesting performers. There were also about fifteen observers: directors, producers, teachers, and one critic, Albert Bermel, who offered to be the group's literary manager.

I figured that a full four-hour meeting every Sunday for the whole class plus midweek coaching sessions with smaller groups for a complete season would approximate that all-important first Group Theatre summer of training and orientation we had enjoyed early in the thirties.

The artistic nourishment the actors of the Westchester Laboratory Theatre and I enjoyed that winter in Irvington derived from a stretching process demanded by the material chosen to work on. An accomplished actress whose success was earned playing sweet, innocent, vulnerable women was turned loose on Medea. We worked her scene over for weeks until the required "size"—I don't mean physical size, I mean inner size—was achieved.

The great opening scene of Molière's *The Misanthrope* between Alceste and his friend Philinte revealed our basic problem when coping with styles other than contemporary realism. When the scene was first presented in class, one of the actors had completely solved all of the inner problems of his part: he talked, he listened, he connected with his partner, his objectives were strong and clear, his emotion was full and true. As for his sense of the style of the period and the problems of language—forget it. His physical behavior would have been appropriate for a contemporary kitchen drama, and Molière's rhymed couplets, so lovingly translated by Richard Wilbur, were hopelessly mangled.

The other actor had a genuine feeling for the period, which he had obviously researched to a fare-thee-well. Even in his rehearsal sneakers, one felt in his posture the effect of the raised heels of period shoes. I could swear I saw a bit of white emerging from his sleeve, where eventually the costumer would tuck an elegant lace kerchief. He spoke with precision, rhythm, and relish of the language. But as for acting out the truth of the scene's situation with his partner, he could just as well have phoned it in.

Our work then consisted of training the first actor to accomplish the stylistic requirements of the material without losing his sense of psychological truth: that inner line of the scene he understood so well. He began to see how the nature of that truth was altered by, and bound in with, the physical behavior of the period and the verse. The second actor, when pressed to uncover the subtext of his part, began to realize that his means of expression—voice, speech, movement—were no longer rigid stylistic mannerisms, but rather manifestations of his character's particular kind of thinking. This continual attempt to work on, and justify, the "inside" and the "outside" in the performance of these roles requiring a sense of style led to an organic approach to the whole problem. We would no longer settle for just inner truth or outer representation of style. Nor would we—and this is the important point—brush up our speech and movement and then try to paste the results onto our personal feeling and thinking. We would, however, study the ways of preserving our sense of truth, but use it to create the truth of the behavior of those characters in that time and place. We were on our way to the "third force" I had talked about. Even if nothing further had been accomplished toward establishing an acting company, we all felt the season of training was important and highly productive.

But I pressed on to the next steps: to find a viable theater to operate in and a general manager who would take charge of business matters and the all-important task of fund raising. The first search was for some large, industrial space that could be converted into a theater where the playing area and the patrons' seats could be easily rearranged for all possible kinds of staging. At the same time I investigated two unused former movie houses in the area which might be renovated for our use. Then one day I was shown the little theater on the campus of the College of New Rochelle and at once I knew it was perfect for our needs. It seated slightly less than one hundred and could operate under the least expensive LORT (League of Resident Theatres) contract. The limited capacity appealed to me on other grounds. I felt it would be better at the start to pack a small house rather than risk a half-empty large one. If we succeeded in the first season we could then move to larger quarters.

The auditorium was in the arena style with stage areas comprising most of the space. I immediately made an appointment to meet the president of the college, Sister Dorothy Ann Kelly. When I explained the objectives of my proposed enterprise Sister Dorothy Ann not only caught on at once but offered me the theater and two offices in the college (one for me and one for our business department) for no money at all. It was a perfect price, since that was the exact amount the project had in the bank at that point.

The other crucial problem in getting the project off the ground was the selection of a business manager. I had to be very careful about this. Even if I had any great expertise in management (which I didn't) I wanted to be free as artistic director to prepare repertory, organize the company, keep up the training program, and direct plays. I needed someone to take full charge of business matters, not the least of which was to expand our capital from ground zero to the point where at least one full season (more if possible) could be guaranteed. Until that first year milestone was passed we could not apply for state or federal grants. I knew several expert Broadway business managers, but even their minimum union wage was way out of the ball park for a small regional theater.

Helen Harrelson, one of the actresses in the Westchester Laboratory Theatre class, was married to Peter Zeisler, head of TCG (Theatre Communications Group), which services regional theaters, and she suggested I contact him. I knew Peter from the Yale Drama School, where he gave a course in theater administration. He promptly recommended six possibilities for the job I discussed with him and suggested I interview them all. I did. Carefully. One twenty-six year old man was light miles ahead of the others. He had run his own summer theater, was confident of his money-raising talent (a friend of his had $25,000 he was eager to invest in anything he did) and most important of all, he seemed to have an understanding of the nature of the enterprise I outlined and was enthusiastic in his endorsement of the objectives. I took a deep breath and put the project I had been building for a year into his hopefully capable managerial hands.

There developed some delay in the actual depositing in the bank of that gentleman's $25,000, which we needed to put our production activities into operation. So, although I had hoped to avoid any fiscal worries and concentrate on artistic problems, I persuaded the Westchester Council for the Arts, which had underwritten our previous year of training, to donate another five grand as front money, this time to help get our producing project off the ground.

The Westchester Laboratory Theatre was incorporated, modestly enough, as a non-profit-making organization. Shortly thereafter I was asked if the theater could be called the Robert Lewis Acting Company as it was felt the word "laboratory" was inhibiting all those potential contributors. I agreed.

When it became clear to me that the long-awaited $25,000 from my business manager's friend would never appear and that our meager exchequer made any hope of starting the planned six-play season unlikely, I compromised on a program of three plays to start midseason in January. This would give us a breathing spell to fill up our coffers. Although I had promised myself to stay away from money raising, I did agree to send a tantalizing brochure, plus a begging letter, to a number of well-heeled theater people who had been associated with me in the past as students or as actors in my productions. Some were just generous friends like Johnny Mathis, who contributed the largest individual amount ($5,000). Among those sending in $1,000 contributions were Henry Winkler (former Yale Drama School student), Martin Ritt (former Group Theatre Studio member), Phil Mathias (formerly stage manager of *My Heart's in the Highlands*), Harris Masterson III (formerly producer of *Traveller Without Luggage*), and Walter Matthau. Other donors were Eli Wallach and Karl Malden (former students) and Tad Adoue (the superstitious *Cock-a-doodle Dandy* man). This time his check ($25) arrived safely.

So, about sixty friends and colleagues helped to launch the Robert Lewis Acting Company. All told their contributions added up to about $13,000, and the $5,000 of the Westchester Council for the Arts brought my money-raising efforts to $18,000. Through his lawyer, the business manager got $2,500 from the Lambs Club plus a couple of smaller donations. By the time he submitted a projected budget of $185,000 for the three-play half-season, we were well into production and I had no time to go into cardiac arrest. Besides, being of an eternally optimistic (some might say dumb) nature, whenever I got a sinking fiscal feeling I looked at the wistful page headed Projected Earned Income, listing potential ticket sales, concession stand, school fees, and individual and corporate contributions. Miraculously that page added up to exactly $185,000, too: the exact figure of the projected budget. The two pages held side by side had a gratifying placebo effect that kept me floating along in my dream preparations for the theater company's inaugural season.

The first and third of the proposed repertory of plays were to be directed by me and the middle one by Austin Pendleton. He had an interesting concept for Shaw's *Saint Joan,* and the play would feature Linda Hunt, the diminutive but powerful actress, who was one of my former pupils. The season would finish with Earle Hyman in the title role of *Othello,* which he had played before and was anxious to tackle again as a result of the kind of work we did in our winter workshop in Irvington. Now about the opening bill: everyone agreed that so many groups had started up and failed in Westchester that it was mandatory to make our identity clear at the outset. Local theatergoers were used to going the short distance into New York City for professional entertainment and were inclined to look on local endeavors as community theater. In order to sell out our subscription season, some way had to be found to nail down the idea that the patrons were to get "Broadway" quality in their own backyard.

To the rescue came Maureen Stapleton, who volunteered to open our theater for us. There were two reasons why I leapt at the idea, aside from the obvious value of her talent. I didn't feel I was going away from my "company" idea just to have an attractive name. After all, Maureen had been in my classes even before the one that inaugurated the Actors Studio. She had been "family" for a long time.

The second reason was a sad one. It was my first big disillusioning experience of the enterprise. As I conducted my initial casting interviews with the Irvington trainees for the first season's plays, I found that, of the actors I wanted most for the leading parts in the proposed repertory, only Earle Hyman accepted. It seemed most of them were happy to enjoy the training work we did the previous season, but to tie themselves up for rehearsals and five-week runs in a regional theater at our modest salaries—well, they just couldn't afford it. One had a mortgage on a new house to pay off, and although he didn't have a better offer, he had to keep himself free in case one turned up. Another had a TV conflict, and so on, and on. I stopped interviewing my former "winter soldiers" and decided to cast the three plays as best I could, using available Westchester Laboratory Theatre people when feasible but not limiting myself to them. I put the idea of a "group" company on the back burner for the time being and thought of those I had worked with in the training program as a "pool" to be drawn upon when needed.

Maureen and I agreed on her playing Eric Bentley's translation of the

Italian playwright De Filippo's *Filumena* as our theater's opener, to be followed by *Saint Joan* and *Othello.* Not a bad half of a first season, eh? Trouble was, not one of those plays ever saw the light of Sister Dorothy Ann's little theater. The first defection was Austin, who could not promise me the time slot needed for his *Saint Joan* project due to other pressing offers. Then I heard that Earle Hyman, who was acting at the time in Norway, had accepted an offer to do *Othello* for an off-Broadway theater during the season and that, of course, made our Westchester presentation impossible. And finally, Joan Plowright, who was playing a British translation of the De Filippo play in London, decided to bring her version to New York, nipping our negotiations for the American rights in the bud.

Al Bermel, our dramaturge, and I made lists of plays that were available and would, at least, hint at our future artistic objectives, if not fulfill them one hundred percent in this first season. What we were trying to do was prove that good American actors could conquer problems of style in the world repertory. Bermel was an expert in the translation and adaptation of French dramatic literature, and after examining many plays in that category, we agreed to take a stab at *Caligula* by Camus, which we could cast and for which our resident designer, Beeb Salzer, had some good ideas for décor.

Searching through anthologies, I had come upon an interesting Spanish play by Alejandro Casona, who, during the Franco regime, had gone into exile in Argentina, where he died. It was called *Suicide Prohibited in Springtime,* and this would be its first performance in this country.

To find a substitute play for Maureen's appearance was top priority, since I didn't want to lose her. I bombarded her with possible choices, from Ibsen to Synge. While this was going on, the happy information arrived that John Ford Noonan, a playwright whom I knew from the Yale Drama School, had just finished a play written with Maureen in mind. I read the play. Maureen read the play. I liked the play. Maureen liked the play. I grabbed it. So we'd open with a new play by an up-and-coming American playwright, go on to a French drama by Camus, and end the season with an American premiere of a work by a little-known Spanish writer. Next year we'd tackle Shakespeare, Molière, the Greeks—all those fellows. Life was beginning to look up again.

The inaugural production of Noonan's *The Club Champion's Widow* (January 1977), with Maureen Stapleton in the title role, not only filled our tiny house with subscribers and individual ticket buyers, but necessitated extra chairs being put in every night of the run up to the limit allowed by the fire department. It also afforded me the great pleasure of directing Maureen again and watching her work. Some actors want to analyze and understand their characters completely in their heads first, make choices from that understanding, and gradually fill those choices in with justified experience and behavior. Maureen adopts a more instinctive approach.

Without deciding on any specific path, she allows the character to grow day by day, using her extraordinary ability to believe in the situations of her part as they're revealed to her in rehearsal. In four weeks then, she seemed able to discover all those past events in the widow's life that led up to the situations in the script. Fellow actors as well as audience members sense this complete identification Maureen can make with the character she's playing. Harold Clurman in the *Nation* took time out in his review of the production to give Maureen a long overdue tribute to her specific talent: "Hers is an essentially lyric temperament; it is composed of the vulnerability I associate with Laurette Taylor and some of the same humor. . . . It is worth the trip to New Rochelle to see her."

Of the play itself Clurman said, "[It] is written as farce bordering on

*The Club Champion's Widow,* 1978. Maureen Stapleton and John Braden: "It is worth the trip to New Rochelle to see her."

fantasy. But the 'fantasy' or plain wackiness is not a literary trick: it is native to Noonan. Madcaps, oddballs, grotesques are his 'family.' Thus, though they are all impossible, they all become real to us, because they are real to him. These cartoon figures inhabit naturally his cockeyed world.

"Lewis has directed the play fittingly at a frenzied pace, without, by the way, a word becoming unintelligible."

The pleasure I experienced launching the theater with this first production was short-lived. It was all downhill after that. As soon as *The Club Champion's Widow* opened, I had to plunge into rehearsals with *Caligula,* our second play, and had no time to investigate the state of the business end of our operation. I knew the theater was so small that the crowded houses could only account for a small amount of our weekly payroll, plus other producing expenses. The business manager, however, assured me we were in good shape financially. I now realize he probably didn't want to worry me when I was deep in rehearsal with a complicated production. However, things had gotten so bad that the moment *Caligula* opened on March 28 the true story was revealed to me. No more money had been raised, and we not only didn't have enough to produce the third play, but we were well into debt. I was advised to cancel the May production of the Casona play and throw in the towel. *Suicide Prohibited in Springtime,* indeed.

Earle Hyman, Annie Murray, and Michael Lipton in *Suicide Prohibited in Springtime.*

Without batting an eyelash, I refused at once to cancel the rest of the season. First of all, our subscribers had paid for three plays, and having to return all that money would only put us further in the hole. Secondly, I had promised David Rotenberg, a directing pupil of mine from the Yale School of Drama, that he could make his professional début as director of the Spanish play. He had quit his university job in Canada and come down to New Rochelle for this opportunity and had his complete production plan worked out.

"How much do we need immediately to keep going?" I asked the manager. "Ten thousand," he replied. "Come on," I said, "let's go over to the bank, take out a loan and while David is directing the Casona play I will give a course in acting in New York City, take no fee myself, and in a short time we can pay back the loan and have some money left over." A separate account of the payments received from the course would be kept so that when the bank loan was due the ten thousand would be there to pay it back.

The scene in the bank left me a little puzzled. The bank officer asked me to fill out a form indicating my personal resources, and I did. My understanding was that this was a loan to the corporation of which I was the president and the business manager was vice-president and fiscal officer. As collateral I cited the acting course itself, which would more than cover the amount of the loan. The smiling bank officer handed me the paper to sign. I did and handed it to the business manager. "I don't have to sign," he said. I thought this was odd, because he and I both signed actors' and authors' contracts, although he alone had been signing all checks so as to relieve me of onerous business details. I looked at the bank officer to ascertain if my manager was right, and he indicated that was so. I handed the loan paper back, and that was that. Since you've already guessed it, you don't need to be told that Bobby, this lummox of a corporation president, signed a personal loan. Further, as the money came in from the classes I was schlepping myself to New York City to give, it was all used to keep the faltering exchequer of the theater breathing. Therefore, when the loan came due I was stuck for the ten grand. It was the only time I paid ten thousand dollars for the privilege of conducting an acting course. The day I brought my checkbook to the bank to cough up the money, the same bank officer, obviously sorry for the shnook who allowed this to happen to him, took pity on me. "Just a minute," he said, and made a call upstairs. "I've gotten permission," he informed me, "to forego the two hundred and fifty dollars interest due on this. You don't have to pay that." Don't tell me banks have no heart.

It was beginning to dawn on me that, as a money raiser and a business genius, my manager was no Roger Stevens. Apparently everyone else, in the organization and out, had suspected it for some time. Further, he had not leveled with me about our fiscal situation. When I asked him to report to me in person continuously on what was happening in the administration while I was busy directing or teaching, he said he couldn't; it would make him feel like an underling instead of a Business Manager, which title by the way he soon changed to "Managing Director." "All right," I said, "put a typed report on my desk for me to read whenever I have a moment so I can know what's going on." He didn't do that, either.

One particular business maneuver on the Managing Director's part caused me acute personal embarrassment. It had to do with a long-time friend of mine, Charles Marowitz, an American running a highly respected avant-garde theater in London. When Charles heard of my New Rochelle activities he sent me a copy of his book *The Act of Being,* inscribed "To Bobby Lewis, the only man from the thirties who's made it into the seventies," and asked me if he could do one of his experimental Shakespeare productions in my theater. In London he had taken scenes from *Othello* and interspersed them with commenting contemporary material. Now he had a version of *The Taming of the Shrew* treated in the same manner, and when he sent me a copy of the script I was intrigued by it. I asked Charles if he would like to open our second season with his *Shrew.*

When he had occasion to visit the United States, Marowitz came to see our production of *The Club Champion's Widow* and liked it, as well as the whole idea of the theater. He proceeded to hold a series of auditions to determine how our actors could respond to his particular approach to Shakespeare, and then he returned to England. When the dismal fiscal situation of our company began to be apparent to me, I told the Managing Director to be sure not to make any contractual deal with Marowitz as we could not be absolutely certain there would be a second season. He assured me he had not and would not set anything with Marowitz.

After the Casona play opened on May 16, our financial plight was so bleak that I asked the Managing Director for his resignation, on the grounds that our collaboration was no longer possible. He had no compunction about leaving the sinking ship. I grabbed a life preserver called Linda Strohmeier. She had been recommended highly by a friend from the Group Theatre days, photographer Ralph Steiner. Linda and I sat in the Managing Director's office as he turned over all the papers, books, accounts, and contracts of his regime. Patiently he described each item as he briefed Linda. I was impressed with this generous gesture, and I thanked him and asked, "Is that everything there is, now?" "Everything," he said, and we parted.

I had written Marowitz on April 13, 1978, informing him that our financial position was so rocky that, at the moment, I could not set up the second season I had envisioned. I had asked the managing director to write Charles, but by then I was covering all bases myself. "At this writing," my letter to Charles said, "I don't know how next season might shape up, so it looks like our plans for your *Shrew* are put off as of now." Charles replied from Bergen, Norway, with a very understanding letter. After all, who knew better than he the financial problems of small theater companies?

You can imagine my shock, then, when Barry Kramer, who had been assistant managing director and was now helping Linda carry on, showed me a letter from Charles, dated May 19, stating he had a written contract with our company and expected the terms of it to be honored. I called the former managing director, who again professed no knowledge of any contract. I wrote this information to Charles on June 14, 1978. Back came a Xerox copy of a contract on Robert Lewis Acting Company stationery dated February 14, 1978. This letter of agreement contained rehearsal, preview, opening, and closing dates for the *Shrew*, starting August 14, 1978, and going through October 29, 1978. It contained fees and royalties to be paid to Mr. Marowitz, hotel expenses and transportation money for him "and spouse" from England to the United States and from his American hotel in New York City to the New Rochelle theater by "minibus." The deal also included a daily stipend plus an extra amount for a side trip to Boston that Charles apparently had to make. Finally, there was an option to take the production to New York City, in which case the parties would enter into a new Dramatists' Guild Agreement. The document was signed on the left by Charles Marowitz and on the right by my Managing Director.

Of the various occasions in my career when I smelled that familiar whiff of death gas, this time I was nearly asphyxiated. I wrote Charles a full explanation at once. He called off his agent, who had been instructed to institute proceedings against us claiming Charles had refused other engagements for the time slot he had been contracted for by our corporation. Charles didn't sue me, which he could have, but he didn't remain my friend, either. This was the kind of loss that hurt the most.

The one big push I instigated toward the end of the season was to investigate with Linda something I had heard about earlier in the season. There was an abandoned church and parish house on North Avenue in New Rochelle, and the city fathers were looking for some community enterprise to take over the premises. The setup, I discovered, was ideal. The church could easily be converted into a theater, and Beeb Salzer, our designer, immediately created blueprints for renovation. The parish house contained space for a small experimental theater, classrooms, offices, costume and scene construction facilities, and a fully equipped restaurant kitchen.

I immediately drew up plans for a self-supporting center, which would include, in addition to our theater, training classes for professional as well as local residents, a children's theater, and a cabaret. I met with the superintendent of schools and discussed a plan of cooperation with the large local high school whereby we would present plays (Shakespeare, for instance) that would coincide with English courses. I rushed all this over to the New Rochelle city manager, who, after a cool start (he showed me a curt turn-down letter he had received from my former Managing Director) warmed to the idea. The city manager promised me he'd sell my idea to the city council members and then turn the two magnificent buildings over to me if I could get up enough money to guarantee the heating bills for at least a year. All in all, Linda figured, we'd need about forty thousand dollars to take possession and to ensure getting some of our proposed money-making projects off the ground.

I now sat in my office, my second wind blowing strong, and called every VIP in Westchester I knew, to form a committee that would guarantee the front money for the community project. It was uphill effort, as I discovered how many local people had been turned off by cavalier treatment from our administrative people during the season. After about a hundred calls I finally got twenty, including the superintendent of schools and a prominent member of the city council, to agree to attend a meeting in a local home. Linda and I arrived with our project for a New Rochelle Center for the Performing Arts minutely documented, and Beeb Salzer brought along beautiful drawing plans of the church in various stages of its proposed renovation into a theater. In order to save money, he had devised three different time periods of building that would permit us to start production modestly and then add to the construction as money came in from our activities in the parish house.

A half hour after the time our committee had promised to start the meeting, only four people had turned up. Nothing daunted, I began my presentation. One of the ladies dropped off to sleep at once and stayed that way to the end of the evening. The other three scowled until I finished and then launched into diatribes describing how their previous attempts to help our theater had been thwarted by our business management. I pleaded with them to understand that all that was over, that our new project would not only save our theater but make a contribution to the life of the community. In my heart I heard Luther Adler's prophetic words during the Group's rehearsals of *Gold Eagle Guy,* "Boys, I think we're working on a stiff." As I went home that night I knew the Robert Lewis Acting Company was dead.

How could I, business genius that I was, not know that, in changing the name of the Westchester Laboratory Theatre to the Robert Lewis Acting Company, I had made it easy for the IRS, the New York State Tax Department, the unemployment insurance folk, the Westchester small shop creditors, the New York Telephone Company, IBM, and a lady from Larchmont (who wanted her ten-dollar deposit on the second season back) to beat a path to my (actual) door, while the ex-business manager and the other corporate signatories faded away into the fog? Why didn't I get legal advice at the outset, you say? Well, I did. You see, my ex-business manager's lawyer friend was not only generously guiding us for free, but the lawyer himself was one of the signers of the corporation papers.

On June 8, 1978, all the office material was moved from the College of

New Rochelle to my garage in Irvington-on-Hudson. As with the demise of the Dollar Top Theatre, the leftover stationery served for some time as scrap paper. There was also a collection of newspaper clippings one of which, written by Jacques le Sourd of the Westchester-Rockland Newspapers, proclaimed, "Little Orphan Westchester has found her Daddy Warbucks, and his name is Robert Lewis."

Disappointment at the failure of my home-grown theater made me feel like going somewhere on the other side of the world to operate. I not only felt like it. I did it. I accepted an offer from Australia. But before I went down under I conducted another semester of the Robert Lewis Theatre Workshop (this time at the Manhattan Theatre Club) and enjoyed a Golden Anniversary party at my sister's loft in Union Square celebrating my seventieth birthday as well as fifty years in the theater. I found it easier to believe it was my fiftieth birthday and my seventieth year in the theater. Among many faithful friends who turned up were Stella Adler, Boris Aronson, Harold Clurman, Elia Kazan, Earle Hyman, Stanley Kauffmann, Anita Loos, Leo Lerman, Maureen Stapleton, Eli Wallach, and Robert Whitehead. Susan Reed, with her Irish harp, sang lovely folk songs; a former student from the Yale School of Drama, Brian McEleney, gave a hilarious impersonation of me conducting an acting class, and Gadget and Harold Clurman made speeches. I was particularly touched by Harold's remark that, although he might take the occasion to review my theatrical career, he would rather comment on the lifetime friendships I had been able to keep in a profession noted for temporary attachments.

Now to Australia. Hayes Gordon had played a small part in *Brigadoon* in 1947 so well that I gave him the understudy to the lead, which he subsequently played on the road tour. He was then engaged to do the Alfred Drake part in *Kiss Me, Kate* in the Australian company and has remained in Sydney ever since. By now he is the leading musical comedy star there, having had long runs as Tevye in *Fiddler on the Roof*, Warbucks in *Annie*, and so on. More important, he has established the successful Ensemble Theatre, which specializes in the production of American plays. In 1979, having been awarded the Order of the British Empire by the queen of England, Hayes was asked to produce (under the auspices of his Ensemble Theatre) a representative American play for an international season to be held in the Sydney Opera House. In a letter to me Hayes asked if I would choose and direct such a play with Australian actors, and while I was there, conduct a seminar on acting at the Ensemble Theatre. I agreed and settled on *Long Day's Journey into Night* as the play choice.

For the first time in my life I cast a play by videotape. Hayes chose a number of actors for each part and taped their audition scenes in Australia. Having worked with me, he sensed what I might be looking for in the actors and instructed them expertly, even stepping into the picture occa-

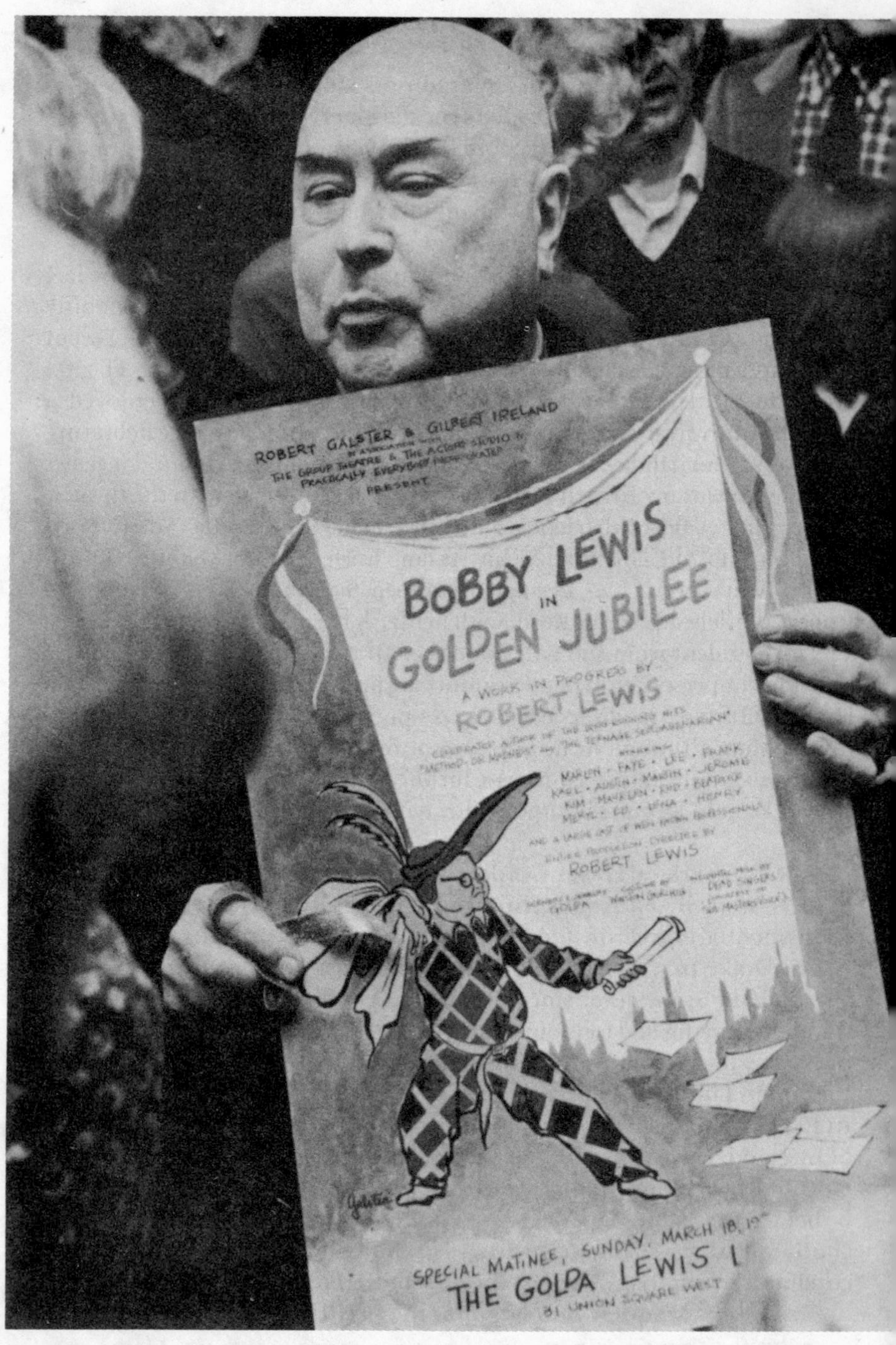


1979, Golden Anniversary. "I found it easier to believe it was my fiftieth birthday and my seventieth year in the theater."

sionally to stop the stage action, talk to the actor a bit, and then let the scene go on, the camera rolling all the time. I thus had a good idea of how the actor responded to direction, too. The tapes, when I viewed them at home, were so good that I had no trouble picking an interesting cast for the proposed production.

On July 31, 1979, I conducted the first session of my Australian seminar for actors at the Ensemble Theatre. The cast of *Long Day's Journey* was there, as well as performers from other shows playing in Sydney. The questions after the talk revealed the very same anxieties about the Method that the American actors expressed during my 1957 "Method—or Madness?" lectures in New York. The Australian seminar turned out to be a *Reader's Digest* version of those talks.

While waiting for the start of rehearsals and giving press interviews, I attended plays and opera productions (Joan Sutherland on her home turf). Two of the plays were by Brecht: *The Caucasian Chalk Circle* and *Galileo*. About the latter, I find an entry in my overseas diary: "Three and a half hours of not talking, not listening, not playing one situation; just line readings and mostly poor ones. Critics raved. It's worrying." The program notes of *Galileo* contained the strange assertion that Charles Laughton, "not wanting to hang out in bad company," had canceled the New York opening (after he had played *Galileo* in California) because of Brecht's appearance before the House Un-American Activities Committee. I thought this odd, since I was at the opening of *Galileo* at the Belasco Theatre in New York and remember very well Laughton's curtain speech, in which he said he would immediately cable Brecht, who had gone home to Germany, the news of the audience's enthusiastic reception. Of such careless program notes is theater history made.

At the first read-through of the play when the rehearsals of *Long Day's Journey* began on August 10, 1979, I realized that I had a cast of interesting actors, each of whom came from different backgrounds and possessed diverse techniques and approaches. My job, clearly, was to make them into a family. By all odds, the older son, Jamie (Max Phipps) was the most gifted actor. Possessed of towering emotional power, he made the great last act confessional scene with his brother, Edmund, a shattering experience—the best I've ever seen it played. Phipps was also blessed with a powerful imagination and lusty humor—a Jamie to remember.

Young David Webb, who played Edmund, was the least experienced actor in the group, but had unusual qualities for the part. He had the exterior appearance of a bookworm, but you sensed a waiting volcano inside him, which one day would erupt into a play about this doomed family. Physically he seemed to be put together with safety pins. Scrunched over in his chair, book in hand, with metal eyeglasses, he evoked a believable picture of the young O'Neill. As an actor he had one problem that nearly drove Kevin Miles, who played his father, up the wall during the early rehearsals. As he studied the behavior of his unhappy family from his chair, David's fingers, hands, and feet were seldom still, drumming a continuous beat, disturbing the concentration of his partners. I didn't want to lose the marvelous inner life that was causing these mannerisms and begged the indulgence of the other cast members as I removed one nervous movement after another, without having to adopt Kevin's suggestion to nail David's hands to his chair and his feet to the floor.

Kevin had his own problems. He was most successful in delineating the remains of the popular nineteenth-century Shakespearean actor who wrecked his fine career for the safety of endlessly repeating his success in a favorite melodrama. The larger-than-life characterization, which emerged in moments such as those when Tyrone recalls the exciting performances when he costarred with Edwin Booth, was splendid. The simple, unadorned depths of emotional agony needed in his scenes of realization of his failures as artist, husband, and father were more difficult for Kevin.

My most illuminating experience was in directing the interesting Patricia Conolly as Mary Tyrone. Having once seen Ruth Nelson in a definitive performance in this part (in a Springfield, Massachusetts, regional theater presentation directed by her stepson, Jamie Cromwell), I had high hopes of being able to accomplish an equal, if not better, result with this part in my production. Not, mind you, that Miss Conolly didn't have a triumph in the part. She did. She got far and away the most enthusiastic notices from all the critics (Phipps was practically ignored) as well as the most vociferous applause nightly from a good part of the audience. This almost universal acceptance of her performance as topdrawer was a tribute to Patricia's uncanny technical prowess. Although she had a limited range of truthful emotional expression, there was no feeling in the book that she could not simulate with such devastating accuracy that not only was it possible for her to make the audience and the critics enjoy her, but she could fool herself into thinking she was actually experiencing what she was only delineating with technique. Well, what the hell else do you want, you may well ask.

First, there are certain extraordinary emotions that come suddenly to great actors and overwhelm them in a given moment. These are distinct from the normal feelings that result from the usual playing out of the situations. Such a moment of being "washed over" by emotion occurred in *The Glass Menagerie,* when Laurette Taylor asked her daughter, on the fire escape, to make a wish on the moon. "What shall I wish for, Mother?" asks Laura. Amanda replies, "Happiness! Good fortune!" Such a moment was also achieved when Laurence Olivier leaned against the proscenium at the end of the second act of *The Entertainer* and moaned a Negro blues. These were occasions when you felt that, instead of the artists playing the parts, the parts were playing them, so to speak.

I needed something like that to happen at the curtain line of act 2 in

*Long Day's Journey* when Mary Tyrone says, "Then Mother of God, why do I feel so lonely?" She maintains she's glad the rest of the family, with their suspicious looks, has left the house, but suddenly she is overcome by a feeling of desperate loneliness. This was the kind of emotion that had to be truly experienced and no ammunition in Patricia's huge arsenal worked convincingly. I finally substituted an emotion that she *could* simulate brilliantly. This resulted from her looking up, shaking her fist to heaven, and bawling out the Mother of God for Mary Tyrone's pitiable condition. It made a startling substitute curtain, which brought the act to a satisfying conclusion.

There is another phenomenon resulting from this distinction between truthfully experienced emotion and simulated feeling, no matter how brilliantly executed, in this old battle of Emotionalists versus Anti-Emotionalists. I remember how worried I was when I awoke the morning after listening to Maurice Evans's "For God's sake, let us sit upon the ground / And tell sad stories of the death of kings" speech on the opening night of his *Richard the Second,* to read that John Mason Brown had been so moved by this passage that, for a moment, he felt he might have to leave his seat and repair to the lobby to collect himself. As for me, I had only admired the way in which Maurice, with his mellifluous voice and technical witchcraft gave the *impression* that Richard was experiencing something more than what an opera singer senses as he lets out a gorgeous high C for its own sake and not as a result of his character's situation. I finally came to the conclusion that, after all, an intelligent and sensitive theatergoer like John Mason Brown brings his *own* understanding and his own reactive sensations to what he is witnessing on the stage. The combination of these is what helps set off his emotional responses. I stopped worrying. But, in the final analysis, one must point out that no matter how successfully a simulated diamond might fool the onlooker, a diamond expert will know the difference—because there *is* a difference. It's the difference between the craftsman and the artist. Hayes Gordon, artistic head of the Ensemble Theatre, who sat next to me watching the cast of *Long Day's Journey* perform, knew that it was Max Phipps who was the real article and Patricia Conolly the brilliant substitute. She had taken Joseph Jefferson's advice to "keep your heart warm and your head cool" and reversed it.

I was so happy exercising my artistic muscles directing the O'Neill play in Australia and conducting the Ensemble Theatre seminar for actors that I kept up the good work by interrupting the flight home in Honolulu to deliver a lecture at the University of Hawaii, where a former pupil of mine, Glenn Cannon, was the head of the drama department.

I was soon to discover why the little koala bear in the TV advertisement says "I hate Qantas," for the plane dropped me down in the middle of the worst Broadway commercial theater disaster in my experience.

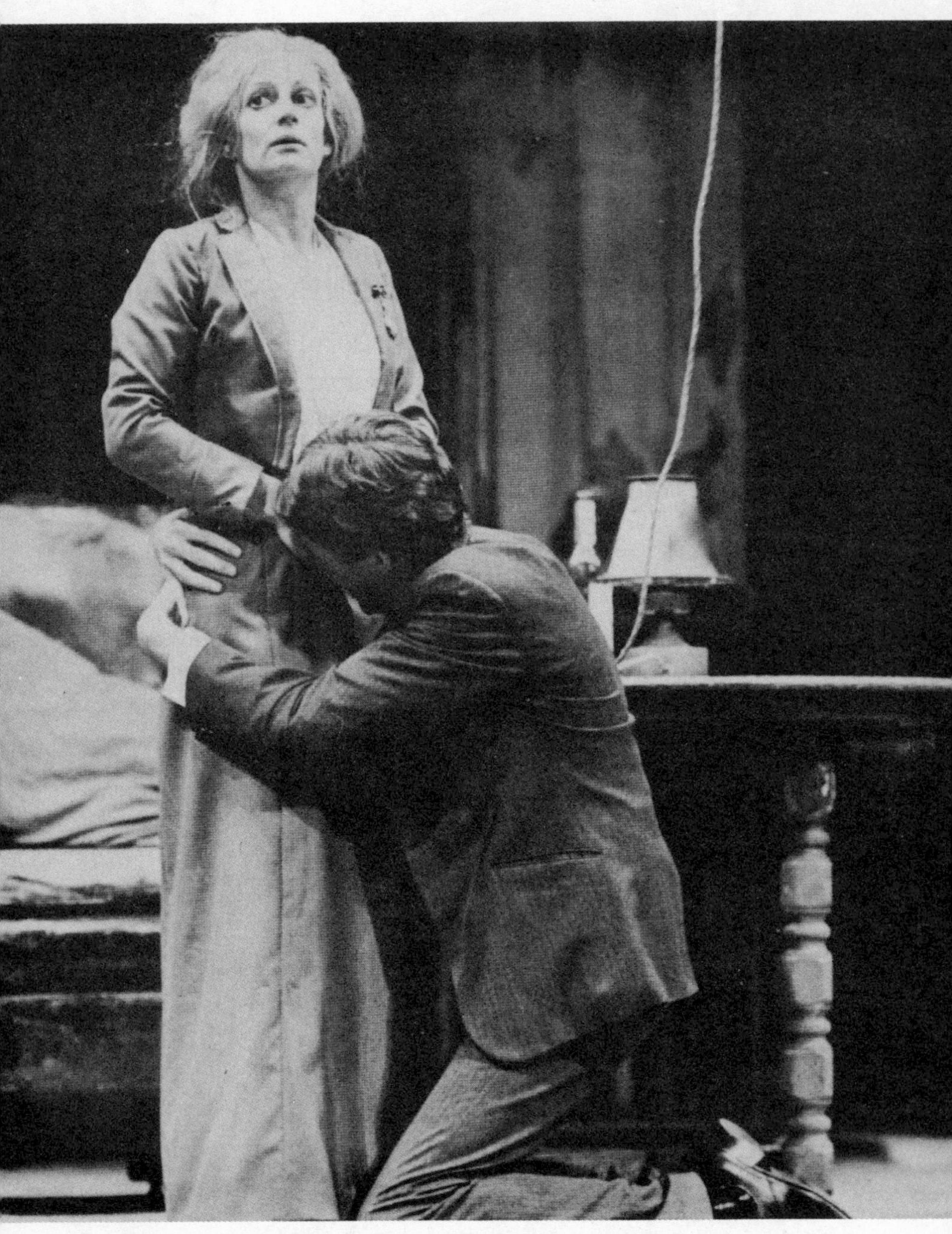

Patricia Conolly and David Webb in the Sydney (Australia) Opera House production of *Long Day's Journey into Night*: "A simulated diamond."

CHAPTER 21

# The Titanic 1980

THREE-QUARTERS OF A million dollars down the drain, huge pieces of scenery that squashed whatever life the scenes might have contained by stalling as they emerged from the wings, causing half of the characters' bodies to be offstage, speeches that unexpectedly turned the audience off with an audible click, critical reviews that literally pounded the poor little show to smithereens—when you have a towering disaster like that, friends are bound to ask, "Why did you do it, Bobby?" The implication seems to be that when I read the script I said to myself, "Oh, boy! Is this a stinker. When do I start rehearsals?"

What happens, though, is more like this. The sick feeling that the ship is sinking starts almost imperceptibly one day when you are already in production. As it grows you become more and more suicidal, knowing that, as the captain, you can't desert all those dear people who are going down with you. In the case of *Harold and Maude,* there was a moment before rehearsals started when I had a premonition of disaster and tried to get out, but unfortunately I was trapped.

Shortly before I was to depart for Australia to direct *Long Day's Journey,* I received a phone call from Frank Milton asking me if I would read a stage version of the Ruth Gordon cult film *Harold and Maude* with a view to directing it after my return from Sydney. Years earlier, Milton had been an acting student in a class of mine, and I remembered him as trying to emulate Noël Coward in every scene he presented. There wasn't too much future in this, as Frank was far too small to fit into Noël's shoes and not blessed with the Britisher's razor-sharp wit. Independently wealthy, Frank had turned to investing in Broadway shows (mostly British imports) and was now about to take a flyer as a producer.

I read the script through once, while packing suitcases for my imminent departure, and found the story innocuous enough and with some possibil-

The *Harold and Maude* company: "Why did you do it?"

ity of making an entertaining production. Further, I had heard people bragging of the number of times they had seen the film. Jean-Louis Barrault apparently persuaded the author, Colin Higgins, to turn the film script into a play for Madeleine Renaud, Barrault's wife; she had acted it on and off for seven years, and it was still running in Paris. Productions had been presented in Canada (with Glynis Johns), as well as in Japan, West Germany, Spain, Argentina, and Czechoslovakia. It must have had something that was attractive to audiences. Mainly though, this would be a perfect financial windfall for me, I reasoned. With huge royalties pouring in weekly, I could spend the next year writing this present memoir by being able to wipe my slate clean of teaching and lecturing chores. Also there was a fee but no royalties for the limited (five-week) Australian engagement of *Long Day's Journey*, so *Harold and Maude* was just the insurance I needed to write my book when I got back. I signed up right before the plane took off, but not without leaving a handwritten note behind to be sure that no production decisions would be set in the months I would be away. I didn't want to be locked into artistic choices that I couldn't live with after I had had a chance to study the project on my return. On the basis of my first reading of the script I left careful typed admonitions for the creators of the sets, costumes, lights, sounds, music, props, and effects, who would be thinking up their contributions while I was away. I ended with this warning: "Nothing in the production, visual or sound, should overpower *in size* the fragility of the emotional story, played out mostly by only two or three characters at a time. All must move as fluidly as music, so the play will appear to be in *two* acts rather than *twenty* scenes."

On my return to America, the first element to explore in the production of *Harold and Maude* was its star, Glynis Johns. She was built into the package, having been signed up before I was. Frank Milton showed me the photos of the Canadian production of the play Glynis had appeared in and my first feelings of doubt were born. Here was Maude who, in the play, decides on her eightieth birthday that that is a good number to go out on and commits suicide. The question of her age, therefore, was of the essence. She completes the cycle of her existence after instilling a despairing young man with a desire to live and he, in the process, falls in love with her.

In the production photographs I looked at, there was Glynis Johns, with her blonde hair, lovely face, and sensuous figure, in an outfit obviously designed by a leading light of haute couture rather than bits and pieces picked off racks or put together by Maude's hands and needles.

"She's not going to want to look that young and chic in our production, is she?" I asked Frank. "The whole idea of the play won't make sense. It'll be the story of an attractive cradle snatcher."

"You won't get her to play old," said Frank.

"How about a beautiful face crowned by silvery white hair?" I asked, thinking of how lovely Aline Bernstein, the stage designer, looked in her great age, with a girlish, pretty face topped with white hair.

"You won't get white hair," said Frank.

"Before I go any further, I think we'd better have a conference," I advised. Frank promptly set one up in his apartment in the Olympic Towers for Glynis, Colin Higgins, the playwright, who was summoned from Hollywood, and myself.

The conference was a huge success. Everybody behaved beautifully. I kept referring to "silvery" hair instead of white or gray. Glynis, who, in the Canadian production, had removed all references to Maude's having been in a concentration camp in the Second World War, didn't even blink when informed that Colin and I planned to clarify and enlarge on this aspect of the character. The author could (and did) return to Hollywood secure in the feeling that the production was off to a flying start. When Glynis and I got down to the street after the pow-wow, she asked me to go back to the

Mayflower Hotel with her right then to discuss her part in detail. I begged off, explaining I hadn't yet had time to study the script sufficiently or to prepare my production, having just come back from directing the Australian *Long Day's Journey*. As soon as I was ready I would call her and we'd make a date.

Next day Florence Klotz, our costume designer, called me to report that Glynis had phoned and asked Florence to go with her to pick out Maude's costumes. I told Florence to hold off as I was just then working on my ideas for the costumes of all the parts based on their characterizations and the points I was trying to make with the play as a whole.

Frank reported that, when she discovered I had called Florence off, Glynis was furious. "I'll call her at once," I said. I tried to explain to Glynis the way I worked: arrive at an overall production concept and then zero in on the specific manifestations of that idea in terms of sets, costumes, characterizations, and so on.

Glynis maintained that Maude's clothes—some English actresses still refer to costumes as clothes—had nothing to do with the rest of the play, as Maude was an individual.

"Exactly," I agreed. "It's for that very reason I want to think about the choices of what she will wear that will dramatize her difference from the other characters."

"There is no way I can talk to you," was Glynis's astonishing reply as she hung up.

This was my moment. I had that recurring feeling in the pit of my stomach that this kind of show business arrangement was not for me and I wanted out. Let me go back to my teaching, writing, and lecturing; I would only direct plays in those parts of the world where I could function as an artist in the way I was brought up.

Picking up the telephone, I called Frank and told him the setup wasn't going to work, that I knew he was unalterably committed to Glynis, and please to release me. He said he'd get back to me, and I went to bed with a great sigh of relief.

The next day I was stunned to hear from Frank that he had spoken to his producing partner in New York and to Colin Higgins in California and that they had all decided to go ahead with me and pay Glynis off. As it turned out, she was the luckiest one in the lot. She averted the disaster to come, and she was the only one who made any money out of it, her agent having procured an enormous sum from the producers to cancel her contract.

To her great credit I must report that, after her successor was duly found, signed, and announced, I received a remarkable telephone call late one night from Glynis. She wished me good luck, told me she had a picture postcard she had planned to give me on the opening but would send me now. Then she said, "I was stupid—I smothered you." Do you know how rare this is? Has any one of you directors, in a similar situation on a Broadway production, ever received such a call? You bet you haven't. I was genuinely moved and let Glynis know what a courageous and gracious gesture I thought she was making.

The search for a replacement for Glynis had started with a typewritten page of suggestions of old stage and screen stars, prepared by the producers and presented to me for my comments. My first comment was that eight of those listed were dead. Naturally they felt the actress to play Maude had to be someone with a big draw, since *Variety* had reported the capitalization of *Harold and Maude* as $525,000, "an exceptionally high amount" for a straight play. (It was to go even higher.) Most of the other names on the list that might bring the customers flocking to the theater (Greta Garbo, for example) were simply out of the question, for one reason or another. Katharine Hepburn's reason was, "Ruth did that already. Remember?"

One name mentioned struck me as possible: Janet Gaynor. I remembered her as the first Oscar winner, but with a personality too sweet for Maude. However, I figured, maybe life had toughened her up a bit by now. Ruth Gordon reportedly had said that when a house of Janet's caught fire, the diminutive movie star stopped for a minute deciding what treasure to save, grabbed some eight-by-ten glossies of herself, and ran out. That bit of gossip encouraged me enough to call Paul Gregory, Janet's husband, whom I knew in Hollywood in the forties. Janet would be interested to read the script, he said. She did, and loved it. Would we come out to California and talk with her?

Frank and I boarded a plane (first class, of course), flew to Los Angeles, picked up Colin Higgins, and the three of us drove to Janet's house in Palm Springs. The actress made a satisfactory impression on me for the part. She revealed a good sense of humor, was in fine physical condition, of an age which made Maude's no problem, and was still mighty pretty. Wanting to be sure I could get the toughness of a survivor the part needed, I took Janet into a study and the two of us worked alone for a while. That room itself, containing a mixture of artifacts Janet brought back from her many travels around the world, was not unlike a room Maude would live in. I became a little worried when Janet showed me a number of paintings she herself had made. They were all of tiny, colorful, pretty flowers. However, she responded to direction well, and I was persuaded I could, with work, toughen her up sufficiently for the part.

Rehearsals for *Harold and Maude* got under way after the rest of the casting was completed and I had seen the sketches of the sets. Everything was designed on the basis of the large stage and wide auditorium of the Martin Beck Theatre, where we had to play to accommodate the huge budget. I experienced a fleeting pang of jealousy as I remembered the simple physical means Jean-Louis Barrault was able to use in the videotape I had seen of his Paris stage production of the play. When Madeleine

Renaud, as Maude, had to play a scene with Harold out on the limb of a tree, she simply climbed up a ladder to the balcony of the theater and sat among the ever-present students in the audience up there. In my early days, would I not have approached this material with the same kind of imagination? But here I was, in a different kind of show business, wildly expensive, with an enormous realistic tree that needed a complicated set of engineering components to bring it on stage for its scene. I couldn't know, from the sketch, that the huge tree would lumber out very slowly, electrical machinery rumbling audibly all the way. I didn't know how many times the machinery would get stuck halfway on the tree's journey, or not work at all, necessitating the operator to round up all the available stage crew to crank it on by hand with agonizing slowness. I didn't know then that Janet Gaynor, when supposedly climbing the tree, would have to go around the back of it, mount a tiny elevator (electrically operated, too), stand on it with one foot, and, with the other, make pathetic little motions supposed to indicate that she was climbing the tree as the elevator rose.

Also, how could I tell from the sketches that my original plan to have continuous stage action would be fouled up by a turntable that would revolve with the speed of molasses while changing from Maude's house to Harold's and back again, taking a noisy eternity each time? How could I know how many times it would turn late or not at all? How could I know that the two platforms coming on from either side to meet the turntable, and so complete the set, would never synchronize with the turntable, being either too fast or too slow to make the transition without a crash? How could I know how many times one or another or both of these platforms wouldn't come on at all, revealing actors arriving for, or leaving from, their positions on the turntable; or worse, show stage hands scurrying to tend to the newest breakdown? And finally, how could I know that all these disasters would occur mainly on nights when the critics were covering the show, including the opening night?

But, more important, how did I *not* know in rehearsal the passages in the script that I later discovered offended some audience members, including the critics. It all seemed bland enough to me. Colin Higgins, the playwright, arrived for a hurried look-see from Hollywood when we were having our run-throughs. He had to go back before the play's opening, as he was directing his film *Nine to Five* at the time and so he never saw the show with an audience. But he enjoyed the run-through, made only tiny alterations in a couple of lines, and went back to California a seemingly happy man.

Then came the audiences and the critics. During the previews, aside from the loss of attention due to mechanical failures (the special effects of Harold hanging himself, Harold's huge exploding sticks of dynamite, Harold immolating himself, and so on, were invariably attacked by gremlins, too) the audiences seemed to enjoy the scenes themselves. There were certain passages during which I thought I detected some resistance from a few of the playgoers, but I'll get back to that in a moment. Janet Gaynor won hearts, though, and got a standing ovation nightly. True, standing ovations have become increasingly more frequent in the theater. Soon the ushers will be getting them. (The first such reception I encountered was the truest I have witnessed. Toward the end of the thirties, at a mass meeting against war and fascism, Thomas Mann was suddenly led on to the stage. As on a single inner cue all the people in the audience rose to their feet spontaneously to honor a giant of literature who was aligning himself with their just cause.) As for Janet's standing ovation, I consoled myself with the thought that, up to then at least, not *every* actor on Broadway was getting one.

Finally, the critical notices arrived. Never in my long theater life have I witnessed an innocuous little number like *Harold and Maude* attacked with such savagery. It was like using an atomic bomb to destroy an insect. The poor little play was pulverized to bits; then the tiny pieces were powdered and blown away to be sure no one would ever hear of the offender again.

I know you won't believe me when I tell you I reacted quite impassively to it all. But I did. Over and over I asked myself why I was feeling no pain. I came to certain conclusions. First, the attack on the play was ridiculously out of proportion to its aspirations. Second, I obviously didn't have a deep enough feeling for the material myself. Third, there must have been resentment on the part of the critics about the boasting of the huge amount of money put into the production. Fourth, the original movie had not received good notices, yet went on to be an audience favorite. The critical fraternity (now why do they call it that?) was not about to let the same thing happen with the play. Best to kill it real dead at once. Fifth, some critics, as well as a number of playgoers, must have been offended by the very idea of a young boy going to bed with an old woman. I was as careful as I could be in that delicate scene, with Harold and Maude sitting on the side of the bed (feet on the floor as in the old movie days of the Hays censorship), to have Harold very slowly lean Maude back toward her pillow as the lights dimmed out. There was also that speech a priest delivered trying to dissuade Harold from marrying Maude by describing the effect of aging on a woman's body. It was fairly explicit, but the actor (Jack Bittner) who played the part was so sincere, his graphic description even causing him to faint, that many in the audience (myself included) enjoyed the moment hugely. Some obviously didn't, thought it in poor taste, and among these, undoubtedly, were the critics.

If a play gets a particularly sarcastic review, it's usually because something in the show has deeply offended the personal taste of the critic. When I directed *Five Alarm Waltz* in 1941, with Gadget Kazan playing the leading part, the prototype of which was William Saroyan, I thought that

Brooks Atkinson might have been upset that I, who had directed *My Heart's in the Highlands,* Saroyan's beautiful first play, had allowed myself to be connected with a takeoff of the Armenian playwright. Not at all. Atkinson wrote, "Cast as the mad genius of the play, he (Gadget) has to act several scenes costumed in a pair of drawers, and it is pleasant to observe that he has a nice little thicket of black curlicues smack in the middle of his chest. Since nature gave him those, he is entitled to them and is herewith handsomely congratulated."

Brooks, a valued friend, was obviously offended. I'm sorry.

## CHAPTER 22

# Speaking of Critics . . .

SPEAKING OF CRITICS . . . Harold Clurman died while I was writing this book. To my mind the theater lost a man who, in his role as critic, combined all the qualities that drama reviewing needs for respectability. He was an acute dissector of play scripts, having worked closely over half a century with any number of playwrights in bringing their plays to the stage. His whole life long, Harold studied the world literature of drama, and he taught many playwrighting classes. A fine director, he dealt with the practical mechanics of the theater: acting, design, all the elements of production. In so doing, he became one of the few professional observers of performances who could take apart a production clinically and understand who contributed what to the result. But over and above all this expertise, there was the humaneness he brought to his observations of the artists, whether it was in praise or censure. He chose to be a companion to the artists, not an adversary. It is to this point that I want to address myself, since I fear that the last vestiges of that attitude may have died with Harold, making his loss even more unbearable.

Of all the bastards who "won't let you live," our drama critics are certainly at the top of the heap. All right, all right, I know it's unfair to lump them all together. But what's the choice? Your work can be successfully savaged by rapier thrusts from self-styled elitist John Simon or by TV's Stewart Klein, a cultural pisher.

Why, you may well ask, am I now going to complain about critics when I have quoted them all through this book? Well, it's not *what* they say that I'm concerned with here. You can agree or disagree with that. It is a certain poisonous *attitude* that I believe has helped to weaken the theater until it is near death. Death, he says? What about the so-called boom Broadway is enjoying? I'm not talking about business. I'm talking about an infection that has crippled good theater artistically.

Constructive critics, starting way back with George Henry Lewes, right up to Harold Clurman, even in their severest moments never lost their respectful tone with proven artists in the manner our reviewers had, for example, with Tennessee Williams. Lewes complained of Kean's gabbling over the less important sections of his roles, but the critic did this from the point of view of his reverence for the magnificence of the high points. Shaw chided Adelina Patti for her flirtatious concert platform manner, but only after making it clear that, as she was the foremost soprano of her day, the critic couldn't stand the slightest blemish in the behavior of one he revered. Donal Henahan, today's *New York Times* music critic, in his November 15, 1981, review of *The Complete Musical Criticism* of Bernard Shaw admits, "He (Shaw) did not think, apparently, that it was necessary to be rude—merely witty, clear and right."

Harold Clurman was sorely disappointed in Lee J. Cobb's *King Lear*, which he felt was too prosaic, too "small" inside for the grandeur of Shakespeare's text. But Clurman didn't finish his scolding review without reminding us of Cobb's worth as an actor in other roles. Harold believed an artist, unlike a chain, should be judged by his strongest, not his weakest, link. Further, Clurman's explication, in his review of the technical problem of what happens when American naturalistic actors meet up with Shakespearean verse, instructed all actors.

In everyday terms, the simple difference I am trying to point out is this: one type of critic feels bad when he has to pan an artist who has paid his dues; the other type gets his jollies. There is not that special kind of pain in criticism that there is in creation. The professional murderer-critic will never know that pain the way the artist does. And don't fall for that it-hurts-me-more-than-it-does-you crap.

Ask mature theater people what they have ever learned from those drama critics who don't have Clurman's expertise and humanity, and they'll tell you: outside of what box-office action can be expected from their reviews—nothing. Here are but three major theater dropouts who had suffered from critical flip-flops: one playwright, William Saroyan; one director, Orson Welles; one actor, Stella Adler. Personally I think dropping out is a mistake—it gives destructive critics more power. Rather, when pummeled, repeat Gertrude Stein's words: "No artist needs criticism, he only needs appreciation. If he needs criticism he is no artist." Sam Behrman, in *Portrait of Max*, tells of discussing Virginia Woolf's diary with Beerbohm. Max found "distasteful" her acute and incessant concern with what reviewers felt about her work. He said she should have read Henry James on Turgenev's opinion. Beerbohm said, "Turgenev appreciated that criticism is a delightful pastime for the critics—that, even, it may be delightful to their readers. But, he says, it has nothing whatever to do with the artist, nor with the process by which art is achieved."

It is not altogether impossible, of course, to learn something from expert and knowledgeable critical evaluations. I'm thinking, as one famous example, of what theater folk have learned from Shaw's brilliant comparison of the acting techniques of Duse and Bernhardt when they appeared during the same week in the title role of Sudermann's *Magda*.

To go from a heavyweight like Shaw to the opposite end of the critical spectrum, let's dispose, quickly, of today's featherweights—most, although not all, of them working on TV and radio. Not, mind you, that those do less damage. As a result of their enormous exposure, the influence they have on the state of the theater is considerable, and it's growing daily. These birds not only often don't do their homework properly, but they mostly have no fund of knowledge of their subject. They do, however, entertain us with some howlers.

TV's Katie Kelly, whose parameters of art don't extend a quarter of an inch beyond the purely naturalistic, announced, with the pride of a confirmed dummkopf, that she prefers the Fonz's "Happy Days" to Samuel Beckett's, whose gem of a play she was reviewing. Giggling foolishly, she informed her TV viewers that in the first part of the Beckett play Irene Worth is half-buried in sand, and in the second part she is buried up to her neck. "I don't like Beckett," cried Katie, whose head is completely buried in sand. (Hey, John Simon, this is fun!) What kind of theater civilization can you expect when a Katie Kelly helps shape the artistic taste of millions of TV watchers?

And now everybody's favorite, Stewart Klein. He not only reviews theater, on and off Broadway, but films, ballet, and music—the lot. He comes to this monumental task of all-round surgeon with no more equipment than a nail file. His pronunciation, for example, would make English language protector John Simon squirm in agony. Since it's just possible that John may not catch Stewart's nightly exhibition, here's a sampling. For beginners, "hang gout" is the way our New York boy delivers the two words "hang out." In a review of a ballet performance Klein referred to the pas de deux as the "pass de doo." How'd you like to hear Anatole Broyard pronounce *Les Misèrables* "Less Miserable"? Stew doesn't bother to check the pronunciation of the names of the artists he's talking about, either. Kenneth Haigh, who pronounces his last name Haig, is called Kenneth High. So much for Stewart Klone.

If, as Gore Vidal has said, there is nothing John Simon "cannot find to hate," there is nothing Clive Barnes cannot find to love. Mostly, of course, it's love for himself he is pleading for. There is hardly a raggle-taggle group of young hopefuls in a cellar (has to be on MacDougal Street or below) that Mr. Barnes doesn't hail as the future National Theatre of America. His ever-bountiful hand has even, on occasion, stretched uptown to Broadway. Covering Clifford Odets' *The Country Girl*, Barnes delivered the following: "This is precisely the kind of gorgeous mediocrity we need on Broadway." With friends like Clive, who needs enemies?

"Excellence is all," says elegant hangman, John Simon, in an attempt to justify his executions. Is it possible *he* is always excellent? If he's not, who is to criticize the critic? I admit I'm not completely qualified but, what the hell, here goes. Simon, at least, might enjoy himself, since he loves bad notices, even when they're about himself. I remember one opening night, during the intermission, he spotted me and asked, with obvious relish, "Did you read what Gore wrote about Bob and me?" John knew I was teaching at the time at the Yale School of Drama where Bob Brustein was the dean. Whipping out a copy of an article Gore Vidal had written in the March 1970 *Commentary* magazine, Simon handed it to me proudly. It was titled "Literary Gangsters," and a glance told me it raked Brustein, Simon, and Richard Gilman over the coals. Since it was four pages long there wasn't time to read the whole article right then, but I promised John I'd get a copy of the magazine and read it later. I did.

Naughty Gore obviously decided to give these fellows a lesson in mayhem, an art Vidal was known to practice himself—with a particularly sharp instrument, too. Here are excerpts from Gore's piece in *Commentary*. On Simon: after the aforementioned "There is nothing he cannot find to hate," Gore goes on with, "Yet, in his way, Mr. Simon is pure; a compulsive rogue criminal, more sadistic Gilles de Rais than neighborhood thug."

On Brustein: "A failed theatre person, he had—has—ambitions not only as director but as an actor. . . . Mr. Brustein's ambition has now translated him from literary gangster to academic bureaucrat but I'm sure he'll be back one of these days. Recidivism is a hundred percent in such cases."

On Gilman: "He has a tendency to get himself hung on as his slow, bumbling sentences unfold like bolts of wet wool . . . a profound thinker were his mind not shallow . . . makes one long for the good old days of Bonnie and Clyde, of Simon and Brustein."

How'd the fellows like them apples? Simon, of course, swelled with gleeful pride. Brustein, when I discussed Gore's piece with him, seemed genuinely hurt. Critics can be human, too.

How can I follow an act like Gore's? I can't. But I'll press on, for the reason that I have a point to make different from simply striking back.

Actor baiting is by no means a new sport. Even such benign writers as Franklin P. Adams couldn't resist the following sweetmeat after witnessing an acting performance by Olga Nethersole:

I love little Olga
Her plays are so warm.
And if I don't see them
They'll do me no harm.

Who is allowed to forget Dorothy Parker's barb at the leading lady of

*The Lake*? "Katharine Hepburn runs the gamut of emotions from A to B." Could a case be made to credit Mrs. Parker for encouraging Hepburn to develop into the powerhouse of emotion from A to Z that she is now?

Eugene Field was responsible for one of the most quoted smart-ass jibes at a hopeful King Lear: "Mr. Clarke played the king all evening as though under constant fear that someone else was about to play the ace."

One critic who anticipated dear John in the gallant art of Simonizing the anatomies of actresses was Percy Hammond: "I have knocked everything but the knees of the chorus girls, and God anticipated me there."

Is this Roman circus fun? Not to the victims being torn at by the lions.

I learned early in my career how hurtful powerful critics could be. George Jean Nathan cost me my production of *The Time of Your Life* by siding with the ravagers of my concept—Theresa Helburn and Lawrence Langner of the Theatre Guild, Saroyan, Julie Haydon, Eddie Dowling—all pals of Nathan. In a later year he would give me a "best stage director" award for my work on *Regina*. It's always overpraise or overkill. From an early age, my attempted solution to this state of affairs was simple. When I wanted real critical evaluation I talked to fine artists in my field, or in related fields (Stieglitz, for instance), or to critics who were also artists, like Harold Clurman.

Sad indeed was the depressing effect incompetent bad reviews could have on even so confident a producer and director as Jed Harris. He had mounted Phillip Barry's *Spring Dance*. Every time I saw Jed before the play opened he expressed his joy in the script and the whole project. I hadn't been to the opening but went to the first matinée after the poor reviews had come out. During the intermission I spotted Jed in the lobby. Running up to him with real enthusiasm, I told Jed what an original idea I thought the play propounded; namely, that the young people, not the parents, were, in reactionary fashion, attempting to sabotage a young man's effort to go abroad for special study in engineering and trying to force him to stay home and marry into a respectable family. Also, I said, the acting, under Jed's direction, was marvelous, with the young José Ferrer, brilliant in one of his first parts, as a cynical friend. Jed looked at me. "You're crazy," he said. "It stinks."

Now, criticizing the critics has a sparse but honorable history. One of the most memorable was Maxwell Anderson's designation of the drama reviewers as the Jukes Family of Journalism. Protective lawyers and agents will always warn you not to challenge the critics, because "they have the last word" and they'll murder you the next time you get up to bat. Not to worry. The next time you get up to bat, the critic's tendency is to go easy on you so no one, including himself, will think he's vindictive. But the time *after* that—watch out, brother.

When Kenneth Tynan arrived in the States to take over the post of drama critic for the *New Yorker*, I gave a welcoming party for him in my house. I was a friend of his and of Elaine Dundy, his wife at the time. Ken was hipped on the idea that certain roles required certain voice ranges. Famous less-than-ideal voices like those of Grasso, the great Sicilian tragedian, or Mihoels, the exciting Russian-Jewish King Lear, would not have met Tynan's criterion. In writing of Olivier's *Othello,* Tynan quotes Orson Welles: "Larry's a natural tenor and Othello's a natural baritone." (Robeson was a bass.)

Our friendship flowered until the night Tynan took me to the opening of John Gielgud's *Ages of Man* recital. During one selection Ken turned to me and said, "The trouble with John is he has no baritone in his voice." "So what," I quipped. "Chaliapin has no soprano in his." Ken's eyes widened, the color drained from his face, and I knew our friendship was over. I had dared to criticize a critic. I didn't see him again until the day before he left for England. He and Elaine gave a farewell party for their American friends. Ken had not invited me but, at the last moment, someone (Elaine?) called my number and left a message that my name had inadvertently been omitted from the guest list and would I please come to the party. I went and was able to thank Ken for his admonition to me in his review of my book *Method—or Madness?* not to use so many exclamation points in my writing. (The punctuation, in this case, was an attempt to recreate on paper my vocal emphases since the book was a transcription of taped lectures.) I promised that never, never, do you hear, would I commit a sin like that again!!!

Unaccountably, Ken, a theater critic who always did his homework, accused me, in his review of *Chéri,* of upgrading Léa's friend the Baroness's cigar to a pipe. Yet, in Colette's novel, from which I did my homework, you'll find the Baroness smoking a "short briar pipe." You can't win 'em all.

Another incident in which I was involved where critical feathers were ruffled took place in the Yale School of Drama. John Simon and Bob Brustein had long been buddies, two champion swordsmen admiring each other's ability to parry and thrust. Bob had invited John to address the drama school students one afternoon. That same morning, Arthur Miller was scheduled to speak to the university undergraduates. Arthur and I had lunch together, and I asked him if he'd like to drop in and partake of a bit of Simon for dessert. Miller and I crept into the back row of the auditorium, and Arthur slid his lanky body into a seat, throwing his legs over the back of the chair in front of him. It was an obvious attempt to conceal himself from the two critics standing in the front row of the house. Brustein gave Simon a glowing introduction referring to him as "Simon the good."

After a few minutes of John's lecture, Arthur uncurled himself, whispering, "Come on, I can't listen to any more of this shit." As we escaped through the rear door I noticed the eyes of both Simon and Brustein catching our precipitous departure. I have often tried to measure how much this incident contributed to the particular pleasure the two critics seem to experience when murdering everything Miller puts his hand to. One day at Brustein's house, when Bob was making a case for the proposition that everything Miller ever wrote was dishonest, I asked, "Including *Death of a Salesman*?" "Yes," said Bob. Even his wife, Norma, took exception to that.

The Brustein-Simon axis collapsed one day when John wrote an embarrassingly brief review of one of Bob's productions at Yale, in which Simon announced he would no longer go up to New Haven to cover productions of the Yale Rep because he didn't review amateur theater. A stiletto to the jugular! From that moment on, Brustein's published comments on Simon's collections of reviews betrayed daggerlike thrusts that the master, John himself, might envy. In *The New York Times* of January 4, 1976, Brustein referred to Simon's style as "murderous brutality."

It has been proven by John Leonard in his *Times* review of a Brustein book, however, that it is possible to criticize drama critics without resorting to their particular stock-in-trade: slashing. (Could it be that sitting comfortably at home with a beer—no, in the case of John Leonard I would guess a glass of cool, white wine—poring over a book you're reviewing is less conducive to the paranoiac feeling the theater critic has, namely, that all the people connected with the production in question have banded together just to see how close to insanity they can drive the reviewer?) Trying to analyze why Brustein's *The Culture Watch* was a "depressing book," Mr. Leonard quotes some examples of the prose in the book which, he says, "clinks about." Then he gives his summation: "Harrassed, combative, indignant, and not a little self-serving, Mr. Brustein has a vision. He prescribes for the future, a chaste, seminal, and poetic theatre, which for the moment, exists only at a brave and labyrinthine Yale, under the auspices of Mr. Brustein." How can we get the immaculate Mr. Leonard on a drama page?

Enough pussyfooting. Let's get down to more specific evidence of the serious damage done to theater artists through the gratuitous cruelty of drama critics. Is any play important enough to justify crucifying a leading playwright the way Tennessee Williams has been? Is any performance important enough to rip a serious actress to pieces in the way John Simon has Zoe Caldwell? Tennessee contributed enough to American drama in the past to be dubbed a national treasure forever. How dare any critic talk of him as though he were a cretin? Respect must be paid. I don't care whether reviewers think his last plays were shit or not. His shit is more interesting than some of the perfumed garbage the critical fraternity turn into hits. I'm not interested in what John Simon thinks of Zoe Caldwell's acting, but in the old days he would have been run through in a duel for writing, "Miss Caldwell is fat and unattractive in every part of the face, body and limbs, though I must admit that I have not examined her teeth.

When she climactically bares her sprawlingly uberous left breast, the sight is almost enough to drive the heterosexual third of the audience screaming into the camp of the majority." Did John get his jollies writing that one?

(Dear Zoe: Forgive me for repeating Simon's quote. "I must be cruel, only to be kind," as the fella said.)

What would Simon have done to Laurette Taylor in her role of Candida, the one that Sandy Meisner and I trekked up to see in Mt. Kisco every day for a whole week in the Group Theatre days? Taylor's face, marked with lines honorably won in her fierce battle with a difficult life, was lit up from inside with the beauty of her thought and feeling. Because she was unable to pass his special standard of feminine pulchritude, would Simon not have had to remark that Taylor looked run over? And with the poverty of the summer stock costume department would her less-than-Katharine-Cornell outfit not appear to Simon like drapes torn down from the window of a barroom? To Sandy and me she was an incandescent revelation in the part and made an impression of artistry and beauty that lasted a lifetime.

If I have used John as a stick to beat the critical fraternity with, it is only because he has raised mayhem to a fine art and so becomes the most quotable. But the tendency to destroy artists is built into the unmindful criticism practiced today in the theatrical shooting gallery. You cannot tell me that a critic wouldn't change places with an artist if he could. The mechanism of the artist has to do with creation. He can't begin unless he has a gift. Then he works his whole life nurturing it, developing it, finding techniques to express it. Once in a blue moon there is a moment of exaltation. Most of the time it's just agony. But he can't stop. He's hooked.

Now what of the critic? I'm talking of knowledgeable ones. To begin with, he should have a good mind. But the artist's mind functions because it's being pumped by the heart, an organ of little use to the likes of most of our reviewers.

The critic should have exemplary taste. Shaw had it. Stark Young had it. Clurman had it. From Simon to Stew, try to name some who have it nowadays.

The critic should do his homework. John does. Stew doesn't.

The critic should point the way. Shaw did, alerting us to the values of Ibsen, Duse, and others.

Try to think of any "way" pointed to by modern theater critics. They'll tell you what they liked or didn't like about a play or production. For that you need only a good dinner before and the ability to keep awake during the performance. Incidentally, not all reviewers can do even that. "Clive Sleeps" whispers a headline in the July 15, 1981, *Village Voice*. Apparently, at a premiere, the director of the play in question *(Wally's Café)* sat next to Barnes, who kept falling asleep during the entire performance, and the director kept trying to nudge him awake. The play didn't turn out to be a sleeper, but the critic did.

When I foolishly accepted that offer from the *New Leader* in 1961 to be the magazine's drama critic, my problem was not sleeping through performances but not sleeping at all when I got home from sheer worry at what my friends that I had to criticize would think of me. In my review of *How to Succeed in Business Without Really Trying,* I had chastized Abe Burrows ever so cautiously for his being careful not to offend anyone in his spoof of the business world. So worried was I at possibly having upset my friend Abe that, when I saw him going down the aisle at a subsequent Broadway second night performance, I slid down in my seat so he wouldn't see me. A little later, looking back to where I was sitting, Abe did spot me and gave me his usual friendly smile of greeting. Relieved as I was to realize the high probability that Abe might not be a faithful subscriber to the *New Leader,* I determined in that moment that my skin was not tough enough to be a successful drama critic. I quit a few editions later. The magazine paid me off with a lifetime subscription. I had probably set some kind of precedent when I reviewed my own production of *Kwamina* and panned it solidly. But I felt slightly purged for my traitorous sin in accepting the job in the first place.

The infliction of pain by the brutal language of theater critics used on performers and playwrights can reach dangerous proportions. In reviewing Robert Brustein's Yale Repertory Theatre production of *The Sea Gull,* Richard Eder, in *The New York Times,* wasn't satisfied that he could not find one iota of Norma Brustein's performance as Arkadina acceptable. Pointing out that Norma "is the director's wife," Mr. Eder went on, "Mrs. Brustein has played important roles in a number of the company's productions and, at least in the ones I've seen, she has tended to sink them." With these words carved on her heart, Norma had, for the length of the engagement, to face her fellow actors as well as her acting students in the drama school. As soon as the play's run ended, Norma had a massive heart attack and died. In the book on his Yale experience, Bob Brustein says the medical diagnosis was "unbearable stress." He had previously remarked that, as theater people, Norma and he "would always be vulnerable to critics and we had to harden our skins." Obviously some theater people can't harden theirs enough. Brustein movingly adds, "I had been pretty harsh myself in my time."

Drama critics are fond of underrating their power over the success or failure of a production. Yet I have seen producers go to the bulletin board after the opening night performance and put up the closing notice of the play as soon as someone at the city desk of *The New York Times* finished reading the review over the telephone as it came off the critic's typewriter. What serious major playwright is going to give two years of his life (the approximate time it takes from starting the first draft of the play to the New York opening) if everything hangs on a throw of the dice like that?

Well, take heart, laddies. In the long line of history there have been good critics and there have been bad critics. But the theater itself has been kept alive by nourishment from Shakespeare, Molière, Ibsen, and O'Neill; Stanislavski, Meyerhold, Reinhardt, and Copeau; Kean, Salvini, Duse, and Laurette Taylor.

In conclusion may I ask you to clap your eye on this paragraph:

"I had the blood lust of a boy. On Christmas vacation, when I was up visiting the farm, I asked to be the one to stick the knife in the hog's throat when they were butchering it. They agreed because they needed me. There were two men on the farm, Walt and Orrie, and two neighbors. It took four men to catch the hog, to turn it on its back and hold it there, each man hanging on to a leg. Then I took a knife, slimmed to a stiletto by years of sharpening, and as Walt directed, I felt along the underthroat for the hard spot, then for the soft spot just below it. I slit the skin gently. Then, with my left hand, I poised the knife in the slit and rammed it in with my right palm. I turned it, sunk to the hilt, round and round. I loved it. Then I pulled it out and we all ran for the fence. The hog got up quickly, furious, charged about the pigpen leaking sloshes of blood all over the mud, grew tipsy, then wildly drunk, then fell on its side, twitched, shit, and died. The men hung it up in the barn by the hind legs to dress it, and I helped scoop out the yards and yards of slippery red and yellow tubing."

The Marquis de Sade, you say? Not at all. It's my good friend, Stanley Kauffmann, in his memoir that he was kind enough to send me, recalling that boyhood scene as though it were a usual one for kids in their early teens. "I had the blood lust of a boy." Doesn't everyone? That chilling paragraph haunted me all through Stanley's autobiographical book as I watched him proceed, after his boyhood butchering, to try his hand at poetry, run a serious theater group, become a novelist—but finally end up a critic.

**At Duse's tomb in Asolo.**

# Epilogue: Upbeat to the Finale 1980s

WHEN THE LETTER came asking me to accept a Mellon Chair in Drama for the academic year 1981-82 at Rice University in Houston, Texas, I telephoned the sender. "What kind of drama department do you have at Rice?" I inquired. "Actually," came the reply, "we have none." "Stay right there," I said. "I'm coming down." Here was a university that could have done nothing wrong in the field of theater training.

The setup turned out to be perfect for my needs of the moment. With a light schedule of lectures, I had plenty of free time to finish this memoir. Rice is a small, very pretty campus, ideal for walking about and contemplating a long life in the theater. I spent only a short time considering the irony of awarding a generous Mellon Professorship in Drama to a university that had no graduate, or undergraduate, theater courses while so many performing arts colleges were aching for more funding. An American paradox.

As I mused upon more than a half century of changing American theater, the many threads of my own life in that theater gained definition. I saw them stretching out, curving, folding back, ripping, and starting up again and again. The many years became a bank from which I could withdraw material as I needed it. I was surprised—strictly professional authors probably aren't—at how certain characters emerged as more villainous and others as more heroic than I had thought them to be originally. Mostly though, an old maxim was reaffirmed: *Plus ça change, plus c'est la même chose.* An example: Richard Schechner, one of the most avant of the garde, had suggested a "Theatre of the Subways," where one scene of a play would be performed on a certain subway platform and then the audience would board a train and proceed to the next station for the following scene, and so on. Well, in July 1908, Stanislavski conceived a project for Maeterlinck's *Pélleas and Mélisande* to be performed on the abbey grounds where Maeterlinck and his wife, Georgette Leblanc, lived. Stanislavski said there was lots of greenery there and even an underground cave for Golaud and Pélleas's scene, and "we decided to stage the show in the course of which the spectators and the actors would proceed from one place to another for each of the scenes." So what else is new?

The only two styles of acting, directing, playwrighting, designing, and so on, I decided, were Good and Bad. To paraphrase friend Carlyle, "good" is that creativity that grows out of the nature of the work and "bad" is that which is arbitrarily pasted on. "Nature strikes back with a vengeance at those who violate it," Stanislavski had said.

As I strolled over the Rice campus I thought how much I missed being part of a theater as defined in the Group days by Harold Clurman: not a building, not a producing organization, but a place where an idea is propounded by a dedicated permanent company of players, headed by a strong, visionary artistic leadership, and nourished by a supportive audience. And if luck is with it, at least one critic who'll understand and fight for it. Also important: that this group be an *alternative* to Broadway (West End, Boulevard, etc.), not a secret repository of hope for the main chance; that is, to find and produce a play that will make it to Broadway.

Nowadays, I meditated, the boundary line dividing show business from theater seemed to be disappearing altogether. Have you noticed how more and more actors are referring to theater as "the business?" Witness this announcement in *The New York Times* of December 18, 1981, stating that, following her staggering box-office success with *The Little Foxes,* Elizabeth Taylor "is suddenly taken with the theatre" and plans, with her producer Zev Bufman, to establish the Elizabeth Repertory Company, dedicated to the production of classics and new works "as vehicles for major stars." Dedicated also to today's "bottom line" psychology, Mr. Bufman is predicting a total profit of ten million dollars from *The Little Foxes* and expects each play of the Elizabeth Repertory Company to pay for its own production cost of $1,200,000 "with a lucrative deal for cable television and video-cassette rights." One of Liz's biggest contributions, said Zev, "will be her contacts with other stars. It is very easy for her to call Gregory Peck or Al Pacino. I've learned the power of a star on Broadway. Now I'm looking for a play for Sophia Loren. She wants to do one."

This news item reminded me of a story Stella Adler once told of a flea-bitten hotel she was ushered into during her days on the road with a Yiddish touring company. After examining her room, Stella went to the telephone and called the front desk. "This is Miss Adler," she said. "I have just noticed a roach in my bed and a bedbug in the sink. Now I can understand a bedbug in my bed and a roach in the sink. But I find this too confusing." As I read the piece on Bufman's "Elizabethan" theater I wondered if the bedbugs weren't in the sink again.

Having preceded the commercial debacle of *Harold and Maude* with the more soul-satisfying Australian *Long Day's Journey*, I hastened to readjust my seesaw by following the Broadway failure with the publication of a book on the craft of acting, *Advice to the Players*. I was reminded that it was over twenty years since the publication of *Method—or Madness?* by a remark of NYU's School of the Arts' Theodore Hoffman in a dissertation I came across: "*Method—or Madness?* was one of the healthiest books of the decade—nobody who was serious about training in the sixties was uninfluenced." Since it was based on a single subject, the American application of the Stanislavski System, I decided to supplement *Method—or Madness?* with a manual containing exercises, improvisations, and role analyses from tapes made in my workshop. Harold Clurman provided the excellent introduction as he had for *Method—or Madness?*

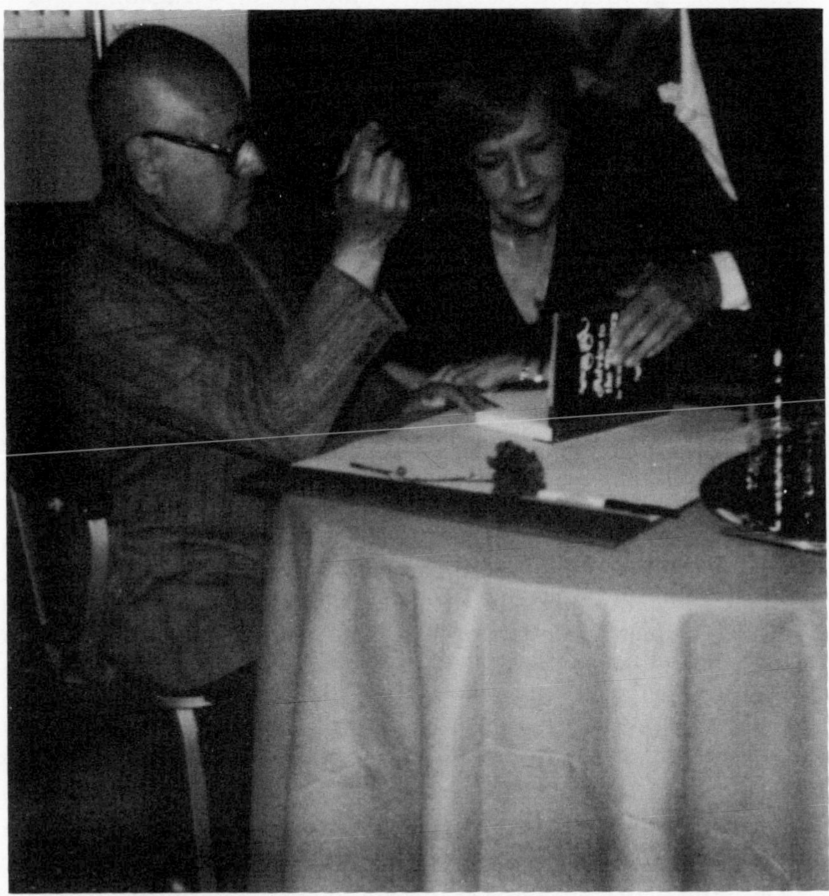

Signing Ruth Ford's copy of *Advice to the Players* in Brentano's, 1980.

It is widely acknowledged to be the toughest job to get any two acting teachers to agree about anything. Therefore it was particularly rewarding, after the appearance of *Advice to the Players,* to read the quote of Stella Adler, one of the great acting coaches in the world: "The book shines with clarity, which should for once and all establish a reasonable and sane approach to acting. I shall use it and ask everybody I know to use it."

From Hollywood, formerly the scene of my swollen stomach, came this healing balm from the *Los Angeles Times*'s Dan Sullivan: "The best theatre book I read this year was a craft book, Robert Lewis' *Advice to the Players.* . . . The remarkable thing about this book is its lack of bunk. . . . Actors and watchers of actors will find it a book to mark up and read again. Yet Lewis' tone is easy, informal, I-may-be-wrong. Only the masters admit it."

The book's publication made me feel more like myself again. But what was that self? I mean artistic self. Although I had taken many detours, sometimes getting lost jogging through the brush, my circuitous road map had led me chiefly on a lifelong search for the answers to the problems of theater style. Right after *My Heart's in the Highlands* opened in 1939, I contributed an article on the fusion of all theater disciplines to John Gassner's *Producing the Play.* This preoccupation with Total Theater, and especially Total Acting, seemed to obsess me from the beginning. Brought up in the realistic school of the Group Theatre, I rebelled at the premise that truthful feeling for the actor was the whole answer. I felt that the performer must use his sense of truth to create a specific character in all its stylistic manifestations, inside and out; that the behavior of that character must be created as well as the emotion. In other words, the actor must be able to *transform* himself. Only then can he face up to the problems of the world repertory so necessary in modern theater life. Only then can he become an artist as well as an Equity member. And for this result we had to examine and expand our training methods.

My stabs at this task progressed from the Group Theatre Studio, through the first year of the Actors Studio, the Lincoln Center Training Program, The Yale School of Drama, the Westchester Laboratory Theatre classes in style, and my numerous other theater workshops. The *Los Angeles Times* review of *Advice to the Players* having led to a rash of requests to create a West Coast operation. I flew out in 1982 for an exploratory visit. I was astounded at how many good actors from my former productions and classes were living in Hollywood and clamoring for some activity different from film and TV chores. I set up interviews immediately.

One actress, upon being asked with whom she had studied, replied, "No one."

"Have you played any parts in films or on TV?" I inquired.

"None."

"Well, did you ever appear in any stage plays?"

"Only in high school."

"Then you've had practically no experience at all?"

"That's right," she said, "but when I'm up on that stage I know exactly what I'm doing."

As I eased the confident one out the door, Anne Bancroft entered.

"Annie," I cried. "How are you? What are you doing here?"

"Bobby," said the highly gifted, very experienced, award-winning star, "when I'm up on that stage, I don't know what the hell I'm doing."

"Welcome, Annie," I said. "Sit down and sign up. We'll have fun."

While it's true that I had occasionally run away from projects to escape the fetid air resulting from artistic mayhem, I'd always bounce back immediately with crazy optimism in an attempt to find the answer some other way. Since I'm still bouncing, that guy who took my picture for *The New York Times* morgue when *My Heart's in the Highlands* opened is just going to have to wait.

Finally, although I had sometimes reeled from the blows of "the bastards [who] won't let you live" in show business, I invariably got a rewarding lift from witnessing some actor's breakthrough in a class. Then to notice that actor benefiting from just such a breakthrough in a subsequent performance is a special kind of joy. Marty Ritt said of his term as an actor in the Group Theatre Studio, "With Bobby there was a joy in the work—fun in work, which, considering that the work was always on a high level, is a very significant achievement."

For this, Marty, I'm grateful. I hope that when I do make my exit the final line won't be, as my father's was, "Excuse me."

# Index

# UNFINISHED BUSINESS

## A Memoir: 1902–1988

**by John Houseman**

For over half a century, John Houseman played a commanding role on the American cultural scene. The *dramatis personae* of Houseman's chronicle represents an awesome roster of arts in twentieth century America. When he isn't conspiring with Orson Welles, Virgil Thomson, Archibald McLeish or a dozen others to launch one of five major new theatre organizations, we find him in Hollywood with David O. Selznick, Alfred Hitchcock or Herman Mankiewicz producing one of his eighteen feature films.

In *Unfinished Business,* the 1500 pages of his earlier memoirs, *Run-Through, Front and Center* and *Final Dress* have been distilled into one astonishing volume, with fresh revelations throughout and a riveting new final chapter which brings the Houseman saga to a close.

paper•ISBN 1-55783-024-X